CONTEMPORARY CRISIS OF THE NATION STATE?

D1086137

B

CONTEMPORARY CRISIS OF THE NATION STATE?

Edited by John Dunn

BLACKWELL
Oxford UK & Cambridge USA

ISBN 0 631 19263-8

First published 1995

Blackwell Publishers
108 Cowley Road, Oxford, OX4 1JF, U.K.

and

238 Main Street,
Cambridge, MA 02142, USA.

British Library Cataloguing in Publication Data
Applied for

Library of Congress Cataloguing in Publication Data
Applied for

Printed in Great Britain by Page Bros, Norwich

This book is printed on acid-free paper

CONTENTS

Preface

There are two very different ways in which one might wonder if there really is a crisis of the nation state today. The first is detached and dispassionate: an inquiry into what just happens to be going on in the world at present, without the least suggestion that there must be anything which human beings can or should do about this (and indeed without any special attention either to the powers of human beings deliberately to affect it or to the ways in which it bears upon their interests). The second, by contrast, focuses precisely on the question of what human beings can and should do about the historical setting which now confronts them. The first, broadly, corresponds to the perspective of theoretical reason; the second to that of practical reason. The first aspires to discover facts and to explain them (and to predict merely if it deems so doing a prerequisite for explanation); the second hopes to guide judgement and perhaps even to prompt action.

The term crisis itself, as Istvan Hont makes clear, is strongly linked to the second orientation. Its initial semantic setting and much of its subsequent imaginative career have each been deeply involved with burning issues of practical judgement. But the strongest of all demands on practical judgment is that it face reality the way it is: that it identify and take account of objective constraints. So it is hard (and manifestly undesirable) for practical reason to part company too permanently with its theoretical counterpart. Political science, too, has always been especially uneasy in its sense of how the two perspectives ultimately relate to one another: unclear what reason really does demand in either or both of these two guises, and unsure quite how much authority to accord its demands in each of them.

In politics the most plausible antithesis to crisis is routine politics, a settled, ongoing assemblage of practices and habits of mind, judgement and conduct, in which the reasonably near future is confidently expected to prove very much like at least the recent past. Subjectively, therefore, and at its most superficial, crisis in politics is simply the acknowledgement of some degree of real challenge to existing routines, a diffuse awareness that practices may have to change and change sharply if even their core purposes are to be sustained; that it may no longer be possible, in Lenin's lapidary phrase, 'to go on in the old way'. Unfortunately, however, political science has never been (and perhaps could never hope to become) wholly at ease once it moves any great distance from routine politics. The more acute the demands placed upon political judgement, the less dependable the resources which that judgement can hope to bring to bear to meet them. The very best political science can only be as good as the quality of political judgement which underlies it. A political science which had made real progress in the main dimension which matters to its potential human users would be one that cast some real light not just on the circumstances under which the historically encountered routines of an existing polity are likely to face challenge, but above all on which polities are likely to prove able to meet such challenges by transforming themselves with fluency and decisiveness, and what types of challenge are likely to prove lethal to even the most resilient and hallowed polity. Unfortunately, this is scarcely the political science we at present have. In the western intellectual tradition (as in several others of comparable antiquity) the question itself is as old as articulated political thinking. In recent decades, it has continued to engage the active energies of, amongst others, literally thousands of political scientists. But it is still unclear that the profession at large (or its amateur forerunners) have made decisive headway with it over this huge timespan.

In the present collection of essays, we can certainly not pretend to have succeeded more handsomely. What we have done is to consider anew a very old question, in a variety of settings in which it has at present some resonance or urgency, and from a variety of viewpoints. None of the contributors has settled exclusively either for the perspective of theoretical reason or for that of practical reason. But some (perhaps especially Paul Bracken in his pungent essay on the potential dynamic of Asian militarization, Istvan Hont in his masterly synoptic survey of the theoretical roots of our contemporary vision of politics, and Sudipta Kaviraj in his splendidly calm and lucid treatment of the unfolding of modern Indian political culture) have laid their main analytical emphasis on the need for detached explanation. Others (David Calleo in his vivid and illuminating exploration of the growing strains on the American polity, Andrew Hurrell on the challenge of ecological crisis to the efficacy of state agency, James Tully on the ongoing constitutional crisis of Canada, William Wallace on the political development and stasis of the European Community) are clearly more deeply concerned with the issue of how we should try to act. One or two (perhaps Geoffrey Hawthorn on the states of the South and John Barber on the fate of Russia) balance the two more evenly against one another. From an editor's viewpoint this heterogeneity is just as it should be. Between them, we hope that these essays put some intellectual shape into the contemporary pertinence of this old question and cast some light, by so doing, on the difficulty of genuinely strategic judgement in modern politics.

As editor I should like to thank the editorial board of *Political Studies*, its editor at the time of initial invitation, Jack Hayward, and its present editor Mick Moran, for their encouragement, support and tolerance throughout. I should also like to acknowledge the material support of the Political Studies Association, the British Academy and the Kings's College Research Centre in facilitating the preparatory work for the collection, the kind and thoughtful aid, administrative and logistical, of Silvana Dean, Rosemarie Baines and Tasmin Shaw, and the friendly solidarity (once more) of the Research Centre's Convenor Martin Hyland. I am grateful, too, to the other participants in the preparatory conference held at King's College in September 1993 (especially to Bhikhu Parekh, Michael Clark, Mike McGwire and Jonathan Haslam). But my principal debt, unsurprisingly, is to the energy, forbearance and goodwill of the contributors.

JOHN DUNN
King's College, Cambridge
(12 March 1994)

Introduction: Crisis of the Nation State?

JOHN DUNN

King's College, Cambridge

Formulating the Question

Nations consist of those who belong together by birth (genetically, lineally, through familially inherited language and culture). States consist of those who are fully subject to their own sovereign legal authority. A true nation state, therefore, would consist only of those who belonged to it by birth and of those who were fully subject to its sovereign legal authority. By this (for practical purposes, no doubt absurdly stipulative) criterion it is unlikely that there is a single nation state in the world at present, and moderately unlikely that any such state has ever existed. But, as with most political ideas, the force of the idea of the nation state has never come principally from its descriptive precision. What it offers is a precarious fusion of two very different modes of thinking: one explicitly subjective, urgent and identificatory, and the other presumptively objective, detached and independent of the vagaries of popular consciousness. (It is hard to exaggerate the shaping impact of this second mode in forming the category of state.)[1] Common birth is both a ground for, and a source of, allegiance. External authority is a device for furnishing protection. Taken together, they furnish a basis for rulers and subjects to live together with greater imaginative ease than either party would be likely to draw from the other taken separately: a contemporary version of the *pactum subjectionis*.[2]

It is unsurprising that this unsteady mixture has proved unsuitable for clear analytical thought. But its analytical debility has been no bar to ideological or practical potency. The ideas that every nation should have its own state and that every state should be a single nation[3] may not have much solid merit either as normative or as practical proposals. But between them they have made a great deal of the political history of the twentieth century.[4] Each of the three great geopolitical shifts of this century – the First

---

[1] Quentin Skinner, 'The state', in Terence Ball, James Farr and Russell Hanson (eds), *Political Innovation and Conceptual Change* (Cambridge, Cambridge University Press, 1989), pp. 90–131.

[2] John Dunn, 'Contrattualismo', *Enciclopedia delle scienze sociali* (Rome, Istituto dell'Enciclopedia Italiana, 1992), Vol. 2, pp. 404–17.

[3] Ernest Gellner, *Nations and Nationalism* (Oxford, Blackwell, 1983); Benedict Anderson, *Imagined Communities* (London, Verso, 1983).

[4] For a helpful and balanced résumé see Eric Hobsbawm, *Nations and Nationalism since* 1780 (Cambridge, Cambridge University Press, 1990) and compare Liah Greenfeld, *Nationalism: Five Roads to Modernity* (Cambridge, Mass., Harvard University Press, 1992).

World War and its aftermath, the Second World War and the unravelling of European empire which succeeded it, and the collapse of Communism in Eastern Europe and decomposition of the Soviet Union – has drastically extended the nation state as a political format and strongly reinforced it as an ideological option.

Why, then, has it come to be a commonplace of contemporary political journalism that the nation state is today somehow in crisis: palpably unable to master problems which it once handled with aplomb, incapable of ensuring an order of its own (ecological, economic, civil, even spiritual) on its subjects' behalf, baffled by the novel challenges of a turbulent global economy and a decaying global habitat?

The first question to press in this context is whether the journalistic commonplace is in fact valid. Has there been, for some specifiable set of reasons, a clear deterioration in the capacity of the nation state format to master the hazards to the security and prosperity of its subjects, in comparison with some distinct and earlier phase in modern history? Has there been some definite change in the sources or intensity of such hazards, sufficient to render a long-serviceable formula, normative or practical, palpably inadequate to control dangers which it once met with relative serenity? The first view locates the crisis in a diminution of the power of the nation state as such – a clear lessening in either its normative appeal or its practical capacity (or, of course, in both). The second locates the crisis in a sharp rise in the acuity or scale of the hazards which now confront its subjects.

The least plausible of these hypotheses is the claim that the practical capabilities of states today in any general fashion fall short of those of their predecessors. Such a claim is not simply absurd. There have been forceful arguments that modern political and economic organization has a strong internal impetus towards immobilism, an impetus which can be reversed only by massive disruption (war, conquest, perhaps large-scale natural disaster).[5] At a more ideological level, also, the right-wing economistic critique of rent-seeking and of the allegedly inherent economic inefficiency of state as opposed to market distribution[6] has achieved considerable impact in many settings over the last two decades. But it is hard to see firm grounds in any of these lines of thought for judging that the intrinsic practical efficacy of modern state forms has deteriorated over the last half century.

Far more plausible is the judgement that the present sense of crisis in the efficacy of the nation state comes from a resonance between two very different types of shift: a fading in all but the most extreme settings (typically those of armed conflict) in the normative appeals of the idea of the nation state, and a brusque rise in awareness of a series of new and formidable challenges (economic, ecological, military, political, even cultural) the scope of which

---

[5] Mancur Olson, *The Rise and Decline of Nations* (New Haven, Yale University Press, 1982).

[6] James Buchanan, *Liberty, Market and State: Political Economy in the 1980s* (New York, New York University Press, 1986); or, at a more refined level, Friedrich von Hayek [John Gray, *Hayek on Liberty* (Oxford, Blackwell, 1984); F. A. Hayek, *New Studies in Philosophy, Politics, Economics and the History of Ideas* (London, Routledge, 1978); *Law, Legislation and Liberty*, 3 vols (London, Routledge, 1973–9)].

plainly extends far beyond national boundaries and effectively ensures that they cannot be successfully met within such boundaries. Seen this way, the sense of crisis, whether well judged or otherwise, is at least easy to understand. It is a sense, above all, of political crisis: crisis in the efficacy of political action.[7]

It is in the nature of politics that new political challenges should arise all the time. But some such challenges are manifestly far more formidable than others. It is most unlikely that the causal capabilities of the nation state as an organizational format should have declined significantly and persistently in conditions of peace and appreciable long term economic growth. But even in these conditions the combination of drastic new challenges and inherently limited inherited powers of action might easily have lessened the normative appeal of the repository of those powers and should rationally have impaired the practical self-confidence of national governing elites. Even if this emergent sense of political inadequacy did not in itself impair the normative appeal of the state form in question, it might readily expose the intrinsic limitations of that appeal in the face of the far harsher demands which are now placed upon it. Whatever else might be needed to meet them effectively, the drastic new challenges of global interdependence plainly require vigorous political action: a preparedness on the part of immense numbers of human beings to alter substantially and rapidly major aspects of how they choose to behave. Such changes place formidable strains on the political capacities of any human population. There may be a reason (perhaps inherent in global economic rationalization or in the dawning awareness of environmental peril) why the normative appeal of the idea of the nation state as such is already weakening. But even if it were not (indeed, even if it *is* not), it might still be true that the novel challenges of rapid global transformation would pose strains on the nation state, as an arena in which to concert political action, far greater (and perhaps unmanageably more severe) than those which have previously faced it.

The immediate appeal of the idea of nation has nothing in particular to do with efficacy. We may not like, or choose to espouse, the social relations into which we are born. But we are born into them, whether we like it or not; and their claims are there, to embrace or to reject, quite independently of any practical impact on our own life chances. But the immediate appeal of the idea of the state is virtually confined to the latter's presumed efficacy.[8] States which are in fact effective in promoting the security of their subjects undoubtedly win (and deserve[9]) a higher degree of loyalty than those that fail lamentably to furnish anything of the kind. But even states that notably fail to furnish security (even Iraq,[10] or Mynamar, or the Republic of Somalia) are compelled today to pretend not merely to wish to do so, but to be within realistic reach of at least becoming able to do so. Because this is so, the normative appeal of the idea of the state is inherently vulnerable to a sense of political crisis, and the practical dissipation of such a sense through effective political action is greatly

[7] Cf. John Dunn, *Interpreting Political Responsibility* (Cambridge, Polity, 1990), ch. 8.

[8] Skinner, 'The state'.

[9] John Dunn, 'Political obligation', in David Held (ed.), *Political Theory Today* (Cambridge, Polity, 1991), pp. 23–47; John Dunn, *Political Obligation in its Historical Context* (Cambridge, Cambridge University Press, 1980), esp. Conclusion.

[10] Kanan Makiya, *Cruelty and Silence* (London, Jonathan Cape, 1993).

impeded by any prolonged weakening in the normative appeal of the state as a system of agency.

It may be difficult to judge whether or not particular states (or even all states considered together) are or are not for the present gaining or losing in the practical ability to handle the collective predicaments of their own subjects.[11] But it is extremely easy to judge that there is widespread and disagreeable suspicion across the even minimally politically concerned populations of most countries in the world at present, from career politicians and high-ranking state officials to the most reluctant and despondent of voters, that their own states (and perhaps most other states also) are at present palpably weakening in their capacity to cope with these predicaments. At the limit, a sense of political crisis converges with the objective dynamics of state collapse – with revolution[12] or descent into the state of nature (Liberia, Somalia, much of Afghanistan). It is clear for the present that all the OECD states (for example) are very far indeed from collapse, and even further from revolution. But it is perhaps equally clear not merely that their practical adequacy for many purposes is genuinely subjectively in doubt in the eyes of their own subjects, but also that this adequacy may in addition be quite objectively in doubt.

A prevailing sense of political crisis is volatile and potentially misleading, an unreliable tracer of real changes in economic, social or even political circumstances. But it is also a political factor in itself, and capable under some conditions of exerting its own causal force in reshaping or dismantling political arenas: consider the recent decomposition of Italy's postwar political system and the emergent challenge to Japan's for long remarkably successful postwar conservative hegemony).[13] At this level, accordingly, the journalistic commonplace that there exists a contemporary crisis of the nation state might well prove virtually self-validating. By being reiterated, and through coming to be believed, it could make itself true: consider, for example, the backwash from the Maastricht agreement. Because a sense of political crisis is itself an important political phenomenon, it is certainly pertinent to study its sources and its potential consequences. But, if we wish to understand what is going on in contemporary politics, it is likely in the long run to prove more rewarding to concentrate principally on the more external and objective features of the contemporary situation of nation states.

Locating Crisis

Every actual nation state is both a somewhat hazy amalgam of at least two constitutive ideas and a disorderly, complex and profoundly opaque fact.[14] If

[11] John Dunn, 'Political theory, political science and policy-making in an interdependent world', *Government and Opposition*, 28 (1993), 242–60.

[12] Cf. John Dunn, *Modern Revolutions* (Cambridge, Cambridge University Press, 2nd ed., 1989); Dunn, *Interpreting Political Responsibility*, ch. 6.

[13] The importance of crisis as a mechanism of adjustment in postwar Japanese politics has been illuminatingly emphasized by Kent E. Calder, *Crisis and Compensation* (Princeton, Princeton University Press, 1988). Compare Chalmers Johnson, *MITI and the Japanese Miracle* (Stanford, Stanford University Press, 1982) and Daniel I. Okimoto, *Between MITI and the Market* (Stanford, Stanford University Press, 1989).

[14] Dunn, *Interpreting Political Responsibility*, Introduction; John Dunn, *Rethinking Modern Political Theory* (Cambridge, Cambridge University Press, 1985), Introduction.

we are to determine how far, and in what sense, the nation state is today in crisis, we first need to consider whether the prevailing sense of its being in crisis (if and where this does prevail) comes principally from the ideas or principally from the facts. Whether at the level of ideas or at the level of facts, it is inherently unlikely that all nation states should ever be equally in crisis at the same time. (A world in which they were so would already have become one in which the hazards to the human species were palpably beyond the reach of human powers to meet: a condition of uncontrollable biological or physical catastrophe, a planet which now precluded life, the heat death of the universe.) In the world of today, incontrovertibly, some states (Liberia, Somalia, Angola, Afghanistan) are far more in crisis than others (Switzerland, Singapore). As far as we know, this has always been true in the past; and we still have dismayingly little reason to expect that it will ever cease to be true in the future.

The judgement that the nation state is today in crisis is not founded on the experience of the feeblest of contemporary states.[15] There is nothing either in the idea of a nation or in that of a state to ensure that Liberia or Chad will ever be firmly viable again (even though Liberia, for example, had in some respects a longer continuous political history than any other single Sub-Saharan state in Africa before it first slipped into anomic military tyranny and then dissolved into competitive banditry).[16] We should not be surprised that ideas alone prove insufficient to ensure peace and prosperity for any human population, even though the idea of the state, both at the level of ideological pretension and at the level of international law,[17] inhibits the acknowledgement of such insufficiency with some obduracy. But in a world in which human populations are technically compelled to live on terms of ever greater intimacy with one another, the inability to guarantee minimal security to particular populations may prove over time an important threat to the appeals of ideas through which their interests are supposedly protected.

In this respect there is an important asymmetry between the ideas of nation and state. In conditions of adversity, nation might become a purely passive category, a pure community of suffering. But even in conditions of adversity, the category of state retains in itself both a claim to be an agent and a corresponding burden of responsibility. Settings in which the idea of the state carries no factual structure of effective agency along with it[18] threaten the chances of their inhabitants to act together strategically and effectively in the face of their predicament. But they also threaten the prospects for the

---

[15] Cf. Donal Cruise O'Brien, John Dunn and Richard Rathbone (eds), *Contemporary West African States* (Cambridge, Cambridge University Press), Introduction and Conclusion.

[16] See the chapters by Christopher Clapham in John Dunn (ed.), *West African States: Failure and Promise* (Cambridge, Cambridge University Press, 1978) and in Cruise O'Brien *et al.*, *Contemporary West African states*; and contrast Clapham's treatment of the fate of the other longest lived of Sub-Saharan Africa's extant polities [C. Clapham, *Haile-Selassie's Government* (London, Longman, 1969) and C. Clapham, *Continuity and Transformation in Revolutionary Ethiopia* (Cambridge, Cambridge University Press, 1988).]

[17] R. J. Vincent, 'Grotius, human rights and intervention', in Hedley Bull, Benedict Kingsbury and Adam Roberts (eds), *Hugo Grotius and the Theory of International Relations* (Oxford, Oxford University Press, 1990), pp. 241–56.

[18] See Cruise O'Brien *et al.* (eds), *Contemporary West African States*, Conclusion; and Geoffrey Hawthorn, The crises of southern states, *Political Studies*, XLII (1994) 130–145.

normalizing political instruments of the world economy (the IMF, the World Bank) to prevent concomitant disruption in the latter's trade and credit flows. The ending of the Cold War has left a world of less imminent eschatological horror,[19] but also one of even more discomfiting tension between social intimacy, gross disparities in human misery, and limited political and military capability and will to alleviate the misery or even suspend the intimacy.[20]

In itself the fact that some parts of the world are at present in no condition to instantiate convincingly the category of the state is conspicuously worse news for those parts of the world than it is for the category of the state. But if we consider the role of that category in articulating relations between states – horizontally and globally, rather than vertically and locally – local inefficacy may in the end prove a major impediment to the capacity of states in happier settings to furnish the services which they too purport to supply. (It is an important question about the realist strand in the understanding of international relations whether (or how far) its trenchantly zero-sum conception of the nature of these relations makes it obtuse to this possibility.) Where it plainly is unviable in practice, therefore, there is more than one way in which the failure of the nation state may react back on its appeal as an idea in less beleaguered settings. But even if these negative reactions do more on balance to impair its appeal than they do to reinforce it (which is far from evident), we can be confident that a sense of political crisis in the core countries of the OECD has not arisen from the travails of Liberia or Somalia (or indeed even from the uncomfortable experience of post-communism from Saxony to Bosnia and Vladivostok).

Nationhood

In this ampler, and for the moment altogether more comfortable, setting is it reasonable to see a sense of political crisis as emanating in any degree from the properties of the idea of the nation state? To answer this question, we need to consider its two core constitutive ideas in turn. The idea of a nation is that of a community of birth (in more liberal interpretation, perhaps, a community of birth and mutual choice). But actually existing nation states (as with actually existing socialism)[21] are altogether scruffier than this: medleys of birth, mutual choice, provisional instrumental exploitation approximately within the law, and vigorous manipulative penetration from well outside it. In idea, membership of a nation should be wholly uncontentious; a brute matter of fact, and prior to (a premiss of) any conceptualization of interest. In fact, however, few things are more contentious (already) in the more prosperous of modern nation states than who exactly at any particular time is entitled to full membership of the nation; and conflicts of interest over this question (while hard to demarcate either stably or accurately) are acute and intensely inflammatory.[22] (Consider

---

[19] Compare Paul Bracken, *The Command and Control of Nuclear Forces* (New Haven, Yale University Press, 1982).

[20] John Dunn, The dilemma of humanitarian intervention: the executive power of the law of nature after God, *Government and Opposition*, 29 (1994), 248–61.

[21] Cf. John Dunn, *The Politics of Socialism* (Cambridge, Cambridge University Press, 1984).

[22] John Dunn, 'The paradoxes of racism', *Government and Opposition*, 28 (1993), 512–25.

the prospective impact of the NAFTA free trade agreement, especially upon relations between Mexico and the USA.) These conflicts have increased; they are increasing; and there is no reason whatever to expect them to diminish for the foreseeable future.

As a fact, the nation state is a rough and ready mechanism for furnishing a set of real services.[23] But the relation between fact and idea is increasingly slack; and there are no imaginative or analytical resources within the idea to alleviate the increasingly prominent strains within the fact. It may in the end prove important that the idea of nation should be so conspicuously exposed from two very different angles. From a realist viewpoint it is too vague and too sentimental to serve convincingly as a device for assessing interests.[24] From a liberal viewpoint it is too particularist in taste and too recklessly submissive to contingency to serve as a device for interpreting value for human beings.[25] But these threats, if threats they are, are as yet scarcely imminent. While it is reasonable to suppose that the idea of nationhood should be under somewhat greater practical strain as a framework for organizing collective action in conditions of massive and (at the receiving end) largely involuntary external penetration of citizenship as well as with unpleasantly slack national labour markets, the strictly civic aspect of such conditions is still in most OECD countries more a fear about the future than a fact about the present.

Statehood

Insofar as a sense of crisis emanates from the properties of these two key ideas, therefore, it is reasonable to assume that it must be coming less from a weakening in the appeals of the idea of the nation than from a lessening in the cogency (normative or practical) of the idea of the state.

Crisis at the Periphery

There are two main doubts about the state, both certainly as old as the concept itself, and each clearly foreshadowed in the historical experience of the miscellany of large-scale political units which preceded its full formulation and to which the concept has since been regularly applied.[26] The first is a doubt about the intentions of those who at any given time direct state power: a scepticism that these intentions are in the case in question (or usually, or often, or ever), as benign as they are fulsomely proclaimed to be. We can be confident in the face of this doubt, that there remain ample grounds for entertaining it; but we can be at least equally confident that the chances of the doubt's being in general better founded now than it has been for the last three and a half

[23] Gellner, *Nations and Nationalism*.
[24] But cf. Max Weber, The national state and economic policy (Freiburg address), *Economy and Society*, 9 (1980), 428–49.
[25] Note, however, the increasingly strenuous and protracted struggle of John Rawls to surmount these impediments; and compare the more realist assessment in Dunn, *Western Political Theory in the Face of the Future* (Cambridge, Cambridge University Press, 2nd ed., 1993), ch. 3.
[26] Cf. Dunn, 'Political obligation'.

centuries are slight.[27] The second (and perhaps even weightier) doubt concerns the state's efficacy in relation to its expressed intentions: above all as a device for furnishing security to its subjects. Here too, while there continues to be massive reason for entertaining the doubt, it is inordinately unlikely that the grounds for doing so have strengthened greatly since the seventeenth century.

Certainly the concept of state is applied more widely (and perhaps more promiscuously) to political units in the world today than it was in the days of Hobbes: not least for its convenience in imposing a minimal framework of order on social interactions and economic transactions which bind human populations ever closer together. In the settings of modern international law and international relations the sufficient conditions for applying the concept manifestly do not at present entail a level of practical efficacy in state performance adequate to guarantee the security of anyone.[28]

Some portion of the sense of crisis in the nation state today, accordingly, may well derive in this way from two types of threat to state legitimacy. The first, stemming principally from the diffusion of a variety of secular rationalist theories of political value and political possibility,[29] foments excessively high political expectations, and vents its disappointment at the failure of history to live up to them on the state powers which are (in fantasy at any rate) the most concrete facilities for at least attempting to realize them. It is inherently difficult to pin down a relation of this character.[30] But it remains a plausible diagnosis of anomalies within the modern understanding of politics, albeit more convincingly seen as a permanent dimension of vulnerability than as an at present especially dynamic source of novel hazard. As we have already noted, the second variety of threat to legitimacy, arising from the overextension of the category of the state, its relentless application to what are often grimly inappropriate referents, occurs principally at the periphery of the world political and economic system. The dismal realities to which the term 'state' frequently refers in these settings (President Mobutu on his river boat), do nothing for the majesty of the idea of the state. (They are not what Hobbes or Hegel had in mind.) But it is hard to believe that they inflict much damage upon its standing or authority closer to the centre of world political economy. (What would you expect of the Heart of Darkness?)

[27] Compare the darkest suspicions which can be plausibly entertained about the purposes of state élites in France and Spain today with J. H. Elliott, *Richelieu and Olivares* (Cambridge, Cambridge University Press, 1984); and consider the haunting English Civil War fear of 'a German devastation' [David Underdown, *Revel, Riot and Rebellion* (Oxford, Oxford University Press, pb. ed., 1987), p. 154].
[28] For the importance of this predicament see John Dunn, 'The nation state and human community: obligation, life-chances and the boundaries of society [unpublished lecture Wendy & Emery Reves Center, College of William and Mary, March (1993); Italian edition forthcoming Edizioni Anabasi, Milan (1994)].
[29] Cf. John Dunn, The heritage and future of the European Left, *Economy and Society*, 22 (1993), pp. 516–24; John Dunn, *The Politics of Socialism* (Cambridge, Cambridge University Press, 1984); Dunn, *Western Political Theory in the Face of the Future*, Conclusion.
[30] Cf. Jurgen Habermas, (trans. Thomas McCarthy) *Legitimation Crisis* (London, Heinemann, 1976).

Crisis at the Centre?

If there really is a contemporary crisis of the nation state, it must in the end be a crisis not of the periphery but of the centre. At that centre, too, there is good reason to suppose that it must stem not from diminishing intrinsic powers on the part of particular nation states[31] but from a growing gap between the causal capabilities of even the more advanced nation states and the effective demands placed upon those powers. This is as we should expect. All power is relational. It is apparent enough that in many concrete ways the powers of advanced states today to carry out particular actions vastly exceed those of their predecessors. They can move their armed forces far more rapidly from place to place. They can communicate with (and spy upon) each other with a speed, intensity and amplitude which are wholly unprecedented. They can shift earth, raise buildings or unleash explosive power on a scale which no past ruler could have seriously imagined. But these awesome powers are not focused on fixed and stable targets. Indeed, now that the Cold War is over, they are no longer even aimed crucially at the rapidly rising powers of other human agencies. Instead, they need to be assessed (and to an increasing degree they are already coming to be assessed), in relation to a range of formidable new threats to human security of which we are belatedly becoming aware.[32] If there really is a contemporary crisis of the nation state (and not merely a transitory, quasi-cyclical decline in political self-confidence, prompted by recession or by reaction to the brief euphoria of 1989), this is where it must emanate from.

There is no reason to assume any clear relation between the degree to which human populations at any time are aware of the threats which they face and the scale of those threats themselves. Neither political theory nor political science offers much special aid in judging that scale.[33] But, between them, they may reasonably hope to capture some aspects of the structures from which the threats arise. Two of these structures are essentially external to state agency: a product of global economic dynamics and ecological degradation. But one is itself in part a consequence of state action: not an immediate product of state agency itself, but an interactive effect between states, generated by the extremity of the challenges now posed by global economic dynamics and ecological pressure.

It is hard to judge the acuity of all three threats, but easy to appreciate how each could readily exacerbate the others. Because of these two features of the situation, we can be reasonably confident at present that no one is in a position to assess accurately quite how severe the contemporary crisis of the nation state really is (or even whether the term 'crisis' is genuinely appropriate). But none of us should have much difficulty in seeing that the sense of crisis, however frivolously generated or insecurely grounded, may well turn out to be all too apposite.

The economic threat has been most extensively explored. We can catch the subjective flavour of it clearly enough in the petulant tones of M. Balladur at

---

[31] Or even from diminishing powers in relation to one another: cf. Paul Kennedy, *The Rise and Fall of the Great Powers* (London, Unwin Hyman, 1988) and Joseph S. Nye, Jr, *Bound to Lead: the Changing Nature of American Power* (New York, Basic, 1990).

[32] Cf. Andrew Hurrell and Benedict Kingsbury (eds), *The International Politics of the Environment* (Oxford, Oxford University Press, 1992).

[33] Dunn, 'Political theory, political science and policy-making'.

the obsequies of the *franc fort*: 'We can't allow a situation to continue where so much money can change hands in a very short time and threaten a nation's security'.[34] (Those who live by the market need not be surprised if they prove to die by the market.) It is still difficult to judge the full impact of the vast expansion in trade flows, the dramatic increase in the scale and speed of capital movements, or the dizzy volatility of currency markets, on the capacity of state élites to realize their own purposes; not least because the starkly unintended consequences of market liberalization will certainly continue to promote vigorous attempts to reverse many of the changes that have produced these outcomes. The accents of M. Balladur are those of a humiliated (and politically exposed) representative of a peculiarly proud state. But they serve to epitomize the discomforts of an entire political class. We can trace the resulting stigmata of impotence already in many prominent political processes: the effective blunting of the Social Democratic project,[35] the recoil from European monetary union,[36] the faltering of the Uruguay round of the GATT,[37] the sharpening (though ultimately contained) challenge under the Clinton Presidency to the NAFTA agreements between Canada, Mexico and the United States.

The central challenge of global economic liberalization is to the Keynesian conception of the welfare state; the promise, reaching back at least to Lorenz von Stein, to take full responsibility for the economic welfare of a given population through the deft exercise of the power of its state. The existing and anticipated unemployment levels of the OECD countries, and of Western Europe in particular, are a notable setback not merely to Keynes's own hopes and expectations in the aftermath of the *General Theory*,[38] but also to the variety of expedients eventually deployed by other western governments in face of the Great Depression,[39] and still more to the levels of employment achieved and welfare publicly provided across most of Western Europe over most of the period since the Second World War ended. Since there is such a clear elective affinity between the Keynesian conception of macroeconomic management to deliver popular welfare and the idea of the nation state (with its claim to embody a relatively intimate relation between ruler and ruled), it is unsurprising that these experiences should have spread anxiety well beyond the ranks of career politicians or state officials. Insofar as the political formula of the welfare state proves to be economically unsustainable (or even insofar as it proves to be unsustainable in the competitive political conditions of modern representative democracy),[40] doubts about the normative legitimacy of capitalism which have dogged it throughout its history (and which have never been fully resolved

---

[34] *Financial Times*, 13 Aug. 1993, p. 1.

[35] Cf. Gøsta Esping-Andersen, *Politics against Markets: the Social Democratic Road to Power* (Princeton, Princeton University Press, 1985).

[36] Compare the oversanguine expectations of John Dunn, 'Democracia: la politica de construir, defender y ejemplificar una comunidad: Europa hoy', *Revista Internacional de Filosofia Politica*, 1 (1993), 21–39.

[37] Contrast Gilbert Winham, *International Trade and the Tokyo Round Negotiation* (Princeton, Princeton University Press, 1986).

[38] Peter Clarke, *The Keynesian Revolution in the Making* (Oxford, Clarendon, 1988).

[39] Cf. William J. Barber, *From New Era to New Deal* (Cambridge, Cambridge University Press, 1985); Peter A. Hall (ed.), *The Political Power of Economic Ideas* (Princeton, Princeton University Press, 1989).

[40] Cf. John Dunn (ed.), *Democracy; the Unfinished Journey* (Oxford, Oxford University Press, 1992), Conclusion.

even at a purely intellectual level),[41] will press against it once more, and with increasing force.[42] While they are most unlikely to place the state as a political format objectively in jeopardy, there is far greater likelihood of their disturbing the comfort of political incumbency (and thus of sharpening a sense of political crisis, not least amongst incumbents).

A less immediate, but potentially more profound, threat to state viability is already beginning to arise from the challenges of environmental degradation. In the sphere of economics, the threat to the political standing of the nation state comes essentially from the tension between a national framework of sovereign authority and governmental responsibility and an uncompromisingly international field of economic causality. In the sphere of ecology, the national framework of sovereign power and governmental responsibility is also in some tension with ecological causality. (Acid rain, the ozone layer, still more global warming, are no respecters of boundaries.) But the principal residual obstacle to effective action in face of ecological hazard (over and above the key elements of sheer expense and painfully limited scientific comprehension) is less an incapacity on the part of governments to meet locally generated ecological threats within their own borders than a difficulty in cooperating effectively together to guarantee one another against the involuntary importation of pollution from elsewhere. Their problem, in this context, is not a deficiency in domestic power but a disinclination or incapacity for effective collective action. Even domestically, the ecological threat to state viability may in the end prove quite formidable. The scale of cost already palpably involved in any attempt to reverse many major instances of environmental degradation,[43] the bitter conflicts which will certainly arise over distributing the costs of any such reversal, even the widespread doubts whether states can readily be equipped to find out what should best be done over matters where powerful interest groups are so drastically at risk, all ensure severe pressures on the state's capacity for effective agency.

But the main ecological challenge to state viability is likely to come not from domestic limits to the state's power, but from the difficulties of securing effective and trustworthy international cooperation.[44] The problem of collective action[45] permeates all politics. It is at least as easy to pick up in the domestic politics of the United States[46] as it is in the General Assembly of the United Nations. But the problems of collective action are peculiarly intractable where there is little realistic prospect of creating an effective enforcement agency and where the rational appeal of seeking to ride free is often devastatingly apparent. It is a complicated and unobvious question about many ecological issues whether or not the structure of costs and rewards of cooperation yields a clear balance

---

[41] John Dunn, 'Property, justice and common good after socialism', John Hall and I. C. Jarvie (eds), *Transition to Modernity* (Cambridge, Cambridge University Press, 1992), pp. 281–96.

[42] John Dunn (ed.), *The Economic Limits to Modern Politics* (Cambridge, Cambridge University Press, 1990), esp. Introduction and Conclusion.

[43] Already heavy enough to imperil the future of the oldest surviving international insurance market.

[44] Hurrell and Kingsbury (eds), *International Politics*.

[45] Russell Hardin, *Collective Action* (Baltimore, Johns Hopkins University Press, 1982).

[46] For the historical antecedents of this feature of the American state see Stephen Skowronek's exceptionally illuminating *Building the New American State* (Cambridge, Cambridge University Press, 1982).

of advantage for state actors to cooperate or to defect:[47] to form binding collective agreements to restrict environmental damage to one another and abide strictly by their terms, or to participate, in the spirit of Callicles,[48] like skulking brigands, in the complex processes of global negotiations, affix their signatures slyly to such treaty documents as emerge from them, and resolutely ignore their terms thereafter, whenever it is more convenient to do so. One element of this complexity lies in the prospective costs and rewards of punctilious observance of the agreements themselves. But a second, which may in practice be every bit as important, lies in the strategic dilemmas delineated in the theory of games. What might be starkly irrational in the case of a single pay-off Prisoner's Dilemma could well be strategically optimal in a frequently repeated game, with no definite terminal point, and with conspicuous relations to many other concurrent repeated games.

If human beings are to re-establish control over the ecological dangers of which they are now becoming aware, they will certainly need to act together more deftly and patiently than they have usually contrived to do in the past. For the present, there is no serious possibility of their either discovering or fashioning a discrete new instrument of action which can supplant the nation state in this struggle against the recalcitrance of nature. If they do eventually learn how to behave in a consequentially less self-destructive manner, there is little reason to expect that the sites of their learning will have any especially intimate relation to states as such. But the agencies required to implement this learning in the last instance are likely to continue for the foreseeable future to be states. *Faute de mieux*: either states or nothing.

If states fail, by and large, to make, enforce, or abide by effective inter-national agreements restraining the environmental destructiveness of modern economic activity, it may be an analytical error to blame them for this failure.[49] The fault may lie principally elsewhere: in the cognitive limitations (or intemperate and inveterate greed) of their subjects – the ultimately ruling *demos* – or in the fundamental features of the pay-off matrix of environmental costs and damage. But their subjects are unlikely to be prepared to acknowledge the former; and most of them will usually be unequipped to recognize the latter.

At the receiving end, therefore, the consequences of state inaction or breach of faith are likely, as they come out, to appear both avoidable and discreditable. While this need in itself have no instantaneous effect on the material or organizational components of state power, it would quite rapidly impair the residual normative appeal of states as such. Every state is many other things too; but the key feature of each state is that it is a potential structure for political action. Damage to the normative appeal of a state is not merely damage to an idea. It also impairs (and can at the limit simply eliminate) the capacity of a state to serve as a structure of political action. If there is a crisis of the nation state today, it cannot result merely from speculative guesses about future possibilities. But even if it is right to conclude that there is no clearly

[47] Geoffrey Heal, 'Formation of international environmental agreements', *Economics and Politics*, unpublished paper, International School of Economic Research, Università di Siena, July (1993), 191–211.
[48] Plato, (trans. Terence Irwin) *Gorgias* (Oxford, Clarendon, 1979), 507e, cf. 483a–4b, pp. 56–7, 86.
[49] Cf. Dunn, *Interpreting Political Responsibility*, ch. 12.

delineated crisis of the nation state today (no objective feature of its location which explains why it must now be in crisis), that is no guarantee that there will not be such a crisis tomorrow. We do not yet know that the political challenge of arresting environmental degradation is any threat at all to the nation state as a format for political life or political action. But just in case it does prove to pose such a threat, we would be well advised to consider that possibility in advance. That at least would give us an opportunity to see why exactly it might do so, while there was still time to do something about it.

America's Federal Nation State: a Crisis of Post-imperial Viability?

David P. Calleo

Does the end of the Cold War point less to the triumph of one superpower over the other than to the collapse of both? Intriguing symmetries aside, are there serious reasons to see the United States as entering its own crisis as a continental nation state?

While the United States is hardly about to follow the Soviet Union into rapid disintegration, it does have problems as a nation state that are causing serious trouble now and will almost certainly bring great difficulty in the future. America's problems are not, however, the result of ending its hegemonic global role of the Cold War. Rather they result from bad habits picked up while prolonging that role. But are these problems sufficient to raise serious questions about America's continuing viability as a nation state?

Addressing this issue requires some sense of the traditional problems and performance of the American federal state. In the long run, a state's viability is presumably connected with its performance. A state is meant to preserve physical peace and security for its citizens and their property against external or domestic disorder. A state is also meant to foster economic prosperity and security. And a state is supposed to provide its citizens with a source of pride, awe and idealism – or at least emotional and psychological satisfaction – a function that grows in importance when traditional religions are in relative decline.

Historically, the United States is often thought to have had a relatively easy task meeting these criteria. The point should not be exaggerated. Our Civil War was, after all, a bloodier military struggle than anything else between the Napoleonic Wars and World War I. For us, the death and devastation were much more than in either World War. But the US has certainly had an easier task than European nation states in providing security from external threats, thanks to its physical isolation from other great powers. Prosperity has also been relatively easy, with an abundance of space and resources, an enterprising population and market oriented culture, and a structure of government that encouraged development and did not smother it with controls.

Historically, the United States has not done badly with the third criterion either. The federal nation state was created around its written Constitution, which has endured for two centuries and which many Americans continue to believe embodies the best liberal and constitutional traditions of the Enlightenment. With the terrible exception of the Civil War, pride in the Constitution has been a powerful support to national unity. Americans have also united around the less intellectual satisfactions of their continental 'Manifest Destiny'.

The 'American Dream', a vision combining liberty with economic opportunity, enabled the United States to attract and absorb generations of immigrants, whose numbers and vitality helped the new federal state to assume a pre-eminent position in the world within a mere century and a half. The large and continuously replenished immigrant population naturally posed a particular challenge for American national identity and political consensus. But the US succeeded in developing a viable sense of nationality thanks to the vigour of the dominant Anglo-Saxon culture, which had its own very considerable cosmopolitan and regional diversity, along with the prosperity that made the American Dream a concrete myth for the children and grandchildren of European immigrants and the rest of the country as well. At the same time, America's 'melting pot' has not robbed the nation's culture of a rich ethnic diversity that imparts not only vitality and pride, but also a certain comprehensive identity.

The immigrant stream, of course, continues to the present day, but the sources are not European but Asian and Hispanic – the former easily adaptable if not assimilable, the latter more resistant. The mass influx of Hispanic Indians from Mexico, the Caribbean and Central America takes on certain aspects of 'historical revenge' for Manifest Destiny. And America's Black minority, one of the oldest and largest parts of the imported population, remains a glaring qualification to the largely successful record of cultural consolidation. Given the scale of its racial problem, however, the United States has probably succeeded as well as any other major nation state in bringing Blacks into the national community. In any event, with a population of such extraordinary diversity, the federal state's historic capacity to produce a shared national identity has been as impressive as its gift for prosperity and its good luck with security.

After 1945, however, the basic situation of the American state changed profoundly. This was widely seen as a matter of necessity. After two world wars, isolationism no longer seemed a reasonable way to protect national security. Fulfilling the traditional state functions, particularly once the Cold War had started, no longer appeared possible without remaining a global superpower. Fostering global economic interdependence was widely seen as the best way to preserve America's own peace and prosperity. Intercontinental nuclear weapons were soon to cancel America's old geographic invulnerability.

Changing America's role in the world also changed America's self-image. Alongside the traditional pride in constitutional virtue and economic prosperity, grew up pride in military prowess and political leadership. Manifest Destiny on the North American continent evolved into an 'American Century' for the world. American globalism also changed the face of the nation's government and economy. An enormous peacetime military establishment developed together with a very large imperial political élite occupied with managing or analysing America's international role. The big peacetime military establishment gave new opportunities for significant parts of the aspiring middle class, while the civilian imperial élite absorbed significant portions of traditional social and intellectual élites. Huge military spending reoriented large sections of the American economy and created numerous symbiotic relationships between business and government around the superpower role.

These radical changes were not universally welcomed. Enthusiasm for the superpower role among the public at large was frequently tempered by a sombre reckoning of the burdens and hazards of military service, resentment of élites with greatly enhanced power, and suspicion of foreign 'free-riding'. A considerable part of the intellectual and political élites worried that the world role would distort constitutional, economic, cultural and social balances, endanger constitutional democracy, blight prosperity, or embroil the nation in grandiose and perhaps unworthy projects abroad, which might prove its moral, economic and cultural undoing at home.

Diffidence turned into resistance whenever large-scale fighting was required. This became clear in the Korean War, which probably did more than anything else to end the long ascendancy of the Democratic Party. Public resistance exploded during the Vietnam War and once more drove the Democrats from power. Although a professional army quickly replaced the draft army, it would be twenty years before American forces again engaged in any large-scale military conflict. Nor does American behaviour since the Gulf War suggest that the lessons of Vietnam have been forgotten.

Happily for American political consensus, the Cold War, with its nuclear balance of terror, involved very little actual fighting. There was, however, a great deal of expense for the two superpowers. Arguably, that expense ultimately ruined the Soviet system. It certainly also caused a great deal of difficulty for the American. Just how the imperial role has weakened the huge US economy is naturally a complex and contentious subject. Often, apparently successful policies, based on apparent national strength, have nevertheless worked to undermine the springs of national vitality.

Fiscal conditions are a major point of linkage between world role and national decline. By the time of the Reagan administration (1981–8), as the Soviet Union was entering its death throes, America's long-gathering fiscal disorder was entering a new dimension. By the mid-1980s, annual federal deficits, already at double-digit levels in the 1970s, jumped to the range of $150–200 billions.[1] The immediate reasons were a combination of factors – a big leap in military spending, a cut in income taxes and a failure to do more than slow the rise in civilian spending. While the overall tax level continued to rise during the Reagan years, the rate of increase was greatly reduced. This was primarily the result of ending the rapid inflation of the previous two decades, which had regularly pushed tax-payers into higher brackets with steeply higher rates.[2]

---

[1] *Economic Report of the President* (Washington DC, US Government Printing Office, 1991), p. 375. The deficit figure is artificially lowered by including as income the surplus funds collected for social security, as well as the interest that the Treasury pays to itself for that accumulated surplus. See for example, D. P. Calleo, *The Bankrupting of America* (New York, Morrow, 1992), pp. 44–5; J. White and A. Wildavsky, *The Deficit and the Public Interest: the Search for Responsible Budgeting in the* 1980*s* (Berkeley, University of California Press, 1989), pp. 313–5; and P. Blustein, 'Alternate social security plan gaining: Hill expected to take pension plan out of budget calculations', *The Washington Post*, 16 February (1990), p. A10.

[2] For a discussion of the reasons for the rise in the deficit during the Reagan presidency, see D. A. Stockman, *The Triumph of Politics: why the Reagan Revolution Failed* (New York, Harper and Row, 1986), esp. ch. 12. On unlegislated tax increases, see J. Pechman, *Federal Tax Policy* (Washington DC, Brookings Institution, 1987), pp. 114–6; and D. A. Hibbs, *The American Political Economy: Macroeconomics and Electoral Politics* (Cambridge, MA, Harvard University Press, 1987), p. 296.

America's fiscal predicament did not, however, arise overnight. The progressive failure to match outlays with income results from conditions developing since the early postwar years. America's world role and the heavy military spending that accompany it are undoubtedly a major element in any convincing explanation. Basically, three features in American fiscal practice stand out in sharp contrast to the pattern in most other advanced Western nation states. The first is the relatively high levels of military spending throughout the postwar period – high both as a percentage of GNP and very high as a percentage of government spending.[3] The second is America's relatively low level of civilian entitlements and civil spending generally, particularly by continental European standards. American entitlements seem particularly ungenerous toward the middle classes.[4] A third feature is more elusive but nevertheless palpable: the high level of inefficiency in federal spending programmes. Inefficiency has always seemed particularly egregious in defence spending and, most recently, in the rapidly rising outlay for health care.[5] The reasons for this inefficiency seem both tactical – Congressional pork combined with inappropriate bureaucratic controls – and strategic – the lack of coherent general policies. These three features help to explain why a consensus on fiscal priorities is even harder to reach in the US than in most other Western countries.

The conflict between guns and butter runs all through the postwar fiscal history of the United States, with competing bursts of military and civilian spending. The public has tolerated the world role but been increasingly reluctant to pay for it – in money or blood. Meanwhile the high level of military spending has limited civilian spending and entitlements – and hence, logically enough, public support for higher taxes. The public sector has remained very much smaller in the US than in continental European states, where the taxpaying middle classes receive a far more generous ration of public goods. Finally, the inefficiency of the American public sector not only wastes what resources there are, but also further discourages public provision of social goods. In some cases, notably health care, this results in further inefficiency, i.e., a much higher combined public and private cost for health care in the US than elsewhere, a cost which squeezes private household budgets and further strengthens resistance to taxation.

To these three special features that help explain the fiscal crisis must be added a fourth: the ease with which the US has always been able to finance its

---

[3] For a comprehensive breakdown of federal outlays, including military spending, see *Economic Report of the President* (1991), pp. 376–7. For military expenditure as a proportion of GNP and government spending, see Calleo, *Bankrupting of America*, pp. 199, 210.

[4] Complete data on levels of civilian spending is given in *Economic Report of the President* (1991), pp. 376–7. A comparative analysis is given in OECD, *Public Expenditure on Income Maintenance* (1976) and *Economies in Transition: Structural Adjustment in OECD Countries* (Paris, OECD, 1989). For an account of the relative decline of the American middle classes, see F. Levy, 'Incomes, families and living standards', in R. E. Litan *et al.* (eds), *American Living Standards: Threats and Challenges* (Washington DC, Brookings Institution, 1988), p. 136.

[5] For inefficiency in US defence spending, see E. N. Luttwak, *The Pentagon and the Art of War* (New York, Simon and Schuster, 1984), D. P. Calleo, *Beyond American Hegemony* (New York, Basic, 1987), pp. 115–20 and 256, n. 21, or *Bankrupting of America*, pp. 54–60; for an analysis of health care provision, see *Health Care Systems in Transition* (Paris, OECD, 1990); and *The Changing Health Care Market* (Washington DC, Employee Benefit Research Institute, 1987). In addition, a full description of the US health care system and the need for reform is given in *Economic Report of the President* (1993), pp. 119–69.

deficits – fiscal and external. In the Reagan era, the bulk of the world's private saving went to finance US federal deficits, despite the intense displeasure and discomfort of most European governments.[6] This capacity for manipulating the international economy to remedy the deficiencies of the American was, however, nothing new. It had become a regular part of American policy-making since the 1960s, when the US was already running a troublesome external deficit. External balances continued to decline, and, by the early 1970s, America's long-standing trade surplus had turned into a deficit. By the 1980s, both trade and current-account deficits had reached levels previously difficult to imagine.[7]

No other country in the world could have continued to run such substantial and rising deficits over three decades. The US was able to finance them thanks to the dollar's international status. Here the superpower role provided a solution to the superpower's apparent 'overstretch'. But the endless manipulation of the dollar has proved to be an exercise of power that ultimately has undermined not only the world economy, but the superpower itself.

Broadly speaking, the United States has followed three distinctive formulas for manipulating the dollar to finance deficits. All three have worked for a time and then collapsed. Arguably, all three have left the real US economy weaker than before.[8]

The first formula was developed under the Bretton Woods system of fixed exchange rates. The dollar's status as a formal reserve currency meant that foreign central banks were constrained to accept and hold surplus dollars as reserves in place of gold. The arrangement, the gold-exchange standard, presumed a prudent American monetary policy that would not create excessive international liquidity and thereby transmit inflation to other countries. The requirement to exchange dollars for gold, at the official price, was meant to limit excessive American monetary creation. In the end, it proved powerless to do so. Instead, the system came to rest, in effect, on forced loans to the Americans from their European and Japanese military protectorates. The superpower was asserting its hegemony. The linkage between military protection and supporting the dollar was made explicit.[9]

America's external deficits in this period could not be traced to any imbalance in the current account. The 'basic' deficit arose when trade and current account surpluses were offset by heavy overseas military spending, corporate investment and tourism – all of which gave America's external deficits an obvious imperial character.[10] As de Gaulle put it in 1965, the Bretton

---

[6] See H. Van Buren Cleveland, 'Europe in the economic crisis of our time: macroeconomic policies and microeconomic constraints,' in D. P. Calleo and C. Morgenstern (eds), *Recasting Europe's Economies: National Strategies in the 1980s* (Lanham, MD, University Press of America, 1990), pp. 160–3.

[7] In 1970, the US trade balance was $0.8 billion in surplus. By 1980, this had changed into a deficit of $31.4 billion and by 1989 the deficit had grown to $129.4 billion. The current account deficit grew from $5.87 billion to $99.01 billion between 1982 and 1984. *Economic Report of the President* (1991), pp. 402, 406.

[8] For a fuller description of these formulas, see Calleo, *Bankrupting of America*, pp. 102–21.

[9] In particular, this involved loans from Canada, Germany and Japan; see Calleo, *Bankrupting of America*, pp. 107–8.

[10] The 'imperial' deficit is explained in Calleo, *Beyond American Hegemony*, pp. 85–7. Full statistical tables for 1962–3 can be found in *IMF Balance of Payments Yearbook*, volume 19 (1968), section 1, and for 1964–8 in volume 21 (1970), section 1.

Woods arrangement, by constraining European central banks to accept dollars in place of gold, was forcing Europeans to finance the takeover of their own industries by the Americans.[11] The Americans, of course, argued that they were merely providing 'liquidity' to a world hungry for investment. The fact remained that the funds were tied to the priorities of American investors, who were, thereby, increasing their presence in allied economies. Americans could also claim that their deficits sprang from the high cost of defending Europe. Not surprisingly, the 1960s saw a sharpening of the 'burden-sharing' debate within NATO.

In more purely economic terms, when America's domestic and foreign spending and investment were combined, the US was 'absorbing' more goods, services and investments than its national economy was actually producing. The excess absorption was being financed by inflated credit in the form of dollars exported to other economies. Under the boom conditions of the 1960s, this naturally brought inflationary pressure on the foreign economies.[12] The situation grew progressively unstable as the accommodating of heavy military spending for Vietnam, plus the accelerating costs of Johnson's 'Great Society', began forcing the Federal Reserve into an ever more inflationary creation of credit.[13] But since American balance-of-payments deficits preceded severe domestic price inflation by several years, a good part of America's excessive credit was being dumped into the international economy, where it fed the offshore 'Eurodollar' market.[14] This capital market, free from national regulation, was a magnet attracting still more capital from the US. It permitted large sums to be mobilized not only for overseas investment, but also for speculation against the dollar. Ultimately, this greatly enhanced capacity for speculation was to prove the undoing of the Bretton Woods formula, as waves of private selling overwhelmed central-bank intervention.

[11] Press conference, 4 February 1965, in *Major Addresses, Statements and Press Conferences of Charles de Gaulle* (New York, French Embassy, Press & Information Division, 1967).

[12] De Gaulle speech, above; J. Rueff, 'Le problème monétaire international' and 'Le deficit des balance des paiements des Etats Unis', *Oeuvres complètes*, E. M. Claassen and G. Lane (eds). Tome III, vol. 2, *Politique economique* (Paris, Plon, 1980). See also, Calleo, *Beyond American Hegemony*, pp. 84–5; H. van Buren Cleveland and W. H. Brittain, *The Great Inflation: a Monetarist View* (Washington DC, National Planning Association, 1976), pp. 13–6, and, for international responses, pp. 31–48; and W. M. Corden, *Inflation, Exchange Rates and the World Economy* (Chicago, University of Chicago Press, 1986), pp. 85–94.

[13] See Cleveland and Brittain, *Great Inflation*, pp. 31–5; for data on the growth of the US money supply, see *International Financial Statistics Yearbook* (1980) (Washington DC, International Monetary Fund), pp. 54–5.

[14] For an introduction to the workings of the Eurodollar market, see Susan Strange, 'International monetary relations' in Andrew Shonfield (ed.), *International Monetary Relations of the Western World, 1959–1971* (London, Oxford University Press, 1976), vol 2, pp. 176–94. The estimated net size of the Eurodollar market in 1970 was $57 billion, compared with total US gold reserves of just $11 billion, BIS, *Annual Report*, no. 41 (Basel, Bank for International Settlements, 1971), pp. 127, 157. This does not prove in itself that the Eurodollar market was inflationary. Cleveland and Brittain assert that around 75 percent of the $54 billion was already counted as part of national monetary aggregates. Its size, therefore, did not reflect a commensurate real growth in money stocks beyond that growth already sanctioned by monetary authorities. Cleveland and Brittain therefore argue that the unprecedented price rise of the inflation of 1968–75 cannot be blamed on the Eurodollar market. Nevertheless, so large a volume of newly liberated capital could create instability for exchange rates when mobilized; see Cleveland and Brittain, *Great Inflation*, pp. 22–3.

By the time the Bretton Woods system finally broke down in 1971, the Americans themselves had grown tired of it. Its principal drawback was that it prevented devaluing the 'overvalued' dollar which was a result of the domestic price inflation that began to afflict the US domestic economy during the Vietnam War and meant that American products were disadvantaged against foreign products. Hence the end of the long-standing American trade surplus in 1970. The US tried vainly to persuade its competitors to revalue and finally abandoned its Bretton Woods obligations and permitted the dollar to float.[15]

The transition to a system of floating exchange rates did not, however, cure the American external deficit. It grew much worse.[16] Nor did it dethrone the dollar from its international role, or prevent the US from financing its imbalances by monetary manipulation. Under floating rates, there have been two distinct formulas for doing so. These might be called the Nixon formula and the Reagan-Volcker formula.[17] Like the Bretton Woods formula, both worked for a time but left the real economy weaker than before.

In its essentials, the Nixon formula consisted of an expansive fiscal policy, accommodated by an expansive monetary policy and accompanied by a 'benign neglect' of the dollar's exchange rate. The formula was obviously inflationary – for the US and for the world. It took frank advantage of what might be called America's comparative advantage in competitive inflation. Although foreign central banks resisted it, the dollar did depreciate sharply – almost 50% against the deutschmark from 1971 to 1979, for example.[18] For most countries, such depreciation would have meant an uncontrollable rise of domestic price inflation. Eventually, this is what happened in the US. But the time frame was much longer. In the meantime, it seemed to work very much to America's advantage. It improved competitive prospects for American producers, without hindering America's ability to spend abroad. America's advantage came from its huge and diverse economy which put it in a quite different situation from other European economies. Relative to the economy as a whole, the US trade sector was considerably less than half the size of most European trade sectors. The US, moreover, was a net exporter of food and raw materials, and its major imports – oil for example – were themselves priced in dollars.[19]

[15] For a description of 'benign neglect' and the demise of Bretton Woods, see S. Strange, 'International monetary relations'; R. Solomon, *The International Monetary System, 1945–1976: an Insider's View* (New York, Harper and Row, 1977). A defence of 'benign neglect' is offered by G. Haberler and T. E. Willet, *A Strategy for US Balance of Payments Policies* (Washington DC, American Enterprise Institute, 1971), and L. B. Krause, 'A passive balance of payments strategy', *Brookings Papers on Economic Activity*, no. 3 (Washington DC, Brookings Institution, 1970).

[16] For full data, see *Balance of Payments of OECD Countries*, 1965–1985 (Paris, OECD, 1986), pp. 10, 11.

[17] For a full description of these two formulas, see Calleo, *Bankrupting of America*, pp. 109–21, or *Beyond American Hegemony*, pp. 90–108.

[18] The dollar depreciated against the DM by 46.8 percent between 1971 and 1979. *Economic Report of the President* (1991), p. 410.

[19] The relative size of the US trade sector can be shown roughly by calculating the sum of imports and exports as a proportion of national product. The proportion for the US in 1993 is 19 percent. For Germany, however, it is 51 percent; for the United Kingdom, 52 percent; and for France, 41 percent. OECD, *Economic Outlook*, no. 53 (June 1993), pp. 55, 67, 73, 83.

After the oil price shock, petroleum and petroleum products, priced in dollars, consistently accounted for between a quarter and a third of all US imports. *Economic Report of the President* (1991), p. 404.

Nixon's formula was already being used in 1970, when he encouraged the Federal Reserve to expand the money supply. The dollar crisis of 1971 gave Nixon the occasion to jettison the Bretton Woods system and let the dollar fall substantially. This helped the beleaguered American trade sector, although not enough to prevent trade deficits in 1971 and 1972, and in most other years of the decade.[20] At the same time, Nixon imposed price and wage controls, which suppressed domestic price inflation until after his re-election in 1972. When controls came off at the beginning of 1973, explosive domestic price inflation followed immediately. There succeeded a series of further inflationary shocks – the explosion of grain prices and the four-fold increase of oil prices in 1974. In that year, the level of price inflation throughout the ten major noncommunist industrial countries had reached an astonishing 13%.[21] European governments, inclined to inflate away the ruinous wage settlements made after 1968, were doubtless partly to blame, but the Nixonian Federal Reserve was the world's inflationary engine.[22]

The end of fixed exchange rates had also allowed Nixon to drop all capital controls. This left American corporations free to invest abroad as they wished and American banks free to participate fully in the burgeoning business of the Eurodollar market. After the oil shock, America's swelling liquidity, transferred through its enterprising banks, permitted the relatively easy 'recycling' of loans to oil-importing countries. This mitigated the effects of the oil shock, but also delayed adjustment to it, and saddled banks with a dangerous level of insolvent debt for the next couple of decades.

By late 1973, exploding price inflation was finally prompting a monetary crackdown. A severe recession followed in 1974 and 1975, until the Nixon formula was resurrected by the Ford and Carter administrations throughout most of the latter half of the decade. The dollar continued its sharp fall against the yen and most European currencies.[23] By 1979, inflation had once more reached record levels and a second oil shock followed the first. A general revolt in the oil, gold and currency markets, together with a powerful political reaction against inflation in the US itself, brought on a new period of monetary austerity, associated with the appointment of Paul Volcker to the Chairmanship of the Federal Reserve in 1979. A recession followed to usher in the Reagan era. In effect the US ended the 1970s as it had ended the 1960s – heading into a deep recession exacerbated by stagflation. Meanwhile, a decade of monetary manipulation had helped neither the trade

[20] US net merchandise trade (in billions of dollars): 1970, 2.6; 1971, −2.26; 1972, −6.41; 1973, 0.91; 1974, −5.5; 1975, 8.9; 1976, −9.48; 1977, −31.09; 1978, −33.94; 1979, −27.56. *Economic Report of the President* (1991), p. 402.
[21] Cleveland and Brittain, *Great Inflation*, p. 54.
[22] For a discussion of the relative responsibility of the US and European governments for spiralling inflation, see Cleveland and Brittain, *Great Inflation*. The authors conclude that the Fed's decision in 1971–2 to follow expansionary monetary policies was largely to blame for the subsequent general inflation, but that European finance ministries (with the exception of the fiscally austere Germans) exacerbated the situation by trying to inflate out of recession (pp. 48–51).
[23] Between January 1974 and December 1979, the dollar depreciated from 298.6 Yen/$ to 240.6 Yen/$ and from 2.81 DM/$ to 1.73 DM/$, depreciations of 19.4 and 38.4 percent respectively. P. Volcker and T. Gyohten, *Changing Fortunes: The World's Money and the Threat to American Leadership* (New York, Times Books, 1992), pp. 370–1.

balance – which was in deeper deficit than ever – nor the real economy, whose rates of investment and productivity growth had fallen to new lows.[24]

The new decade soon brought a new formula. This Reagan–Volcker formula consisted of loose fiscal policy combined with tight monetary policy. The combination brought record interest rates and attracted a huge inflow of foreign capital. In effect, the US borrowed back much of the credit it had created and exported under the Nixon formula. The capital inflows meant a very high exchange rate for the dollar, which kept down domestic price inflation. A moderate boom ultimately followed, financed by the inflow of foreign capital.[25]

In due course, the formula's longer-term costs forced its abandonment. These sprang from the unnaturally high dollar, which fell heavily on those parts of American industry subject to foreign competition. The result was a 'rust belt' of bankrupt industries, principally in the Middle West. The costs were also catastrophic for dollar debtors of the previous decade, along with the financial institutions that held their debts. Hence the various domestic and foreign debt crises – most spectacularly the collapse of a good part of the American savings and loan industry, a financial disaster estimated at the time to cost the Treasury at least \$325 billion in outlays.[26] As early as 1984, the Federal Reserve felt constrained to loosen its monetary policy.[27] As the decade continued, bursts of credit to avoid various financial disasters and lower the exchange rate alternated with returns to monetary austerity in the interest of preventing runaway speculation. By the end of the decade, the US was falling into a deep and stubborn recession, from which recovery remains, in mid-1993, still very feeble.

Thus, the end of the 1980s, like the last years of the two previous decades, saw the US caught in a period of recession and chronic stagflation – with oscillating monetary policy trying to avoid both inflation and a deeper recession.

[24] For the trade balance, see note 20. Output per hour rose by just 0.9 percent in 1978 then fell by 1.1 percent and 0.2 percent in 1979 and 1980. *Economic Report of the President* (1991) p. 339.

[25] Private foreign investment in the United States rose sharply after 1982. Between 1982 and 1989, private holdings of government securities by non-US citizens rose from \$25.8 to \$134.8 billion; of securities other than government bonds from \$25.8 to \$134.8 billion; of corporate bonds from \$16.7 to \$229.6 billion; and of corporate stocks from \$76.3 to \$260.2 billion. This capital inflow was supported by high real interest rates and the consequent appreciation of the dollar. When the dollar began to weaken in 1985, partly as a result of deliberate US government policy, private holdings fell, but foreign official holdings of US assets began to increase dramatically. Official investment grew from \$202.5 billion to \$337.2 billion between 1985 and 1989, reflecting attempts to support the dollar and protect dollar investments. *Economic Report of the President* (1991), p. 401.

[26] The minimum cost of \$325 billion over four decades was reckoned by the GAO. Some estimates went as high as \$500 billion. This included the interest cost of the additional borrowing that would be needed. See D. E. Rosenbaum, 'A financial disaster with many culprits', *The New York Times*, June 6, 1990, A1. R. D. Brumbaugh Jr. and A. S. Carron, 'The thrift industry crisis: causes and solutions', *Brookings Papers on Economic Activity*, No. 2 (Washington DC, Brookings Institution, 1987), p. 354. A later government estimate was \$130–76 billion, which did not include future interest payments [*Economic Report of the President* (1991), p. 173]. Others have questioned whether the capital involved in the bailout should be seen as a *cost*, rather than merely a transfer of funds that will be reinvested at the same level, thus having no net effect on the economy. This appears to assume that there are no opportunity costs for malinvestment; see, Calleo, *Bankrupting of America*, pp. 46, 135–8 and 234n.

[27] In 1984, the federal funds rate, a general indicator of the Fed's monetary policy, was 10.23 percent, up from 9.09 percent in 1983. By the beginning of 1985, it had fallen to 8.35 percent. *Economic Report of the President* (1991), p. 368. For a discussion of Federal Reserve policy in this period, see W. Greider, *Secrets of the Temple: How the Fed Runs the Country* (New York, Simon and Schuster, 1987), p. 17; or Cleveland, 'Europe in the economic crisis of our time', in Calleo and Morgenstern (eds), *Recasting Europe's Economies*, pp. 163–5.

Not surprisingly, the early 1990s saw a serious public malaise over the state of the economy. The 1980s had left the US with radically increased fiscal deficits of a structural kind. The national debt, which had been roughly one trillion dollars in 1980, was over four trillion in 1992, and had been growing since 1989 at the rate of $400 billion annually. Debt service had risen, as a percent of federal spending, from 8.89% in 1980 to 14.77% in 1990.[28] In effect, the US had entered an era of 'Ponzi finance'.[29] An increasing part of the government's borrowing was being used to cover interest payments. The debt had grown self-propelled. With the collapse of the Soviet empire, the continuing American hunger for capital seemed likely to be more difficult for the rest of the world to accommodate. The opening of Eastern Europe and Russia to investment promised greater competing demands in the future. Meanwhile, Germany's reunification and Japan's own severe financial difficulties robbed world capital markets of two major savers. The Gulf War had similar effects on Middle Eastern savings.

Meanwhile, the growing share of US budgetary resources eaten up by debt service grew harder and harder to square with growing demands for public-sector investments in infrastructure and education – needed, it was argued, to restore the economy to competitiveness.[30] At the same time, the lack of adequate public provision for health care in America, together with the rapidly escalating costs of the existing private system, began to be regarded as a major crisis for the federal system itself. Added to the clamour over health care was a broad public unease over increasing poverty and homelessness, rising crime, growing anger and despair in the urban underclass, and increasing racial and ethnic tension throughout the society.

Giving new force to these perennial arguments over the size and responsibility of the public sector was a growing public sense that the real economy was not performing well. While the US had been notable for its capacity to produce new jobs, most were in the low-paying services. Despite the large increase in the number of wives at work, real incomes for American families had been stagnant for well over a decade.[31] The huge current-account deficit, despite the dollar's sharp depreciation, suggested a radical decline in American competitiveness in precisely those high value-added industries that could support higher wages. Decades of statistics showing relatively low US investment and productivity growth gave substance to those fears of decline.[32] America's poor long-term

[28] *Budget of the US Government, Fiscal Year* 1992 (Washington DC, US Government Printing Office, 1991), Tables 1.3 and 3.1, Part Seven, p. 17, 31–6. For comparative statistics, see OECD, *Economic Outlook*, 53 (June 1993), p. 142. For the growth of the US government debt, see *Economic Report of the President* (1991), p. 377.

[29] For an explanation of Ponzi Finance, see Cleveland, 'Europe in the economic crisis of our time', in *Recasting Europe's Economies*, pp. 164–5; see also Calleo, *Bankrupting of America*, p. 268n.

[30] See for example, R. Reich, *The Work of Nations* (New York, Alfred Knopf, 1991), ch. 21, 'The decline of public investment', pp. 253–61; or E. N. Luttwak, *The Endangered American Dream* (New York, Simon and Schuster, 1993).

[31] See, for example, F. Levy, 'Incomes, families and living standards'; J. Minarik, 'Family income' in I. V. Sawhill (ed.), *Challenge to Leadership* (Washington DC, Urban Institute Press, 1988), pp. 33–67; and L. Uchitelle, 'US wages: not getting ahead? Better get used to it', *The New York Times*, 16 December (1990), section 4, pp. 1, 6.

[32] For example, real GDP per employed person did not grow at all between 1973 and 1979, and from 1979 to 1988 by just 1.1 percent per annum. In comparison, the OECD average growth rates (without the US) for the same periods were 2.4 and 1.9 percent and those of Japan, 2.9 and 3.0 percent. The effect of the move to service sector employment and of low investment is discussed in Calleo, *Bankrupting of America*, pp. 127–8, 171.

investment and productivity performance began to be traced, not implausibly, to the bad fiscal and monetary habits I have been describing. All the formulas for manipulating the dollar had, after periods of minimal success, ended up in stagflation. Perpetual oscillation between austerity and inflation could be seen, in itself, as a great inducement to speculation rather than to serious investment in the real economy.

All these issues began to form a giant cloud over the Bush administration, which had succeeded the Reagan administration in 1989. While Bush had the good fortune to be in office for the Soviet collapse, it brought him surprisingly little political benefit. The public was proving much more concerned with stagnant living standards, declining competitiveness and financial fragility. It had grown commonplace to blame the outsized fiscal deficit. Durable economic improvement was thought to be unlikely without serious fiscal reform. Bush, who had once described Reaganite macroeconomic ideas as 'voodoo economics', tried to bring the deficit under better control by agreeing to modest tax increases and cuts in military spending.[33] But he seemingly lacked the concentration and determination to push through major budgetary improvements. Saddled as he was with his own Reaganite party and a Democratic Congress, he probably also lacked the political means.

Instead of fiscal reform, Bush tried to capitalize on America's triumph in the Gulf War. He began to pin the fate of his administration to a commanding American global role in the 'New World Order'.[34] Some of his rhetoric seemed to have been borrowed from Henry Luce's 'American Century' of the 1940s. In this, Bush misjudged both the international situation and the American political mood.

The Gulf War proved less the harbinger of a 'unipolar' Pax Americana, as Bush claimed, than the 'last hurrah' for unilateral American global interventionism. The conditions did provide a near perfect occasion to demonstrate American power. Iraq threatened the vital interests not only of its neighbours in the region, but also of all the Western powers and Japan. Thus the US had willing military allies, eager to participate in order to exert influence over the outcome, and financial allies able to defray the costs. The Soviet collapse meant that the ample US forces still in Europe could be withdrawn without fear. The military situation was ideal for demonstrating the prowess of American air, naval and land forces developed in the long Carter–Reagan build-up. The

---

[33] For details of the October 1990 budget agreement, see *Omnibus Budget Reconciliation Act of 1990* (Washington DC, US Government Printing Office, 1990). The package agreed by Congress aimed at reducing the federal deficit by $492 billion over a five-year period. However, it optimistically assumed a real growth rate of 3.3 percent, falling interest rates, and did not take account of either the Resolution Trust Corporation or Gulf War expenditures. For further details, see M. Feldstein, 'Bush's budget deal made the deficit bigger', *The Wall Street Journal*, 29 November (1990), A12.

[34] On August 8, 1990, President Bush spoke of a 'new era' when deploying troops for Operation Desert Shield. The concept of a New World Order was introduced in a speech to Congress on 11 September 1990. *US Department of State Dispatch* 1, no. 3 (17 September 1990), pp. 91–4; cited in L. Freedman and E. Karsh, *The Gulf Conflict, 1990–1991: Diplomacy and War in the New World Order* (Princeton, Princeton University Press, 1993), p. 215. For a broader discussion, see R. W. Tucker and D. C. Hendrickson, *The Imperial Temptation: the New World Order and America's Purpose* (New York, Council on Foreign Relations, 1993), chs 1–4.

terrain lent itself to effective use of sophisticated weapons and there was no need to take and hold hostile urban areas. Some analysts argued there was no need for a land war at all. Militarily and geopolitically, however, these were not conditions that could be generalized into a new American-dominated world order.

In fact, the US would soon have difficulty hanging on to its hegemonic position in Western Europe. As the Yugoslav crisis demonstrated, Europe after the Cold War had new security problems, with new complex political and economic dimensions that the Americans were neither well-suited nor much disposed to take the lead in addressing. Nor did the major West European powers seem eager to legitimize a renewed American hegemony.

In any event, the New World Order had little durable appeal with Americans at home. The American public was not inclined to see the end of the Cold War as an historic opportunity to extend and consolidate American global hegemony. It was more inclined to see it as the long-delayed opportunity to rejuvenate America's national political economy.

Clinton's campaign was adept at focusing on the long deterioration of America's economic competitiveness and social harmony. His solution was selective public investment in infrastructure and education, together with a radical reform of the health care system. It was not really Clinton, however, who set the campaign debate but Ross Perot, whose primary focus was on the budget deficit itself. Perot was able to convince a substantial part of the electorate that the deficit was at the bottom of many of the nation's long-term economic ills. He was not opposed to reforms along the lines that Clinton was suggesting, but argued that nothing would succeed without repairing the basic macroeconomic framework by sharply reversing the growing fiscal deficit.

As Perot proceeded with his campaign, his analysis grew more radical. Unlike Clinton, Perot was not shy about making obvious linkages between cutting the budget deficit, finding money for necessary public investment and welfare, making sharp cuts in the military budget and pursuing a less grandiose foreign policy. Controlling the deficit or having serious policies of any kind, Perot began to argue, was not imaginable without a reform of constitutional practices. Something would have to be done about the habitual 'gridlock' between the executive branch and the Congress. And something would have to be done about the highly corrupt Congressional system, whose election campaigns required huge funds and left individual Congressmen free to tailor legislation to suit those who could buy influence.[35]

In effect, it was Perot who made explicit the links between economic decline, world role and constitutional practice. His basic message was that the American political system was growing increasingly unviable. The basic problems of the American political system raised by Perot are as old as the system itself. They involve the principal issue of the Federalist Papers – balance between executive energy and Congressional resistance. While the executive's tenure does not depend on a legislative majority, without such a majority it is difficult to carry through any kind of coherent programme. In current circumstances, a genuine working majority is difficult to imagine. At best, an administration can bargain and compromise and hope that some semblance of its original plans will emerge

---

[35] For Perot's campaign platform, see H. Ross Perot, *United We Stand: How We Can Take Back Our Country* (New York, Hyperion, 1992).

through a process over which it has little real control. It is not, of course, that a directing power is located elsewhere in the system. Rather, the legislation and policy that emerges is the serendipitous result of innumerable private bargains. The consequences of such a system for the government's ability to control its own bureaucracy are what might be expected. At the moment, the American political process is merely a market – where every legislator is a private entrepreneur working on his own account. His imperative need is to accumulate enough clients to meet the voracious demands for funds to finance his own election campaign. In the House of Representatives these elections take place every other year. Under such circumstances, party loyalty is minimal. The budget crisis thus emerges as a metaphor for the dysfunctionality of the system as a whole.

Obviously, all political systems have strong elements of bargaining and compromise. But, as the budget crisis suggests, the US has lost its balance between the power to govern coherently and the power to obstruct. The result is large-scale waste and plunder of public resources. Under such circumstances, it is not surprising that budgets can never be balanced and that unresolved domestic problems continue to accumulate and fester.

In some respects, the present American situation resembles conditions at the beginning of the century, when the inadequacy of the constitutional system was much discussed and reform movements and third parties sprouted on all sides. The resolution came through a strengthening of presidential power – a process often associated with various domestic reform movements – Theodore Roosevelt's 'Square Deal', Woodrow Wilson's 'New Freedom', and later, Franklin Delano Roosevelt's 'New Deal'. But the more durable strengthening of presidential power came as the US adopted a major global role. That evolution was prefigured in the roles played by Wilson and Roosevelt in two world wars and reached its peacetime fulfillment with what might be called the Cold War constitution in the early postwar era. An 'imperial presidency' became the solution to the inadequacies of the traditional constitution.[36]

The problem with such a solution was that it remained inadequate for civilian policy. Except in war or quasi-war, the presidency lacked either the institutional base or the political prestige to develop and impose coherent domestic policies. While presidents became all-powerful figures abroad, they grew increasingly impotent at home. This was a situation that could only reinforce the already dangerous tendency to divert too many resources and too much attention to the global role, while neglecting domestic civilian needs and undermining the real economy. Hence the national 'decline' that has been so fruitful a topic over the past few decades.[37] Hence, too, the use of external power to compensate for internal imbalance and weakness. Thanks in part to its own constitutional

---

[36] For a broad, learned and possibly more optimistic discussion of cycles in presidential activism, see A. M. Schlesinger, *The Imperial Presidency* (Boston, Houghton Mifflin, 1973) and *The Cycles of American History* (Boston, Houghton Mifflin, 1986).

[37] See for example, P. Kennedy, *Rise and Fall of the Great Powers* (New York, Random House, 1987), and *Preparing for the Twenty-First Century* (New York, Random House, 1993), ch. 13; S. Schlosstein, *The End of the American Century*; Calleo, *Beyond American Hegemony*; Report of the comparison of the skills of the average work force, *America's Choice: High Skills or Low Wages* (Rochester, 1990); R. Rosecrantz (ed.), *America as an Ordinary Power* (Ithaca, Cornell University Press, 1976); M. Green and M. Pinsky, *America's Transition: Blueprints for the 1990s* (Lanham, MD, University Press of America, 1990).

inadequacies, the US became a 'hegemon in decline', relying on its power in the world system to compensate for its growing weakness at home.[38]

The imperial solution began to break down seriously as early as the 1960s. This was the decade in which the American public revolted against the human cost of the imperial role, while the political system demanded a redirection of resources to civilian needs. This was also the decade when Europe began to mobilize itself to resist the exactions of its declining hegemon. The next two decades have witnessed the playing out of the struggles that followed from these reactions. The Soviet collapse and the American fiscal crisis have now brought our constitutional game to its present phase.

Where will it go from here? Clinton's election did register wide public recognition that a crisis is in view. But Clinton received considerably less than a majority of the votes cast.[39] Much of the public has probably doubted from the start that he could resolve the worsening problems that he and Perot brought into the open. The hopeful have counted on a Democratic president to instil some return to party discipline within a nominally Democratic House and Senate. It is obviously too early to see how well Clinton may succeed. But the protracted struggle over a 'budget agreement' shows him to have, at best, only a tenuous majority in Congress. So much compromise is required to sustain that majority that any coherent and radical policies from the administration are unlikely to be carried. Clinton's budget agreement bears out such a prognosis. Although it does raise upper-middle class and corporate taxes, it promises no more deficit reduction than a similar agreement negotiated by the Bush administration two years earlier. At best, it will merely stabilize the deficit at its present high level.[40] In the process of achieving it, moreover, the new administration was forced to jettison a good part of its plan for targeted public

[38] See Calleo, *Beyond American Hegemony*, p. 149. See also C. Kindleberger, 'Systems of international organization', in Calleo (ed.), *Money and the Coming World Order* (New York, 1976); B. Buzan, *Peoples, States and Fear: the National Security Problem in International Relations* (Chapel Hill, University of North Carolina Press, 1983). For historical parallels, see C. M. Cipolla, *The Economic Decline of Empires* (London, 1970).

[39] President Clinton was elected with just 43 percent of the popular vote, the lowest figure since Woodrow Wilson in 1912 (42 percent). A survey showed that 57 percent of the population were concerned or scared by the prospect of a Clinton presidency. On the eve of inauguration, a *Time*/CNN survey showed that only 41 percent of the public thought that Clinton was completely trustworthy, 50 percent said they still had reservations. For an analysis of the 1992 election results, see 'The 1992 vote for Clinton: another brittle mandate', *Political Science Quarterly*, Spring (1993), 1–28.

[40] The Senate finally approved Clinton's budget plan on 25 June 1993 after a 50–49 vote with Vice President Al Gore casting the deciding vote. The package of spending cuts and tax increases will reduce the deficit by an estimated $500 billion through fiscal year 1998. The plan has been criticized, like the Bush plan of 1990, because it relies on optimistic assumptions about US economic performance. The OECD, assuming weaker growth, low inflation rates and higher interest rates than those used by the Clinton administration, estimates that the 1998 fiscal deficit will be 15 percent higher than official US forecasts suggest. *World Economic Outlook* (Washington DC, International Monetary Fund, October 1993), p. 54.

[41] During his election campaign, Clinton, emphasizing that government should borrow only to invest, announced a plan to target investment of $219 billion on education, skills training and infrastructure development. See R. Reich in *The American Prospect*, Fall (1992), 61–4. The plan in its original integrated form was, however, reduced in scale during Congressional budget negotiations, and finally represented an increase in Federal investment of just $7.1 billion for fiscal year 1994. *The Budget of the United States Government: Fiscal Year 1994* (Washington DC, US Government Printing Office, 1993), p. 72. A supplementary plan announced early in the Clinton administration to boost growth and create jobs and to cost over $18 billion a year was killed by a Republican filibuster in April 1993.

investment, arguably its own best idea in the campaign.[41] It still faces the enormous challenge of conceiving and carrying through Congress a basic reform of the health care system. Given the tenuousness of its majority, the prospects are scarcely reassuring.

If Clinton is seen to fail, what will follow? The American malaise may well move to a more radical stage. Without a revival of the imperial presidency, what other direction could reform take? Serious efforts at reform can be found stirring in the Congress itself. Campaign financing rules have been debated with unusual acuteness and a balanced-budget amendment last year came within a handful of votes of achieving a two-thirds majority in the House.[42] The great and sudden strength of the Perot movement indicates, in itself, widespread disaffection from normal political parties and, indeed, from normal political practices and structures.

Within the federal government itself, the root ailment seems to be the lack of an efficacious balance between the executive and legislative branches. Woodrow Wilson, as a young professor, once suggested a parliamentary system, with a prime minister depending on a majority.[43] In recent times, France seems to have found a reasonable arrangement to combine presidential power with a strong government with a majority. In the French system, and indeed in most European systems, the legislature can throw out a government but not change the details of its budget or meddle with the details of its policies.[44] Such a change would be a revolution in American constitutional practice, but perhaps no greater than what the French experienced in 1958.

In all such fanciful discussions of reform, America's continental scale and diversity is the reality that distinguishes the American system from most other Western or Westernized democratic nation states. Rather than a comparison of the US with a European nation state, perhaps a more appropriate parallel is between the US and Europe's own nascent confederation built around the European Community. Put in this perspective, both the failings and the achievements of America's federal system can be better understood. To some, the parallel also suggests that the US has grown too centralized to be governed properly.

The relative power of the states and the federal government is, of course, another ancient topic of American constitutional debate. Today, it is easy enough to argue that America's federal government is 'overloaded'. The problem with redistributing power is that the states lack the legitimacy or,

[42] The House of Representatives voted on the balanced budget amendment sponsored by Senator Paul Simon, a Democrat from Illinois, on 11 June 1992. It failed by nine votes to achieve the required two-thirds majority. A Senate version failed by four votes to reach a two-thirds majority in March 1994.

[43] Wilson's advocacy of a British-style Cabinet system stemmed from his perception that the power of the presidency had been seriously diminished by a succession of weak presidents following the assassination of Abraham Lincoln. A Cabinet drawn from the Congress itself would, Wilson believed, control the power of individual committees and ensure a strong, decisive and accountable executive, regardless of the character of the President himself. His enthusiasm for reform along such lines, however, declined after the election of Grover Cleveland and then Theodore Roosevelt, two strong, charismatic presidents. See Woodrow Wilson, *Congressional Government: a Study in American Politics* (Baltimore, Johns Hopkins University Press, 1981). For a brief introduction to Wilson's early views, see A. S. Link, *Woodrow Wilson*, vol. 1, *The Road to the White House* (Princeton, Princeton University Press, 1947), pp. 14–9.

[44] For an explanation of French constitutional arrangements, see R. Hadas-Lebel, 'The governmental structure of the Fifth Republic', *SAIS Review*, Special Issue; Fall (1993).

in most cases, the scale to cope successfully with the major social and economic problems of a modern society. In this respect, the European Community's 'Europe of States' possesses a more promising distribution of central and 'regional' power for the kind of articulated governance that a large continental system requires. Obviously, the more centralized American system also has features and powers that Europe has not achieved, or does not want. In any event, no one can legislate that America's existing states become the cultural, political, economic or moral equivalents of Europe's nation states.

George Kennan, among others, has recently been advocating bold steps in a European direction. He suggests a regrouping of American states into thirteen regional entities – including three large urban agglomerations – New York, Chicago and Los Angeles. These super-states would be more like German Laender than American states, and would therefore assume many current federal powers. This would not only permit solutions better adapted to what are often quite different regional conditions and propensities in America, but also allow greater experimentation with diverse solutions. Kennan imagines that the super-states on the Latin border (Florida/Puerto Rico, Texas, or the Southwest – including Southern California) might grow increasingly Hispanic in their population and culture. He leaves open the nature of their relationship with neighbouring Latin American states – except to suggest that intimate relations would be natural and in everyone's best interest.[45]

Kennan's suggestive if Delphic comments about the Hispanic presence in the United States raise the familiar issues of 'multi-culturalism' and 'historic revenge', issues that currently bedevil many American universities. They can be used either to support a relaxation of central control, which is Kennan's position, or a strengthening of it. Traditionally, the United States has always sought to impose English through 'Americanization' in the schools. This part of the tradition will probably continue to prevail. Most Hispanic immigrant families are poor and lack formal education. Mastering English is likely to remain their obvious route to economic success and cultural advancement. But there seems no reason why Spanish language and Latin American culture cannot be taught in schools as well. If this means that regions of the US ultimately become bilingual, it is hard to see this as a diminution of American culture.

Such a prospect will undoubtedly frighten many people. The reaction could at least indirectly reinforce the tendency to strengthen the federal government, perhaps also to retain or seek new hegemonic duties abroad. Among American political élites of the older generation, moreover, there remains a strong feeling that only attachment to the world role can keep America's motley population in some kind of civic discipline. And the American role in the world is not, after all, the product merely of American ambition to fulfill it. There remains always the possibility of some major new geopolitical enemy who will return American priorities to a Cold War pattern. The situation in Asia, for example, seems strangely unbalanced and could become chaotic, with China an obvious threat.

---

[45] G. Kennan, *Around the Cragged Peak: a Personal and Political Philosophy* (New York, Norton, 1993).

Reluctance to see Japan become militarily independent – particularly as a nuclear power – could easily be used to justify a continuing American protectorate, given a more aggressive Chinese military posture. China, too, may find an external enemy necessary for maintaining inner cohesion.

It may be doubted, of course, whether the American public feels a sufficient attachment to Asia to support the sort of existential commitment that was made to Europe in the Cold War. Nor are America's economic interests in Asia as promising as is often assumed. In many respects, Asia is the source of America's economic problems rather than the solution. Trade remains highly unfavourable to the US, nor is it clear what will make the balance improve in the foreseeable future.[46] If American business needs a large area for lucrative investment and cheap labour, Latin America may seem a safer bet. This is not to suggest that Americans will lose interest in Asia, merely that they will not mobilize their society to remain the dominant power there.

In any event, there is no reason to accept the familiar dichotomy of the 1930s – between an America that is imperial and an America that is 'isolationist'. The present American mood might better be described as 'measured internationalism'. Students of American public opinion have long noted the decline of sentiments that can properly be called isolationist.[47] The great bulk of the public accept the need to play a major external role, less from a craving for grandeur than to protect the nation's own security and prosperity. But there is also the deep suspicion that America's allies have been 'free-riding' too long for their own good, or for the health of the United States.

A policy of regional coalition-building and devolution fits well with such a mood of measured internationalism. Logically, it should mean support for European integration, including efforts to build a 'European pillar' in the Alliance, preferably within NATO. These are long-standing American positions, but they may be advanced in the future with fewer second thoughts. America's role in the Yugoslav crisis seems to fit this pattern. It certainly shows a strong American diffidence toward pulling Europe's chestnuts out of the fire. Yugoslavia also illustrates a renewed American interest in using the United Nations. Engagement in the Security Council's machinery has a certain logical drift of its own – toward multilateralism and away from hegemony.

In summary, so long as no enemy superpower threatens the US, the drift toward regional self-help in Europe and multilateralism in the world seems to suit the current American mood. That this mood is both an opportunity and a challenge for European confederalism seems obvious. It should not, however, lend much encouragement to nationalist European policies that count on an American safety net.

Ideally, the new era will lead to a rejuvenation of state institutions on both sides of the Atlantic – perhaps even to a certain convergence of structures. Europe's nation-states need to strengthen their collective arrangements for

---

[46] In 1992, the US trade balance with Asia was $−84.05 billion compared with $−73.4 billion in the previous year. In contrast, trade with the two NAFTA countries, Canada and Mexico, had deficits of $−3.95 billion in 1991 and $−0.45 billion in 1992. Trade with Western Europe showed a positive balance of $16.13 billion for 1991 and $6.19 billion for 1992. *Survey of Current Business*, July (1993), pp. 16–7. The average annual trade balance between the US and Latin America for the period 1989–92 was $2.1 billion in surplus. OECD, *Economic Outlook*, 53, June (1993), 186.

[47] D. Yankelovich, 'Foreign policy after the election', *Foreign Affairs*, Fall (1992), 1–12.

ordering a continental market, maintaining regional security and taking an effective role in sustaining global order and balances. The US, by contrast, needs to devolve power from its overloaded central system, while at the same time making the federal machinery more efficient, politically and administratively.

To return to the observation made at the outset, America's current economic, political and social problems do not arise from no longer being a hegemonic superpower. Rather, they are the result of having been one for too long. The end of the Cold War gives the US a splendid opportunity to recoup its inner strength and balance. It means more resources should be available for civilian needs. It should permit the gradual reform of what has become an excessively wasteful and overcentralized federal system. It should also help encourage America's élites to devote more of their attention to domestic rejuvenation than to world management. Such a shift will doubtless be inconvenient. In the end, however, it may prove no bad thing – either for the US, or for its friends in the world.

Such a view may reflect an American inclination for more optimism than seems reasonable. But even if the United States is entering, as I think, a certain crisis as a continental nation state, nothing ordains that its government and people cannot rise to the occasion. Given the history of the past century, the nature of America's current predicament is not difficult to grasp, nor is there any reason to be greatly surprised at it. The remedies require some imagination, courage and luck – but not to a degree that makes success unimaginable. The United States was founded, two centuries ago, as an experiment 'to decide the important question, whether societies of men are really capable of establishing good government from reflection and choice, or whether they are forever destined to depend for their political constitution on accident and force'.[48] The experiment is certainly not over.

---

[48] Alexander Hamilton, *The Federalist Papers*, no. 1, R. Fairfield (ed.) (New York, Doubleday, 1966), p. 1.

Russia: a Crisis of Post-imperial Viability

JOHN BARBER

Crisis may be an overused term in political analysis, but nobody applying it to the Soviet Union and Russia since the late 1980s could be accused of exaggeration. In the most literal sense of the word, it describes the period of intensifying political conflict and accelerating economic decline which ended in the collapse of the Soviet state in December 1991. Whether the even steeper economic decline and bitter political confrontation seen in post-Communist Russia since then will similarly culminate in the collapse of the new Russian state remains to be seen; at present, this appears no less possible an outcome than any other. In a more general sense, crisis captures the striking contrast between the remarkable stability which characterized the Soviet state and society for four decades following World War II, punctuated occasionally by brief succession struggles, and the political turmoil and social unrest resulting from the failed policies of perestroika. (The latter has more parallels with Russia in the first two decades of the twentieth century.) It also points to the wider significance of events in Russia. Given the size of the population and territory involved, and the potential repercussions beyond the borders of the former Soviet Union, they may well constitute the greatest crisis of the state in the contemporary world.

Analysing the politics of the Russian crisis poses major problems, which arise from the fact that the crisis is not only a series of conflicts and upheavals, but also an acute phase in a process of change affecting all structures of society. These are in a state of flux, at times changing with great rapidity. The difficulty of understanding the connections between developments in different spheres, of identifying key institutions and actors at any given time, are substantial – as the repeated inability of both participants and observers to anticipate the course of events suggests. Failure to predict the sudden break up of the Soviet Union and the collapse of the Communist system, or the breach between Yeltsin and his allies, or the rise of Zhirinovsky and the Liberal Democrats, are a reflection less of analytical incompetence than of the role of contingency in crises on the one hand and the virtual unknowability of key factors at such moments on the other. (As the example of an earlier Russian crisis indicates. No-one in February 1917, including Lenin, envisaged that the Bolsheviks would take power only eight months later. In October, few Bolsheviks, excluding Lenin, imagined that they would retain power for long).

With the advantage of historical perspective, the patterns of causality may be easier to discern. For the present, it is less useful to attempt to explain why the Russian crisis has happened as it has than to focus on the context of that crisis, and specifically to examine the changing character of the state, which has been and remains at its epicentre. It will be argued that in the first phase of the crisis, an imperial state collapsed, or rather was destroyed. In the second, current phase, the building of a new state, a nation state, has begun. This process, however, is far from complete, and the hazards involved pose major threats to its viability.

There are few better illustrations of what E. H. Carr called 'the familiar reaction of the principle of continuity against the onset of revolutionary change'[1] than the evolution of the Soviet state. Lenin's insistence in 1917 that the proletarian revolution would smash the existing state machine and his assertion that under socialism the state would disappear challenged the whole political tradition of Tsarist Russia, where (as Gramsci remarked) 'the state was everything'. But within weeks of taking power he had shelved indefinitely any notion of the state withering away. Almost immediately the exigencies of economic collapse and civil war led the Bolsheviks to adopt many of the institutions, personnel and practices of the Tsarist state, and to intermesh them with those of their party to produce the party-state which ruled Soviet Russia for the next three-quarters of a century. Like its predecessor this state took the leading role in the country's economic modernization, in the process vastly expanding its own size, scope and powers.[2] This all-embracing state was central to the rise of the Soviet system, as it would be to its fall.

Continuity in the Russian state's pre- and post-revolutionary role was equally a feature of the political relationship between the Russian half of the population and the numerous ethnic minorities. For geo-political reasons (that from the sixteenth to the nineteenth centuries it expanded into adjacent territories), Russia evolved as an imperial state. But it was an empire with a difference. The emergence of Russia as a modern state, as part of the European political system, under Peter the Great (the first tsar to adopt the title of emperor) had not accidentally been accompanied by the appearance of new words to distinguish the Russian state (*Rossiia*) and its citizens (*rossiane*) from the historic Russian heartland (*Rus'*) and ethnic Russians (*russkie*). The concept of the Russian empire (*rossiiskaia imperiia*) was explicitly not one of an ethnic Russian empire, but of an autocracy whose citizens regardless of nationality owed allegiance to the tsar and could be employed in the service of the state[3] (In the eighteenth and nineteenth centuries non-Russians, particularly from the Baltic provinces and Armenia, occupied prominent positions in the state bureaucracy.) Only in the late nineteenth century did an ideology of Russian nationalism develop, and with it the policy of the Russification of non-Russian provinces. The latter, however, was only selectively applied. Neither in theory nor practice did the idea of Russia as a nation state have a significant political impact.

If in general World War I extended the ideological and political importance of the nation state, then Russia was the outstanding exception. The Bolsheviks proclaimed the obsolescence of the nation as the basis for a society's political

---

[1] E. H. Carr, *Socialism in One Country* 1924–1926, vol. 1 (New York, Macmillan, 1958), p.8.

[2] Moshe Lewin, *The Making of the Soviet System* (London, Methuen, 1985); Lewis Siegelbaum, *Soviet State and Society between Revolutions*, 1918–1929 (Cambridge, Cambridge University Press, 1992).

[3] John Dunlop, 'Russia: confronting a loss of empire', in Ian Bremmer and Ray Taras, *Nations and Politics in the Soviet Successor States* (Cambridge, Cambridge University Press, 1992), p. 45.

arrangements. The very word Russia was absent from the original title of their own regime, which was described simply as 'the workers' and peasants' government'.[4] The state they created on the somewhat reduced territory of the former Russian empire was a multi-national, supra-national one. In the process of its formation, however, Leninist realism, recognizing that the idea of the nation state had far from exhausted its strength produced the compromise on which the Union of Soviet Socialist Republics was based: between the *de jure* federal state, consisting of nationally defined territorial units, and the *de facto* unitary state governed by the central party-state apparatus. Throughout the USSR's existence, centralism prevailed in every important political and economic respect; expression of national identity in the republics was permitted in culture alone, and then only to a limited degree. At the same time, the idea of the nation state, though essentially a fiction, was treated with respect. All-union republics possessed the right of secession and were provided with attributes and symbols of statehood; their own constitutions and laws, governments and capitals.[5]

Though it emphatically repudiated the suggestion, the Soviet Union like its predecessor was in essence an empire. The multi-national society was ruled by a highly centralized state, by a Moscow-based bureaucracy, with Russians or other Slavs generally holding the key political and economic, military and security appointments in the non-Russian republics. Russians were settled there in their millions, often playing a leading part in the process of modernization. Russian language and culture were promoted among the ethnic minorities, while reminders of Russia's leading role, past and present, among the nations constituting the USSR were ubiquitous: 'Great Russia [*Rus'*] united for ever the indestructible union of free republics', ran the opening lines of the Soviet national anthem. Russian patriotism, when it served the regime's purposes, was stimulated; overtly between 1941 and 1945 to mobilize support for the war effort, covertly in the Brezhnev period, when conventional ideological themes had lost their appeal.[6]

Unlike Tsarist Russia, the Soviet Union after 1945 acquired an external empire as well as a global political and military role. But its internal empire, like that of its predecessor, eschewed in theory if not in practice any ethnic basis. While Russians were encouraged to see their national interests as subsumed in those of the Soviet Union, the only patriotic identification officially permitted was with the Soviet motherland (*sovetskaia rodina*). Any manifestation of a Russian nation state as fact or idea was firmly suppressed. In this respect, Russia was deliberately discriminated against compared with the other union republics. Unlike them, it was allowed neither a capital, a Communist Party, an Academy of Sciences, nor its own KGB or Ministry of the Interior. Even its territorial composition was treated as a matter of political

[4] Carr, *Socialism in One Country*, vol. 1, p. 15.

[5] W. Connor, *The National Question in Marxist-Leninist Theory and Strategy* (Princeton, NJ, Princeton University Press, 1984); R. Pipes, *The Formation of the Soviet Union* (Cambridge, MA, Harvard University Press, 1964); Graham Smith, 'Nationalities policy from Lenin to Gorbachev', in G. Smith (ed.), *The Nationalities Question in the Soviet Union* (London, Longman, 1990).

[6] F. C. Barghoorn, *Soviet Russian Nationalism* (New York, Oxford University Press, 1956); J. B. Dunlop, *The Faces of Contemporary Russian Nationalism* (Princeton, NJ, Princeton University Press, 1983); R. Szporluk, 'Nationalities and the Russian problem in the USSR: an historical outline', *Journal of International Affairs*, 27, no. 1 (1973).

convenience; in 1954 the Crimea, with its largely Russian population, was detached from the Russian republic and incorporated in the Ukraine.[7] And for all the advantages Russians enjoyed in terms of access to positions of influence in the Soviet state and society, their living conditions were no better than those of non-Russians, their ecology was no less despoiled, and they were no more immune from political repression, cultural control or religious persecution. If the Soviet Union was an empire, the Russians were a distinctly underprivileged imperial people.

Given its eventual fate, it is tempting to portray the Soviet Union as an anachronistic continuation of the Russian empire, doomed from the outset, which postponed its inevitable disintegration mainly due to highly developed forms of state coercion. This seriously distorts the historical record. For well over half a century the Soviet system provided the basis for rapid economic growth and social change, for improved living standards, for the establishment of a welfare state, for the creation of cultural, educational and scientific structures of international quality, for stable relations for the greatest diversity of ethnic groups in any country in the world, and for a defence establishment able to maintain the country's security in the face of the greatest imaginable threats. Whatever the cost of these achievements, they do not suggest a state whose viability was always in question.

Concern that the Soviet political structure and the bureaucracy's practices impeded the efficient functioning of the economy was a recurrent theme of public debate from the late Stalin period onwards. The reform associated with Kosygin in the latter half of the 1960s was the last major attempt to decentralize economic management. Like earlier attempts it failed both because of opposition from the party apparatus, afraid that a reduction in its executive power would diminish its political influence, and because until well into the 1970s the Soviet economy, for all its failings, had proved capable of simultaneously enabling military parity with the West to be achieved, providing the Soviet population with a slow but steady increase in consumption, and generating sufficient surplus for capital investment.[8]

By the 1980s, however, the Soviet system was visibly ailing. Immobility in the top echelons of government, institutional stagnation, the virtual cessation of economic growth, and adverse developments in the Soviet bloc (particularly in Afghanistan and Poland) combined with a drive by the USA under Reagan to break the nuclear stalemate by developing new weapon systems of potentially unmatchable sophistication to force reform back on to the Soviet political agenda. Under Andropov the Soviet leadership began to confront the implications of the Soviet Union's worsening economic performance for its vast range of military, political and social commitments. Only with Gorbachev's election as General Secretary in March 1985, however, did the scale of the problem become apparent.[9] At this time he frequently referred to the 'pre-crisis'

---

[7] For the peremptory character of the transfer, see 'Iskliuchitel'no zamechatel'nyi akt bratskoi pomoshchi', *Istoricheskii arkhiv*, no. 1 (1992), 39–54.

[8] Ed. A. Hewett, *Reforming the Soviet Economy* (Washington, DC, Brookings Institution, 1988); Alec Nove, *The Soviet Economic System*, (London, Allen and Unwin Hyman, 3rd ed., 1986).

[9] Archie Brown, 'Gorbachev and reform of the Soviet system', *Political Quarterly*, 1987; Jerry Hough, *Soviet Leadership in Transition* (Washington, DC, Brookings Institution, 1980).

situation in the Soviet Union; the term would be more appropriate than he could have imagined.

Perestroika was often described by Gorbachev as 'revolutionary' – but only in terms of its consequences does this seem a valid description.[10] The motives for perestroika appear typically reformist – to preserve the basic elements of the Soviet system (the party's political monopoly, central planning, state owned industry and agriculture), but to increase its efficiency by adding market mechanisms as well as cultural, and to a lesser extent political, pluralism. Fundamental structural change, such as ending the political leadership of the country by the Communist Party guaranteed by article 6 of the Soviet constitution, was opposed by Gorbachev until the pressure was overwhelming. Whether perestroika amounted to a strategy is doubtful. It was less a coordinated set of measures aimed at a clearly defined goal (such as the policies of the Chinese Communist Party since the late 1970s) than an attitude of mind ('new thinking'), consisting of a highly critical assessment of Soviet institutions and policies, a rejection of traditional beliefs and values, and an openness to discussion of alternatives. This gave perestroika its radical image, and was more than enough to destabilize the existing system, without providing a feasible alternative. Opponents who accused Gorbachev of inconsistency and vacillation were correct, with three exceptions – in foreign policy, where the policies of furthering *détente* and achieving arms reductions produced favourable Western responses; in promoting glasnost, whose momentum became irreversible because of the need to maintain the support of the intelligentsia and of Western public opinion; and in preserving the unitary state.

Why did pre-crisis turn into terminal crisis? The strains resulting from the imperial structure of the Soviet state may have provided powerful incentives to change the system, but they also created an unpropitious climate in which to undertake reform. The structure was much more frail than it appeared. The claims of Soviet ideologues and Western Sovietologists notwithstanding, the Soviet state in its final decade was far from monolithic. It is now clear that by the 1980s the political system was becoming increasingly differentiated. At the centre, power was divided between the main political institutions, of which the party apparatus, theoretically the heart of the system, was only one. During the Brezhnev period, power had moved to major ministries (defence, the KGB, industry), over which the party apparatus had only limited control. In the republics and regions, meanwhile, a feudalization of the power structure had taken place, with autonomy traded for political loyalty and nominal fulfilment of the Plan. Given that the Gorbachev group's power base was the central party apparatus, it was natural that in the name of eliminating corruption from the system they should seek to bring the ministerial bureaucracies, republics and regions back under its control, initially through purges and new appointments, later by means of glasnost and democratization. But with the party élite itself

[10] Anders Aslund, *Gorbachev's Struggle for Economic Reform* (London, Pinter, 1989); Seweryn Bialer (ed.), *Politics, Society and Nationality inside Gorbachev's Russia* (London, Westview, 1989); Michael Ellman and V. Kontorovich (eds), *The Disintegration of the Soviet Economic System* (London, Routledge, 1992); Geoffrey Hosking, *The Awakening of the Soviet Union* (London, Mandarin, 1991); Eugene Huskey, *Executive Power and Soviet Politics* (London, Sharpe, 1992); Stephen White, Alex Pravda and Zvi Gitelman, *Developments in Soviet Politics* (Basingstoke, Macmillan, 1990); Stephen White, *After Gorbachev* (Cambridge, Cambridge University Press, 1993).

deeply divided, the attempt failed, and the reaction to it only strengthened the centrifugal tendencies in the system.[11]

The external empire added to the problems facing the Soviet leadership. The heavy costs, financial and political, of maintaining Soviet control of Eastern Europe (and between 1979 and 1989, of Afghanistan) aggravated their domestic dilemmas; while the example of oppositional movements such as Solidarity added to the momentum of change in Soviet society. 1989 was above all the crucial turning point. The Soviet government's decision not to veto the rejection of the Communist regimes of Eastern Europe by their populations created a powerful precedent for challenges to its own policies of maintaining the Communist Party's political monopoly and denying independence to the nominally sovereign Soviet republics. In the event, both the abrogation of article 6 of the constitution and the first declaration of independence by a Soviet republic, Lithuania, took place in March 1990.

The manifest existence of serious structural strains together with the subsequent collapse of the Soviet state provide grounds for the argument that the Soviet system was intrinsically unreformable, and that (as conservatives in the party leadership warned with growing vehemence) the dangers involved in attempting reform were bound to prove lethal. It is certainly unlikely that the Soviet Union could have survived indefinitely in its pre-perestroika form. But it is equally improbable that other policies than those adopted by the Gorbachev group would not have had different consequences, which might, as in the Chinese case, have produced a more than short-term revival. In retrospect it seems clear that the abandonment of the Communist Party as the main vehicle for policy making and implementation and the discarding of Marxism-Leninism as the official ideology destroyed both the political base and the legitimacy of the Soviet leadership. Political choice in these and other areas appears to have had a substantial impact on the course of events – though how much real choice Gorbachev and his associates had is difficult to know, when self-serving memoirs and highly selective archival documents are the main sources of primary information about the reasons for the adoption of policies which ended in the demise of the USSR.

What is clear, however, is that while the role of agency in this process was crucial, to focus exclusively on the mistakes of the Gorbachev leadership is misleading. The Soviet Union did not simply collapse; it was destroyed by the action of its opponents. The crisis of the Soviet state in its decisive phase, 1990–1, consisted of an intense struggle for power. This had the state-breaking outcome that it did because what had begun as a struggle for power within the existing political system became, for the part of the political élite which broke within Gorbachev, a struggle against the existing political system. The alliance of reform Communists and anti-Communist 'democrats', led by Boris Yeltsin, did not obtain state power in Russia by default. By appealing to widespread disillusion with the Soviet system in general and the policies of the Gorbachev government in particular, they gained a majority in the Russian parliament in the elections of spring 1990 and thus took control of the state apparatus of the Russian republic. With this, limited though its powers were, together with the legitimacy conferred by their electoral success, they proceeded to activate step

---

[11] For a revealing account of this process by one of the main architects of perestroika, see A. N. Yakovlev, *Predislovie, Obval, Posleslovie* (Moscow, Novosty, 1992).

by step the Russian government's potential capacity, inherent in the constitution, to challenge the authority of the Soviet government and to erode its ability to rule the country. The Russian republic's declaration of sovereignty in June 1990, the bilateral political and economic agreements signed with other republics, the March 1991 referendum approving the establishment of a Russian presidency, Yeltsin's election to this post in June 1991, the formation of Russian state committees on defence and security, the creation of a Russian television channel and radio station, all steadily advanced the Russian republic towards full statehood.

Parallel developments were taking place in other republics. In some, particularly the Baltic republics, Georgia and the Ukraine, the undermining of the central government went still faster, with leading officials of the Communist Party collaborating with nationalists to work for full independence; though by virtue of its economic and political strength it was the Russian republic's growing assertiveness which posed the greatest threat. One factor, however, distinguished Russia from the other republics challenging the Soviet government's authority. Elsewhere mass organizations had emerged from 1988 onwards to campaign for nationalist demands and had played an important role in the all-union election of 1989 and the republican elections of 1990. In Russia, attempts to establish a nationalist popular front in 1989 failed because of divisions between 'empire-savers' and 'nation-builders'. It is doubtful in any case how successful such a movement would have been in attracting mass support. While the Soviet government was increasingly unpopular, the idea of the Soviet state was far from discredited. In March 1991, the referendum on the future of the USSR produced a vote of 71% in the Russian republic in favour of the preservation of the union.[12] Even with due allowance made for the vagueness of the question put to the electorate and for the absence of any breakdown of the results by nationality, the idea of a separate Russian nation state does not appear to have commanded widespread allegiance before the Soviet Union's collapse. While support among Russians for the 'democrats' in their opposition to the Soviet government was evidently substantial, there is no evidence that it included support on a large scale either for separation from the union or for the radical economic policies which would subsequently be adopted.

How far in any case was securing Russia's independence for Yeltsin and the democrats an end in itself, as opposed to the only available means to dispose of the Gorbachev government and with it the Soviet economic and political system? It is possible that they shared the common view among Russians that Russian subsidies maintained the living standards of the ungrateful ethnic minorities, and that Russia would do better to cut itself off from the other republics. Alternatively, they may have judged that the separatist trend in the republics was irreversible, and decided to take Russia down the same path. Yeltsin during 1990–1 repeatedly denied any intention of planning the break-up of the Soviet Union, which might have been true at least in the short run. It might well have been to Russia's and the other republics' advantage for the transition to full independence to have been effected over a period of years rather than months.

[12]Dunlop, 'Russia: confronting a loss of empire', pp. 57–8, 65.

But the essential point is that the decline in the Soviet state's capacity to maintain itself was already well advanced by the time of the abortive coup in August 1991 which precipitated its collapse. Faced with growing resistance from republican governments, including the withholding of tax revenue, Gorbachev in April agreed to the '9 + 1' talks between the centre and most of the republics over a new union treaty. In August these resulted in a treaty which would effectively have turned the USSR into a confederation, with substantial power delegated to the republics and the imperial structure of the USSR largely demolished. It was to prevent the signing of this treaty and to preserve the union in its traditional form that the leaders of the central state institutions (the government, the armed forces, the KGB, the ministry of the interior, the party apparatus) staged their coup. And with its collapse Yeltsin seized the moment, uninhibited by questions of constitutional legality, to ban the Communist Party and take control of the central state apparatus and armed forces. Three months later, together with the leaders of Belarus and the Ukraine he established the Confederation of Independent States and declared the dissolution of the USSR.

If Gorbachev had called an essentially reformist project 'revolutionary', Yeltsin did exactly the opposite. In the name of carrying through economic reforms, he and his government, led in the first year by an advocate of free market economics, Yegor Gaidar, launched Russia down the path of rapid transformation.[13] Continuity in some of the leading personnel (including many members of the old political élite, the *nomenklatura*, headed by Yeltsin himself) and institutions (the presidency, parliament, soviets) should not obscure the fact that the aim was to destroy the remaining structures of state socialism, any more than the return to traditional Russian values, symbols, names (the reincorporation of the Orthodox Church into public life, the renaming of cities and streets, the adoption of pre-revolutionary administrative terms such as guberniia and duma) should conceal the intention to create a new capitalist social and economic order. The new Russian Revolution may have had more in common with 1688 than with 1789 or 1917, but it still represented a conscious and fundamental break with the past. To the new Russian leadership, Gorbachev's fate was the inevitable consequence of reformist procrastination; it therefore had to implement irreversible changes at the maximum possible speed.

Given this, the turbulent politics of post-Communist Russia are not surprising. In post-revolutionary situations, a new regime invariably faces major problems in establishing control of the administration of the country, there are bitter disputes over means and ends, and protracted struggles for power within the new élite, as well as between it and former rulers unwilling to accept their defeat. Attempting the wholesale implementation of an ambitious programme, underestimating the obstacles in the way of creating the new order, and learning from painful experience (generally most painful for the population) what is feasible are also familiar features of such a regime. The Yeltsin government, moreover, has been firmly in the Russian tradition of state-directed social and economic change, of revolution from above. It has obviously differed from its Stalinist predecessor in the extent of violence, coercion and suffering; and its financial and ideological indebtedness to the West contrasts strikingly with the

[13] Richard Sakwa, *Russian Politics and Society* (London, Routledge, 1993); White, *After Gorbachev*.

hostile capitalist encirclement that accompanied the Soviet industrialization drive of the 1930s. But like Stalin's modernization strategy, Yeltsin's was imposed with minimal regard for its social consequences, and with the urgent insistence (for the benefit perhaps of the rulers as much as the ruled) that time was not on their side. The common lack of popular support for the process was even more marked in Yeltsin's case. (The enthusiastic participants and beneficiaries of the early five year plans were undoubtedly more numerous than those of the reforms implemented since January 1992).

This is not to deny that Yeltsin succeeded in retaining sufficient of his initially substantial support to win two crucial referendums; in April 1993 on confidence in the president, in December 1993 on his draft of the constitution. But it is probable that this support owed more to charismatic appeal and the absence of feasible alternatives (and also probably to Western electioneering techniques) than to approval of his government's economic policies. In the December 1993 elections to the State Duma, the humiliating defeat of the main pro-governmental party, Russia's Choice, and the success of the anti-government Liberal Democratic Party and Communist Party provided Yeltsin with sobering evidence of the public's hostility to the effects of shock therapy.[14] Whether the subsequent withdrawal of Gaidar and Fedorov from the government and the apparent moderation of economic policy signify an abandonment of the strategy of radical change or merely a temporary retreat remains to be seen.

The conflicts which have plagued Russian political life since the collapse of the Soviet Union are in the first instance the result of the unpopular policies applied since January 1992. But their traumatic impact – which reached a climax in the storming of the parliament building on 4 October 1993, though not an end, as the renewed confrontation between the government and parliament after the December elections would show – was the product of the legacy of the previous regime: a fragmented élite and an unworkable constitution.

The Soviet political élite in its last years had been no more united than the system it managed was monolithic. Factions, interest groups, clientalist networks had always existed, even under Stalin, and they had proliferated in the Brezhnev period.[15] But until perestroika they were kept within bounds, and out of the public's awareness, by the tradition of party discipline and by the controls at the disposal of the central party apparatus. This situation changed rapidly under the impact of glasnost. Differences within the ruling group were clearly discernible by 1987, and from 1989 fractions, 'platforms', were being openly organized; regardless of the leadership's will, political pluralism was emerging in the party itself. Meanwhile, thousands of *neformaly*, informal political or social groups, were being founded. By themselves these did not constitute an immediate political threat to the existing order. But when dissident groups in the party began to form alliances with them, counter-élites appeared which first challenged and then deposed the old élite.

---

[14] Vera Tolz, 'Russia's parliamentary elections: what happened and why', *RFE/RL Research Report*, vol. 3, no. 2, 14 January (1994).

[15] V. Bunce and J. Echolls, "'Pluralism' or 'Corporatism'?", in Donald Kelley (ed.), *Soviet Politics in the Brezhnev Era* (New York, Praeger, 1980); H. G. Skilling and F. Griffiths, *Interest Groups in Soviet Politics* (Princeton, NJ, Toronto University Press, 1971); Susan Solomon (ed.), *Pluralism in the Soviet Union* (London, Macmillan, 1983).

In Post-Communist Russia, however, from the start the political élite was significantly less unified than its predecessor had been until its final phase. The defeat of the conservative wing of the Soviet establishment with the failure of the August 1991 coup, soon followed by the downfall of the Gorbachev centrists, removed the forces which had served to unite radicals of various shades in opposition to the older order. Even before the Soviet Union finally disappeared, Yeltsin had lost his guaranteed majority in the Russian parliament. In November the latter reversed his decision to use troops to put down a rebellion in the Chechen-Ingushetian republic; and while in the same month it voted him special powers for a year to issue decrees with the force of law on economic matters, it reserved for itself the right to veto these. Within weeks of the introduction of radical economic reform, the political élite had become polarized between the supporters of such reforms, who dominated the government, and their opponents, who constituted the parliamentary majority. Nothing better reflected the élite's fragmentation than the emergence as leaders of the opposition to Yeltsin's policies of Ruslan Khasbulatov, his chosen successor as chairman of the Supreme Soviet of the Russian Federation, and Alexander Rutskoi, his vice-president. As the conflict deepened, a process similar to that which had occurred under Gorbachev took place; namely the formation of alliances between alienated factions of the political élite and non-establishment groups ranging from Communists to centrists to right-wing nationalists. The smashing of parliamentary resistance in October 1993 halted the rise of a counter-élite; but the potential evidently remained.[16]

Meanwhile the ruling group was slow to develop mechanisms for ensuring its own unity. Apart from the powers of appointment and patronage, these seem conspicuous by their absence. Yeltsin has occasionally talked about founding a party, but in the event has chosen to remain at least in theory 'above parties'. As a result ministers were to be found in rival parties contesting the December 1993 elections, to the confusion of the electorate and the detriment of the government. Within the government the notion of collective responsibility is weakly developed, with disagreements over economic policy openly paraded. For an élite attempting to implement a radical strategy, moreover, its sources of active support seem narrow. These basically comprise part of the old *nomenklatura*, with its strong network of connections (which however also includes members of the opposition), a rapidly diminishing section of the intelligentsia, and the small but growing new entrepreneurial class. What appears to be totally absent is any link, institutional or other, with the working class, a constituency which the Communist Party, with the largest registered membership of any party, and its nationalist counterparts have not ignored. The risks of attempting to carry through unpopular policies with a relatively weak social and political base and in the face of organized opposition would appear to dictate either a modification of those policies and/or the formation of a coalition with other political tendencies – or a retreat to authoritarianism.

That political conflict has posed so great a threat to the stability of the Russian state is largely due to the political structure inherited from the Soviet period. It is for this reason that the question of the constitution became the central issue in Russian politics in the second year of the new state's existence.

[16] David Lane, 'Political élites and leadership under Yeltsin' *RFE/RL Research Report*, vol. 2, no. 30, 23 July (1993).

As opposition within the party apparatus towards the policies of perestroika mounted, Gorbachev had made two major constitutional innovations. In summer 1988 he persuaded the 19th party conference to end the party's direct involvement in government and transfer its executive role to the soviets. The following March after nationwide elections a new body, the Congress of People's Deputies, came into being which in turn elected a new Supreme Soviet. This body was already sovereign according to the Soviet constitution, although its role had been largely formal. It now became a working parliament, with a major legislative role and some control over ministers. As its chairman Gorbachev had direct influence over legislation as well as exercising executive powers. A parliamentary system of government seemed to be evolving. But as opposition in the country, and particularly in the Congress and Supreme Soviet increased, Gorbachev changed course. In March 1990 the new post of executive president was created with Gorbachev as its incumbent. This was endowed with substantial powers, increased at the end of the year, including making government appointments, issuing decrees and dissolving parliament, and was supported with a large secretariat and advisory bodies. The presidential system now in the making, however, was unable to reverse the decline in Gorbachev's position. Although he exercised his power to issue decrees widely, so too did the increasingly assertive union and republican parliaments. The Soviet crisis moved towards its climax against the background of a 'war of laws'. Meanwhile, in 1990–1 parallel institutions, parliamentary and presidential, were established in the republics.

The new Russian state thus inherited a hybrid system of government. It was headed by an elected president (unlike Gorbachev, appointed to the Soviet presidency by the Supreme Soviet, Yeltsin had won an absolute majority in the Russian presidential election of June 1991) with substantial power to implement sweeping changes – but given him temporarily by a sovereign parliament (which had also been elected, in 1990). The political conflict which soon developed over the government's economic reforms inevitably took the form of a struggle for power between the executive and the legislature. Yeltsin and his ministers made extensive use of decree powers to bypass the legislative process and force through the reforms; while parliament attempted to use its constitutional powers of control over the government to influence its composition and policies, exploiting in the process the executive powers of its chairman, which were modelled on those originally possessed by Gorbachev. With a substantial apparatus of his own and exercising his right to issue his decrees, Khasbulatov formed what came to be virtually a shadow government.

This situation of dual power produced a series of political crises.[17] At the sixth Congress of People's Deputies in April 1992 parliamentary pressure resulted in the appointment of representatives of the heavy and defence industry sectors to the government. Over the following months there were attempts to incorporate the centrist block, Civic Union, in government, but

---

[17] See Alexander Rahr, 'Yeltsin and Khasbulatov: analysis of a political struggle', *RFE/RL Research Report*, vol. 2, no. 12, 19 March (1993), and 'The roots of the power struggle', *RFE/RL Research Report*, vol. 2, no. 20, 15 May (1993); Nina Belyaeva and Vera Tolz, 'Crisis as a form of political development', *RFE/RL Research Report*, vol. 2, no. 20, 14 May (1993); Dominic qualtieri, 'Russian Parliament renews power struggle with Yeltsin', *RFE/RL Research Report*, vol. 2, no. 32, 13 August (1993).

these failed. At the seventh Congress in December parliament threatened to remove the president's special power, securing instead the replacement of Gaidar as prime minister by Victor Chernomyrdin, and an agreement to hold a referendum on a new constitution. In February 1993 this compromise broke down, with Khasbulatov instead calling for early elections for both parliament and president. Yeltsin's reaction in March was to proclaim 'special rule', in effect a state of emergency, but then immediately to retreat. This time the compromise took the form of holding a referendum in April on the questions of confidence in the president and his policies, which Yeltsin won, and early elections, where the result was negative. Yeltsin used his victory to bypass parliament, the only body with the legal right to amend the constitution, and convene a Constitutional Assembly in July. This debated, without approving, a draft of a new constitution, which was instead referred to the parliaments of the Russian Federation.

In the meantime, a new 'war of laws', was in progress.[18] Literally thousands of laws, decrees, directives were being issued by conflicting authorities, by government and parliament, president and vice-president, prime minister and chairman of the Supreme Soviet. Often deliberately, sometimes simply through ignorance or incompetence, these contradicted each other on major policy issues, such as the state budget and privatization, and on appointments. With political deadlock threatening administrative chaos, Yeltsin in August called for 'immediate action against the opposition' and declared that September would be 'a month of serious political struggle'. Fulfilling his own prediction, on 21 September he announced the dissolution of parliament and the holding of new elections. Parliament's response to what the Constitutional Court immediately declared was an illegal act was to impeach Yeltsin and appoint Rutskoi acting president. Negotiations to resolve the crisis, mediated by the Patriarch, were in progress when on 3 October fighting broke out between government and parliamentary forces. Claims of armed uprising and government provocation seem equally improbable; spontaneous action by militant para-military units appears to have swept the parliamentary leadership into endorsing it (as happened to the Bolshevik leadership in July 1917), bringing devastating retribution the following day.[19]

The immediate outcome of the crisis was to allow Yeltsin to seize the political initiative and bring the debate over the new constitution to an end. The final draft, published in November and approved in a referendum in December, removed any ambiguity about the location of power in the Russian state by creating an unequivocally presidential system.[20] Under the new constitution, the president has decisive powers over government appointments and policy. He controls defence and foreign policy, and has power to declare war and states of emergency, issue decrees, call referendums, veto legislation and dissolve parliament. The power of the latter (comprising the State Duma and the Federation Council) is limited to the right to oversee government appoint-

---

[18] Dominic Gualtieri, 'Russia's new "War of Love"', *RFE/RL Research Report*, vol. 2, no. 35, 3 September (1993), pp. 10–5.

[19] Alexander Rahr, 'The October Revolt: mass unrest or putsch?', *RFE/RL Research Report*, vol. 2, no. 44, 5 November (1993).

[20] Carla Thorson, 'Russia's draft constitution', *RFE/RL Research Report*, vol. 2, no. 48, 3 December (1993).

ments, initiate legislation, approve the budget and economic policy, and impeach the president (though the procedure involved would make this difficult if not impossible). Parliament has lost the ability directly to challenge the president's exercise of power, though not the capacity to obstruct government – particularly since there exists no mechanism other than review by the Constitutional Court to resolve clashes between presidential and parliamentary decisions. The new constitution makes no pretence to a balance of power between the central institutions of the state; like that of the first French Republic, its priority is to ensure a stable basis for government.

Any hope that the combination of a presidential system and a docile parliament would provide political stability, however, was rudely shaken by the results of the December 1993 elections and the renewed conflict between government and parliament when the latter convened in January 1994. The new constitution no more ensures that the executive can exercise its powers than the constitutional changes introduced by Gorbachev enabled him to survive. For all Chernomyrdin's claim at the opening of the State Duma that 'the state has acquired a solid legal foundation',[21] the legitimacy of the constitution remains in doubt. Not only did the process of its approval contradict the former constitution by bypassing the Congress of People's Deputies; it contradicted the rules originally accepted by Yeltsin himself, under which it had to be approved by a majority of the electorate. (In the event it was approved by 58.4% of those voting, who were 54% of registered electors, that is by less than a third of the electorate.[22]) But this would not be the first constitution to be enacted in controversial circumstances. Whether it can provide a viable structure for governing the country would appear to depend on the willingness of the executive and legislature to observe its provisions, and on the success of the government's economic policies. The past record does not give strong grounds for optimism.

Dangerous though the effects of the political struggle between government and parliament have been and remain, the greatest threat to the survival of the Russian state as presently constituted probably comes less from this source than from the relationship between the centre and the provinces. In the aftermath of the Soviet Union's collapse, central control over the provinces has reached its weakest point since the civil war of 1918–20. The possibility exists that the Russian Federation could experience the fate of the USSR and fragment into its component parts.[23] The problem lies in Russia's vast size (comprising 75% of the territory of the former Soviet Union it is the largest country in the world), its great heterogeneity (the Russian Federation consists of 21 ethnic republics and 68 regions, including another 13 national territories), and the effect of the Soviet Union's collapse.

The way in which the USSR disintegrated had a highly destructive impact on the patterns of subordination binding Russia's provinces to its central government. While in practice local élites already enjoyed some autonomy, the

---

[21] BBC Summary of World Broadcasts SU.1893/B2 (11 January 1994).

[22] SWB SU.1877/B1 (21 December 1993).

[23] For an assessment of the possibility of the Russian Federation's republics following the example of those of the USSR, see L. M. Drobizheva, 'Povtorit li Rossiia put' soiuza?', in *Sotsial'nye konflikty* no. 2, part 1 (Moscow, Russian Academy of Sciences Institute of Ethnography, 1992).

example of the union republics' successful challenge to Moscow's authority inevitably stimulated aspirations both to greater practical independence and its formal recognition. These were encouraged by the protagonists in the final stages of the Soviet state's crisis for their own purposes. Yeltsin in March 1991 imprudently declared that the republics within Russia 'can take as much independence as they can administer. We can agree to all of it'; while the Gorbachev group, to undercut the Russian government's position, proposed recognition of the sovereignty of all national territories in the Russian republic and their subordination directly to the USSR.[24] Somewhat belatedly Yeltsin recognized the danger of Russia disintegrating. With local government still in the hands of the old *nomenklatura* despite the banning of the Communist Party after the August 1991 coup, since it largely controlled the soviets in which power was legally vested, Yeltsin attempted to strengthen the centre's control by appointing 'heads of administration' in the republics and regions, supplementing them with 'presidential representatives'.

Soon after the Soviet Union's collapse, the Russian government declared its intention to create a new federal structure, and took an important step in this direction in March 1992 with a Federal Treaty between the central government and the constituent members of the Russian Federation (the republics, regions, autonomous districts, and the cities of Moscow and St. Petersburg).[25] This gave new rights to the republics, including some control over foreign policy and foreign trade, and recognized that the land and natural resources belonged to the peoples of the republics. It did not, however, extend such rights or recognition to the regions (which comprise over 80% of the population and 70% of the territory). And since the treaty was essentially a declaration of intent, it had no direct impact on the position of the provinces, where centrifugal trends continued. Two republics (Chechnya and Tartastan) refused to sign the treaty; Chechnya in any case claimed to have seceded from Russia. The regions demanded rights equal to those of the republics, some asserting claims to sovereignty. (In summer 1993 the Sverdlovsk region unilaterally declared itself a republic, a move immediately vetoed by Yeltsin.) And following the earlier example of the union republics, some of the Russian republics and regions withheld taxation revenue from central government.

The provinces also became a factor in the power struggle at the centre, with both sides trying to gain their support for their versions of the constitution; the president concentrating on the republics, parliament on the regions. The presidential draft presented to the Constitutional Assembly in July 1993 went so far as to recognize the republics as 'sovereign states', and allowed their inhabitants to hold joint citizenship, republican and federal. But the dominant tendency in the provinces remained hostile to central government. In the April 1993 referendum more than half the republics produced majorities against the president. When Yeltsin dissolved the parliament in September most of the republican and regional soviets condemned the decision; and in the ensuing crisis an attempt was made to displace the government altogether. On 30 September 93 provincial leaders set up a Council of Members of the Russian

---

[24] Dunlop, 'Russia: confronting a loss of empire', pp. 51, 53.
[25] Vera Tolz, 'Thorny road towards federalism in Russia', *RFE/RL Research Report*, vol. 2, no. 48, 3 December (1993).

Federation to take control of the government of the country pending the holding of elections for parliament and president.

The suppression of parliament's resistance produced an immediate reassertion of central authority over the provinces. Yeltsin dissolved all soviets at city levels and below; ordered elections to regional and district soviets and 'recommended' elections to republican parliaments. Heads of administration were given extra powers; some who had sided with parliament were dismissed. A presidential envoy was sent to one particularly rebellious republic, Mordovia, to 'supervise' its parliament and government. When the final draft of the constitution was published, several of the earlier concessions to the republics had been dropped, including their description as sovereign states and the introduction of republican citizenship, and the equal status of republics and regions was stressed. When in January 1994 Yeltsin addressed the opening session of the upper house of the new parliament, the Federal Council, he declared that the results of the referendum on the constitution showed that the voters 'were unanimous that the Russian Federation should continue to be an integral state'.[26] The evident falsity of this assertion is less important than its significance as a statement of the centre's intent.

To what extent the government will succeed in regaining political control over the provinces is unclear. The spirit of independence unleashed by the Soviet Union's collapse is still in evidence. The supposedly unanimous result of the referendum in fact included votes in 24 republics and regions which were either against the constitution or invalid because of low turn-outs.[27] Three republics (Bashkortastan, Tatarstan and Tyva) simultaneously voted for constitutions of their own which proclaimed their sovereignty, and in the case of Tyva its right to secede.[28] Such actions do not have a great deal of practical significance; for economic and geographical reasons, separation is a feasible option for few if any of the Russian republics; though for some of the larger and richer regions it might be. But they reflect an attitude which is likely to be a major obstacle for a government set on re-establishing central authority – without which neither the successful implementation of its policies, nor the control of local resources, including the lifeblood of government, taxation, will be possible

The existence of strong attitudes of local independence points to one of the key issues for the Russian state: the problem of national identity. For many Russians the end of the Soviet empire and birth of the Russian nation state has been a disorienting experience. It begs the question – what is Russia? What is the political community with which the citizens of the new state are supposed to identify? What are its national interests?[29] By contrast with other former Soviet republics, several with a history of independent statehood and a strong sense of national identity, in Russia consensus is conspicuous by its absence – even on questions of territory and demography. With the exception of the small number of separatists among the ethnic minorities, there is agreement that the territories at present in the Russian Federation are Russian (and for

[26] SWB SU.1893/B2 (12 January 1993).

[27] Tolz, 'Russia's parliamentary elections', p.3.

[28] SWB SU.1878/B5 (22 December 1993), 1891/B4 (10 January 1994), 1892/B4 (11 January 1993).

[29] Vera Tolz, 'Russia: Westernizers continue to challenge national patriots', *RFE/RL Research Report*, vol. 1, no. 49, 11 December (1992).

this reason there is strong opposition to returning the Kurile islands to Japan). But what about territories beyond the borders of the Russian Federation, in Estonia, Latvia, Kazakhstan, Moldova, the Ukraine, with predominantly Russian populations? What about the 25 million ethnic Russians living outside Russia? Although they do not yet have Russian citizenship, they are widely seen as being entitled to the protection of the Russian state. If they vote for the reunification of their territory with Russia, as for example the people of the Crimea are likely to do,[30] does it become part of Russia? The question of Russian identity is both conceptually and politically a complex one.

In the periods immediately preceding and following the collapse of the Soviet Union, an acceptance of a Russia defined by its existing borders and an isolationist view of its national interests were common. Opinion polls revealed approval in Russia for the secession of the non-Russian republics from the Soviet Union.[31] An imperial concept of Russia continued to be disseminated by nationalist groups and by some of the Communist Party's successor organizations, and no doubt had many adherents, not least among the old Soviet *nomenklatura*. But the view that Russians were 'tired of empire' seems not unfounded. Popular attitudes, however, can alter, particularly at times of major social and political change. The electoral success of Zhirinovsky's Liberal Democrats in the December 1993 elections, with their unequivocal message of a Russia 'within its historic borders', provides some evidence for a resurgence of the idea of Russia as empire.

In any case, the belief that Russia because of its size and geographical position is bound to exercise a leading role in the region comprising the former Soviet Union is not confined to the 'red-brown' extremes of the Russian political spectrum. The Civic Union has argued for a more assertive Russian foreign policy towards the CIS, and has advocated the latter's transformation into a confederation which would promote economic integration. Many opposition leaders, notably Rutskoi, demanded action to defend the rights of Russian minorities in the 'near abroad'.[32] Yeltsin belatedly took up the issue in his New Year broadcast in January 1994, telling them that 'we defend and will defend your and our common interests'.[33] During 1993 the CIS signed agreements on economic union and collective security; although implementation was delayed. In September, Vyacheslav Kostikov, a presidential spokesman, predicted that the former Soviet republics would eventually form a new political and economic union; by uprooting a 'few prickly nationalist weeds' a new commonwealth could be created.[34] And in his address to the Federation Council on 11 January, Yeltsin said of the CIS, 'our countries are already being linked together, and in the process it is Russia's calling to be first among equals'.[35]

In more concrete ways as well, developments during 1993 suggested that Russia's post-imperial aversion to close involvement with countries of the

[30] On 30 January 1994, a Russian nationalist, Iuri Meshkov was elected the first president of the Crimea, committed to holding a referendum in March on the question of the Crimea rejoining Russia. *The Independent*, 1 February (1994).

[31] Dunlop, 'Russia: confronting the loss of empire', pp. 63–5.

[32] Tolz, 'Russia: Westernizers continue to challenge Russian patriots'.

[33] RFE/RL News Briefs, 27 December 1993–4 January 1994.

[34] Elizabeth Teague, 'The CIS: an upredictable future', *RFE/RL Research Report*, vol. 3, no. 1.

[35] SWB SU.1893/B2 (12 January 1994).

former Soviet Union might be at an end. Russian troops were in action in peace-keeping roles in Georgia, Moldova and Tajikistan. In the first two cases at least, there are grounds for suspecting that Russia's involvement was in part directed at bringing the republics concerned back into the Russian orbit; in December Georgia joined the CIS. Earlier in the year, Azerbaijan rejoined. Several countries remained in the rouble zone, giving Russia considerable influence over their economies; at the end of the year Belarus applied to rejoin, as Georgia also seems likely to do. The remark of the Russian foreign minister, Andrei Kozyrev, in a speech to Russian ambassadors to the CIS countries and the ex-Soviet Baltic countries in January 1994, that 'we should not withdraw from those regions which have been the sphere of Russian interests for centuries; we should not fear the words "military presence" ', was a far cry from the relative isolationism of two years earlier.[36]

These developments do not necessarily point to imperialist aspirations on the Russian government's part, to a restoration of empire. The costs, economic and political, would be almost certainly too high. But they do suggest that Russian hegemony over its immediate neighbours, in cases where economic, historical and strategic factors coincide, may be inevitable, and may even be sought by local élites.[37] At any rate, it may be premature to speak of Russia as a post-imperial state.

It is in any case impossible to say that a Russian nation state in the full sense of the term has yet been created. What exists at present is a weak, semi-federal and semi-imperial state, lacking stability and predictability. Its institutions are in conflict and in flux, while its government is liable to be forced into sudden changes of course, and possesses a distinctly limited capacity to implement its own decisions.

None of this, however, is particularly surprising. Crises as deep as that of the Soviet/Russian state are not usually resolved speedily or with little conflict. A crisis involving the collapse of an empire, the transition from an authoritarian to a democratic form of government, and the transformation of a centrally planned economy to a market economy might be expected to involve considerable turmoil over an extended period of time. From this perspective it might be argued that the Yeltsin government in a short time has had a reasonable degree of success. Major changes have been set in motion, at a cost but not to date a fatal one. The Russian state's ability to discharge its functions has been impaired but not destroyed. Economic decline has produced hardship, but not mass unemployment or starvation. Security of life and property has diminished, but the rise in crime has not turned into anarchy. Political conflict has not erupted into civil war or large-scale inter-ethnic violence. Troops have been involved in military action on the periphery of the country, but Russia's territorial integrity has been preserved. There has been suffering and violence; but the people of Russia, unlike those of Armenia or Azerbaijan, Georgia or Moldova, Afghanistan or Yugoslavia, have not been exposed to the catastrophes of war, famine or genocide.

---

[36] RFE/RL News Briefs, 10–21 January (1994)

[37] As reflected in the words of the Speaker of the Georgian parliament at the beginning of 1994. 'Georgia must ally more closely with Russia ... We shall not find a more reliable brother than Russia ... I am asking Russia to support my country actively in order to save it.' SWB SU.1892/F4, (11 January 1994).

The record to date provides grounds for expecting that the Russian state will continue to maintain itself. From the present period of crisis, however extended it may be, a new and more stable order will eventually emerge. In what political form is a matter for speculation; whether democratic or authoritarian, unitary or federal, in its present territorial shape or smaller or larger, is impossible to predict. Given the prominence of the state in Russian history and political culture, and the appeal of the idea of the nation to a society suffering a crisis of identity, it is likely that Russia's future will be as a nation state. And though no longer an empire, Russia, for economic, geo-political and strategic reasons, appears destined (or doomed) to continue to play an imperial role.

Rescue or Retreat? The Nation State in Western Europe, 1945–93

WILLIAM WALLACE*

'My first guideline is this: willing and active cooperation between independent sovereign states is the best way to build a successful European Community. To try to suppress nationhood and concentrate power at the centre of a European conglomerate would be highly damaging. ... Europe will be stronger precisely because it has France as France, Spain as Spain, Britain as Britain, each with its own customs, traditions and identity.'

Margaret Thatcher, British Prime Minister, speech to College of Europe in Bruges, 20 September 1988.

'The nation state was the twin of the industrial society, and like industrial society it is becoming outworn. ... The evolution of Europe in the next decades will be shaped by the phasing in of the information society to replace the industrial culture and industrial technology which have served us so well for almost two hundred years.'

Poul Schluter, Danish Prime Minister, speech to the America–European Community Association, London, 20 September 1988.

'Nations are not everlasting. They have a beginning, they will have an end. Probably a European confederation will replace them.'

Ernest Renan, *Qu'est-ce qu'une nation?* Lecture to Sorbonne, Paris, 11 March 1882.

'Both the nation state and integration appear as fortunate accidents of the time, fundamentally contradictory tendencies, which nevertheless in promoting economic growth fortuitously complemented each other.'

Alan Milward, *The European Rescue of the Nation State* (London, Routledge, 1992), p. 24.

The European State and West European Integration

The tension between the nation state and international integration is central to any discussion of the development of the European political system since the Second World War – as to its likely development during the 1990s. Three overlapping questions are at stake. How far were the processes of European integration deliberately designed to undermine national sovereignty and create instead a European federal state? How have the autonomy and integrity of European nation states been affected by the evolution of economic, social, technological and political integration over the past 45 years? How far were

*I am grateful for comments and advice on an earlier draft from participants in the *Political Studies* conference on 'the crisis of the nation state' in Cambridge, September 1993; and also to Anne Deighton, Ralf Dahrendorf, Anthony Forster, Jack Hayward, Alan Milward, Julie Smith, Helen Wallace and Vincent Wright.

both the reconstruction of West European nation states and their development of intense patterns of cooperative management and formal and informal integration dependent upon the provision of security and hegemonic political and economic leadership by the United States within the Cold War 'Western' order, rather than on the efforts of European leaders themselves or the dynamics of intra-European politics?

The main concern of this paper is with the second of these questions rather than with the first or the third – though it notes that the passion with which proponents of federalism and defenders of sovereignty argued their case in the 1950s and 1960s served to obscure the more subtle impact of economic, social and technological trends, and it notes the extent to which the American role and the importance of the stable security framework were underplayed in the analysis of West European integration in the 1960s and 1970s. It argues (with Milward, Hoffmann and others) that there was – at least until the end of the 1960s – a positive-sum relationship between the security and economic frameworks which the institutions of European integration (including those American-sponsored frameworks for European cooperation, NATO and OEEC/OECD) had built, and the maintenance – or re-establishment – of national legitimacy and autonomy.[1] The ability of national governments to satisfy the aspirations of their citizens and to achieve their own economic and political objectives was strengthened, not weakened, by the institutional containment of West Germany within the EEC, the confidence in continuing economic growth which progress in economic integration provided, and the additional resources which that continuing growth gave national governments to spend on welfare, industrial and technological policies, and defence.

Two definitional points must briefly be noted before our discussion proceeds. First, there is a subtle but vital distinction between the concepts of sovereignty and autonomy. Some nineteenth century theorists, building on seventeenth and eighteenth century models, claimed for the state itself as the expression of the nation an authority unchecked by internal or external constraints; others saw sovereignty as both legitimized and checked by 'the consolidation of the community-state relationship' in the democratic nation-state. Both saw the essence of sovereignty in 'the ultimate primacy of the power of the state': its formal independence from any superior authority.[2] Autonomy is a relative, not an absolute, concept: to be assessed in comparative terms with reference to external constraints and domestic vulnerabilities to outside developments. Sovereignty is formal, legal; autonomy informal, shaped by economic, social and security factors. Second, the processes of regional international integration within Western Europe must be placed within the context of the wider – but looser – processes of globalization which flow from the transformation of communications and the emergence of a global economy. Distinctive elements of West European experience since 1945 include: the presence of an accepted external hegemon (the USA) with surplus security and economic resources available to lessen the costs of integration to the participating states; a degree

[1] Stanley Hoffmann, 'Obstinate or obsolete? The fate of the nation state and the case of Western Europe', *Daedalus* Summer 1966, 862–915. Alan Milward, *The European Rescue of the Nation State* (London, Routledge, 1992); Alan Milward (ed.), *The Frontier of National Sovereignty* (London, Routledge, 1993).
[2] F. H. Hinsley, *Sovereignty* (London, Watts, 1966), p. 230.

of shared identity and community sufficient to support compliance with common rules and the limited transfer of resources within the region; the establishment of formal institutions for regional international cooperation – OEEC, NATO, and for the core states the EC (and WEU) – marking mutual limitation of sovereignty for mutual benefit; and the marked demographic and geographical concentration of the region, above all of its core area around the Rhine valley and delta.[3]

'There is', Karl Deutsch wrote 40 years ago, 'apt to be confusion about the term "integration" ' – most of all between the deliberate political process of institution-building which constitutes formal integration and the largely un-directed processes of economic and social interaction which constitute informal integration.[4] The early theorists of European integration saw the institution-building framework as setting in train new patterns of cross-border transactions which would in time create new cross-border shared interests, and so raise perceptions of political community, identity and loyalty 'beyond the nation state'.[5] Working together, through the newly-established structure of inter-governmental committees and through the economic associations and social and political groups which increasing interactions would encourage, would lead to a process of informal political integration, through which participants would come to recognize their common interests and to transfer their loyalties to this wider European entity. This constituted – as will be argued in the section following – an ideology of integration much more than an analytical theory.[6]

The relationship between formal and informal integration, it is now clear, is much more complex. The framework of rules and regulations which formal institution-building establishes serves to channel and direct – as well as to inhibit and redirect – informal flows. But economic and social development, aided by technical change, may in time raise those flows to an intensity which faces governments with the dilemma of limiting further development or adjusting rules to accommodate their consequences; so setting off a push-pull process between formal and informal integration, moving from partial bargains among governments to adjust the formal balance between autonomy and common policies to further intensification of informal exchanges, and so to renewed pressures for changes in rules and structures.[7]

The impact of economic and political integration on national autonomy since the end of the 1960s is much more open to question. Paradoxically the years

---

[3] The distinctiveness of West European integration is explored further in W. Wallace, *Regional Integration: the West European Experience* (Washington, Brookings, forthcoming 1994).

[4] Karl Deutsch *et al.*, *Political Community and the North Atlantic Area* (Princeton, NJ, Princeton University Press, 1957), p. 2. Mica Panic, in *National Management of the International Economy* (London, Macmillan, 1988), p. 142, uses the term 'spontaneous integration' to describe informal economic integration.

[5] Ernst Haas, *Beyond the Nation State* (Stanford, CA, Stanford University Press, 1964). For a survey of the extensive theoretical literature on West European integration see Carole Webb, 'Theoretical perspectives and problems', in Helen Wallace *et al.* (eds), *Policy-making in the European Communities* (New York, Wiley, 1983).

[6] Theorists, largely American, and Commission officials shared these perceptions of the dynamics of the process; see for example Walter Hallstein, *Europe in the Making* (London, Allen and Unwin, 1972). Its original German title was *Der Unvollendete Bundesstaat*.

[7] William Wallace, 'Introduction: the dynamics of European integration', and Robert O. Keohane and Stanley Hoffmann, 'Conclusions: Community politics and institutional change', in William Wallace (ed.), *The Dynamics of European Integration* (London, RIIA/Pinter, 1990).

in which *formal* political integration seemed to be making least progress –
between 1972 and 1984–5 – appear in retrospect to have witnessed a progressive
erosion of national autonomy, arising out of changes in technology (particularly in its impact on communications), in methods of production and
management, and in the explosion of cross-border movement throughout
Western Europe. These trends have been reinforced by the integration of
financial markets and investment flows, which has been such a marked
development during the 1980s.[8]

The dramatic clashes between proponents and opponents of European
Union in the early 1960s obscured the relatively limited incursions on national
autonomy then proposed. Conversely, the relative caution with which most
national governments in the 1980s approached formal proposals for the
transfer of power and authority from states to European agencies and
institutions obscured the progressive erosion of national autonomy through
informal (economic and social) integration and the increasingly intensive
interlocking of governments and administrations which has marked the
nation-state response to these trends.[9]

Any assessment of how far these developments have undermined the core
functions of the nation state – or, alternatively, forced nation states to
adapt to increasing interdependence without severely affecting their core
functions – depends partly on one's perception of the role and function of
the nation state as such: a perception which differs to some degree from
one European state to another, reflecting the distinctive historical
experience of different European states. States have probably lost most
autonomy in the economic sphere: where 'national champion' strategies have
given way, to one degree or another, to acceptance of multinational cooperation and external and internal investment, and where the instruments of
national economic management have been blunted by economic integration.
They have lost considerable autonomy over national defence – and more over
defence procurement; and are beginning to lose autonomy over the central state
functions of public order and maintenance of territorial boundaries. Rule-making and decision-making – law and government – are increasingly becoming
caught up in multilateral bargaining: not (as postwar idealists hoped) bypassing
the nation state, but collectivizing national decisions through intergovernmental negotiations.

For the nation state as a focus for popular identity and a basis for legitimacy,
by contrast, little has changed; despite the remarkable increase of a social
interchange and media integration over the past 20 years. A certain diffusion
of loyalties, a certain expansion of horizons from the national to the European
(and the global), are evident both among élites and – more faintly – among
mass publics. But challenges to the legitimacy of national institutions and élites
have come largely from within existing states: leading to fragmentation, not
integration. Throughout Western Europe the national community remains the

---

[8] Richard O'Brien, *Global Financial Integration: the End of Geography* (London, RIIA/Pinter,
1992); Albert Bressand, 'Regional integration in a networked world economy', Margaret Sharp,
'Technology and the dynamics of integration', in Wallace, *Dynamics of European Integration*.

[9] For the distinction between formal and informal integration, see William Wallace, *The
Transformation of Western Europe* (London, RIIA/Pinter, 1990), ch. 4.

broadest focus for political life and group identity. This growing discrepancy between the political sphere and the economic and social (and even military and public order) spheres was already unsettling national politics in some Community member states in the late 1980s, and became a focus for argument over national autonomy, and even national identity, during the ratification process for the Treaty on European Union in 1992–3.

Assessment of the impact of political and economic integration on the nation state depends partly upon the observer's perception of the stability or developmental character of the European state. Margaret Thatcher (and Charles de Gaulle), seeing the nation state as a natural and permanent framework for political life, have seen both the creeping flow of informal integration and the deliberate bargaining and rule-making of formal integration as a fundamental threat – and an impossible dream. Poul Schluter, and those who see the modern nation state as itself the creation of an earlier process of political, economic and social integration over the past 100–200 years, are less fundamentalist; the nation state for them is a product of modernization, and technological and economic innovation may indeed be rendering the concept of the autonomous nation state obsolete. Academic analysts can be found in both camps, defending the state as the only political reality or emphasizing the relative novelty of the developed nation state and the radical implications of the adjustments West European states are gradually making in the face of rapid internal and external changes.[10]

Ideology and Integration

The idealists who defined the rhetoric of European integration were anti-nationalists: shaped by the bitter experiences of World War Two, the pathological mutation of nationalism into Fascism and National Socialism, the military defeat of Germany's neighbours and the corrosive impact of occupation. Later historians have questioned whether the reality of intergovernmental bargaining – over the Schuman Plan, the European Defence Community proposals, the Messina 'relaunch' – ever approached the rosy picture of Euro-idealism which the early apologists painted. But the enthusiasm which suffused the Commission in its early years represented an explicit challenge to national governments – and to the opposing rhetoric of national sovereignty – which aroused (under President de Gaulle) the French Government's vigorous opposition, and made the British and Scandinavian Governments deeply suspicious of the whole process of institutionalized integration.[11]

---

[10] Thus Milward starts 'from the realist position that the modern nation state is still the arbiter of its own destiny' (*The Frontier of National Sovereignty*, p. 20), and – in spite of including Belgium within his compass – equates nation with state throughout. Compare W. Wallace, *The Transformation of Western Europe*, chs 3 and 4.

[11] Alan Milward, *The Reconstruction of Western Europe*, 1945–51 (London, Methuen, 1984), provides the most vigorous – and convincing – presentation of the 'revisionist' interpretation against those who portrayed the history of European integration in terms of the intellectual leadership and influence of the 'Europeans'. Contributors to Raymond Poidevin (ed.), *Histoire des Débuts de la Construction Européenne* (Brussels, Bruylant, 1986) support the same view that the influence of intellectual idealists was limited, the role of national governments central.

The characteristically 'technocratic' approach of the early theorists and practitioners of 'the Community Method' was not only implicitly anti-national, but also anti-political.

> 'It relied on technology as the fuel, and on the logic of the market as the motor of integration: the drive for economic modernization would lead to political unity. It was the old Saint-Simonian dream of depoliticized progress, accompanied by one idea that, at first sight, seemed quite political: the idea that the gradual dispossession of the nation-state and the transfer of allegiance to the new Community would be hastened by the establishment of a central quasi-federal political system.'[12]

But the new system was itself conceived of in largely technocratic terms: its dynamism to be derived from a professional élite within the Commission, to whose disinterested proposals national governments had to respond. The immediate model was the post-World War Two French planning system, which was successfully rebuilding the state and modernizing the economy even while the political class was squabbling over the disintegrating institutions of the Fourth Republic. 'The development of French planning in the 1950s can be viewed as an act of voluntary collusion between senior civil servants and the senior managers of business. The politicians and the representatives of organized labour were both largely passed by.'[13]

The drama of institutionalized (or formal) European integration as a challenge to the nation state was thus played out in the early years of the European Community, most directly in the clash of perspectives and wills between the first Commission President, Walter Hallstein (a German *Beamte* rather than a French *Fonctionnaire*), and President de Gaulle. The Commission package of proposals of 1964–5 on EEC revenues and expenditure, linked to the completion of the Common Agricultural Policy, majority voting in the Council of Ministers, and increased powers for the European Parliament/ Assembly represented a dash towards supranationalism; and as such aroused an intransigent response from de Gaulle and the French Government. The Luxembourg Compromise, on this interpretation, represented a clear victory for intergovernmental cooperation under the careful control of state administrations over supranational integration. That was, after all, how it was interpreted in the Commission, which issued defiant statements on its continuing commitment to the 'European ideal', as well as within most national governments. British politicians and officials, for example, were much reassured; a Community in which national governments retained firm vetoes over undesired developments was a Community which it might be safe to enter without jeopardizing parliamentary sovereignty.

This was however a Brussels-centred drama: enthralling for those who looked to the Community and its institutions as *the* focus for European politics, but of only secondary importance to the large majority of national politicians and officials on whose responsibilities and concerns the three Communities (ECSC, Euratom and the EEC) had not yet impinged. Once we step outside the committed perspective of those who battled over the Brussels institutions,

---

[12] Stanley Hoffmann, 'Reflections on the nation-state in Western Europe today', *Journal of Common Market Studies*, 21 (1982), 29.

[13] Ralph Miliband, *The State in Capitalist Society* (London, Weidenfeld, 1969), p. 53.

it becomes clear that national political systems throughout most of Western Europe were more strongly entrenched, and more effective in delivering material and symbolic benefits to their citizens, in the 1960s than they had ever been before.

A major element in this was due to sustained economic growth: international cooperation plus Keynesian demand management, with national economies still for most purposes firmly under national control while benefitting from increasing *trade* across national frontiers. Governments large and small across Western Europe sponsored nationally-owned companies and followed different interpretations of corporatism both in their handling of relations among government, workers and managers and in the relations between government, public and private financial institutions and industry. The percentage of each national economy accounted for by the public sector was high; the percentage of national income accounted for by taxation and by the distributive and redistributive impacts of public expenditure was far higher in almost mixed democratic 'mixed economies' than in their predecessor regimes of the interwar period. This in turn enabled state administrations to provide substantial welfare benefits to all their citizens: the nation state strengthening its legitimacy and its hold on its citizens' loyalty by becoming 'the welfare state'.[14]

The contrast with the interwar period is evident. Then, national governments and state administrations which found themselves unable to guarantee employment to a large minority of their citizens, and cut welfare benefits as recession set in and public revenues fell, suffered revolutionary challenges from right and left. Some collapsed into authoritarianism, even into civil war. The stable framework of rules which the OEEC provided, and the confidence that stability would continue, gave governments a far stronger base for national economic development. The acceptance of Keynesian economic policy – or more broadly of social partnership, economic management and social democracy – legitimized the active state. National industrial development and rising public revenues also enabled West European governments to spend more on defence, and on nationally-designed and manufactured military equipment. Alan Milward, deliberately attacking the historical school of 'Euro-enthusiasts', concludes that 'the power of the European nation-state reached its highest point at the end of the 1960s ... the period 1945–1968 may be considered as that of its [final] achievement: the apogee of a pre-existing process and not the beginning of a new phenomenon'.[15]

One may expand on this image of the consolidated nation state, 20 years after the end of World War Two, reinforced in its ability to meet the expectations of its population. Modernization had rebuilt national infrastructures, without yet developing extensive new communication channels across national boundaries. Europe's motorway network was developing on a national pattern, radiating out from capitals to provinces without stretching beyond the national boundary – following the pattern of Europe's railways of 60–80 years before,

---

[14] On the role of the major West European states in economic planning and management, see Peter Hall, *Governing the Economy: the Politics of State Intervention in Britain and France* (New York, Oxford University Press, 1986), and the classic work by Andrew Shonfield, *Modern Capitalism* (London, Oxford University Press, 1964).

[15] Alan Milward, 'Etats-nations et communauté: le paradoxe de l'Europe?', *Revue de Synthèse* Juillet/Sept. (1990), p. 255. (My translation.)

which had thinned out towards each border (and each well-manned border post) as they integrated each national territory. National telephone networks (without exception national monopolies) had expanded, international links were only beginning to be built. International STD across Europe was initiated from the early 1960s, to revolutionize contacts among businesses and governments over the following decade.[16]

National education shaped perceptions, with only a small minority involved in cross-border study and exchanges. The massive Franco-German exchanges started in the mid-1960s; rising numbers in further education throughout Europe during that decade brought an increase in foreign student flows. But the largest body of students from abroad in Britain and France came from their former imperial possessions, not from other European states; and the first country of destination for European university students going abroad was the United States.[17] Migration within Europe was rising, as economic growth and labour demand in rich northern Europe drew in *Gastarbeiter* from southern Europe; but it had not yet reached a point where it was seen as threatening national solidarity. Mass tourism began to shift balance from an intra-national to an inter-national phenomenon in the course of the 1960s, but it was not until the late 1960s and early 1970s that large numbers of young people across Europe began to treat their continent – rather than their country – as the space within which they expected to move.

Both the apologists for the idealistic project of European Union as pursued in the 1950s and 1960s and the revisionists underplay the immense importance of the American presence in shaping the structure of postwar Western Europe, and in influencing the character of its politics. American wartime planning for a postwar Europe promoted the idea of a 'United States of Europe'; John Foster Dulles was the secretary of 'the American Committee for a United States of Europe' in 1947–8.[18] The conditions attached to Marshall Plan aid forced its European recipients into close cooperation, through the Organization for European Economic Cooperation and the European Payments Union. American pressure on the European allies to integrate the reconstructed West German economy, without which (they argued) a prosperous pattern of European economic growth could not be established, did much to push the French Government into the proposal for a European Coal and Steel Community, as the only way to reconcile national security with economic recovery.[19] Intense American pressure, after the

[16] Interviewing British civil servants in 1972 about the impact on British government of Community membership, I was struck by the official who answered that the revolution in relations with the continent had already happened, over the previous ten years, with the shift from formal despatches through embassies to telephone conversations with opposite numbers in other capitals.
[17] Federico Romero, 'Cross-border population movements', in Wallace, *The Dynamics of European Integration*, surveys these and other flows.
[18] On American wartime plans, see David Ellwood, 'The American challenge and the politics of growth', in M. L. Smith and P. M. R. Stirk (eds), *Making the New Europe: European Unity and the Second World War* (London, Pinter, 1990). See also Max Beloff, *The United States and the Unity of Europe* (Washington, Brookings, 1963). Jean Monnet's wartime position in Washington gave him and his associates – Robert Marjolin and others – privileged access to postwar US Administrations as close as those which British officials enjoyed.
[19] On the central importance of the US-German relationship in this period, see Thomas A. Schwartz, *America's Germany: John J. McCloy and the Federal Republic of Germany* (Cambridge, MA, Harvard University Press, 1991).

North Korean invasion of South Korea, to allow the rearmament of West Germany similarly pushed the governments of France and the Low Countries into pursuing the directly federal proposal for a European Defence Community, with the necessary corollary of a European Political Community to follow.

The collapse of the EDC proposals left security issues firmly within the Atlantic framework, with the commitment of six American (and four British) divisions to Germany providing a guarantee of German good behaviour as well as protection against the Soviet threat; while political integration was pursued less directly through 'functional' economic channels. But the argument between de Gaulle and Hallstein (and the governments of the 'other five') was as much about rejection of American patronage and the American-dominated political and security framework as it was about the integrative or inter-governmental character of European Union. The Fouchet proposals were intended to displace NATO as the main framework for foreign policy cooperation; a third of the Elysée Treaty of 1963 was devoted to defence and foreign policy cooperation.[20] Looking back, Milward indeed sees the alliance between American theorists and Commission institution-builders as an aspect of the Cold War, through which 'neo-functionalism in the 1950s and 1960s became the intellectual foundation for a hegemonic foreign policy architecture'.[21]

Western Europe was 'America's Europe'. The reconstruction of the nation state in a postwar Western Europe was built on a number of contradictions and compromises between the reassertion of sovereignty and the acceptance of integration. Acceptance of a degree of dependence on the USA – direct and substantial for Italy and Federal Germany, indirect for Britain and France – was the first of these compromises; from which West European states gained a great deal, not only in terms of security but also in terms of the transformation of their economies through the transfer of American technology, the introduction of American managerial and production methods, and the stimulus of American investment. Acceptance of a semi-sovereign Germany, with which its neighbours around the Rhine valley and delta agreed to share sovereignty, rather than risk full independence for the successor to Europe's would-be hegemon of the previous half-century, was for them as significant a compromise. A further self-conscious compromise was the recognition, most directly by the Benelux states, that the only way to provide their citizens with the full employment and economic growth – and the public services which the revenue generated through economic growth would finance – was through acceptance of intensified international trade regulated through tighter international regimes. Paul-Henri Spaak, speaking as foreign minister in the Belgian Government-in-exile to the Belgian Institute in London in the bleak winter of 1941 spelt out the limitations of autonomy necessary to re-establish post-war autonomy: 'What we shall have

---

[20] H. van B. Cleveland, *The Atlantic Idea and its European Rivals* (New York, McGraw-Hill/Council on Foreign Relations, 1966). Atlanticists in the Bundestag added a rider to the Elysée Treaty on ratification, to de Gaulle's fury, which delayed the activation of this chapter until the early 1980s; William Wallace, 'European defence cooperation: the reopening debate', *Survival*, 26 (1984), 251–61.

[21] Milward, *The Frontier of National Sovereignty*, p. 5.

to combine is a certain reawakening of nationalism and an indispensable internationalism'.[22]

If we nevertheless accept on the above evidence that the 1960s *were* the high point of national consolidation and state management of economy and society, the crucial question to pose is: what trends have strengthened or weakened the centrality of states in the European political system since then? The forces of economic integration, industrial modernization, and technological innovation had so far operated to reinforce national political systems; have they continued to do so, or has there been a qualitative shift in their impact over the 20–25 years following? But before we address that question it may be useful to consider whether we can talk about a single model of *the* European nation state, or whether we should accept that different relations between state, economy and society, different national traditions and myths, make it necessary to treat the concept of 'the nation state' and 'national sovereignty' as to some extent contingent on the particular states to which they are applied.

Nation-states – and Nation-states

'The nation state' is an artificial construct, an ideal type heavily dependent upon the historical experience of only two of Western Europe's states: Britain and France.[23] Since Britain and France have developed very different traditions on the role of the state and the relationship between state and society, and state and economy, it is not easy to construct a universally-agreed model of the nation state and its core functions against which to test the impact of formal and informal integration over the past 20 – or 40 – years. Any such attempt is complicated further by the weight of German (and Austrian) theory on the authority and functions of the state, from Hegel and von Humboldt to Weber via Marx and many others – and still further by the evolution of Catholic doctrine as Germany and Italy were unified as secular states.[24] To some extent, as Dyson argues, Britain has been the 'odd state out' in comparison with the continent, never developing a full concept of the state as an autonomous entity, nor achieving any stable consensus on the economic role of the state. But it would be enormously rash to suggest that German concepts of statehood and nationhood obtained unmodified in protestant Norway and Catholic Portugal, in orthodox Greece or in the consociational Netherlands.

We have to recognize that there is *no* permanently-valid corpus of sovereign powers and state authority – though it has been a frequent assertion of national politicians and political theorists that there is. One may see the late-nineteenth century European nation-state as representing one apogee of centralized authority and territorial integrity, the states of

[22] Quoted in Milward, *European Rescue*, p. 320.

[23] 'It is . . . a case of Western myopia: we have equated the "nation" and the "state", because that is the form they took in the two historically influential societies – Britain and France – at the very moment when nationalism burst forth.' A. D. Smith, 'State-making and nation-building', in J. A. Hall (ed.), *States in History* (Oxford, Blackwell, 1986), p. 230. See also Charles Tilly, 'Reflections on the history of European state-making', in Charles Tilly (ed.), *The Formation of National States in Western Europe* (Princeton, NJ, Princeton University Press, 1975).

[24] Kenneth Dyson, *The State Tradition in Western Europe* (Oxford, Martin Robertson, 1980).

the 'Trente Glorieuses' of postwar growth as representing another: each taking advantage of advances in technology, administration and communication, and each adapting to changes in the external environment.[25] But it must be emphasized that the West European states of the 1960s differed substantially from those of 60–70 years before, not only in their size and territorial boundaries but also in their military, foreign policy, economic and social characteristics. Just as industrialization, railways, the telegraph, and the development of efficient state administration transformed the capacities of the nineteenth-century state and its relations with its citizens, so mass-production, the telephone, Keynesian techniques for national economic management, technological advance (often also under state sponsorship, and defence-led) and the development of the 'welfare state' transformed those capacities again in the 1950s and 1960s. 'The basis of the rescue of the nation state was an economic one', Milward argues – though the economic necessity of including the German economy within the broader framework required to sustain growth imposed underlying political, as well as economic, constraints on that rescue. 'The combination of welfare state and employment policy' which northern European states were enabled through sustained growth to pursue 'represents the apogee of the concept of the nation [state] as the improver of man's lot'.[26]

Even within the same time period and under the same domestic and international constraints, the diversity of state/society, state/economy and state/interdependence or autonomy relations is striking. 'Economic viability and political legitimacy can be secured in many ways ... and these ways are shaped by history and politics'.[27] Large states have more resources with which to maintain national autonomy, defend national integrity, and promote national prosperity than small states; but such small states as Sweden, Austria and Finland have managed to maintain (and even expand) a high degree of autonomy over the past forty years through the pursuit of carefully-judged mercantilist and welfare policies within the limits imposed by the rules of the postwar Western order.

The irreducible minimum of the concept of a state is a body which exercises an accepted monopoly of violence within its boundaries, and a willingness to use violence against outsiders to defend those boundaries. Internal order, external defence (and the diplomacy needed to maintain and reinforce that defence): Hobbes, Machiavelli, Austin and Dicey all recognize that necessity. The concept of sovereignty asserted that no other authority had the right to summon or convict those under the protection of the sovereign, and that the sovereign conversely had the sole right to conduct political – or military – relations with other territorially-organized states. 'This realm of England

---

[25] Hinsley's classic *Sovereignty* provides a developmental interpretation of the rise of the nineteenth century sovereign state on the back of improvements in administration and education, industry and communication; but then draws back in the final chapter from accepting the parallel logic that 'these [contemporary] changes in international conditions [which] have proceeded from precisely those technical, social and economic forces which have been producing the highly integrated community and the modern nation state' would progressively weaken the community-state link which an earlier stage of development had supported a century before (p. 221).

[26] Milward, *European Rescue of the Nation-State*, pp. 43, 45.

[27] Peter Katzenstein, *Corporatism and Change: Austria, Switzerland and the Politics of Industry* (Ithaca, NY, Cornell University Press, 1984), p. 246.

is an Empire' (the Act of Supremacy of 1534: arguably a more important document in the evolution of the English state than the much more-frequently quoted Magna Carta) excluded the claim of the Roman Church to exercise jurisdiction – and to mete out punishment – in England alongside the temporal power.

Legitimacy is as much a part of the core concept of the state: *accepted* authority, laying down and applying rules which have the status of law.[28] Early European states rested their claim to legitimacy – to acceptance by their subjects as representing and identifying them as a 'community', a 'commonwealth', a 'nation' – on sacred or mythical claims: 'the divine right of kings', the inheritance of ancient kingship symbolized by investiture and ritual. Modern states have increasingly rested their claim to internal legitimacy on two different grounds, one ideological, the other rational: first, their identification with (or, personification of) 'the nation'; and second, their ability to deliver security, prosperity and welfare to their citizens.

The immensely-powerful idea of the nation state as providing a focus for social and political identity in mass urban societies was a development of the 19th century in Western Europe – and of the early 20th century in Eastern Europe. The integrating power of national identity, propagated through 'national education' and national history by an active state, was perhaps most sharply demonstrated in July and August 1914, when the populations of European states mobilized in response to their governments' commands to defend their nation state against each other. The harrowing experience of a Second World War brought a wave of revulsion against this mutual identification of nation and state; but the intellectuals who led this revolt aroused little response from populations who continued to live almost entirely within the boundaries of their particular nation state, to work for companies owned within that state, and to buy products manufactured within that state.

The promotion of national wealth was a central part of most states' aims and activities in the 17th and 18th centuries – the mercantilist era, in which European governments fought for control of trade routes, sugar and spice islands, and saw tariffs as a means of raising revenue from each other and of protecting national agriculture and manufactures from foreign attack.[29] Mercantilist aims were central to Hamilton's vision – in *The Federalist Papers* – of a strong United States, and to List's vision of a powerful united Germany. The rapid industrialization of Germany in the final decades of the nineteenth century was, after all, a case study in public and private interests mobilized in pursuit of common national objectives – as was the similarly rapid industrialization of Japan. Bismarck saw it as sound policy to give all German subjects a strong sense of common benefits from common citizenship by developing the foundations of national welfare policies; an example soon copied by others. Well before the postwar period, therefore, the pursuit of prosperity and the provision of welfare were seen by

---

[28] I am drawing on the extensive discussion in Dyson, *The State Tradition in Western Europe*, here.

[29] Istvan Hont, 'Free trade and the economic limits to national politics', in John Dunn (ed.), *The Economic Limits to Modern Politics* (Cambridge, Cambridge University Press, 1990), pp. 121–41.

European states as essential tasks for the nation state.[30] Keynesianism however added to their confidence in promoting state-guided capitalism in 'mixed economies'.

The *core* functions of the nation state may thus be seen as: the preservation of internal order, the maintenance of national boundaries and the defence of national territory against foreign attack; the provision of 'legitimate' government, through an established and well-ordered state apparatus, equipped with the symbols and institutions needed to 'represent' the nation and to give its citizens a sense of participation in the national community; the provision of services, and of welfare, to reinforce this sense of national community; and the promotion of national prosperity – which in the Keynesian era became the pursuit of balanced and sustained economic growth. All of these were successfully provided to their citizens by West European states in the 1960s. How successfully were they still being provided in the 1980s? How likely is it that West European states will still be successfully providing these over the next decade?

After the Apogee: the Long Retreat?

Just as the apparent early successes of formal European integration and the reconsolidation of the nation state had gone together, so at the end of the 1960s and through the early 1970s both faltered. Part of the explanation for both is to be found in a more disturbed global environment, with international economic recession and changes in US policies – still, as in the 1950s, a crucial factor in West European political and economic developments. The student revolts which flashed across Western Europe in 1968–9 – shaking the state itself in France, shaking authority and hierarchy elsewhere – were at once imitative of the American student revolt which the Vietnam war had inspired, and fuelled by domestic discontents and the impatience of the first entirely postwar generation. The legacy they left behind into the 1970s, of student radicalism souring into terrorism, presented a longer-term challenge to state authority.

A more pervasive loss of self-confidence was reflected in the widespread concern over 'ungovernability' which burst out in the 1970s. Sustained economic growth had fuelled popular and interest group expectations of increasing state provision; social democracy had granted representatives of organized interests an entrenched position in the policy-making process. With slower growth such expectations could be satisfied only through rising levels of taxation, instead of the hoped-for dividends from expanding revenue. Industrial restructuring, needed as heavy industries lost their place as the 'commanding heights of the economy', was inhibited by the mechanism of corporatist consultation. Economic adjustment, necessary to cope with the successive shocks of the US suspension of dollar convertibility and the rise in

---

[30] Mercantilist policies and state-building thus went together. Deliberate promotion of national competitiveness, and the protection of the national economy against over-dependence on foreign investors or suppliers, were part of the doctrine of state sovereignty – against which free traders argued a deliberately internationalist, anti-strong state, line. The Thatcher Government's attempt to defend state sovereignty while at the same time pursuing free market policies thus led to a number of fundamental contradictions in British policy. See W. Wallace and H. Wallace, 'Strong state or weak state in foreign policy? The contradictions of Conservative liberalism, 1979–87', *Public Administration*, 68 (1990), 83–102.

the oil price, was inhibited by the ethos of social democracy as well as by the entrenchment of economic interests in national policy-making. Technical advance and managerial innovation were enabling transnational companies to move towards multinational production for regional and global markets, while bargaining with competing national governments over the location of production and new investment. 'Ungovernability' was followed by 'Euro-sclerosis' as a Europe-wide fear. European nation states appeared to be losing power and authority not to any new supranational authority to which decision-making capacities and loyalties were being transferred (as the neo-functionalists had hoped) but into a void.

Yet from the perspective of the early 1980s 'the most striking reality' was 'not the frequent and well-noted impotence of the nation-state'. It was its 'survival, despite the turmoil'.[31] The passing of deference left governments more dependent on the provision of services and visible economic benefits than their predecessors – but did not destroy their legitimacy. The challenge which terrorism presented to several of the larger European states was successfully withstood. Both political and administrative élites, shaken by the turmoil of 1968–74, adjusted through generational change and the turnover of government office, without weakening the state apparatus as such – in sharp contrast to the debilitating stagnation of élites throughout Eastern Europe.

The 1980s, however, have been marked by increasing awareness within West European states of the contradictions in which they are caught up: with governments negotiating new bargains over the decision-making rules and regulations of formal integration, while attempting to satisfy electorates who wished to gain the benefits of continuing prosperity and welfare – and of easy access across West European frontiers – without accepting the costs in reductions in national autonomy. The Single European Act was a classic compromise, in which governments committed to the maintenance of as much autonomy as possible nevertheless agreed a new package of rules under what seemed to them powerful economic and political imperatives.[32] The impetus which carried them on to agree on a further Inter-governmental Conference, and then to negotiate and sign the Maastricht Treaty on European Union, followed from the same pattern of adjustment to the flow of intensifying economic and social interaction, complicated in the course of 1990–1 by the transformation of the security context within which the whole framework of 'civilian' political integration in Western Europe had developed, with the unification of Germany and the beginnings of American (and Soviet) military withdrawal.

Economic logic made for moves towards a single currency, and for the transfer of competition rules and market regulation to the European level. The transformed *security logic* supported closer cooperation among police and intelligence agencies as well as among armed forces. The Maastricht Treaty, it should be noted, touches on almost all the core functions of the European nation state: control of the national territory and borders, police, citizenship and immigration, currency, taxation, financial transfers, management of the

---

[31] Hoffmann, 'Reflections on the nation state today', p. 22.

[32] Andrew Moravcsik, 'Negotiating the single European Act', in R. O. Keohane and S. Hoffmann (eds), *The New European Community: Decision-making and Institutional Change* (Boulder, CO Westview, 1991).

economy, promotion of industry, representation and accountability, foreign policy and defence. Only welfare remained securely in the hands of national governments: though even there the argument over the 'Social Chapter' showed the determination of some participants to transfer rule-making and standard-setting to the Community level. But *political logic* imposed a contradictory impulse, with governments attempting to reassure their publics that this was only a further limited package, and that the focus for political identity and accountability would remain firmly at the national level: a message which their publics, now able through the integration of communications and élites to understand very well what other governments were telling *their* domestic publics and what was being claimed in Brussels, were reluctant to accept.[33]

Perhaps the most striking shift has been in *the pursuit of national prosperity*: the recognition – throughout Western Europe – of the futility of national industrial strategies, and of the increasing limitations on national economic policies. 'National champions' – Phillips, Rolls-Royce, Dassault – had been the focus for much industrial (and technological) policy in the 1960s. Government commitment began to falter during the 1970s, most strikingly in Britain (and least so in France and in several of Europe's smaller states); and to give way in the 1980s to deregulation and (or) collaboration, through strategic alliances, even mergers. Industrial 'sponsorship' shifted from the national to the European plane, with governmental and company support for the plethora of initiatives which began with the 'Esprit' programme and developed with 'Eureka', FAST, JESSI and a lectionary of other acronyms. Indeed, many observers see this shift of industrial and technological imperatives as a key factor in the 'revival' of formal European integration in the 1980s.[34]

National governments continued to fight, and to win or lose, national elections on their 'record' of national economic management – or their promises of superior achievement. But the contrasting experiences of the governments of Britain and France which came into power in 1979 and 1981 provide powerful evidence of the erosion of national control. Britain's domestic monetary squeeze of 1979–81 led to a 30% rise in the external value of sterling, sparking off a much sharper recession than anticipated: the beginning of a long learning process in the limits of national autonomy in pursuing deregulation and free market policies which led, through the (remarkably successful) efforts of the mid-1980s to extend deregulation from the national to the European plane with a programme to 'complete' the internal market and through pressure for stricter Community policies on competition and state aids, to acceptance of membership of the exchange rate mechanism of the European Monetary System in 1990. The French experience of a 'dash for growth' in 1981–3, complete with programmes for the 'reconquest of the domestic market', provided a more direct shock – and thus a more rapid learning process, demonstrating vividly to every West European Government that it was no

---

[33] The best description of the Maastricht negotiating process so far available is Philippe de Schoutheete, 'The Treaty of Maastricht and its significance for third countries,' *Österreichische Zeitschrift für Politikwissenschaft* Winter (1992–3), 247–60. On Danish reactions see Morten Kelstrup (ed.), *European Integration and Denmark's Participation* (Copenhagen, Political Studies Press, 1992).

[34] Wayne Sandholtz and John Zysman, '1992: recasting the European bargain', *World Politics*, 42 (1989), 95–128; Margaret Sharp, 'Technology and the dynamics of integration', in Wallace, *Dynamics of European Integration*.

longer possible even for major European economies to pursue national priorities without careful coordination with their partners. If monetary sovereignty is indeed 'the core of the core' of national sovereignty, as Mrs Thatcher once remarked, then both Western Europe's most sovereignty-conscious states are losing control of that core: the British in 1992–3 deeply confused over national or European monetary strategy, the French more determined than ever to gain a degree of compensating control over dominant German monetary policy through closer integration – even monetary union.

Nation states no longer control national economies in Western Europe. Advances in technology, communication, management of multinational companies and techniques of multinational production, as well as the integration of financial markets through electronic communications and the displacement of inter-national trade by flows of foreign direct investment linked to intra-company trade, have irreversibly undermined their autonomy.[35] Smaller states which had survived the downturn of the 1970s through national policies of industrial adjustment and social/corporatist partnership shifted during the late 1980s towards an acceptance that regional integration was now the only viable national economic strategy. The neutral states of EFTA excluded the question of full membership in the EC before 1989, seeing the EC as too closely linked to the US-led Atlantic Alliance; but their need for as close an involvement as possible in setting the rules of the regional economy within which they lived led them to pursue all forms of association short of membership.[36] After the revolution in European security of 1989–90 such political inhibitions no longer held them back. First Austria, then Sweden and Finland, applied for full membership, even before the EC/EFTA European Economic Area (EEA) agreement had been implemented. The Swiss Government's announced intention to follow suit, under the same pressures of economic logic, was undermined by the political logic which holds the Swiss Federation together; all but two of its German-speaking cantons produced a majority against ratifying even the EEA in a referendum in December 1992.[37] The gap between government recognition of the advantages of trading a degree of autonomy for the benefits of full access to EC markets, free movement, and shared decision-making, and popular resistance to the loss of autonomy (and the feared implications for national identity) was as evident within states approaching EC membership in the 1990s as within existing member states.

Yet it would be rash to conclude that national economic policies have been *entirely* displaced by the pressure of financial markets, multinational investment and production flows, instant communication and market integration. The

[35] Albert Bressand, 'Regional integration in a networked world economy', in Wallace, *Dynamics of European Integration*; R. O'Brien, *Global Financial Integration: the End of Geography*; Deanne Julius, *Global Companies and Public Policy: the Growing Challenge of Foreign Direct Investment* (London, RIIA/Pinter, 1990).

[36] Helen S. Wallace (ed.), *The Wider Western Europe: Reshaping the EC/EFTA Relationship* (London, RIIA/Pinter, 1991).

[37] Anna Michalski and Helen Wallace, *The European Community: the Challenge of Enlargement* (London, RIIA, 1992). Katzenstein, *Corporatism and Change: Austria, Switzerland and the Politics of Industry* provides an excellent study of the struggles of small European states to balance economic autonomy and interdependence as the European economy was transformed by industrial, financial and technological innovation. I am drawing here also on draft chapters of the Oxford D.Phil. in progress by Olli Rehn, 'The Nation State revisited: small European states in the new dynamics of world economy and integration'.

successful partnership between several German Laender Governments – most notably Baden-Wurtemberg – and high technology industries, involving co-operation with financial institutions, support for research institutes and relevant university education, shows that adaptive strategies are still practicable. The support given by several European governments to state-owned industries to become European 'multinationals' – Nokia, Matra, Thomson, most recently Renault – provides further evidence. The arguments advanced by Michael Porter[38] on the importance of 'the home base' to multinational company success will be music to the ears of those governments pursuing such 'multinational-national' policies. National economic *autonomy*, we may conclude, has now substantially been lost. But national abilities to shape the balance of advantage within European and global markets, through education and training expenditure, research and development, partnerships with banks and (private or public sector) companies, remains; and is likely to remain for some years to come. French European strategy is the clearest example of government moving onto a European plane in pursuit of national objectives no longer achievable on a national basis; but there are elements in German, Dutch, Italian and Spanish industrial and economic strategies which illustrate the same pursuit of harnessing European cooperation to national ends. The development of a common agricultural policy thirty years earlier, and the development of common policies on coal and steel even earlier, had after all attempted the same trade-off between national interests and European cooperation.[39]

A 'crisis of the welfare state' has been identified – and examined – since the early 1970s. Facing a shift in the age balance of their populations as well as rising expectations from their younger generation, all West European governments have to differing degrees cut back on *the provision of welfare*. Further ageing of Western Europe's population will force them to economize more during the coming decade. Recent reforms in Sweden mark a major retreat from the principle of universal welfare provision through financial transfers and benefits. But what is remarkable here is how much of the structure of national welfare provision – in unemployment benefits, old-age pensions, health insurance and housing subsidies – has survived, despite the gloomy predictions of the 1970s. What we have seen has been retrenchment and adjustment, rather than retreat or abandonment. 'Compared to most aspects of the postwar political economy . . . the welfare state has proved to be remarkably durable . . . in large part because of a broad and deep base of political support' which serves also to maintain the instrumental legitimacy of the nation state as welfare provider.

> This strength at the national level helps to explain why social initiatives have lagged behind other actions in Brussels. But at the same time, the popularity of social protection means that if national welfare states should falter under the mounting pressures of regional and global integration, the European Community will be under intense popular pressure to extend its activities[40]

[38] Michael Porter, *The Comparative Advantage of Nations* (London, Macmillan, 1990).

[39] Milward, *European Rescue*, chs 3 and 5, provides an excellent description of the trade-offs involved in the development of the ECSC and CAP.

[40] Stephan Liebfried and Paul Pierson, 'Prospects for Social Europe', *Politics and Society*, 20 (1992), 356–7.

– or, more disruptively, to demand a return to the protection of national economies and of national social standards seen to be threatened by international integration. The arguments over the 'social chapter' of the Maastricht Treaty rehearsed these possible developments, with German trade union leaders pressing their government to insist on common employment standards to discourage the movement of production from *Standort* Germany to less regulated states.

Loss of control over national economies, and the declining importance of national defence, has left the provision of welfare and related public goods as the most significant function of West European nation states: legitimizing national government and national taxation, redistributing resources among the national community. The combination of slow growth, high unemployment and huge deficits in social budgets which emerged in the early 1980s therefore represented not only a crisis of the European welfare state but also a potential crisis for the nation state as such. So far that crisis has been managed, despite persisting high unemployment and consequent heavy demands for redistribution of income through taxation throughout Western Europe. Adverse demographic trends suggest that the strains on national budgets and on popular acceptance of high levels of redistribution will grow further over the next decade.[41] The close link between national solidarity and social welfare in the evolution of the modern nation state suggests that any substantive moves to dismantle the structures of national redistribution would undermine this legitimizing link between community and state.

The development of modern nation states was accompanied by the development of *national communications and national media*, formally controlled by domestic censorship laws and informally constrained by domestic political and social pressures. National values and perspectives were fostered through state support for national theatres and literature, and through close relations between the national press and the government. The barriers of language maintained a high degree of autonomy among European media despite the increasing social interactions of the 1970s and 1980s. International newspapers were slow to emerge; the *Financial Times* sold less than 17,000 copies in Germany in 1993, after fourteen years of printing in Frankfurt. National licensing arrangements for radio and television also helped to maintain separate national styles (and ownership).

Yet improvements in television transmission, and the spread of cable networks offering a range of channels from several countries, have gone some way to erode national autonomy in this sphere in the geographically-concentrated European region. Most of the population of the German Democratic Republic received, and watched, West German television in preference to their own by the mid-1980s: a development which deprived their government of influence over the news their citizens heard or the symbols and images they acquired.[42] Development of satellite television is accentuating this loss of national control, and increasing the incentives to produce 'international'

---

[41] Jean-Pierre Jallade, 'Is the crisis behind us? Issues facing social security systems in Western Europe', in Z. Ferge and J. E. Kolberg (eds), *Social Policy in a Changing Europe* (Frankfurt, Campus, 1992), pp. 37–56.

[42] Richard Davy, 'The central European dimension', in Wallace, *Dynamics of European Integration*, ch. 8.

programmes rather than transmissions which relate to specifically national myths and values. The French Government's resistance to American demands for deregulation of the audio-visual sector reflected its acute awareness of the threat to national particularity posed by this combination of technological and entrepreneurial challenges. But it was less clear whether any West European state had the financial capacity – or the support of its viewing public – to resist these globalizing pressures.

In *defence and public order*, in contrast, little has happened on the surface of European politics in the 1970s and 1980s to alter the perception of clear national responsibility, subject to straightforward national accountability and control. I want to suggest however that these were the areas in which sovereignty – this *is* the most appropriate term for areas so fundamental to any concept of the state – was most undermined during that period, though formally registered only in the 1985 Schengen Agreement and in Titles V and VI of the Maastricht Treaty.

The explosion of cross-border movement which was such a remarkable European phenomenon in these years forced governments progressively to ease, and now in some cases to abandon, protection of their national territories through control of their boundaries. Jet aircraft and cross-border motorways, complemented by improvements in cross-border railway links, allowed for a massive increase in trans-European travel: for business, for tourism, for study, even commuting across borders to work. The 5 million journeys across the Channel made by British subjects and residents in the mid-1960s allowed for careful controls both of their passports and their luggage at either end – complete with chalkmarks on each suitcase and a thorough examination of each passport. For the 40–45 million journeys made annually in the early 1990s the small increase in immigration officers (and reduced numbers of customs officers) attempted in most cases a brief glance and a cursory nod as the waves of tourists, students and business people swept through: mute acceptance, perhaps, that the European continent is no longer regarded as 'foreign' or hostile territory, and symbolized by the single queue for 'European Community Nationals' at British ports and airports.[43]

First five, now nine countries on the European Continent went further, in the Schengen Agreement of 1985; which provides for the abolition of internal frontier controls both on goods and on people, together with consequent measures for cooperation among police, immigration, customs and intelligence services, for common procedures on rights of entry and residence. This involves the abandonment of one of the most basic tenets of the nation state; and as such was vigorously resisted by many within national administrations and politics, delaying implementation of the provisions of the agreement again and again. Yet national police forces, and intelligence services, had come to cooperate extensively with their counterparts in other European countries during the 1970s and 1980s (through the intergovernmental Trevi and Pompidou groups, and other little-reported bodies) against terrorism, drugs traffic, international money-laundering and financial fraud, and against the growth of cross-border organized crime. There is a powerful security logic in this

---

[43] I am drawing on material from a seminar organized by the Royal Institute of International Affairs in collaboration with the Association of Chief Police Officers and the Home Office in the Spring of 1989.

development: that the internationalization of crime necessitates the internationalization of police work, and that the freer movement of goods, people, information and money across frontiers necessarily means that national police forces must move also. Chancellor Kohl in a speech in 1988 even floated a proposal for a European Federal Bureau of Investigation, as a necessary response to the internationalization of crime. The 'third pillar' of the Maastricht Treaty set out to formalize the extensive existing patterns of 'Cooperation in the fields of Justice and Home Affairs', while retaining control of that formalized structure within an inter-governmental framework beyond the reach of the European Parliament and with only a consultative role for the Commission.[44] Before either full implementation of the Schengen Agreement or ratification of the Treaty on European Union, the Schengen Bureau, the newly-established European office of Interpol and the complex network of committees which link governments and executive services in dealing with terrorism, drug-smugglers, asylum-seekers and immigrants have taken Western Europe a long way from the traditional concept of the territorially-sovereign state.[45]

European defence integration was an early aspiration, forced onto the agenda by American insistence on the rearmament of West Germany. The traumatic failure of the European Defence Community proposals, in 1954, took the issue off the agenda – its taboo status strengthened by French Gaullist polarization of the choices between *European* and *Atlantic* defence cooperation in the 1960s. Western European Union was revived, in the mid-1980s, into a sickly life as a vehicle for intergovernmental cooperation – and as a framework for European defence cooperation, under American leadership, in the Red Sea and the Gulf. Demolition of the Berlin Wall, and the prospect of German unification, led the French and German Governments in April 1990 to add defence and foreign policy explicitly to the agenda of the planned Inter-governmental Conferences (supporting and expanding on the earlier Belgian proposal for a 'Political' IGC to meet and negotiate in parallel with the Economic IGC already agreed). Redefinition of NATO strategy in the course of 1991 interacted with competing Franco-German and Italian-British proposals for bringing defence and security more closely together with the civilian framework of European Union. The 'Provisions on a Common Foreign and Security Policy' in the Maastricht Treaty are tortuously worded and deliberately ambiguous: faithfully representing the immense sensitivity of this area for sovereign nation states, and the consequent contradictions of almost every government's position. Yet, with the dissolution of the Soviet Union almost as the European Council met in Maastricht, and with the run-down of US forces in Europe well under way, the strengthening of WEU and its relocation in Brussels agreed in a protocol to the treaty moved ahead during 1992 without waiting for national ratification.[46]

---

[44] Title VI, *Treaty on European Union*, Official Publications of the EC, 1992.

[45] So far very little has been published on this whole field. But see Malcolm Anderson and Monica den Boer (eds), *European Police Cooperation: proceedings of a seminar* (Edinburgh University, Department of Politics, 1992), and working papers V and VIII of their series on 'A system of European Police Cooperation in 1992'; and Malcolm Anderson and Monica den Boer (eds), *Policing across National Boundaries* (London, Pinter, 1994).

[46] A. Menon, A. Forster and W. Wallace, 'A common European defence?' *Survival*, 34 (1992), 98–118.

The pressures which have been pushing European governments together on defence issues have come much more, however, from technological and budgetary factors than from intergovernmental agreement. The increasing inefficiency of national procurement, producing limited numbers of sophisticated and highly expensive weapons, has pushed the major European countries – France, Britain, Germany, to a lesser extent Italy and even Spain – into collaboration. Joint procurement requires some agreement on tasks and threats to be met by the weapons systems to be produced, and so consultations on strategy and tactics: half way towards coordination of policy as such. Shrinking numbers, and hopes of reducing defence expenditure, pushed governments during the 1970s and 1980s further together: into joint training, into mutual dependence for logistical support, and increasingly into specialization of roles. The Anglo-Dutch Marine Force and the Franco-German brigade represented the most visible indicators of a trend about which *all* West European governments were schizophrenic, with many defence professionals acknowledging the irrationality of attempting to maintain the myth of independent national capabilities while also acknowledging the immense symbolic and practical (command) obstacles to moving much further.[47] Until the security revolution of 1989–91 American leadership, and the ability of European contingents to fit into American-led forces with all-round capabilities, enabled European defence ministries to avoid difficult choices. The unification of Germany, the disappearance of the Soviet threat, the shift in American security priorities away from Europe, domestic expectations of cuts in national defence budgets, the challenges posed by the growing conflict in Yugoslavia and by outbreaks of disorder in Africa and in the former Soviet Union: all these posed central questions to West European states about the role and purpose of national military forces and about appropriate responses to threats which, while diffuse and distant, nevertheless affected long-term national security. Even before 1989, Western Europe had already passed well beyond the traditional model of the independent nation state, or even the model which France and Britain proudly presented in the 1950s and 1960s of independent military power. After 1991 West European states were moving, no longer under firm leadership from the USA, into previously uncharted waters.

States themselves, the very apparatus of government, have in many ways been most transformed by the developments of the past 20 years. No British Prime Minister before Edward Heath thought it a necessary part of his duties to travel round the capitals of Europe on a regular basis, or to devote a considerable amount of his time to the intricacies of European affairs. Scarcely any members of the British Cabinet beyond the Foreign Secretary and the President of the Board of Trade found it useful to devote much time to continental travel – nor, below them, did more than a few of their officials. NATO from 1949–50 provided a framework for consultations on security and defence – involving a small and discrete group of officials from foreign and defence ministries – and for biannual ministerial Councils and occasional heads

---

[47] Pierre Lellouche and Karl Kaiser (eds), *Le Couple Franco-Allemand et la Défense d'Europe* (Paris, IFRI, 1986); Karl Kaiser and John Roper (eds), *British-German Defence Cooperation: Partners within the Alliance* (London, RIIA/Jane's, 1988); Yves Boyer, P. Lellouche and J. Roper (eds), *Franco-British Defence Cooperation: a new Entente Cordiale?* (London, RIIA/Routledge, 1989).

of government summits. For their six member governments, the ECSC and the EEC from the early 1950s had demanded multilateral diplomacy – though the numbers of officials and ministers involved remained limited to the areas of national policy over which competence had been transferred to these institutions. France and Germany had deliberately created an intensive bilateral network of consultations alongside this multilateral network, under the 1963 Elysée Treaty. By the end of the 1960s all EEC member governments were concerned to maintain national control over these spreading transgovernmental links – the French government, with its strong sense of state sovereignty and national interest, more than its partners.[48]

But the interpenetration of governments across Western Europe has advanced astonishingly since the early 1970s, as governments have responded to international economic disturbances, political crises and new cross-border issues – if initially largely by calling conferences and setting up working groups. Direct and secure telex and telephone linked foreign offices and central banks; officials from every department of state developed regular contacts with their counterparts in other European capitals, bilaterally and multilaterally, assisted by improvements in telephone links, telex and fax; embassies, previously the main channel of communication between European states, found themselves arranging hotels and appointments for a constant flow of ministers and officials; local authorities skirted round national governments in their contacts with each other and with the European Community; national officials took training courses together, and even began to work on exchange within other national administrations.[49] This gradual transformation crept up on European governments so imperceptibly that the cumulative impact has been easy to overlook – except where such prominent innovations as the creation of the European Council or the institution of the rotating Community Presidency reveal the reorientation of national business and ministerial and official time. But, again, it has taken us far from the nation state model as, for example, Anthony Eden or Harold Macmillan knew it, and a good deal further than President de Gaulle, a pioneer of summitry and intergovernmental consultations, would ever have wished to go.[50]

The sharpest and most formal incursion into national sovereignty, however, has been the acceptance of European Community law as superior to domestic law in all areas of Community competence under the Treaties. The high level of compliance with Community law throughout the EC – and beyond, in its effective incorporation into domestic law by EFTA associates and aspiring ex-socialist 'Europe Agreement' states, and in the gradual spread of extra-territorial jurisdiction – is one of the most remarkable and distinctive aspects of

---

[48] H. S. Wallace, *National Governments and the European Communities* (London, RIIA/PEP, 1973).

[49] The largest number of exchanges so far among major European governments have been between France and Germany; some smaller countries, in particular the Scandinavians, have exchanged officials for many years. There have to my knowledge also been exchanges between the British and German foreign ministries; a German official was working in the (British) FCO Planning Staff in 1993–4.

[50] Wolfgang Wessels, 'Administrative interaction', in Wallace, *Dynamics*, provides detailed figures for multilateral meetings within the EC and other European organizations. William Wallace, *Britain's Bilateral Links within Western Europe* (London, RIIA/Routledge, 1984), detailed the growth of bilateral consultations in parallel with these multilateral meetings.

West European regional integration over the past 25 years.[51] The federal quality of Community law was remarked by the British Foreign Secretary, who told Conservative students in February 1992 that it is 'now right to think of the Treaties as part of the [British] Constitution'.[52] This clear emergence of an operating legal order above the nation state negates the absolutist concept of unitary sovereignty propounded by nineteenth century theorists; it has to be understood in terms of relations among multiple levels of government, not between sovereign powers.[53]

Multi-level government implies multiple loyalties and identities, distributing a degree of legitimacy to each: citizens who define themselves as Bavarian in some contexts, German in others, and European in perhaps the broadest political context (or Catalan, Spanish and European – or Scots, British and European . . .). European élites move easily between such levels, benefitting from the cosmopolitan patterns of their work while holding on to national and regional roots – where they wish to do so – in their private lives. European publics are much less convinced of the benefits which integration has brought, and conscious of its psychological costs: national identities shaken, the link between citizens and accountable governments weakened by the displacement of policy-making into the transgovernmental maze of the Community process. There is an underlying crisis of national identity in most West European states, expressed in different forms of popular disillusion with established institutions and élites – but without any indication of the transfer of loyalties to any new, European, institutions for which the early idealists of European integration had hoped. Intermarriage, migration, cross-border movement, even the purchase of large numbers of second homes by West European nationals in other countries and the emergence of a significant north-south 'drift' of the well-to-do elderly from Germany, Britain and Sweden to Spain, Italy and Portugal have diffused identities, and shaken established assumptions about national political communities.[54] A degree of disorientation is evident within the domestic politics of most West European states: demands for the reassertion – or redefinition – of national identity in the light of the development of 'multicultural' societies or transformed relations with other European countries, or for its restatement in resistance to these 'cosmopolitanizing'

---

[51] The leading case on extra-territoriality is Ahlström Osakyhtio v Commission, ECR 5193 1988: the 'Woodpulp' case, in which Finnish, Swedish, Canadian and American suppliers of wood pulp were fined for infractions to EC competition rules for concertation of pricing on sales into the EC.

[52] Speech to Cambridge University Conservative Association, 7 February 1992 (FCO Verbatim Service).

[53] Joseph Weiler, 'Journey to an unknown destination: a retrospective and prospective of the European Court of Justice in the arena of European integration', *Journal of Common Market Studies*, 31 (1993), 417–46; Ann-Marie Burley and Walter Mattli, 'Europe before the Court: a political theory of legal integration', *International Organization*, 47, (1993), 41–76.

[54] Occasional papers 34, 35 and 36 of the Department of Geography, King's College London (1992) illustrate an interesting dimension of this move towards living across borders: the growth of British second-home ownership in France. BNP and Barclays Bank estimated in 1990 that in 1989, 15,000 British subjects brought property in France, bringing the total of British owners of French property to over 200,000; *Independent*, 31 March 1990. Between 75,000 and 100,000 more owned property in Spain, Italy, Portugal and Greece; for some these were retirement homes, from which (under recent British legislation) they retained the right to vote in British elections. Large numbers of Germans and Dutch also owned property outside their own national boundaries.

trends.[55] The single focus for loyalty and identity which the nation state model promoted has loosened; but it has not been replaced by any clear pattern of multiple loyalties and identities, like that which predominated in West European Christendom before the seventeenth century and which idealists hoped would come again to characterize the modern European Community.[56]

Is there an Underlying Crisis?

The great achievement of the late-nineteenth century West European nation state – the very model of the nation state which aspirant nationalists in eastern Europe and their imitators beyond attempted to emulate – was to link accountability, loyalty and legitimacy to authority and power: to tie political community to state power, as Hinsley put it. The experience of Western Europe over the past 25 years is that this link is now loosening. The nation as a political and social community is disconnecting from the state as provider of security and welfare. Both nation and state have lost coherence, as borders have become more permeable, national myths harder to maintain, ethnic diversity more evident, personal prosperity more dependent on local or transnational factors than on national protection.

State administrations have struggled to adapt to the implications of technical change and economic and social integration. They have adapted relatively successfully to the demands of shared policy-making, but at the cost of losing the confidence of a rising proportion of their national publics. The territorial and administrative congruence of state, society and economy which Germany, France, Britain, Belgium represented 100 years ago has given way to an almost Marxian contradiction: between forces of production (and of services) operating across wider spaces, social communities seeking to revive regional loyalties or splintering into divided ethnic and social groups, and states attempting to maintain the old territorial and authoritative patterns. The rescue of the West European nation state after 1945 was guided and assisted by the benevolent hegemony of the United States, and contained by common recognition of a clear and present danger from the Soviet Union. Half a century later there is no definable threat to focus civic loyalty on the state, or to provide nation states with a common purpose and a shared sense of direction; and there is no benevolent hegemon to redefine objectives or to distribute resources to gain wider consent.

'The strength of the European Community ... lies in the weakness of the nation state'.[57] The weakness of the European Community lies in the strength of national and sub-national identities. Economic integration, driven by technological change and global competition, is counterbalanced by political

---

[55] William Wallace, 'Foreign policy and national identity in the United Kingdom', *International Affairs*, 67 (1991), 65–80; Emmanuel Le Roy Ladurie *et al.*, *Entrer dans le XXIeme Siècle: essai sur l'avenir de l'identité française* (Paris, Documentation Française, 1990); Peter Merkl, 'A new German identity?' in Gordon Smith *et al.*, *Developments in German Politics* (London, Macmillan, 1992), ch.17; William Wallace, 'British foreign policy after the Cold War', *International Affairs*, 68 (1992), 423–42.

[56] A. D. Smith, 'National identity and the idea of European unity', *International Affairs*, 68 (1992), 55–76; Smith, *National Identity* (London, Penguin, 1991), ch.7.

[57] Milward, *European Rescue of the Nation State*, p. 446.

disintegration. The crisis of the Belgian nation state – that model of nineteenth century modernization – may well be terminal. The crisis in the Italian state, never entirely integrated, may yet prove less severe. The maintenance of the United Kingdom of Great Britain and Northern Ireland has been questioned by its own government, signalling a willingness to reconsider the 'Union' with Northern Ireland for which its Conservative predecessors of 80 years ago were prepared to fight. Disintegrative tendencies in Spain and elsewhere appear, at the end of 1993, much less severe. Integrative capacity however, in a region faced with complex and difficult demands for political adaptation – to integrate the former socialist countries of central and Eastern Europe, with all the redistributive and security consequences that implies – is low.

The European nation state is in retreat. It might again be rescued, through striking a further bargain between sovereignty and integration and adjusting the idea of national sovereignty to a more explicitly confederal regional framework. But that would require a redefinition of the European nation state, and a political leadership to persuade disillusioned publics to accept that redefinition, of which in 1993 there was little sign.

The Crisis of Identification: the Case of Canada

JAMES TULLY

Political identification in a culturally diverse society

Since 1960 there have been five inconclusive and turbulent rounds of democratic constitutional negotiations in Canada.[1] The aim of the negotiations is to reach agreement on a renewed form of federal constitution which recognizes and affirms the 'cultural diversity' of Canada: that is, the overlapping cultural differences and similarities of its citizens. The fifth and most recent proposed constitutional amendment which sought to accommodate the diverse demands for recognition, the *Charlottetown Accord*, was negotiated and agreed to by the federal government, the three federal parties, the ten provincial prime ministers, the leaders of the Northwest and Yukon territories, and the leaders of the four main Aboriginal peoples' political organizations. Yet, the Accord was voted down in a referendum on 26 October 1992 by a majority in Quebec and the predominantly English-speaking provinces, and a majority among the Aboriginal peoples.

Despite this impasse, constitutional negotiation was set aside in 1993 as a new federal government was elected, the politicians associated with the failed *Charlottetown Accord* were swept out of office, and Canadians turned their attention to the devastating economic recession. However, the constitutional demands remain unresolved and are likely to return in the near future. In the federal election of 1993, the Liberal Party won a clear majority with 177 seats. The Bloc Québécois, the first federal party dedicated to the achievement of Québec sovereignty by separation from the rest of Canada, elected 54 members to Parliament and became the Official Opposition in Ottawa. The new Reform Party, with their base in western Canada, elected 52 members to Parliament. They are opposed to any special constitutional status for Quebec within Canada. In addition, there will be a provincial election in Quebec in 1994 and polls suggests that the separatist Parti Québécois will be victorious. They have promised to hold a referendum on sovereignty within one year of the election. Moreover, the Royal Commission on Aboriginal Peoples will table their report in 1994 and, judging from the recent publications of the Commission, the commissioners will recommend constitutional recognition of Aboriginal self-government.[2]

---

[1] For two excellent accounts see P. H. Russel, *Constitutional Odyssey: can Canadians be a Sovereign People?* (Toronto, University of Toronto Press, 1992) and J. Webber, *Re-imagining Canada* (Montréal, McGill-Queens University Press, 1994).

[2] See Royal Commission on Aboriginal Peoples, *Partners in Confederation: Aboriginal Peoples, Self-government, and the Constitution* (Ottawa, Canadian Communication Group, 1993).

The constitutional impasse is, to use John Dunn's phrase, a 'crisis of political identification' in the sense that the citizens who advance demands cannot identify with and give their allegiance to the Canadian federation until their cultural differences are recognized and affirmed in the constitution and legal and political structures of Canada. However, the demands cannot be accommodated within the vocabulary and institutions of political identity *standardly* associated with the modern constitutional nation state. The inherited vocabulary and institutions that are standardly associated with the nation state would have to be revised in order to accommodate the various demands for recognition of cultural diversity.

The demands for constitutional recognition of cultural diversity can be seen as demands for a range of overlapping *forms* of self-government.[3] The majority of the citizens of Quebec demand recognition not only as a province but also as a predominantly French-speaking 'distinct society' or nation, of equal constitutional status to the predominantly English-speaking provinces as a whole, thereby giving recognition to the equality of the two non-Aboriginal founding cultures of Canada. The government of Quebec thus requires special constitutional powers, normally exercised by the federal government, to preserve and promote Quebec's French language, culture and civil law. The Aboriginal peoples demand recognition as independent, self-governing *First Nations* with their own original legal and political systems and land base, and in international treaty relations of equality and co-existence with the federal government and, to a lesser extent, with the provincial governments. The French language minorities in the predominantly English-speaking provinces and the English language minority in predominantly French-speaking Quebec demand constitutional recognition as official language minorities with the acquired right to schools and social services in their languages and the use of their languages in the courts, provincial parliaments and the public sphere. The women's movement demands that women's formal and substantive equality be recognized and affirmed in the constitution and the basic institutions of Canadian society, as well as in the authoritative traditions of interpretation of these institutions. The wide variety and growing number of multicultural (or intercultural) citizens in Canada who are not Aboriginal and whose first language is neither French nor English participate in the basic institutions and official languages of the federation. Nonetheless, they demand constitutional protection and promotion of their languages and cultures within these institutions; through the public support for education in their languages and histories, public radio and television, affirmative action, and the right to practice their religion and cultural ways in civil society. They aspire to participate in Canadian society through cultural integration rather than assimilation.

Thus, the demands are for what Charles Taylor calls 'deep diversity': diverse and overlapping ways of participating in and identifying with Canada, from forms of nationhood in the cases of Quebec and the First Nations (including Métis, Indians and Inuit) to acting in accord with one's first culture in public in the case of multicultural citizens.[4] According to the opponents of deep

---

[3] For a survey of the major spokespeople see J. Simpson, *Faultlines: Struggling for a Canadian Vision* (Toronto, Harpers Collins, 1993).

[4] C. Taylor, 'Shared and divergent values', in G. Laforest (ed.) *Reconciling the Solitudes* (Montréal, McGill-Queens University Press, 1993), pp. 155–86.

diversity, such constitutional recognition and affirmation must be rejected because it would violate the unity and equality of citizens and provinces under a uniform legal and political system, the basic norms of modern constitutional nation states.[5] It would dissolve the Canadian nation state into a disunited and unequal patchwork aggregation. For these opponents, there are only two solutions to the crisis of political identification: either Canadians must embrace constitutional uniformity and equality or the dissenting members, such as Quebec, must separate in order to form their own uniform nation state.

On the first solution, the demands for cultural recognition must be suppressed or severely modified in the name of the pan-Canadian unity of one nation and the formal equality of all citizens and provincial governments. This solution is associated with former Prime Minister Trudeau and *The Charter of Rights and Freedom*, a substantial constitutional amendment which was introduced in 1982 without the consent of the government of Quebec. Although *The Charter* is associated with the vision of Canada as one juristically uniform nation recognizing only individual rights and formally equal provinces, it, along with the Canadian constitution as a whole (called the Constitution Act, 1982), actually contains a number of exceptions which accommodate some demands for diversity. Official language minorities, the formal and substantive equality of women and other disadvantaged groups, multicultural groups, Aboriginal and treaty rights, differences among provinces, and reasonable limits to individual rights are recognized to some degree (the strict adherents of the vision of Canada as one uniform nation would like to eliminate these sections).

Since *The Charter* failed to recognize Quebec's demands for recognition as a distinct nation in Canada, and since the more recent proposals to accommodate Quebec were also voted down by Quebec and the rest of Canada, a minority of Quebec nationalists argue that Quebec must separate to form a uniform French-speaking nation state. Although this second solution is diametrically opposed to pan-Canadian uniformity of English Canadian nationalists, it is based on the same unitary vision of the identity of a nation state. Not surprisingly, therefore, it is supported by many English-speaking Canadians who argue that Quebec must either conform to *The Charter*, and so be recognized as one province like the others, or leave the federation.

From the perspective of deep diversity both of these solutions appear to be impractical and unjust. There is no evidence that the citizens of Quebec will abjure their aspiration for national recognition and assimilate to an uniform Canada. The Aboriginal peoples have been fighting against the interlopers for recognition of their status as self-governing First Nations for over 380 years and there is no sign that they will abandon the struggle. Nor will the women's movement, the growing multicultural groups and the official languages minorities disappear. Quite the opposite. They are here to stay in the face of polices of assimilation and suppression.

The separation of Canada into two uniform nation states would also fail to solve the crisis of political identification. Each new state would face the same problems of cultural diversity within their new borders. There are, for example, eleven Aboriginal First Nations within the present borders of Quebec. They occupy over half the territory of present-day Quebec and claim the right of

---

[5] See, for example, D. Bercuson and B. Cooper, *Deconfederation: Canada without Quebec* (Toronto, Key Porter, 1991).

self-determination in international law if Quebec separates. The same holds for the 500 First Nations in the rest of Canada, some of which may form independent nation states in the event of separation and non-recognition, perhaps precipitating a chain of indigenous movements for self-determination throughout the Americas and the Commonwealth. The disentanglement and negotiation of competing territorial claims would be daunting. There are also 800,000 Anglophones within Quebec, 1,000,000 Francophones outside Quebec, and various multicultural groups who will all aspire to constitutional recognition in the new states.

Despite the wishes of the proponents of the vision of a uniform nation state, neither pan-Canadian uniformity nor separation into two uniform nations solves the constitutional impasse. Only some form of recognition of deep diversity can do that; either within a new Canadian constitution or, if this is blocked, in two separate countries which recognize diversity in their constitutions. The majority of Quebecers and Quebec nationalists are tolerant of cultural diversity, especially with respect to self-government for Aboriginal peoples and the partial protection of the Anglophone minority, and they prefer recognition within a culturally diverse Canada to separation. Yet, since their minimum demands for constitutional amendment have been repeatedly rejected by English-speaking Canadians over the last decade, the option of a sovereign and internally diverse Quebec state, in some sort of association with the rest of Canada, has gained reluctant popularity. Given the historical record and the current political parties in the rest of Canada, it appears less likely (but not impossible) that an independent, predominantly English-speaking Canadian state would constitutionally recognize either its French-speaking minorities or the degree of self-government for Aboriginal peoples that, say, the Cree, Inuit, Naskapi and Mohawk now exercise in Quebec.[6] While the Atlantic provinces and Ontario have an uneven yet improving tradition of respect for the First Nations and the Francophone minorities, a more recent affirmation of multiculturalism, and roughly 50% popular support for Quebec's demands, the majority tradition of the western provinces is assimilation. If the two new states were able to recognize and affirm diversity after separation, then presumably they can do so before separation, and thus separation, is unnecessary. Yet, five rounds of constitutional negotiation have failed to reach agreement on a form of mutual recognition.

Many culturally diverse, post-colonial societies face similar crises of political identification in one form or another. Whether in the former Yugoslavia, Israel-Palestine, the multiculturalism and multinationalism of the United Kingdom, the European Union, the Maori of New Zealand, or the culturally and linguistically diverse United States, the politics of cultural recognition is one of the most common and difficult political problems of the present age.[7] We may call these crisis a historical movement from political identification to political diversification.

---

[6] For a comparative study of the First Nations see B. Morse, *Comparative Assessments of Indigenous Peoples in Québec, Canada and Abroad*, a report prepared for La Commission d'étude sur toute offre d'un nouveau partenariat de nature constitutionelle et la Commission d'études des questions afférentes à l'accession du Québec a la souveraineté, (Ottawa, University of Ottawa, Faculty of Law, 1992).

[7] For an introduction to some Canadian and the US views see A. Gutmann (ed), *Multiculturalism and the Politics of Recognition* (Princeton, Princeton University Press, 1992).

It is therefore worthwhile to explore the Canadian case to discover what revisions in the prevailing normative vocabulary and institutions of the modern nation state and federation are required to accommodate deep diversity. Of course, accommodation need not take form of constitutional amendment. This depends on the political culture of the country. Even Canada may find a practice of accommodation within an acceptable re-interpretation of its current, flexible constitution. Nevertheless, the institutional and theoretical revisions are substantial. They are not, however, as radical as some writers have warned. It is not the case that culturally diverse, post-colonial societies are composed of a multiplicity of incommensurable identities whose recognition would negate the principals of constitutionalism and disunite the country. Still, the revisions are more substantial than simply the acknowledgement of a dimension of pluralism within the prevailing liberal, nationalist and communitarian theories, for these theories rest on some of the inherited norms of political identity that need to be revised.

I

Which of the conditions of political identification standardly associated with the modern nation state need to be questioned and revised to accommodate justifiable aspirations for recognition of cultural differences and similarities? States in the modern age are identified by three main characteristics: they are constitutional, nations, and modern. Each of these characteristics consists of a complex set of features. Some of the more prominent of these are incompatible with the accommodation of diversity.

First, one prominent feature of modern constitutionalism is a uniform and centralized legal and political system which recognizes each citizen as equal (in the sense of being treated identically rather than equitably).[8] This is the condition of legal monism or legal centralism, usually contrasted with the legal pluralism and customary law of pre-modern Europe. Further, the democratic institutions of representative government, the judiciary, the public sphere and constitutional amendment are presumed to rest on and to institutionalize the sovereignty of the people. In the prevailing conceptions and theories of popular sovereignty, the people are presumed to be culturally homogeneous and prior to the constitution in one of three ways: the people are a society of equal individuals in a state of nature, behind a veil of ignorance, or in a quasi-transcendental speech situation, prior to the establishment of a constitution and with the aim of founding one uniform political society; the people are a society of equal individuals who share a set of authoritative institutions and traditions of interpretation derived from European history; or the people is a unified community bound together by a shared set of authoritative institutions, traditions of interpretation and the common good.

Ever since the American and French revolutions these constitutional features have been understood to be a necessary but insufficient characteristic of modern political identity. The second necessary characteristic is a sense of belonging engendered by understanding the constitutional society as a nation – an

---

[8] See H. Berman, *Law and Revolution* (Cambridge, MA, Harvard University Press, 1983), and D. Kelley, *The Human Measure: Social Thought in the Western Legal Tradition* (Cambridge, MA, Harvard University Press, 1990).

imaginary community to which all citizens belong and enjoy equal dignity.[9] Hence, in addition to allegiance to the constitution, citizens also identify with their particular nation and the national historical *narrative* of the public deeds of its citizens. This characteristic of constitutional nationalism fills the need, first noted by Samuel Pufendorf, of a modern constitutional state for its own distinct name and narrative personality to give it corporate unity.

The third necessary characteristic is that the constitutional nation state is modern. This usually means that the government is able to co-ordinate education, science, technology, markets and international relations in such way that the natural environment, understood as a national resource, is brought under rational control and the well-being of citizens is progressively increased. For our purposes the important feature is that since the sixteenth century 'modern' has been defined in contrast to an exotic 'other'; what anthropologists call the savage slot.[10] In various accounts of the making of the modern political identity this contrasting other is called pre-modern, primitive, savage, oriental, hunter-gatherer, underdeveloped, the state of nature, or the radically separate and different other of ethnographic liberalism. A citizen is modern and the member of a modern nation state just insofar as these three characteristics obtain.

Finally, modern political identity involves a specific concept of identity. This is the idea that identity is a distinct and bounded unity. The individual, society and people of liberal constitutionalism; the citizen, nation, community and culture of nationalism; and the primitive and modern states of modernization theories are all identified by means of this concept which has informed European political thought since the early modern period.

These features of constitutionalism, nationhood and modernity are, in some respects, a caricature (as we shall see). Nonetheless they are not merely a caricature. They are part of, and a real presence in, the theory and practice of modern states. They have been, and continue to be, imposed by processes called discipline, rationalization, socialization and state building: for example, the imposition of centralized and uniform constitutional systems over the crazy quilt of early modern legal and customary systems, the spread of similar systems by European colonization and then by independent, post-colonial third world states, the genocide of 90 per cent of the Aboriginal peoples of the Americas over 400 years, the imposition of linguistic and cultural uniformity, and countless programmes of naturalization, assimilation and development to build modern nations.

Constitutionalism, nation building and modernization have been spread by, and are the leading processes of, the historical movement of liberation from imperial rule and the building of states, from the formation of independent nation states in Europe after the Thirty Years War to the War of Independence of 1776 in the thirteen colonies, and from Third World revolutions in the nineteenth and twentieth centuries to the overthrow of the Soviet empire in eastern Europe. This has been the dominant form of global politics over the

---

[9] See L. Greenfield, *Nationalism: Five Roads to Modernity* (Cambridge, MA, Harvard University Press, 1992).

[10] M.-R. Trouillot, 'Anthropology and the savage slot: the poetics and politics of otherness', in R. G. Fox (ed.), *Recapturing Anthropology* (Santa Fe, School of American Research Press, 1991), pp. 17–44.

last 400 years. The politics of recognition of cultural diversity can be seen as a second movement of anti-imperialism by the peoples and cultures that were excluded and suppressed in the first movement of decolonization and state building. These political actors now experience the three characteristics of modern nation states as an imperial yoke imposed over their distinctive cultural ways, in a manner analogous to the way the proponents of the first movement experienced the old imperial structures they overthrew. This continuity between the two movements explains why the older language of imperial oppression and liberation has re-appeared in these newer struggles. The difference from the first movement is that the aim of the new anti-imperialism is not to build nation states in order to gain independence and self-rule, but, as we have seen, to gain forms of cultural recognition and degrees of self-rule within and across existing nation states.[11]

II

I would now like to show how the three characteristics of modern political identification sketched above have been called into question and revised in the course of the constitutional crisis in Canada.[12] To anticipate, the crisis has been precipitated by the conflict between the demands for recognition and the three prevailing characteristics. However, the proponents of cultural recognition have not rejected constitutionalism, nationalism and modernism and embraced a postmodern discourse to justify their claims. The phenomenon is more complex than this. In the first instance, they have appealed to normative conventions which are deeply woven into the constitutional, national and modernist traditions of contemporary societies, but which have been brushed aside by the more prominent features. However, the politics of cultural recognition is not only an exercise in the retrieval of sources available in modern political discourse yet standardly disregarded. In addition, some of the modern concepts themselves have had to be revised in the light of the diversification that the constitutional crisis has brought gradually to light.

To illustrate this, the constitutional demands of Quebec, the Aboriginal peoples, the women's movement, and the official language minorities will be summarized in order to draw out their shared conventions of justification. Then, the revisions of the characteristics of modern political identification that these demands entail will be outlined.

The government of Quebec argued that the citizens of Quebec could not identify with a Canada constituted by *The Charter* of 1982 because it fails to recognize, and threatens to extinguish, Quebec's distinctiveness in an uniform, pan-Canadian national identity. They presented three demands for constitutional amendment: Quebec's status as a distinct society or nation should be recognized in *The Charter* or the constitution; *The Charter* should be interpreted in the federal courts, by judges from Quebec trained in civil law, in a

---

[11] Compare the somewhat similar opinion in E. W. Said, *Culture and Imperialism* (New York, Alfred A. Knopf, 1993).

[12] For a more detailed discussion and set of references for this section see J. Tully, 'Diversity's gambit declined', in C. Cook (ed.), *Canada's Constitutional Predicament after* 1992 (Montréal, McGill-Queens University Press, forthcoming 1994), pp. 200–67. See also A.-G. Gagnon and G. Laforest, 'The future of federalism: lessons from Quebec and Canada', *International Journal*, 48 (1993), 470–91, and note 1 above.

manner that conforms to the civic, linguistic and legal culture of Quebec; and *The Charter* and any other constitutional amendment can apply to Quebec only if it has the consultation and agreement of the sovereign people of Quebec and their representatives in the National Assembly (the Quebec provincial parliament, the oldest non-Aboriginal democratic institution in Canada). If these three demands were met then the citizens of Quebec could identify with Canada because the country would then be seen as a diverse federation which recognizes and affirms their cultural distinctiveness rather than a uniform nation state which threatens to suppress and extinguish it.

In presenting these demands, the proponents appealed to three constitutional conventions of justification that underpin western constitutional theory and practice. The first is that the members of a political association (whether individuals or peoples) should be recognized in their own cultural terms and ways throughout constitutional negotiations and in the constitution itself (the principle of mutual recognition, *audi alteram partem*, or self-identification in international law). Second, the cultures of the members who compose a constitutional association should continue through the establishment of association and not be discontinued or extinguished, even in the case of conquest or capitulation (the principal of legal, political and customary 'continuity' in international law). Third, negotiated constitutional agreements and amendments which alter the cultures of the members require the consent of those affected and/or their representatives (the principal of *quod omnes tangit*, what touches all must be approved by all).

Quebec writers went on to argue that these conventions of recognition, continuity and consent are not a new ideology of multiculturalism and nationalism but the fundamental conventions of constitutional government, with longer usage and practice than the norms of national uniformity and equality the defenders of *The Charter* proclaimed. When Quebec (or Canada) was officially brought into the British imperial system after the capitulation of France in 1760 and fourteen years of negotiation, its French language and Catholic religion, legal and property system, and customary ways were explicitly recognized and continued in *The Quebec Act* of 1774. Once its constitutional culture, so to speak, was recognized, the Crown further acknowledged, as a general principal, that it could not alter it without the consent of Quebec representatives.

As the whig proponents of *The Quebec Act* of 1774 pointed out, these three conventions on which Quebec's allegiance to Canada rests derive from the law of nations and from the common law tradition. They were famously asserted, for example, by William Molyneux, in *The Case of Ireland* (1698), by John Locke in his defence of the recognition and continuity of Anglo-Saxon laws, liberties and forms of local government through the Norman Conquest, in the *Two Treatises of Government* (1690) and Matthew Hale in *The History of the Common Law of England* (1713).[13] The violation of these conventions was also the major justification for the War of Independence of the thirteen colonies. Moreover, when other colonies federated with Quebec to form what is now called Canada in 1791, 1867, and so on, these conventions were applied to the new members. The acts of confederation did not discontinue the long-standing

---

[13] W. Molyneux, *The Case of Ireland being bound by Acts of Parliament of England* (Dublin, 1698), J. Locke, *Two Treatises of Government* (Cambridge, Cambridge University Press, 1988),

legal and political cultures of the former colonies and impose a uniform legal and political culture, but, rather, recognized and continued their constitutional cultures in a diverse federation in which the consent of each province was given.[14]

In this light, the imposition of *The Charter* on Quebec in 1982, affecting its constitutional culture without consultation and consent, appears as an anti-constitutional act of discontinuity and assimilation. Quebecers received a further slap in the face in 1990. They were informed that *The Charter* is binding on them without their provincial consent, yet their proposed amendment to *The Charter*, the Meech Lake Accord in 1987 – 90, was rejected because, even though it had the consent of all the provincial Prime Ministers and the federal parliament, it did not have the ratification of two provincial legislatures. Manitoba and Newfoundland (neither of which were substantively affected by the amendment), and it would have been rejected if only one provincial legislature failed to ratify.

This justification of recognition, with its impressive constitutional and liberal foundation, caused the character of the federation to appear in a different light from that of the defenders of *The Charter*. First, Canada appears to be a federation of provinces, each with their own distinctive culture, rather than a single nation state. The juristic identity of Canada appears to be closer to legal pluralism than to the legal monism that dominates theories and depictions of modern states and charters of rights, with Quebec defending legal diversity against the centralizing tendency of the federal government. Legal scholars and anthropologists went on to reinforce this revision by arguing that legal pluralism is the norm rather than the exception in the contemporary post-colonial world.[15] To formulate this characteristic more accurately, the constitutional identity of Canada appears not to be fixed and uniform at some historical founding moment, as contemporary theories tend to presume, but rather to be an ongoing activity of negotiation among federal and provincial governments in accord with the conventions of recognition, continuity and consent. Moreover, the member provinces of the federation, and not just Quebec, are seen to be equal, not in the sense of identical, but in the Aristotelian sense of equitable constitutional recognition of their similarities and dissimilarities.

The convention of cultural continuity entails that the government of Quebec has the responsibility to preserve and promote a constitutive public good: the French language and culture in Quebec. It has, for example, the authority to limit the written use of English on the public commercial signs if and only if this proves to threaten the survival of French. That is, the limits on the individual freedom of expression in *The Charter* should be interpreted in the light of Canada's commitment to the recognition and continuity of the French language and culture. This request, formulated in the Meech Lake Accord, was rejected by the majority of English-speaking Canadians because it deviated from the norm that all rights and freedoms should be applied to all citizens in

Footnote continued

pp. 384–98, M. Hale, *The History of the Common Law of England* (Chicago, University of Chicago Press, 1971), pp. 47–72.

[14] The classic statement of this Lockean compact theory of federalism is T. J. J. Loranger, *Lettres sur l'interprétation de la consitution fédérale: première lettre* (Québec City, A. Coté, 1883).

[15] See J. Griffiths, 'What is legal pluralism', *Journal of Legal Pluralism and Unofficial Law*, 24, (1986) 1.

an identical manner and independent of circumstances. Yet, research showed that the courts have been involved in contextualized and culturally sensitive legal reasoning and interpretation, in accord with the principle of culture continuity, since confederation with respect to Aboriginal, French and English cultures, and more recently with respect to other cultures. Indeed, scholars further suggested that *The Charter* itself, the supposed embodiment of individual rights and formal equality contains a number of sections which can be used to protect Quebec's culture.[16] Consequently, the drive to abstraction and universalization in much of modern constitutional theory since the seventeenth century, as well as in the standard picture of the legal identity of modern states, seriously misrepresents the legal identity and practice of culturally diverse common law societies.

Finally the arguments advanced by Quebec writers called into question the standard picture of popular sovereignty in Canada. The people were now envisioned neither as culture-free (or culture transcending) and pre-constitutional individuals nor as members of a homogeneous national culture. They are already constituted members of both provincial and federal cultures, with complex and overlapping relations of political identification to both, and deliberating in the constitutional negotiations in terms of their diverse cultural narratives.[17]

The Charter recognizes treaty rights of the Aboriginal peoples and a section added to the constitution in 1982 recognizes Aboriginal rights. However, the meeting with Aboriginal leaders and federal and provincial governments from 1983 to 1986 failed to reach agreement on the meaning of Aboriginal rights. The demands of the Aboriginal peoples for recognition were ignored during the years of the Meech Lake Accord (1987 – 90). The definition of Aboriginal rights as inherent rights of self-government, forming a third order of government in Canada, parallel to some degree to the federal and provincial orders, was negotiated by the leaders of the four main Aboriginal political organizations during the Charlottetown Accord, but, as I mentioned earlier, the Accord was voted down in the referendum of October 26, 1992.

The Aboriginal peoples argued that *The Charter* and the constitution fail to recognize explicitly that Aboriginal peoples as First Nations: that is, independent nations with the inherent right to govern themselves in accordance with their own legal and political traditions and their indigenous languages and cultural ways, and to exercise jurisdiction over the territories they have not ceded to the Canadian government. If they are to identify with Canada then their status as First Nations has to be recognized in the constitution, their constitutional culture has to be continued, rather than discontinued by policies of suppression, extinguishment and genocide, as has so often been the case. Furthermore, if the First Nations delegate some of their inherent powers to the federal government, then this conditional delegation should be based on their agreement, reached by negotiations in accordance with their own traditions of inter-nation diplomacy, and formalized in treaties which preserve their status

---

[16] Two leading scholars in this area are Professor B. Slattery of the Osgoode Hall Law School, York University, and Professor J. Webber of the Faculty of Law, McGill University.

[17] Compare Alain Noel, 'Deliberating a constitution: the meaning of the Canadian referendum of 1992', in Cook, *Canada's Constitutional Predicament*.

as co-existing nations of the Canadian federation. The Aboriginal peoples thus understand the political identity of Canada to be a federation of Aboriginal nations and the federal government based on treaty relations negotiated from time to time in accordance with the conventions of recognition, continuity and consent.

Although it appears that the First Nations appealed to the same three western constitutional conventions as Quebec, they actually appealed to similar Aboriginal conventions that have governed the relations among the First Nations of America for thousands of years.[18] When the Europeans arrived the First Nations entered into treaty negotiations with them, just as they were used to doing among Aboriginal nations, recognizing the Europeans as equal in status to Aboriginal nations. Over 500 treaties have been negotiated in what is now Canada (and over 300 in the United States), first with the French nation, and then with the British, and later Canadian, government. The Aboriginal conventions of recognition, continuity and consent are embodied in these treaty relations (in so far as they have been respected) and are best expressed in the practice of treaty federalism developed by the Haudenosaunee (Iroquois) confederation in its diplomacy with the Dutch, French, British, and (later) US and Canadian governments. This practice is called the *Two Row* treaty system in honour of the belts of two parallel rows of purple wampum beads which are exchanged at the conclusion of a successful negotiation. The two equal rows,

> symbolise two paths or two vessels, travelling down the same river together. One, a birch bark canoe, will be for the Indian people, their laws, their customs and their ways. The other, a ship, will be for the white people and their laws, their customs and ways. We shall each travel the river together, side by side, but in our own boat. Neither of us will try to steer the other's boat.[19]

The Aboriginal peoples thus recognize the European Americans as equal and independent nations, with a right to acquire land and jurisdiction through treaty cessions, just in so far as the European Americans recognize the Aboriginal peoples as equal and independent prior nations. This is the principle of mutual recognition of equality (*Kahswentha*). The second feature is that, as they become bound together by relations of trust, by means of treaties, the Aboriginal traditions and governments continue in co-existence through all the negotiated relations of interdependency over time. This principal of continuity is symbolized by the parallel rows the vessels travelling 'side by side', and by neither people trying to steer the other. The third feature is that the negotiations, whether they are for land cessions to the newcomers, shared resource

---

[18] For the following exposition (based on J. Tully, 'Diversity's gambit declined'), compare Royal Commission on Aboriginal Peoples, *Partners in Confederation*, Ovide Mercredi and Mary Ellen Turpel, *In the Rapids: Navigating the Future of First Nations* (New York, Viking, 1993) and Patrick Macklem, 'Distributing sovereignty: Indian nations and the equality of peoples', *Stanford Law Review* 45, Autumn (1993).

[19] From the submission of the Haudenosaunee confederation to the Canadian House of Commons Committee on Indian Self-Government (1983). I have discussed the Two Row Treaty System of treaty federalism with the Canadian and US governments in 'Aboriginal property and Western theory: recovering a middle ground', in E. F. Paul, J. Paul and F. D. Miller (eds), *Property Rights* (Cambridge, Cambridge University Press, 1994 forthcoming).

management, delegation of some inherent powers from time to time, redress of earlier treaty violations, or whatever, require the consent of the Aboriginal peoples through their own traditions of government by consensus.

The First Nations argue that this vision of the relation of the First Nations to the Crown was understood and recognized in the Royal Proclamation of 1763 (in a manner similar to the recognition of Quebec in the Quebec Act of 1774). In addition, John Marshall, Chief Justice of the US Supreme Court, recognized and reaffirmed the status of Aboriginal peoples as independent, self-governing nations in a treaty federation with the US federal government in the 1820s and 1830s, laying the foundations of Aboriginal-US constitutional law. Since the Royal Proclamation of 1763 is part of the Canadian constitution, the sovereignty of the Canadian government in Canada thus rests on its recognition by the First Nations, not *vice versa* as the non-Aboriginal negotiators tended to assume throughout the 1980s.

Of course, the Aboriginal peoples went on to point out the conventions of recognition, continuity and consent have been violated time after time in practice, especially over the last century. The Aboriginal population has been reduced by over ninety percent as the result of 400 years of oppression. Their land has been stolen and they have been forced on to tiny, polluted reserves with the worst living conditions in the Americas. Their legal and political institutions have been destroyed: their languages, religions and family structures outlawed and demeaned, and they have been forced into English and French speaking schools to become 'civilised'. *The Indian Act* an administrative dictatorship established in 1874, has been imposed without consent and it governs every aspect of their daily lives, devastating their basic sense of self-respect. As a result, they have the highest rates of infant mortality, unemployment, youth suicide, substance abuse, incarceration and school dropout in Canada.[20]

For the Aboriginal peoples, therefore, the imposition of *The Charter* without their negotiation and consent, and without explicit recognition of the inherent right to govern themselves in accordance with their own laws and ways, or to opt into a suitably amended *Charter* if they chose, represented another act of imperialism in a long chain of abuses, giving the lie again to Canada's self image as a constitutional democracy. Like Quebecers, they were not opposed to *The Charter*, but to its imposition without consent and to its individualist and western bias which violated the principal of equality of peoples and their cultures.

Understandably, these claims for recognition caused a further revision of the standard picture of Canadian political identity. First, it reinforced the view presented by Quebec of Canada, at its best, as a negotiated plurality of legal and political cultures. Despite the innumerable attempts to destroy Aboriginal political organizations, legal scholars were able to show that the common law justices, prior to twentieth-century modernization, recognized Aboriginal nationhood and added the Aboriginal systems of customary law and land use to

---

[20] For this paragraph see D. Stannard, *American Holocaust: Columbus and the Conquest of the New World* (Oxford, Oxford University Press, 1992), O. P. Dickason, *Canada's First Nations: a History of Founding Peoples from Earliest Times* (Toronto, McClelland and Stewart, 1992), and Royal Commission on Aboriginal Peoples, *The Path to Healing* (Ottawa, Canada Communication Group, 1993).

the common law as a co-ordinate system. In *Partners in Confederation* The Royal Commission of Aboriginal Peoples argued that the inherent right of self government already exists in the history and practice of the Canadian constitution. It needs only be recovered from beneath the legal monism of the present age. Justices have begun to move in this direction in some recent court cases. Rather than appearing regressive and pre-modern relative to the prevailing picture of the modern nation state, the recognition of Aboriginal law and self-government appears to be just and progressive relative to the three Aboriginal and western constitutional conventions. This new and more complex vision of a modern 'nation' state is also reinforced by the advances in international law with respect to the cultural survival of indigenous peoples (based largely on the recovery of the conventions of recognition, continuity and consent).[21]

The combined effect of this intense public discussion and confrontation was to question the very distinction between modern and pre-modern constitutions on which the standard picture of a modern state rests. The movement towards constitutional centralization, uniformity and national assimilation appeared less enlightened as the debate proceeded. The recognition and affirmation of a plurality of legal and political systems in Canada, some of which are over 5,000 years old and based partly on custom, seemed required by the three conventions underlying constitutional rule, thereby, ironically, re-establishing a continuity between so-called modern and pre-modern constitutionalism.

The struggle of the First Nations challenged another aspect of the distinction between modern and pre-modern societies. Since environmental destruction in Canada, such as clear cut logging on Calyquot Sound in British Columbia, usually involves the destruction of the way of life a First Nation seeks to preserve by constitutional recognition of their jurisdiction, the Aboriginal peoples are at the forefront of the fight to protect the environment. As the environmental battles coincided with the constitutional negotiations, some Canadians discovered the unique relation of 'stewardship' Aboriginal people have to the ecology and how this differs from the western relation of private property, which serves to legitimate environmental destruction.[22] This sharp contrast served to shake the unquestioning faith of some Canadians in the superiority of the modern, systems of private property and resource development, and thus to open to critical review this powerful dogma of modern identity.

When non-Aboriginal Canadians met with Aboriginal people struggling with resource management on their lands they further discovered that they are not the exotic, romanticized other of popular anthropology and the four stages theory of human history, but human beings struggling with problems familiar to all Canadians. This in turn made the distinction between modern societies and the so-called lower and earlier cultural stages of historical development,

---

[21] See the draft *Declaration of the Rights of Indigenous Peoples*, as approved by the members of the Working Group on Indigenous Populations and reported to the United Nations Sub-Commission on Prevention of Discrimination and Protection of Minorities, August (1993).

[22] For the concept of stewardship see M. Jackson, 'Alternatives to extinguishment: a report prepared for the Royal Commission on Aboriginal Peoples', Royal Commission on Aboriginal Peoples (forthcoming).

such as hunting and gathering, on which the modern character of nation states is said to rest, look strikingly implausible and ideological.[23]

The quest for justice of Aboriginal peoples also illustrates the 'tangled' nature of modern political identity. It is not simply that there is a plurality of cultures and legal forms in many modern societies, but also that cultures overlap and interact. The Aboriginal peoples, for instance, do not wish to return to their pre-invasion political identities, nor could they if they so wished. They have interacted culturally for over 400 years with non-Aboriginals and the cultures on both sides have been deeply shaped by this ongoing interaction. Cultures in diverse societies are neither sharply bounded, homogeneous nor static; they are a cluster of intercultural relations negotiated and renegotiated over time.[24]

To define and implement self-government and Aboriginal justice, for example, Aboriginal people have drawn on their own traditions, Canadian law, international law, and even *The Indian Act*, in the course of challenging them. They have forced Canadian courts to recognize international law and they have formed alliances with Aboriginal peoples outside of Canada. The political identity of Aboriginal government is continually debated and modified by Aboriginal peoples. Band Council chiefs, who work within *The Indian Act* regime, disagree with traditionalists; Aboriginal peoples living of the reserves differ from those living on the reserves; Aboriginal men differ from Aboriginal women, who sometimes form alliances with non-Aboriginal women. Aboriginal women differ among themselves. This continual negotiation of cultural identity, common also to multicultural groups, the women's movement, and Quebec and English Canadian nationalists, has revised the prevailing assumption that the identity of any community or nation is single settled and comprehensive.[25]

A third dimension of the constitutional crisis in Canada is the demands of the official language minorities: the Anglophones in Quebec and the Franco-phones in the predominantly English speaking provinces. They argue that their languages, schools and cultures also have been protected by the same three conventions of recognition, continuity and consent since the Constitution Act of 1791. Here, the three conventions are used to recognize minorities, not nations, with a degree of cultural and linguistic self-governance within the political and legal institutions of the two majorities. Like Quebec and the First Nations, they too have historical narratives of the violations of these conventions and innumerable attempts to assimilate them to the dominant language of their province. (It would be unfair to place the two minorities together in this respect. Throughout Canadian history the French language minorities in the English language provinces have suffered more than the English language minority in Quebec.)

Canada's multicultural groups demanded constitutional recognition, continuity and consent in a manner similar to the official language minorities. Although their languages and cultures are not constitutive of the basic institutions of Canada in the way Aboriginal, French and English languages

---

[23] See, for example, M. Boldt, *Surviving as Indians: the Challenge of Self-Government* (Toronto, University of Toronto Press, 1993), and D. Smith, *The Seventh Fire: the Struggle for Aboriginal Government* (Toronto, Key Porter, 1993).

[24] See J. Clifford, *The Predicament of Culture* (Cambridge MA, Harvard University Press, 1988), pp. 277–348.

[25] See Royal Commission on Aboriginal Peoples, *Aboriginal Peoples and the Justice System* (Ottawa, Canadian Communication Group, 1993).

and cultures are, they nonetheless can claim in an analogous fashion constitutional recognition and a degree of public support for the continuity, rather than the assimilation, of the many other languages and cultures that have been, and increasingly will be, woven into the Canadian fabric. Constitutional recognition was given for this recent government practice in *The Charter* and multicultural groups protected it through the later negotiations.[26]

Accordingly, since Quebec, for example, bases its demand for recognition on the same three conventions as the Anglophone minority appeals to in defending its culture, then it follows that Quebec should also be concerned to preserve and promote the Anglophone minority in Quebec and, in a different way, the multicultural groups, just as, to be consistent, it should recognize the claims of the eleven First Nations of Quebec to self government. In each proposed constitutional amendment, the Quebec government has included a clause protecting its Anglophone minority and every Quebec government since 1983 has recognized, to some extent, the self-government and autonomy of the First Nations. The Allophone cultural groups in Quebec also have a degree of recognition and public support; and several of them have their own schools. In the same manner, the predominantly English speaking provinces ought to recognize their French speaking minorities and the respective First Nations, as well as their multicultural groups, since the legal and political continuity of the provinces is founded on the same conventions.

This example shows how the three conventions provide one of the most important requirements of contemporary politics: a cross-cultural normative framework to justify and adjudicate cultural diversity and to invalidate claims to cultural exclusivity and homogeneity. Cultural recognition is not a zero sum game. The courts have developed a distinctive form of common law legal reasoning which enables them to accommodate the differential claims for cultural recognition of, for example, both Quebec and its Anglophone minority while respecting individual and collective rights.

The values of recognizing cultural diversity within the conventions of modern constitutionalism has also inspired one of the most important and promising intellectual movements of our age. This is the revision of nationalism by a group of Quebec scholars so it can accommodate the diversity of modern societies. They are developing a pluralistic form of Quebec civic nationalism which affirms the Quebec nation while including the recognition and affirmation of the eleven First Nations, the multicultural allophone groups of Quebec, the Anglophone minority, the ties to the Francophone minorities outside Quebec, and the fundamental individual rights enshrined in Quebec's own charter. This distinctive liberal and culturally diverse nationalism revises the culturally homogeneous view of a nation given by most modern theories of nationalism.[27]

---

[26] For an overview see W. Kymlicka, *Recent Work in Citizenship Theory: a Report Prepared for Multiculturalism and Citizenship Canada* (Ottawa, Supply and Services Canada, 1992).

[27] Two of the major figures in this movement are Professors A.-G. Gagnon at McGill University and G. Laforest at Université Laval. See G. Laforest, *De la prudence* (Québec, Boréal, 1993), L. Balthazar, G. Laforest, V. Lemieux (eds), *Le Québec et la restructuration du Canada 1980–1992* (Sillery Québec, Septentrion, 1991), A.-G. Gagnon, F. Rocher (eds), *Répliques aux détracteurs de la souveraineté du Québec* (Montréal, VLB, 1992), A.-G. Gagnon and M. Burgess (eds), *Comparative Federalism and Federation: Competing Traditions and Future Directions* (London, Harvester Wheatsheaf, 1993).

The fourth group to challenge the standard features of modern political identification is the women's movement.[28] They justified their demands for constitutional recognition by appealing to the same conventions of recognition, continuity and consent. The women's organizations argued that they cannot identify with Canada unless women are recognized as equal to men, their distinctive cultures or voices are not excluded from the basic institutions and traditions of interpretation, and their consent is secured for any constitutional amendment that affects their position in Canadian society. Since the Canadian constitution was established long ago by men without the participation or consent of women, it is unjust by the conventions the male negotiators appeal to in their own cases. Feminist scholars and justices went on to expose the male bias of the constitution, *The Charter*, and the basic institutions of Canadian society, showing how men systematically overlooked the different situation and constraints on women in establishing and running Canadian political institutions. They concluded that it is insufficient to give women a say and a vote *within* these exclusively male institutions and political discourses, as was done a few decades ago: the equality of women and their concerns must be constitutive of the basic institutions and traditions of interpretation.

The way to do this is to revise the standard view of popular sovereignty. If the key feature of popular sovereignty is that each person has a voice in democratic deliberations, then women should not only have the right to speak but the right to speak as women; to voice their own distinctive political concerns in their own terms and ways. The precondition of having a voice in this sense is that women's culture (political concerns and ways of taking about politics) is recognized and esteemed, rather than excluded and denigrated, by the other participants in public constitutional deliberations, just as *their* cultural ways are recognized.

Accordingly, *The National Action Committee on the Status of Women* (NAC), the umbrella women's organization, took the role of presenting briefs to the negotiators and publicly commenting on the various constitutional proposals as they appeared. They thus acted as an intermediary between negotiators and citizens and ensured, by means of *ad hoc* lobbying, that their consent was seen to be required for any amendment. In this way the bias caused by the predominantly male culture of the negotiators and institutions was constantly challenged and occasionally even corrected. The women's organizations were able to add two last minute clauses to *The Charter* in 1982 – formal gender equality and an affirmative action or equity clause to correct the structural gender equality in Canadian society – and protect these clauses throughout the later rounds. When the *Native Women's Association of Canada* used these clauses to argue that the negotiations for the Charlottetown Accord were unjust because there were not enough Aboriginal women at the table, the Supreme Court ruled in their favour.

The claim that the subordinate position and culture of women needed to be taken into account and remedied, while clearly a deviation from the standard of formal equality alone, was shown to be in conformity with the normal

---

[28] For an introduction see S. Razack, *Canadian Feminism and the Law: the Education and Action Fund and the Pursuit of Equality* (Toronto, Second Story, 1991).

practice of common law judges in analogous cases. Feminist legal scholars argued that even the interpretation and application of individual rights, the seeming bastion of formal and abstract equality, can be, and often is, a matter of discriminating judgements of cultural similarities and dissimilarities in particular contexts, precisely the sort of reasoning that feminists were concerned to promote.[29]

Consequently, the women's movement demonstrated how the three conventions could be used to justify recognition of their cultural difference in a form dissimilar to the recognition of Quebec, the First Nations and the official language minorities (by modifying the basic institutions and practices in accord with their culture rather than establishing their own institutions). But they did more. The recognition of women's cultural identity cuts across the other cultural differences we have discussed. When male negotiators put forward proposals for the recognition of Quebec's or the First Nations' cultural distinctiveness, for example, their portrayals were constantly contested on the ground of gender bias. They thereby confirmed that modern political identity is contested and negotiated along gender lines (among others) and, therefore, that a just political identity is based on these intercultural negotiations, not on their suppression of imaginary transcendence.

The evolution of women's constitution negotiations illustrated yet another aspect of cultural diversity. The negotiations over recognition are not only among overlapping cultures but also within cultures. The women's movement soon came to realize that it could not pretend to speak in one voice for all women. Many women refuse to identify with the movement and the women who do speak with culturally diverse voices, each with, to apply the conventions again, the right to be recognized and heard. The concerns of Aboriginal women, Quebec women, African and Asian Canadian women, and the way they articulate them and relate them to the concerns of other constitutional actors, are significantly different from the concerns of the white middle-class women who dominated the movement in the early rounds. NAC found itself negotiating this diverse federation of voices. To take another important example, Aboriginal women divided over the nature of self-government. Some want *The Charter* to be applied directly to Aboriginal governments to protect Aboriginal women from the male dominated Band Councils and male violence and sexual abuse on Aboriginal territory. Other Aboriginal women want to deal with these problems in Aboriginal systems of justice and healing circles, based on the renewal of Aboriginal traditions of consensus government and gender equality which prevailed in many First Nations before the coming of European majoritarian and patriarchal political and legal institutions.[30]

---

[29] For an excellent survey and original contribution to this field see P. L. Bowden, *Caring: an Investigation in Gender-Sensitive Ethics* (Montréal, McGill University PhD Dissertation, 1993), and M. Minow, *Making All the Difference: Inclusion, Exclusion, and American Law* (Ithaca, Cornell University Press, 1991).

[30] For a helpful discussion of these differences see Royal Commission on Aboriginal Peoples, *Aboriginal Peoples and the Justice System.*

III

In conclusion, what lessons can be drawn about the crisis of identification in modern nation states from the Canadian experience? First, a modern constitution is not separate from culture as some liberals have suggested. Aboriginal, Quebec and feminist scholars have shown that *The Charter*, one of the most modern constitutional documents in the world, is shaped by western, individualist and male cultural biases respectively. For a modern constitution in a culturally diverse, post-imperial society to be just, it should rest on the negotiation and equitable recognition of the cultures of the association. This is just to affirm that earlier liberals such as Locke, Molyneux, Lord Mansfield and Chief Justice Marshall were more tolerant than their later followers in incorporating cultural continuity into modern constitutionalism.[31]

Second, there is not one national culture and narrative which either excludes or stands over and above the 'sub-national' others, as many modern nationalists and communitarians presume. There are many and they are diverse.[32] They criss-cross and overlap in various ways, require different forms of recognition, and exist in a continual process of contestation and change. As a result, citizens are members of (at least) more than one culture and the 'crossing' of cultures is one of the most important phenomena in understanding how they relate to their political associations.[33]

Third, the diversity of modern political identity is obscured by the concept of identity in standard use in theory and practice. One of the most important criticisms of the concept of identity as something bounded, homogeneous and separate was advanced by Wittgenstein in the *Philosophical investigations*. He replaced it with a vocabulary of identity as family resemblance, criss-crossing and overlapping similarities and differences, and the like.[34] As many scholars have since concurred, this language of identity provides a more perspicuous representation of the tangled, intercultural identities of modern societies and citizens than the standard one which continues to inform much of modern political theory.[35]

Wittgenstein summarized the concept he attacked in the following way:

> 'A thing is identical with itself.'–There is no finer example of a useless proposition, which yet is connected with a certain play of the imagination. It is as if in imagination we put a thing into its own shape and saw that it fitted.[36]

[31] For a promising attempt to reconcile contemporary Kantian liberalism to cultural diversity see D. M. Weinstock, 'The political theory of strong evaluation', in J. Tully (ed.), *Philosophy in an Age of Pluralism: Critical Perspectives on the Philosophy of Charles Taylor* (Cambridge, Cambridge University Press, forthcoming 1994).

[32] For the rethinking of nationalism and communitarianism in the light of cultural diversity see G. Laforest, *De la prudence*, A.-G. Gagnon and G. Laforest, 'Federalism: lessons from Canada and Quebec', C. Taylor, 'Shared and divergent values', and the exchange between G. Laforest and C. Taylor in J. Tully (ed.), *Philosophy in an Age of Pluralism*.

[33] For a similar view of the US see R. Takaki, *A Different Mirror: a History of Multicultural America* (Toronto, Little Brown, 1993).

[34] L. Wittgenstein, (trans G. E. M. Anscombe) *Philosophical Investigations* (Oxford, Basil Blackwell, 1988), ss. 65–75.

[35] Two of the most important scholars are C. Geertz and J. Clifford. For a summary see M. Carrithers, *Why Humans Have Cultures: Explaining Anthropology and Social Diversity* (Oxford, Oxford University Press, 1992), pp. 12–33.

[36] L. Wittgenstein, *Philosophical Investigations*, s. 216.

This imaginary identity is still associated with the modern constitutional nation state and its constituent parts, whether these are construed as individuals or communities. It now needs to be abandoned if the multiplicity and intercultural negotiation of modern political identity is to be recognized. A modern nation state, one might say, is a thing that is not identical with itself.

Fourth, Canada's constitutional struggle also suggests that the concept of popular sovereignty should be revised. A culturally homogeneous people does not reach agreement in the state of nature or an ideal situation and then found a constitution in one single act in the distant past. Rather, the culturally diverse peoples here and now seek to reach constitutional agreements from time to time by means of negotiations in which the conventions of recognition, continuity and consent are honoured. Also, this constitutional recognition and affirmation of the diverse cultures in which citizens speak and act is a necessary condition for them to participate in everyday politics. People can acquire the self-respect necessary to act as autonomous citizens and speak about their political association only if the cultures in which they speak and act are affirmed by others. Nothing has driven this elementary point home more than the devastating effects on the Aboriginal peoples of the denigration and attempted destruction of their cultures.

Finally, the Canadian experience suggests on the one hand that the politics of cultural recognition cannot be suppressed or ignored. It is a second type of anti-imperial struggle, just as powerful and durable as the type which built modern constitutional nation states over the last 400 years. The policies of suppression and assimilation simply cause greater resistance, like so many bent but unbreakable twigs, as Sir Isaiah Berlin puts it, and as the courageous resistance of the indigenous peoples of the world exemplify.[37] Cultural recognition may also be disregarded for a time, as in Canada at the present moment, but not for long, for cultural recognition is a deep and abiding human need. When William Knox wrote a pamphlet in 1774 to explain why the Crown recognized and continued the legal and political culture of French Catholic Quebec in *The Quebec Act*, he said simply that the Crown had learned from its mistake in Ireland.[38]

On the other hand, Canada's crisis suggests that the recognition and affirmation of the culturally diverse identities of modern citizens does not lead to disunity and disintegration of modern nation states. Quite the opposite. The steady glacial movement towards disunity and separation in Canada is caused by the failure mutually to recognize and accommodate the aspirations of Quebec and the First Nations along with the just demands of the other cultural groups. This is a complex political task but it is neither hopelessly complex nor a threat to liberal democratic constitutionalism. It is possible by forms of political reasoning and norms of equity available in our constitutional traditions and it is required by, rather than a threat to, the liberal and democratic conventions of constitutionalism. The task appears hopeless and

---

[37] I. Berlin, 'The return of the Volkgeist', *New Perspectives Quarterly*, 4 (1991), 4–10, and D. Maybury-Lewis, *Millenium: Tribal Wisdom and the Modern World* (New York, Viking, 1992).

[38] W. Knox, *The Justice and Policy of the Late Act of Parliament for Making More Effectual Provision for the Government of the Province of Quebec* (London, 1774).

threatening only in the light of the oversimplifications of identity in the standard picture of the modern nation state. This caricature is a major cause of the crisis and a major obstacle to understanding and accommodating the negotiated cultural diversity of modern political identity.

The Military Crisis of the Nation State: will Asia be different from Europe?

PAUL BRACKEN

The state's coercive nature is missing from current accounts of the crisis of the nation state. This neglect is easy to understand in the face of the end of the cold war, and the appearance of many new challenges to the state. But it is unfortunate because in the enthusiasm for identifying new sources of crisis the oldest one has seemingly disappeared, and done so at the very time when the spread of cheap technologies of destruction and a new disciplined ruthlessness in military organization are appearing in the most economically dynamic part of the world, Asia. In Asia a combination of the atavistic forces of capitalism with a profound transformation in the organization of coercion may not produce what happened in Europe at a comparable period of change, but it certainly calls into question any analysis which does not take account of the military character of the state. A prospect that the next century could be a period of organized violence worse than this one, but by Asia rather than by Europe, is a crisis, if that term is to have any meaning, in a form of political organization which has only been dominant for a few centuries in the world, and in Asia only since World War II.

Asia is now an urgent concern of the West for its economic dynamism and for problems which follow from this in the fields of trade and environment. It is as if this one dimension were the unique measure of the nation state. Asian economies *are* changing, shifting more to market and less to state allocations, and in the process undergoing the largest capitalist transformation in world history. Economic growth is the highest in the world, much higher than took place in Europe before 1914. But the social and economic structures which underlie this growth are forever being changed by it. Established equilibria are being strained and broken, in a classic pattern of capitalist development, but with unknown consequences in a setting so very different from Europe's. The outcome of this transformation may be malevolent, or benevolent. Or it could be both in sequence, as has been the case in Western Europe to the present time.

At a minimum it can be said that the foundations on which Asia's more important states were founded after 1945 are changing in ways that will fundamentally alter their character, and pose deep challenges to the West's conception of that character. This conception, either for developing countries like China and India or advanced capitalist countries like Japan and South Korea, argues that they compete for ways to create wealth without aggressive intent toward each other, that they emphasize economic rather than military competencies, and that they are at least gradually moving toward a universalist conception of nationhood which detached citizenship and citizen rights from ethnic and cultural inheritances. It is by no means clear that the capitalist dynamic will produce this outcome in Asia, and to assume that it will do so while searching for new kinds of threats to the nation state risks focusing on secondary, at the expense of primary issues.

One of the most important aspects of a theory is that it tells us what issues to look for. It focuses attention on variables which comport with its view. With the Western conception of Asian modernization, there is little reason to monitor the restructuring of a state's coercive organizations because they do not play much of a role beyond the point where the nation state is firmly established. The military is necessary to create and defend the new nation state, sometimes in revolution and sometimes to administer it during its growing pains of development. In this theory of modernization once a nation state is established the military is an institution which mainly retards economic growth and democracy. It is superfluous, and can be safely neglected as a topic of attention.

This is a comforting perspective, but it altogether misses the changes that capitalism is producing in basic political and economic structures, and the profound transformation which is now beginning to occur in Asian military institutions in contrast to the four decades after World War II. New strategic capacities are being built allowing states to reach one another with military means. After four decades of primitive military capacity compared to the West, Asia is setting out on a path Europe pioneered as its nation states developed: the construction of a deadly outward looking military apparatus which in no way threatens to usurp civilian political power.[1]

Those who wish to assess the crisis of the nation state must come to grips with state institutions, of which its coercive organizations are among the most important. To fail to do so is to neglect basic determinants of state structure and behaviour, and to fail to note changes in what are likely to be among the best early indicators of what is happening. For institutions reveal far more about a state than the policies enunciated by its leaders, which can and do change with great frequency. A focus on institutions, especially coercive ones, is relatively marginal in political science, where issues associated with non-state actors, economic interdependence, and environmental problems, are more prominent. A desire to de-emphasize the military dimensions of the state, especially in a new era where one major military competition is now behind us, can readily lead to missing the importance of their role.

The Military Crisis of the Nation State

Distributive problems now dominate coercive ones among the advanced nations. These states do not consider military action one against the other. They are rapidly reducing their defence burdens to a new and lower level following the collapse of the Soviet Union. And they have entered an era of international distributive relations with each other. Examples dominate the literature of international political economy: how trade increases competition, threatening domestic interest groups; the difficulty of controlling the multi-

[1] The view of Gaetano Mosca in *The Ruling Class* (New York, McGraw-Hill, 1939).

national corporation; the danger that one country's pollution will spill over to another. The absence of competitors who seek to change the status quo by force apparently makes it 'safe' to dismiss coercive crises and focus on distributive ones.

But perhaps it is premature to dismiss in so facile a way the military dimensions of the crisis of the nation state. As capitalism advances in Asia it will greatly expand wealth. This can be directed to any of a number of different purposes. If the spectacular energies which underlie Asian economic dynamism ever turn to military competition, as those which underlay the construction of European states did, then the scale of such competition would dwarf anything seen in European or world history. Drawing from the European experience with any precision is intellectually risky. But several aspects of that experience do seem relevant to Asia. Prognostications by 19th century European social theorists foresaw progress as the order of the day. No one foresaw the effects of nationalism or the spectacular levels of destruction produced during European modernization. It was also foreseen that old institutions would be swept away by the new. This happened, but they did not depart gracefully. Multinational empires lasted too long and the tension between old and new convulsed Europe.

In European modernization the nation state as a form of political community not only survived, it flourished. The concept of a military crisis of the nation state therefore does not necessarily imply an end to this form of political organization. It may or may not be the case that the nation state in general, or in any particular case, will dissolve or transmute into some other kind of political entity. In the middle ages there was a military crisis of the *city* state, and in this instance a new political format, the nation state, replaced it.[2] The nation state was better adapted to military competition, it could draw on more resources and deploy them into a fighting machine better than the city state.

But even without a termination of the nation state as the dominant political format there are crises associated with its military dimensions. The tendency of a nation state system toward what has been vaguely defined as 'systemic violence' has been noted by others:[3] the idea that a system of state actors has an inherent tendency toward violence, and that capitalism and industrialism can put in motion forces which propel it faster in this direction. However much this viewpoint needs to be refined, the European experience after 1789 gives powerful reason to believe that there are important relationships between these variables.

Another potentiality for crisis comes from the observation that states are sometimes peculiarly adept at tapping resources for military purposes. This, in itself, is no crisis. However, a state which is especially effective at doing this can exacerbate crises by harnessing the unholy energies of nationalism or despotic internationalism to military power. The *nation* part of the nation state lacks formal organization of a kind skilled at disciplined ruthlessness. But the state part of these entities carries with it the organization to direct resources against other actors in the international system. This is quite different from the systemic violence of a system of states, because the latter arises from

---

[2] Charles Tilly, *Capital, Coercion, and European States* (Cambridge, MA, Basil Blackwell, 1990).
[3] Anthony Giddens, *The Nation-State and Violence* (Berkeley, CA, University of California Press, 1987); Michael Mann, *States, War, and Capitalism* (Oxford, Basil Blackwell, 1988).

competitive interactions of actors where there is no overarching system of regulation. A propensity to link individual and collective rage, hatred, even madness to an organizational expression should not be underestimated as a source of crisis. Both Adolf Hitler and the Mullahs of Iran were able to exploit nationalist energies. Both had fanatical followers. But the difference between them, and what made Nazi Germany the more dangerous, was her ability to institutionalize these energies into formal killing organizations. In the German case intermediation between her deranged leaders and the expression of their derangement in the wider world was achieved through formal institutions which amplified their psychoses. Poor organizational expression, as little more than an armed mob, eventually humbled the fantasies of Iran's Mullahs, ultimately forcing her to terms against a foe, Iraq, who could draw on fewer human energies but could translate them into relatively better organizational performance.

Lastly, a military crisis of the nation state stems from its inability to change to another better and less crisis prone format. A circular logic applies. City states, tribes, multinational companies, kinship networks and others may be less adept at harnessing resources for malevolent purposes. But the existence of militarily adept nation states may prevent these alternatives from being born. Even if these alternatives are born, and despite their comparative economic advantage, they may be snuffed out of existence by a political organization which is superior in other dimensions of performance. Prosperous Hong Kong is being swallowed by China, and a dream of a purely capitalistic entity where all is subordinated to business will not survive because China will not allow it.

It is not difficult to define a military crisis of the nation state in less abstract ways. It exists first in the scale of violence inherent in this form of political organization. This scale has grown logarithmically. None of the social theorists of the 19th century anticipated its magnitude, and all would be stunned at the hyperbolic levels of organized violence reached in this century. The successive transitions from World Wars I and II to the potential of World War III military institutions of the United States and Soviet Union mark a kind of progress in what the nation state is capable of. Current expectations that this episode has come to an end with the demise of the Soviet state could mask its continuation in the most dynamic part of the world. For if the extraordinary energies which now underwrite economic growth there follow anything like the European path of the past one-hundred and fifty years in being rechannelled to military competition, then the world may be at a very different kind of end of history from the one which that phrase usually implies.

If this does not represent a crisis of the nation state it is hard to see what could. That this crisis is not especially novel is of course true. That the nation state system continues, withstanding world wars, and a potentially even larger one, may be less a testament to the weakness or containability of these shocks than it is to the fact that alternative and safer formats have been precluded from coming into existence. So to see these circumstances as an index of crisis may be less accurate than to see them as normality.[4] Adam Smith foresaw the extension of wealth to the peoples of Asia and their military strengthening to eventually overawe Europe.[5] But like Marx and Weber, Smith did not imagine

---

[4] Istvan Hont of Cambridge University has brought this argument to my attention, and also the views of Adam Smith on the matter.

[5] Adam Smith, *The Nature and Causes of the Wealth of Nations*, pp. 626–7.

the destructive capacities which were to come. If many wars had been fought with the infantry of the 19th century, there would be no military crisis of the nation state of comparable scale that here causes concern. Yet it is hard to see how the current nation state can endure an extended sequence of all out wars if the pattern established in the first half of this century continues on in Asia early in the next.

A military crisis of the nation state exists in other ways that pattern international politics. The Western ideal myth that selfish pursuits reflected in the theory of comparative advantage will produce a socially optimum outcome of trading and investments among states points to a certain kind of international politics. It is a politics that makes sense because individual desires can be directly traced to the resolution of problems in trade, investments, or in adjustments for environmental degradation. An international politics composed entirely of disputes over hormone-fed beef, butter surpluses, and acid rain would be a transparent one where major groups could identify their interests and be able to keep score with fair clarity.

Compare this to the actual world of international politics. Metaphors drawn from games of chicken and prisoner's dilemma haunt international politics. They make a mockery of the notion of personal autonomy and the public good. No economic calculations alone could lead to the state behaviours exhibited in the modern era. A state's military institution is not merely the obedient agent of the state, but by its very existence changes the shape of the strategy space open to states. The existence of a Strategic Air Command poised on hair trigger to attack its Soviet counterpart was something that changed the nature of international politics. The appearance of a 'small' nuclear force in North Korea, a Chinese navy able to isolate Japan, or an India staging nuclear bombing exercises would all change the content of international politics because they would drastically change the fears, hopes, and opportunities of many of the actors in it.

Domestic politics too are changed by the military dimensions of the state. This may not generally create a crisis of the nation state, but on occasion it may well do so in response to external factors, some new political ordering may sweep away the old. The appearance of threatening powers around Japan in the late 19th century changed the basis of her domestic politics, leading to a centralized state intent on transforming itself so as not to be swallowed up like its larger neighbour in China. Domestic politics can be fractured by international pressures. The basis for Japanese politics today rests on minimal military forces and on a security alliance with the United States. One domestic effect of this is that it excludes the kind of extremists from political life who in the 1920s turned Japan upside down with their nationalist and militarist programmes.

Finally, the military nature of the state can lead to pathological linkages between external and internal politics which must amount to a crisis for at least some nation states. Today, North Korea has linked its survival to that of its neighbours through an insidious but carefully designed military structure that makes its survival press sharply on that of its neighbours.[6] The fragility of its internal position – food shortages, economic deprivation and the lack of

---

[6] Paul Bracken, 'Nuclear weapons and state survival in North Korea', *Survival*, Autumn (1993), 135–53.

legitimate succession – becomes a perverse strength when linked to nuclear weapons and an army capable of destroying some significant part of the South, even if it is ultimately defeated. Outsiders had better not pressure North Korea where it may implode, or they will cause it to explode. The crisis of a North Korean state facing extinction becomes a crisis for its neighbours through the mechanism of its military institutions. Following the collapse of communism the increase in the number of dubious states capable of acquiring significant military capacity suggests many new opportunities for establishing similar linkages.

The North Korean example points to the importance once again of the nature of the military institutions that a state deploys. The economically dynamic states of Asia are capable of developing military organizations roughly similar to that which the United States possessed in 1960. India, or China would have little trouble in doing this. North Korea and others can divert disproportionately large resources to their military, thereby creating a force with formidable strategic impact on the region. What will not produce a crisis for any other nation state will be states with premodern forces whose reach extends little beyond their own territory. There *are* many small conflicts of an ethnic and nationalist character in the wake of the collapse of Soviet communism. These do present problems to the West in peace making or nation building. But none of them really matter greatly in a direct way for the advanced nations. On the face of it, the outcome in Somalia, Haiti, or Bosnia may arouse moral revulsion but it is hard to see how it could actually affect international order except by producing large numbers of refugees. Attempts to link these ethnic and third world conflicts to a larger crisis of the nation state are not convincing. Many have tried to draw parallels between Sarajevo in 1914 and today, but the arguments are far fetched without the introduction of militarily more capable actors.

The Nation State in Asia

The nation state is a new form of political organization in Asia. Only in the aftermath of World War II did it take on a significant standing, replacing empires, colonies, and kingdoms. This historical fact has had a great deal to do with its character and current position in the continent. In the West the collapse of Soviet power is seen as the definitive event of the late twentieth century. Its impact on Asia presupposes some power balance adjustments, the elimination of an old score in North Korea, and a continuation of policies which have made many people rich. But from a historical perspective the story looks different. The collapse of the Soviet Union is significant, but must be seen against the larger creation of a nation state system arising from the more important collapse of colonial and imperial rule in 1945. This ended a period of outside domination from the West, and of attempts by insiders to overturn this domination.

De-colonization meant the new nation states of post-1945 Asia were created with a sense of conscious experimentation. Western concepts of state, nation, civil society and class were imported and re-worked for these new creations. The Indian state was built on these concepts, but with greater recognition of the diverse multiethnic makeup of its population. Secular Indian government was intended to integrate these, in a vast project of a state-created nation. In

China a different experiment was undertaken. Marxist ideas were adapted to creation of a unified state from the patchwork fiefdoms of pre-war China. In Japan the democratic experiment took hold with no great reason at the time to believe it would turn out as successfully as it has. The Philippines were another democratic experiment. Indonesia is a case like India where a powerful state tried to create a nation from a diverse ethnic population.

The large variance in Asian nation states reflects this experimentation. European nation states did not have the freedom to experiment in their formative period as they faced vicious military competition from one other. The very large role that armies played in European state development came from *external* pressures. The large *internal*, but small external role (so far) in post-war Asia mark a fundamental difference from European state development. In Asia there has as yet been no such vicious competition. Instead the populations of Asia have had the freedom to test democratic-socialist government in a country of 800 million; Marxism-Leninism in the Chinese empire; democracy in Japan; bureaucratic authoritarianism in Indonesia, and chaos in the Philippines. It is not clear that India's inefficient socialist democracy, the Chinese Cultural Revolution, Japan's economic miracle, or Philippine disorders would have been possible had these nations faced a competitive military environment.

That the idea of a nation state was so novel in Asia made it easier to develop, for it did not come with a historical legacy. Its newness nicely matched the need to wipe the historical slate clean after 1945. For whatever existed in Asia before then were not nations in any sense useful to contemporary political discussion.[7] In the decades after their creation Asian nations ignored each other and developed characteristics which were overwhelmingly domestically determined. The project of most Asian states was nation building, but each such project was separate and unrelated to the others. Their armies (save in the Japanese case) played an important role in these projects, but it was directed inward. In every case these projects required such enormous energy that there was little left over for extensive interaction, yet alone adventures against one another. Finally, Asia's external security environment was structured by the cold war between Moscow and Washington. This competition laid down limits of behaviour for those in the region, lines which they could and did manipulate for their own advantage, but which established a centre of gravity for international security relations among them.

Modernization and Asia

The trend toward capitalism and industrialization first swept maritime Asia in the first three decades after World War II – Japan, South Korea, Singapore, Hong Kong, and Taiwan – and is now shifting to continental Asia – China, India, Pakistan, Southeast Asia. High levels of GNP growth are now *general* features of Asia. The number of exceptions is rapidly being reduced to Mynamar, North Korea, and the mountain states of the Himalayas.

These forces – capitalism and industrialization – are reaching levels of intensity where they are having a definite transformative effect. The Asian economic miracle in the face of large population growth and regional and ethnic divisions rested on a set of balances which are being changed by the very growth which

---

[7] William Pfaff, *The Wrath of Nations* (New York, Simon and Schuster, 1993), pp. 132–60.

they produced. These balances are unique to a certain period of Asian history beginning in the late 1940s, and are being strained if not upset altogether by the movement toward more intense capitalism and industrialization. The foundations for its economic growth are changing in fundamental ways. A new set of foundations will be created to replace earlier ones.

Continuation of Asian growth creates problems of overpopulation, resource availability, environment degradation, and government capacity to handle these challenges. These are new hazards facing the Asian nation state, and it is not difficult to see why many observers question its capacity to deal with them.[8] But the argument presented here is different. While acknowledging the appearance of new hazards – in population, resources, the environment – it is essential to remain alert to a much older crisis of the nation state: its propensity to military rivalry with a complex and complicated relationship to modernization in a nation state structure.

Capitalist Maritime Asia

Maritime Asia first created the economic boom which now captures world attention. It took place through a number of socio-economic innovations which in relative terms were superior to the comparable systems in Western Europe and the United States. These innovations, along with a benign security environment, contributed to the peaceful nature of the economic prosperity in this part of Asia.

There was a balance between market economy and government control. Government share of GNP in Japan, South Korea, and Taiwan was always less than that in Western Europe because these countries were not developing welfare states but were using markets to allocate resources and foster competition. This is what produced the economic boom. It had a single-minded focus on economic growth with a deep consensus in the relevant political classes. What is now taking place is a fragmentation of this consensus. Whether it be in demands for greater rights for certain groups, protection of consumer interests, the environment, or defence, throughout this part of Asia there is a broadening of the national focus to include a more differentiated set of goals.

Capitalist maritime Asia also saw fair distribution of income and wealth along with their high rates of growth. This was a remarkable achievement. Japan, South Korea and Taiwan stand in sharp contrast to countries like Brazil where growth was achieved only with an extraordinary gap between rich and poor. But the achievement is beginning to erode. A new business élite has been created by the capitalist take off. It is an élite which has extensive foreign exposure, and takes less interest in the national development project than the early pioneers of Asian capitalism after the war. A growing complexity of the financial system also contributes to this, by internationalizing the basis of wealth and control.

Many of the innovations admired in the West which underwrote the equitable distribution of income are ebbing. The percentage of the Japanese work force guaranteed lifetime employment by their companies has been declining for years. Layoffs are beginning to occur as a response to the business

---

[8] Paul Kennedy, *Preparing for the Twenty-First Century* (New York, Random House, 1993).

cycles which accompany capitalism. In past cycles, Japan would increase her exports to the West. But strong western resistance to this has necessitated internal adjustments to compensate for slack demand. South Korea and Taiwan face this as well, as their comparative advantage in low cost labour has clearly eroded. Increased disparities in wealth and uncertainty of employment challenge another innovation throughout this region: labour discipline. The discipline of the past decades is attributed by many observers to cultural traits. But experience in many other countries casts doubt on the universality of such traits in the face of economic competition.

Japan, in particular, is entering a period of political instability that could hinder policy making, weaken the economy, and play havoc with regional security. The fragmentation of Japanese politics in the 1990s is generally analysed in terms of a contest between reformists and an old guard. But this is simplistic, because the unique configuration which produced the post-war miracle is something that could not possibly be sustained in the face of changing economic and political conditions. Japan is facing changing defence requirements as well, as US forces withdraw from the Pacific in response to the end of the cold war. This has implications which transcend a need for increased defence expenditures. The Liberal Democratic Party consensus of delegating national defence to the United States effectively removed extremes from Japanese politics. The far right and left were excluded by making their appeals irrelevant in the national debate. Japan's success with its low posture policy in areas like defence and foreign affairs is something which has worked well for itself and others. But it is clear that these policies are approaching the limits of their usefulness because of changes in the world and in Japan itself.

Continental Asia, until 1980

The changes in continental Asia are much greater than those in maritime Asia because this area was so much further removed from capitalism. Shock effects are likely to be larger. At the most basic level of description what is happening is that a vast expanse of the Asian land mass is being introduced to modernization and widespread political activity simultaneously, and in ways which are a sharp change from the past fifty years.

This was a part of the world with a tumultuous history prior to communism. Its removal from the world economy, suppression of individual rights, and isolation from international politics is being speedily reversed. While most discussions focus on the details of economic reform and pace of marketization, the larger point is that a massive part of the earth is now joining the capitalist world. In China, the opening of the economy in a way that attempts to retard political development so as not to cause disorder is a source of tension. In Asian Russia, an even more complicated opening is underway, one which could split Russia into pieces.

Other Asian countries are opening to the world economy as well. India, Indonesia, and Pakistan have moved toward opening their economies to foreign investment, reduction of tariffs, creation of stock exchanges, and large scale (rather than village and craft) industrialization. In India's case this represents a major reversal of its past socialist policies. Students of particular countries may be sceptical about how far such liberalization can go, but they may not be best placed to judge the impact of economic development in the capitalist model. Once set in motion the idea that these forces can be safely restored to government control through changes in policy probably overestimates the power of the state in question. The disruptive impacts of capitalism on a country such as India with its legacy of state allocation, large bureaucracies, and import substitution may be difficult to overstate. Again, our purpose is not to predict what will happen, but merely to emphasize that fundamental change is under way.

In addition to India the newly created central Asian republics arising from the former Soviet Union are new factors changing Asian politics. These countries are drawn by their Islamic ties toward joining in the disputes between Turkey, Iran, Pakistan, and Iraq. India always considered the suppression of fundamentalist Islamic energies in these areas, so that they could not reinforce Pakistan against her, as an important benefit from the Delhi-Moscow alliance. New actors have been brought into the picture who will complicate planning and enlarge the strategy spaces of states in the area.

The Chinese state merits special attention because of the clash of old structures of the communist era with the new requirements of modernization. Eighty percent of the Chinese population were rural peasants, organized into a large number of small villages for greater ease of political control. These villages were isolated from one another by a political communication system where the communist party controlled a public address network deployed in thousands of villages. Access to two-way communication was limited, as even economic development emphasized the interior of the country to remove it from international influences.

China also had a relatively equitable distribution of wealth, or of misery, depending on economic performance. Unlike other developing countries she was able to prevent the massive urbanization found in Rio, Lagos, or Calcutta. Shanghai was large, and a traditional problem in this respect, but it was managed easily during the Maoist period and hence could not serve as a conduit for the outside world to enter China. Hong Kong was used as the centralized vehicle for foreign interactions, with access tightly controlled. This relative absence of urbanization meant that rural areas were not used to subsidize the cities, and that urban pressures on the government were minimal. Economic parity made it possible to keep people in the countryside, something which formed the most important pillar of the revolution. As long as it endured leaders like Mao and Deng could reach over the heads of other institutions in China, such as the Party, the Army, and heavy industry, to institute reforms and to keep these other institutions' power in check. In the 1960s reform was of a malevolent kind – the Cultural Revolution – while in the 1980s it was benevolent – the liberalization of the economy – but in each case it depended on a structure which minimized the potential for opportunism of other important actors in the system.

This structure is now disintegrating. Income disparities are reaching very large levels in China. A new luxury class of businessmen is growing, who get much of their power from *external* ties to foreign business establishments for capital, technology, and expertise. In coastal China it is common today to see BMWs, cellular telephones, luxury apartments, golf courses, and all of the other crass accompaniments of capitalist development. Much more of this is certain to come, and to be extended to larger parts of China. As the situation of the Korean peninsula develops there are notably stronger business ties connecting South Korea with China. Seoul is becoming a virtual conduit for transfer of western ways into northeastern China, promising to transform that region on a scale that is now only seen in the southeast.

The most troubling features of the Chinese transformation arise from changes in the foundations of the Chinese state during the past forty years. It is not merely that income disparities are moving toward 'Brazilian levels', but that cities are growing in population and clout, and rural areas are being left behind. People are fleeing the countryside to move to the cities in a process the world has seen many times before. It is not clear where this immense population will be absorbed. Agricultural productivity will increase as farm prices are decontrolled and as modern methods of farming begin to be adapted. If significant portions of the workforce move to cities, the world will see a drama that makes Dickens's accounts of a similar migration in 19th century Britain pale in comparison.

As Weber noted, modes of production created by mass use of 'freely given' wage labour are far more flexible and efficient than those achieved through coercion. This change is precisely what is now happening in China. It is why China is growing at such a large rate of GNP. But it is also a transforming social problem. What happens when a country has a huge population migrating in search of subsistence wages? Experience in 19th century Europe gives some indication of the social forces unleashed, but in China, and throughout continental Asia, the sheer magnitude of the movement and the radically different cultural and social context means that what is in question is on an entirely different scale from anything in European experience. Nonetheless, the only theories we possess through which to try to understand it are Eurocentric. Barrington Moore points to the way in which agriculture becomes commercial-ized as a signal indicator of whether representative or authoritarian government later evolves. He argues that where exploitative landlords (or 'bosses' in current business Chinese) survived in power when farming moved from coercing peasants to cash crop farming the result was authoritarian government.[9] There are very good indicators that this is just what is taking place in contemporary China.

Region-Wide Changes

Other changing factors cannot easily be fitted to particular geographic areas. Geographic scale and terrain features have made cross border interactions and communication difficult. For example, in the military area the effort needed to fight even tiny skirmishes between India and China demonstrates this. In 1962 each nation had to mobilize large resources to get a few infantry divisions into the high mountains so that they could shoot at each other. Absence of roads and communications lines made intra-regional enterprises extremely difficult, whether military or economic. But this is now changing as some parts of Asia, e.g. Korea, parts of India, and coastal China, are developing dense levels of communication and transportation. Mass air travel, satellite broadcasting and communication, fax machines, all help overcome the limits of distance and terrain.

[9] Barrington Moore, Jr., *Social Origins of Dictatorship and Democracy* (New York, Beacon, 1966).

Another region-wide change is that after a lengthy period of not interacting with each other, both maritime and continental Asia are once again experiencing high levels of intra-regional trade, investment, contact, and movement of people between them. Between 1950 and 1980 Japan, South Korea, Hong Kong, and Taiwan had almost nothing to do with China, India, Pakistan, or Russia and other nations from the former Soviet Union east of the Urals. This is such an obvious change that it is easy to miss. Japan, South Korea, and Taiwan now are being re-Asianized. Hong Kong is being annexed. Japan, like every other developed state is searching for cheap labour in continental Asia.

Benefits of increased interaction are promised by the theory of comparative advantage. But the blessings may not be unmixed. The historical record is not good. And although the Japan of today is far different from the Japan of the 1930s there are still grounds to worry about negative interactions. The racial hatreds in the region are as strong as they have ever been, and in many ways are more intense than those suppressed by the cold war in Eastern Europe and the Soviet Union. Not much is said publicly about this because of its extraordinary sensitivity. But a study of Japanese-Chinese, Korean-Japanese, or Russian-Japanese history and perceptions show that very old stereotypes and hatreds remain. They have been muted in recent times more by the fact of political isolation from one another than by any fundamental changes in perception. Communist China was able to manipulate the image of Japan in a highly controlled way to suit the needs of the revolution with little danger that it would go too far. In Korea, the North Korean threat created a veneer of alliance between Japan and South Korea. The experience of Indonesia in 1965, or in certain aspects of the Vietnam War gave glimpses of what these hatreds are capable of producing.[10] These atrocities were interpreted by the West in cold war categories as a struggle between communists and democrats. The reality was far more complex.

Finally, the ultimate military dominance by outside powers, the United States and the Soviet Union, must be taken into account. United States military supremacy in Asia began in the Philippines in 1898 during the Spanish American War. Its ultimate duration is unknown – remaining to be tested perhaps by North Korea in what would be an ironic end to communism – but there can be little doubt that US military power in Asia is something with about a one-hundred year history and is on the way down. At any time during this period the United States could have inflicted a military defeat on any power in the region. This might have necessitated escalation to nuclear attack, and it may have required virtually unsustainable political burdens at home, but the technical ability to do so remained. China's opening to the US in 1971 was a recognition of American military power, just as was Japan's surrender in 1945.

It is worth noting the way that the United States achieved this military supremacy in Asia throughout the period. During the Spanish American War the US dispatched its newly created Great White Fleet which outgunned and outclassed Spanish ships. In every subsequent decade the United States used a small high technology force against larger Asian forces which were technically primitive. In World War II it used long distance bombing from aircraft carriers and island air bases, and eventually the atomic bomb to defeat the Japanese.

---

[10] Harold Crouch, *The Army and Politics in Indonesia* (Ithaca, NY, Cornell University Press, 1978).

In Korea in 1950–1 American air supremacy offset Chinese infantry superiority. Throughout the cold war its air, naval, and nuclear superiority gave the United States its dominant position. In Vietnam, this technical edge was not enough. But the lesson learned that military forces do not matter in Asia is surely the wrong one to draw.

It is worth thinking about this in the context of an expansion of military competency and modern military technology to Asia. This is exactly what is taking place. Just as fundamental social and economic changes are under way the structure of Asian military institutions is also changing.

Asian Military Institutions

Asian armies during the post World War II era were born of a disharmony between *nation* and *state*. They were not formed in the cauldron of war between *state* and *state* as were European armies during their formative nation-state years. This has had a profound impact on the armies of Asia because it focused their energies not on inter-state competition as the energies of German, French, and Russian armies focused, but on internal nation-state processes. Asian forces have had almost no capacity to project power outside their own borders, or for that matter, to defend their territories with anything but a massive use of manpower. They have been exceptions to Otto Hintze's dicta on the real organization of the state: the claim that states were formed from an internal structure of social classes and the external pressures from other states, and that of the two the latter was the more important.[11]

To focus on coercive organizations offers a singular view of the changing nation state in Asia. Transformation of a state's military organizations to focus more on the relation with other states signals something which is important: that Asian military institutions are beginning to look outward, and that the entire framework for understanding them needs revision. Development of an external orientation is just as important as other changes analysed by state theorists, like juridicial modernization or efficient extraction of taxes. Broadly speaking, scholars of Asia have not considered major structural changes in its military system in relationship to the state because they see the latter as essentially static, with only small adjustments to founding effects present when these nation states came into existence. They allow for a kind of pseudo dynamics with small shifts around starting conditions of tension between nation and state.[12]

Asian military institutions were created in a process of nation-state for-mation where an external power determined the shape of the coercive arms, or in which a nation was emancipated from an external power. In the first case the external power proved decisive in defining the institutional norms and capacities of the new force and in this sense it was a state-produced military. In the latter case national liberation forces, where they were triumphant,

---

[11] See 'Military organization and the real organization of the state', in Felix Gilbert (ed.), *The Historical Essays of Otto Hintze* (New York, Oxford University Press, 1975), p. 183.

[12] Robin Luckham, 'The military, the developmental state and social forces in Asia and the Pacific: issues for comparative analyses', in Viberto Selochan (ed.), *The Military, the State, and Development in Asia and the Pacific* (Boulder, CO, Westview, 1991), pp. 1–49.

defined the norms and capacities, which were taken on by the new revolutionary state. These led to a military produced by the nation itself.

In the first case the new state inherited the military institutions left to them by departing external powers, sometimes with strings attached which limited their future development. Examples include India, Pakistan, Sri Lanka, Malaysia, Singapore, Fiji and most of the Pacific Islands. It also includes the military of states ruled by America: the Philippines and Japan. In all these instances the outside power shaped local military institutions as they thought best. That is, they were shaped less by local dangers and requirements than by the perception of these held by the external power. Britain built armies useful for internal order in India, and later to supply manpower for her efforts in the world wars. The Indian army was an institution where staying above local politics was important, and where acceptance of legitimate orders was paramount. In the case of Japan, Washington disarmed its former enemy and only created small self defence forces useful for domestic order. Unlike Britain, the US did not 'use' Japan's military in its virtual world war against the Soviet Union, but instead decided not to rearm Japan or to increase its military capacities because doing so might lead to other negative consequences. South Korea may appear to be an exception to this trend. But its military was overwhelmingly shaped by the United States after the Korean War. So far, it has had virtually no capabilities beyond manning the line against ground invasion from the North, backed by US air and naval forces.

In the second case the state acquired a military which came from the nation. Examples include the former Dutch and French colonies in Indonesia, Vietnam, Laos, and Cambodia. They also include China and North Korea. The Chinese and the North Korean People's Armies were forged in revolutionary struggle against external rulers. All of these armies have an extensive participation in the national life through their activities in economy and politics. Here civilian control was problematic, if not in the sense of direct military intervention against the state, then certainly in terms of the army's being a force in domestic politics. The military was an instrument of social change, whether in civil construction and agricultural work as in China and North Korea, or in the leadership of economic modernization as in Indonesia. To this day Indonesian military officers are guaranteed a fixed share of the legislature, and officers are frequently given stock in state companies as part of their compensation. The Chinese People's Liberation Army (PLA) is fifty percent self financed from its own businesses. Its revenues derive from non-military businesses in everything from luxury hotels to textile exports to management of coastal smuggling operations.

Deviations from these founding conditions are thought to define the limits of military change in Asia. In Pakistan, for example, the British model developed as in India but quickly turned to something closer to the nation armies of Asia. The Pakistani military became active in politics and commerce, leveraging its powerful position to something that is little different from a political party. In other Asian countries the military was adjudged the most administratively competent institution in the country, and increased political and economic activities were tolerated because of their central role in modernization.[13] Debates today focus on the role of the Chinese PLA in going along

---

[13] Lucian Pye, 'Armies in the process of political modernization', in J. J. Johnson (ed.), *The Role of the Military in Underdeveloped Countries* (Princeton, NJ Princeton University Press, 1962).

with modernization or in influencing leader selection. But in none of these are the dynamics of military state relationships changing in a fundamental and structural way. Rather they represent small shifts and deviations in the real character and situation of the military of Asia.

An absence of external military pressure is an extraordinary environment in which for military institutions to develop. It encourages inefficiencies, corruption, and politicization. European armies did not have this luxury. There are many examples in European history of armies which were politicized and inefficient, but in Europe's case there was a large penalty to pay for this. Asia has not faced this problem in five decades. Interestingly, the only Asian military which has been a definite exception to this pattern of looking inward rather than focusing on external threats since World War II was the North Vietnamese Army between 1945 and 1975.[14]

Changes in the social and economic situation in Asia will drastically effect the armed forces. There is no longer need for mass infantry armies because as the state building process matures these become a cumbersome and inefficient instrument for conducting either political or economic activity. A movement toward capitalism means that the labour force, not the army, becomes the more important mechanism of social control. Capitalism's main effect, here, is its creation of competitor institutions to the military which fill specialized roles in society at which the military is not particularly adept. Allocations of goods and services, internal policing, operation of commercial enterprises, are all better performed by others. The relevance of current Asian military structures is declining. They have served an important, indeed essential role, but it is a role which is changing. They are shifting from low technology, mass agrarian infantry hierarchies to more differentiated and skilled organizations, using higher technology. These changes represent the military arm of a complex bureaucratic society rather than a simple traditional society. There is a change, too, from an overwhelmingly *inward* focus, to an *external* focus. We can see examples of this transformation in some of the more important countries.

China

The history of the PLA after the Korean War is that of a decentralized organization designed first for building the revolution, and second for people's war against an invader. The PLA was the largest army in the world, with an independent cell-like structure based on regional village support. For defensive reasons there were no critical nodes in this army. Its ability to project power was negligible, as was demonstrated in the debacle against Vietnam in 1979. Its ability to defend industrial regions such as Manchuria against armoured attacks by Moscow was doubtful. This is the military reason why China turned to the US for protection against the Soviet Union in the early 1970s.

In the mid-1980s China abandoned its People's War doctrine. It reorganized away from a defensive cell-like structure where single arms units operated from fixed village bases to a new system of group armies. These new group armies were distinguished by their combined arms training – infantry, armour, air, artillery – and their offensive projection of military power over long distances,

---

[14] See Douglas Pike, *People's Army of Vietnam* (Presidio, 1986).

conceivably outside China's borders.[15] The new re-organization also reduced the earlier force by eliminating 1.3 million people, and is now about 2.2 million persons in size. This decline in the scale of the army has been widely misinterpreted as a sign of declining interest in military force. Instead it represents a transition to a smaller more flexible force capable of offensive operations. The group armies signal a change to an external orientation, military rather than political training, and integration with advance technology. On this last point, a People's Army defending in depth without mutual support has no need for helicopters or electronic links to missile bases in the rear. But an advancing group army plainly does, to locate enemy positions for destruction or avoidance, and to call in supporting firepower that is too bulky to carry with the advancing units. The new re-organization is thus the basis for the technological modernization of the army.

The navy is undergoing an even more drastic change, moving from coastal defence to an ocean going fleet which can seize and hold territory thousands of kilometres from China's shore. The Chinese maritime programme represents a development of entirely new organizational capacities. It involves operating air and naval forces far from the coast. Entirely new integrated administrative and intelligence capacities have been built. At-sea re-supply and re-fuelling, coordination with aircraft for protective cover, links to navigation satellites, meteorological intelligence, and long distance communication have been put together. Chinese bombers covering these naval operations have been fitted for aerial re-fuelling, and Chinese Marines have landed on the Spratly Islands in the South China Sea.

These new military capacities are like a company diversifying into new lines of business. Changes in the management structure necessarily follow. They are not examples of a crash effort to threaten neighbours, but a more gradual restructuring of China's military. An *organizational stretch* of the Chinese military is currently in progress.

South Korea

South Korean armed forces are moving to establish what they call an all azimuth defence, one not focused only on the large ground threat from North Korea.[16] The civilian government of President Kim Young Sam has cleaned house of the military old guard, advancing more professional officers. A new Joint Chiefs of Staff Organization for the first time gives South Korean civilian leadership a mechanism to direct the future development of the armed forces and to overcome the bureaucratic power of the services.

The Army has taken over peacetime command and control from the United States. There are major programmes underway in long distance intelligence, an open ocean navy, and air forces covering most of Northeast Asia. Seoul recently launched its first modern diesel submarine, naming it after an admiral who defeated the Japanese Armada centuries ago. Five more modern submarines will be built, all in South Korean shipyards. New military ties with China are forming, and the South Korean Navy is making port calls in Russia.

[15] Paul H. B. Godwin, *The Chinese Communist Armed Forces* (Maxwell Air Force Base, ALA, Air University Press, 1988).
[16] Paul Bracken, 'The Korean state in Northeast Asia', *Strategic Review* 20 (1992), 40–7.

India

The Indian Army was intentionally deprived of resources to minimize its political power within India, and its early history was shaped by a view that India hardly needed an army at all. This changed when it was humiliated in the skirmishes with China in 1962 and performed badly in early wars against Pakistan.[17] But reform has always been minimal, in part because Indian political leaders did not want to create a powerful institution to defeat Pakistan, only to find that it then copied the Pakistan Army in flexing its own political muscle.

Indian armed forces are changing in ways which underscore the complexity of institutional change. Institutions do not always develop in clear strategic ways, but in ways that can be haphazard, incoherent, and, for precisely these reasons, dangerous to others.[18] During the 1980s there were ambitious military expansion plans to modernize the Indian armed forces. By the early 1990s these were greatly scaled back because of gross inefficiencies and costs. A large open ocean shipbuilding programme was cancelled, modernization of the land forces postponed, and production of advanced warning aircraft put on the shelf. According to most observers inefficiencies which plague the general Indian economy penetrated the military programme as well.

But a reorientation of the Indian armed forces is also under way. During the 1980s a very large paramilitary establishment was built to deal with religious and ethnic tensions in a way that would keep the Indian Army out of these highly politicized affairs. The armed forces' attention shifted to the external environment. In 1989 medium range missiles were tested which could be armed with nuclear warheads. The nuclear programme itself was never cut back, but in fact was accelerated as other military programmes were curtailed. India could have an arsenal in the hundreds of warheads.

In addition, a rapid reaction airborne force was created and used successfully in the Maldives. A space programme, although inefficient, was integrated with defence radars looking out from India. Tactical communications systems to coordinate submarine and surface ships were deployed. The largest exercises ever conducted in South Asia, Operation Brass Tacks, was held to test combined arms forces. Finally, India has engaged in military exercises that should be troubling to her neighbours. Delhi has used the Nicobar Islands in the Indian Ocean as a staging area for bomber operations. Old Jaguar, Canberra, and Mirage aircraft have been flown from the mainland to the Nicobars where they landed for re-fueling, maintenance, and arming. A suspicion of many observers is that these exercises were practice runs for aircraft delivery of nuclear weapons.

Conclusion

The restructuring of military organizations in important Asian countries is part of a larger change throughout Asia to adapt economic and military institutions to a new environment. These changes may not presage any immediate military or foreign policy crisis, representing more aggressive

[17] Sukhwant Singh, *India's Wars Since Independence* (New Delhi, Ikas, 1981), vol. II.
[18] Ravi Rikhye, *The Militarization of Mother India* (New Delhi, Chanakya, 1990).

policies or a desire to intimidate neighbours. But Asian military institutions are beginning a structural change which reflects the new domestic and international circumstances in which Asia finds itself. Military organizations are no longer as useful for nation and state building and their role in economic affairs does more harm than good. They are being displaced by better competitors in the new situation, such as private business and the police. The increasing wealth generated by these states however does have military implications. Entirely new coercive strategies have been created which place greater emphasis on technological sophistication and competition with external actors such as the military of other countries.

The current situation is characterized by these transformations, but as yet by no overt use of their new military capacities themselves. It may be that the capacities are too undeveloped, or that the opportunity to use them has not arisen. But there can be little doubt that they do exist, and that the early pattern is not one which warrants unvarnished optimism that the military crisis of the nation state is safely behind us. At bottom the question is whether a capitalist Asia will be more problematic for the nation state system than a communist and developing Asia. A focus on tensions arising from fundamental nation and state structures which are themselves rapidly shifting may obscure the more important, and dangerous, changes inherent in the continent's current economic dynamism.

Crisis of the Nation-state in India

Sudipta Kaviraj

To identify the political form of a state with a nation is common in the analytic literature on modern politics, but to ascribe a single nationalism to that nation is deeply problematic. The nation-state has undoubtedly become the predominant form of modern political identity, but this idea brings together in an historically special and unstable combination two dissimilar things – the tangibility of an institutional organization of force in the state which derives its imaginative and moral justification from the idea of a nation.[1] Besides, this political imagination of the nation is rarely an incontestably simple and single idea; most actual nationalism contains within its apparent singularity conflicting interpretations of what it means to be that nation contesting for space and political expression. The nation state is thus, despite its pretence to permanence and its claims to an immemorial history, a contradictory historical phenomenon: as a state and a political-institutional form, it aspires to historical stability; yet the body of ideas on which its permanence must be based tends to be internally contested and eternally contestable. It is rarely that a clear line of causality and moral empowerment runs from a single homogeneous self-understanding of a people, called its nationalism, to the sovereign state. Behind the state several configurations of nationalism lie indistinctly and jostle for political realization; the dominance of one of those, which then turns into the ideology of the eventual nation-state, is, though decisive, historically contingent. To understand the historical trajectory of the nation-state in India, it is necessary to set this contingency against the state's conceit of permanence and begin from the ambiguities of Indian nationalism – of its origins, its social support, its various ideological forms.[2]

Nationalism evidently bears a specially intimate historical connection with modernity,[3] because the national community was an identity[4] unavailable in earlier political imagination. But modernity does not merely add the form of

---

[1] For a wide-ranging discussion about the idea and its many trajectories in historical practice, see John Dunn, *Western Political Theory in the Face of the Future* (Cambridge, Cambridge University Press, 1993), pp. 57–81.

[2] On the intellectual history of Indian nationalism, P. Chatterjee, *Nationalist Thought and the Colonial World* (Delhi, Oxford University Press, 1986).

[3] One of the most forceful arguments on the connection between nationalism and modern practices comes from Ernest Gellner, *Nations and Nationalism* (Oxford, Blackwell, 1983); but its emphasis on the material side of the connection has to be supplemented by the analysis of political imagination in Benedict Anderson, *Imagined Communities* (London, Verso, 1983).

[4] It is necessary to differentiate between the various senses in which the term identity is used in political analysis. There can be a distinction between identity of a group, which means a cluster of features by means of which they can be marked clearly off from others, and their self-identity, the characteristics by which they recognize themselves. Often this is a crucial difference for political action.

the nation-state to the earlier repertoire of identities, it appears to do something fundamental to the structure and nature of identities in general. Surely, before the coming of modernity people had identities, and if pressed may have been able to provide a fairly clear picture of who they thought they were. Yet it is a safe guess that occasions would not have been very common when they would have been asked to face this most pressing of modern questions. Philosophical schools often urged enquirers to 'know thyself', and there was an instructive abundance of serious reflection on this question of all philosophic questions. But such philosophic reflection was never expected to have political relevance. Political life in precolonial Indian society was structured around a peculiar organization of power.[5] First, the impersonal rules of the caste system vested some critically significant functions in an 'absent' centre of the system, which governed boundaries and controlled transactions between social groups. Royal authority was entrusted with the task of maintaining and invigilating this system, without being empowered seriously to modify its principles. Most significantly, the state could not expand its powers radically; it had to function under the rigid rules of the caste system,[6] nor did all social demands for preferment or redistribution have to be routed through state. Political belonging to territorial states was a rather tenuous affair under traditional conditions. Kingdoms and empires constantly collided and expanded at the expense of each other, so that a group of people stably inhabiting a particular space, could be part of different kingdoms in a short space of time. The ease with which such political inclusion could be achieved also made such 'belonging' rather thin in contrast to modern practices. It was in that sense impossible to achieve the kind of firm identification between people and a form of politicized space which is presupposed in the political ontology of the modern nation-state.

Not only was the connection between people and states tenuous, identity itself meant a somewhat different kind of social adhesion. The logic of traditional identity appears to have been different from its modern counterpart in several respects. Politically, at least, premodern identities tended to be fuzzy in at least two ways. First the identity of an individual was distributed in several different social practices; a kind of layering in which the fact of his distinctive belonging to his village, local community, caste group, religious sect, language, kinship complexes, trade associations would have all figured in a context-dependent fashion.[7] An individual was not exclusively one of these things, nor under pressure to yield an undeniable lexical ordering of such features. It was not only individual identity which was plural and flexible; the structure of

---

[5] If we reserve the term state for the sovereign political centres in modern societies, it is difficult to apply that term to traditional political authority. Political authority and control tended to be dispersed and distributed between various levels of authority – a state of affairs that late medieval historians have sought to capture by the concept of a 'segmentary' as distinct from a 'sovereign' state. It is safer to use the concept of a *power* organization rather than a *state* form.

[6] This is not to deny that the brahminical system allowed occasional liberties with its rules, particularly in the case of successful ruling groups, who always found obliging Brahmins to confirm their belonging to the kshatriya caste from an immemorial past. But the system was understandably more principled in case of those who lacked political power.

[7] I have tried to explain this argument in greater detail in S. Kaviraj, 'The imaginary institution of India' in P. Chatterjee and G. Pandey (eds), *Subaltern Studies*, VII (Delhi, Oxford University Press, 1992), pp. 1–39.

identities in the world itself was fuzzy in a related sense. Although both modern and traditional societies have to structure social differences in a significant order, they arrange such differences in different ways. Traditional societies arrange identities in the way colours are arranged in a spectrum, one shading off into another, without revealing closed systems with clear demarcatable boundaries. It is a world of *transitions* rather than of *boundaries*. And if people live in such worlds the differentiation between the self and the other remains necessarily a fuzzy, unconcluded and inconclusive business. Finally, the ontology of the traditional social world, especially its cognitive constituents were fundamentally different. Traditionally, individuals were equipped with a fairly detailed and sometimes astonishingly intricate system of classificatory categories by which to distinguish the relevantly similar and different, us and them. Still, they simply lacked the cognitive means to generate a global picture of the spaces in which social groups lived. Individuals who could quibble indefinitely about the hierarchical status of two castes in adjacent areas, or define ritual purities with endlessly tedious detail, still had the equipment merely to establish who was a Vaishnava or a Brahmin or when one properly belonged to one among the innumerable and constantly fissile sects. They simply did not have the equipment to know how many Vaishnavas there were in the world, and the means of persuading the members of this group to act together to shape political possibilities in their favour. Conflicts were not rare among religious sects, castes, or other social groups; but in the absence of the fatal knowledge of maps and numbers, they expressed themselves primarily as wars of position in the terrain of everyday life rather than as wars of manoeuvre in the political arena. Conflicts of interest therefore did not take on the scale which modern violence can produce so effortlessly.

British colonial power in India put an end to this traditional social ontology, and replaced it with an ontology of a fundamentally new kind. Colonial control over India was uneven, and in its early years resembled earlier empires, a thin layer sitting rather insecurely on top of an exceptionally resilient social order.[8] But British colonialism commanded historically unprecedented resources in military, political, administrative and cognitive terms; and some of its political initiatives started off a comprehensive social transformation. British administrators brought with them an entire cognitive apparatus from modern Europe, especially mapping and counting, and produced an image of India as a geographic and demographic entity which far surpassed in tangibility and precision the hazier notions with which people transacted business in earlier times. The fundamental transformation involved a picture of the social world in which the organization and perception of social difference was altered: irreversibly changing peoples' images of their collective selves and their occupancy of the social world. Ordinary peasants may be entirely unable to count, but despite this small technical infirmity, they knew exactly what it meant to be a member of a majority or a minority community, and how to act appropriately in these social roles. The political consequences of this new ontology were decisive: this made possible a membership of individuals in abstract religious identities like Hindus and Muslims, and by corollary, a new kind of impersonal and abstract violence, as people began to ascribe to them

---

[8] For a brief critical discussion on the debates about the colonial state, see P. Chatterjee, *The Nation and Its Fragments* (Princeton, NJ, Princeton University Press, 1993), ch.2.

an untraditional capacity to have intentions and undertake action. Once this new ontology of social/political being comes into existence, it becomes impossible to escape the logic of its consequences.

Enumeration processes began in the early nineteenth century, as did the establishment of western-style education for producing a new, collaborating middle class. By the middle of the century, the first unintended consequences of this process of enumeration had become apparent. Sections of the new intelligentsia who were more disgruntled or imaginative than others already grasped the sources of power this enumerated space provided. By the end of the century, the idea that three hundred and fifty million could not be politically helpless had gained such currency that popular patriotic songs constantly reiterated such empowering arithmetic. Still, in the nineteenth century a curious ambiguity remained at the heart of the early sentiments of anti-colonialism. Paradoxically, the earliest writers to create an anti-colonial sensibility, had only resolved to defy colonial power, but had not yet chosen their nation. Among the first Bengali 'nationalist' writers one detects a strange ambivalence about whether the nation that they belonged to was a nation of Bengalis, of Hindus or of Indians. Each one had its distinctive appeals, the decisive advantage of an Indian nation being its enormous size and its shared resentment against foreign rule.

It is common in modern social science to assume a dichotomous classification of identities between modern and primordial. This assumption is subtly fallacious: I should like to argue that the logic of modernity pervades the map of identities: there is no identity that it leaves untouched. People were indeed Muslims or Hindus before; but under conditions of modernity, their way of being Hindus and Muslims changes fundamentally, and acquires new, unconventional implications. First of all, from the traditional point of view, these huge blocs of Hindus and Muslims were entirely new inventions of *political* agency; relevant groups for traditional religious practices were small self-recognizing sects.[9] Modern identities are either directly or potentially political.

Despite its internal complexity, the dominant political imagination of the Indian national movement went primarily in favour of a constructed modern Indian nation, an identity in which both the principle (of modern state-citizenship) and its symbolic markers were modern. Yet it would be wrong to follow some hasty followers of Nehru and give to this movement a deeply anachronistic sanitized history that recognizes secular modernist nationalism alone as 'truly' nationalist and in effect retrospectively derecognizes other, less appealing, exclusivist trends. To understand the full range of political possibilities in the future, it is essential to admit the full range of possibilities that existed in the past. In historical fact, Indian nationalism consisted of a number of competing, jostling constructs of political imagination: one of these was severely modern and secular, but it was surrounded by others which had much

[9] We can perhaps make a rough distinction between formal and practical/agential identities. A formal identity is one like being a Hindu which would have been logically intelligible to an actor in a past society, but which would not have had any practical purchase; i.e., that group of people, though logically classifiable would not be seen as a category for practical action. Agential identity would be one which is not merely formally understandable but which forms part of the generally accepted range of strategies of social life. Thus worshippers of a particular vaishnava sect would have their temples, their religious centres, occasionally, their distinct system of donation collections etc.: the group of Hindus would have none of these and would thus be politically inert.

more ambiguous attitudes towards democracy, secularism, social justice and the entire programme of modernity.

Most nationalist politicians were in love with the narratives of western modernity, especially its dominant hegemonic form which saw the nation-state as an agency of collectively intended social change. Although this narrative made the achievement of a free national state intensely desirable, some aspects of the trajectory of European nationalism could not be replicated under Indian conditions. If the nation-state had to be culturally homogeneous by definition, it did not fit the cultural reality of the Indian subcontinent: and one of the central divisions within nationalist ideology was between a homogenizing and a pluralist trend. Nationhood, the first view held, gave strength because it was the great force of homogeneity and identity. But the more dominant and persuasive strands in Indian nationalism opposed this construction, and interestingly, Gandhi and Nehru were one in upholding a distinctively pluralist idea of the Indian nation though their detailed constructions were vastly different. All cultures in India were of a similar family, and the responsibility of the new state would be, on this view, to provide a political template which could accommodate this enormous diversity, turning this diversity precisely, economically and culturally into the main strength of the future nation. Eventually, it was this political imagination which was translated into the founding institutions of the Indian state with several parallel and mutually reinforcing principles of pluralism. Secularism provided for a pluralism of religious practices; federalism encompassed the pluralism of regional cultures, and democracy allowed expression of plural political ideals. The constitutional form of this nationalism was civic, based on a secular, republican citizenship rather than belongingness to any mystical cultural or ethnic essence; at the same time, with characteristic prudence, it provided for an expression of more ethnic identities within limits. Interestingly, there was no way, in this political arrangement, for any person to be *only* Indian and nothing else; indeed, one could not be an Indian without being some other things at the same time. Being a Bengali or Tamil or Punjabi, or Hindu, or Muslim or agnostic, was not contradictory to being an Indian. Indianness was a complex and multilayered identity which encompassed other such identities without cancelling them.

Translating this humanistic complex imagination of a political community into legal rules was a difficult task, but it was achieved by the heroic labours of a constituent assembly which produced a document that was among the longest and most complex in the world. The enormous intricacies of legal rules which this elaborate construction required, because it did not wish to hurt any sensibility and tried to mediate between different partially conflicting pictures of justice,[10] made the constitution a technical rather than a popular document. Thus there was a mixed, complex, ambiguous imagination of nationalism standing behind the new state. It appeared in 1947 that the secular, pluralist,

[10] One of the major conflicts was between the right to equality and the right of some groups to escape from traditional disabilities, a question that has repeatedly irrupted into political turmoil, the most recent being the disturbances following the declaration by the central government that the recommendations of the Mandal Commission would be implemented. But there were other conflicts as well: for instance some of the rights were conferred and conferrable only on individuals, some others, especially those relating to minorities, could be enjoyed by individuals only by virtue of their being members of particular communities. This can lead to difficult problems at times.

reformist interpretation had won a final victory; but this history always pursued its uneasy career empowering the secular pluralist option but also menacing it. It was not wholly surprising if the Nehruvian form of nationalism failed, its other forms, sent into hiding by its triumph, would reappear and contest its claims.

After independence, the nation-state followed, broadly, three major goals. The first and minimal one was to maintain its own integrity, but the principle of democracy added an implicit rider that this securing of territoriality must imply some exercise of consent.[11] In the context of the postwar political economy, the second, equally significant objective was to defend political sovereignty, preventing a drain of real decisionmaking authority through absorption into the military systems of the cold war. Nehru was particularly convinced, against the shared commonsense of the Soviets and Americans, that the world appeared more bipolar than it actually was, and acting as if it was not bipolar would in fact make it less so.[12] The third objective of the nation state, generally termed economic development, had a complex connection with its explicitly political goals; and its economic aims themselves were complex and involved internal trade-offs. Dependence on more advanced nations for capital and technology was seen to be the major reason for depletion of sovereignty; and the first strand of development, therefore, was to be industrial self-reliance through a strong drive to develop capital goods industries. Amelioration of extreme economic inequality and destitution was immediately necessary as well for the political stability of the new regime. Happily, a strategy of state-led industrialization could answer both needs: the state was the indispensable centre of planning for capital goods industrialization; it was also the primary agency for redistributive policies. For the first generation of nationalist rulers, the nation-state they had established could acquire legitimacy in two different ways: its political legitimacy depended on its constitutional structure being considered fair by most social groups; but its legitimacy would also depend, it was widely acknowledged, on how it performed on the economic indices of import-substituting industrialization, increasing production and supporting redistributive processes.

The Indian nation state did remarkably well in the first twenty years in terms of the objectives it had decided to pursue. Although India's economic perform-ance is routinely derided, compared to the size of the problem of poverty, and the considerable complexity of the goals, its performance during the Nehru era was impressive by any standards.[13] The constitutional structure absorbed some initial shocks from regionalist movements against the ruling Congress party; but these were not so much against its policies as its forgetfulness about past promises of linguistic reorganization of states, which was not pursued energet-

---

[11] The fact that India practised a form of democratic governance added to her problems in retaining territorial control over disaffected areas. This was reflected most recently in the attempts by the Indian government to hold elections in the disturbed state of Panjab.

[12] Nehru showed the greatest political astuteness in his analysis of international relations. This is borne out by the initial difficulties but eventual success of the nonaligned movement. Ultimately the nonaligned idea was a victim of its own success, when inclusion of all third world states, from Pakistan to Cuba made it politically formless.

[13] For a generally sympathetic account of the achievements of Indian economic planning, S. Chakrabarty, *Development Planning: the Indian Experience* (Oxford, Clarendon, 1987); for a more critical and more recent assessment, J. Bhagwati, *India in Transition* (Oxford, Clarendon, 1993).

ically. But these problems were largely settled by a general territorial re-organization of the federal structure in 1956. Upper class professionals often grumbled privately against the reverse discrimination practised in favour of socially backward groups; but hardly anyone questioned the principles behind these policies. Apart from overtly political events, several more silent and less newsworthy processes provided the foundation for the stability of the nation state. During the colonial period, the British administration had, for their own interests, created three major structures for the support of the subcontinental empire. Foremost among these was the British Indian army, a highly disciplined force recruited from all parts of the country, and permeated by an all-India rather than a provincial character. It was complemented by the celebrated bureaucracy of the British raj which, by the time of independence, was largely manned by well trained Indian officers. Finally, and not least significant, the British had patronized the enterprise of indigenous enthusiasts in developing an educational system which worked with a common curriculum all over the country. The élite produced by this educational structure was essentially bilingual, using English for communication across vernacular boundaries. More than its formal curricular structure, this system produced a common culture of educated manners and taste which was appreciated and intelligible across the country. Nationalists under Nehru's leadership in a sense national-ized these British institutions, using their nonparochial (i.e., pan-Indian) character now effectively to nationalist purposes. The army remained instru-mentally effective, despite humiliating defeats in the border war with China, and coped quite successfully with initial military skirmishes with Pakistan. More significantly, it maintained, despite its effectiveness and prestige among certain circles, a scrupulous loyalty to the civil political leadership. The structure of the colonial bureaucracy was altered on crucial points by the constitution, which carefully retained and strengthened its national character, systematically insulating it from temptations of regionalism.[14] Higher education was expanded by massive investments in teaching of high science and technol-ogy, producing both an educational and a labour market for modern pro-fessional skills. Transformed by deliberate nationalist engineering, these structures of erstwhile colonialism performed efficiently for the endurance and legitimacy of the national state in the first twenty years.

But the nation-state inherited the teeming expectations of the nationalist movement. 'To wipe every tear from every eye', even when restricted to socially relevant tears, is not a very practical programme for a new state. Nationalist rhetoric endlessly repeated the idea that colonialism was to blame for economic backwardness and social injustice. Amorphousness and ambiguity of national-ist ideology meant that the state it created had to strive simultaneously to meet several types of expectations, not any single consistent set to the exclusion of everything else.[15] At least three types of state functions, which emerged in the

[14] Recruitment to the Indian Administrative Service is through a national examination; and administrative careers consist of transfers to posts across the country and occasional secondments to serve at the centre. This is meant to provide officers with both the equipment and the incentive to decide on the basis of national rather than regional considerations.
[15] It appears in the light of research in comparative political economy that democracy might impede fast capitalist growth; and certainly the countries of East Asia have done better than India economically at least in part because their search for economic rationalization was not

West in three waves of state-building, were condensed into the new nation-state. It had to perform with almost unconscious fluency the sovereignty functions that absolutist regimes in Europe took two centuries to outline and learn how to perform. This involved, because of the very different organizing principles of the caste system, a massive transfer of social practices from the province of social regulation to state control.[16] Simultaneously, it had to take on the expectations arising out of a democratic process, much like the ones described by Tocqueville for nineteenth century Europe.[17] Finally, it was also a conscious emulator of the social democratic strategies of the Keynesian state of modern Europe which added to its political responsibilities the unprecedented role of engineering economic growth and redistribution. In European history, the paradoxical paradigmatic text that the leaders' imagination wished to re-enact, these processes did not happen at the same time: the winning of modern state sovereignty, the slow wrenching of universal suffrage from reluctant aristocracies, and the preparation of the welfare state through the conversion of the principles of democracy from the political to the social realm, happened in sequence, not in simultaneity. Logically, at least, it could be argued that these processes were not entirely symmetrical or self-evidently consistent with each other. If happening simultaneously, one might in fact impede the progress of others. It is not at all apparent that the logic of secularization and of democracy, or of democracy and primitive accumulation for capitalism are effortlessly consistent and compatible with each other. The pursuit of such complex objectives evidently made the Indian state's success more difficult by its own acknowledged criteria of politico-economic judgement.

Nevertheless, the record of the Indian nation-state in the first three decades was fairly respectable, if not impressive. Political sovereignty, as Nehru believed, was successfully defended through difficult times of hard bipolarity through the nonaligned foreign policy and its intelligent connection within development strategy. The basic format of development planning in the Nehru years was fairly internally consistent. Planning was organized by the state which allocated certain spheres of industrial production exclusively to state control, but allowed ample room for free enterprise for India's commercial and industrial bourgeoisie, assisted by generous protectionist laws.[18] The state monopolized capital goods industries like steels, heavy engineering, petrochemicals, military equipment production, while private enterprise expanded energetically in production of consumer goods and small producers' industries. In the first three five year plans, India achieved a rate of growth which was

Footnote continued

hampered by democratic rights of the population. It is of course a different matter that after achieving growth, these countries might be forced to democratize politically.

[16] The most remarkable instance of the assumption of this new, historically unprecedented power was the legislation abolishing untouchability. This was not merely an unprecedented social policy; this could be attempted only through an utterly different conception of the state.

[17] The most relevant Tocqueville text for Indian democracy appears to be the *Recollections*, which describe the ferment produced by democratic aspirations in a highly unequal society. For a perceptive analysis of India's democratic experiment, Sunil Khilnani, 'India's democratic career', in John Dunn (ed.) *Democracy: the Unfinished Journey* (Oxford, Clarendon, 1993).

[18] It is often forgotten in debates about liberalization of the economy, that indigenous enterprise benefited from state control in some ways and lost in others. License controls by the state obstructed its entrepreneurial spirit certainly, but protectionism shielded them from external competition. The indigenous bourgeoisie's admiration for the free market and trade is not wholly consistent.

unspectacular in gross terms, but this was offset by its impressive differentiation of industrial production, especially self-reliance in heavy industries. Unfortunately, the structure of the world economy changed rapidly from the seventies, creating opportunities which India's self-reliance industrialization made inaccessible. Since the state performed three vital functions relating to the economy: setting out general targets through its powers of planning, fiscal controls to exercise supervision over free market operations of the private sector, and physical production of critical capital goods, this led to a constant expansion of state bureaucracy. Expansion of the state sector in turn impelled greater demand for the production of personnel who could fill these roles through an education system which must be comparable and equal across different regions, a recruitment which spanned its whole territory and their final integration into an appropriately nationalist bureaucratic culture.[19]

The forces of the market, ironically, pulled remarkably in the same direction of greater and deeper integration of Indian society into the organizational structures of the nation state.[20] Indian capitalism had enjoyed remarkable growth during the last years of colonial rule, partly due to the difficulties of international commerce during the prosecution of war. And the years after independence saw a sharp growth of capitalist industrialization, leading again to the growth and integration of the vast territory into a more meaningful national market for goods and for professional and skilled labour. The logic of economic modernity in both its forms, the market and the developmental state, contributed to greater integration of the national structure of state and economy.[21] Occasional crises in foreign relations, especially wars with China and Pakistan, and serious conflicts with the United States over economic and political questions, reinforced this sense of national integration instead of undermining it. Crises created a sense of danger to the nation state and produced paroxysms of patriotism at difficult times; but probably such sentimental intensity was based on the fact that these occasions of crisis called forth an exceptional mobilization of resources of precisely these professional groups in society and their various skills: the army, the bureaucracy, the press and the intelligentsia, the managerial élites. Thus the nation state in India during the Nehru years experienced a general consolidation, although its career was never free of trouble. The two types of trends which have imperilled the health of nation-states recently, internationalization of production and control pressing from above and local resentments undermining it from below, were not absent; but they did not produce the kind of fatal corrosion evident in later years.

It was a mark of the solidity of the nation-state that it could easily absorb the effects of low level political instability and discontent. The electoral hegemony

[19] I use the term nationalist in such cases not to indicate an access of intense patriotic emotion, but to note the much less dramatic fact that they thought and acted in pan-Indian (i.e. national) rather than regional terms. Usually, this is the sense in which everyday political discourse in India differentiates between national/nationalist and regional political parties.

[20] Indian industrialists appreciated the importance of the nation-state for their own purposes quite early in their historical career. See Bipan Chandra, *The Rise and Growth of Economic Nationalism in India* (Delhi, People's Publishing House, 1977), and A. K. Bagchi, *Private Investment in India* 1900–1939 (Cambridge, Cambridge University Press, 1972).

[21] Although their economic functions are dissimilar, the sociological boundaries between the occupational groups serving in the state and managerial bureaucracies are porous; and they collectively constitute a single occupational culture.

of the Congress in all parts of India provided an important source of political stability and order, since the federal character of the party allowed some dissatisfactions to seek recourse inside the party rather than through external opposition. But there were intimations of a new kind of impermanence in this political world in the bitter conflicts of succession after Nehru's death, and in more aggravated form, after Shastri's. Although Indira Gandhi's accession to power provided an appearance of continuity, in fact, she inherited a political world of very different construction.[22]

Ironically, serious difficulties for the Nehruvian system ensued from its successes, not from its inability to achieve the targets it set for itself. Indeed, what happened in Indian political economy is an especially emphatic example of the recursive requirements of political rationality. A scheme of policies presupposes a world within which it is calculated to succeed. But the historical successes of those policies themselves alter, sometimes quite fundamentally, the structure of that world and its conditions. Strategies, consequently, begin to offer diminishing returns, not because they were misconceived in the first place, but because of the more ironical paradox of the necessary obsolescence of success. Politicians and policy makers can, and usually do, maintain plausibly that it would be extremely odd to change policies which have been successful; yet that watchful scepticism is the condition of long term successes in the constantly reforming world of modernity.

In its own historical world, Nehru's regime registered some signal successes. Within a relatively short time, it accomplished a kind of forced march of heavy industrialization, and the complementarity of the state and market brought into secure existence a new, modern burgeoning economy, which because of its close connection, both structural and personal, with the decisionmaking bureaucracy, could bring the rest of the sprawlingly diverse economy under its regulative control. Secondly, this economic change was brought in within the framework of a democratic structure of governance, limited admittedly in its reach, depth and dependability, yet remarkable in the context of the high rates of infant mortality among democracies in the south. Again, remarkably, the Nehru regime was able to receive its legitimacy through periodic elections, without becoming obliged to scatter scarce resources in short-term populist policies. Its legitimacy was sufficiently deep to allow it to make decisions which required long gestation periods – something that a government could undertake only if it was under no immediate pressure to distribute imminent financial benefits in exchange for electoral support. Yet the dominance that modernist processes of economy and politics achieved over other sectors of society was flawed and insecure in several crucial ways. The dominance of state or market capitalism was primarily a regulative one. It did not generate sufficient momentum to transform the rest of the primitive agrarian and artisanal economy into capitalist production; it merely succeeded in imposing the demands of capitalist accumulation on other sectors which remained, in their productive logics, largely untransformed. Capitalist transformation of the whole economy homogenizes the economy and society after a period of social turbulence; capitalist subsumption, which captures more truthfully what happened in India, fails to homogenize the economy's structure, and social

---

[22] I have analysed Indira Gandhi's regime in my 'Indira Gandhi and Indian politics', *Economic and Political Weekly*, XXI, (1986), 1697–1708.

turbulence simmers on instead of coming to a forcible solution. Eventually, a situation of this kind comes to combine the disadvantages of modernity with those of the society it had disturbed without supplanting. In its size, depth, scale, the modern economy in India was an enormous organization, a world in itself; inside its secure, comfortable interior space India's social élites and their supporting professional classes could live out their existence; but in fact, it sat uneasily poised over a statistically vaster, backward, populous, agrarian economy which was riven by more intense contradictions precisely because of the demands that the modern capitalist sector insistently made on its resources. Also, this interior world of middle class comfort was surrounded by processes of modern destitution and squalor, anger and resentment, symbolized by cities increasingly submerged by slums. Besides the classical terms of trade disputes between the two sectors, cultural resentment gradually surfaced. Large parts of the submerged population in the rural economy learnt to make demands on the state through continued use of democracy, and expressed their resentment against the fact that benefits of development were monopolized almost entirely by urban, modern bourgeois classes to their total exclusion. The only rural group which secured benefits out of the development process were the large farmers whose compliance was bought by heavy subsidies, absence of income tax, and slow cooptation into governmental power. The ruling coalition of the bourgeoisie, high managerial élites, state bureaucracy and agrarian magnates[23] came under serious strain as capitalism in agriculture spread unevenly and produced a class of rich farmers who controlled substantial resources and felt unjustly cheated out of their fare share of the privileges of political power. From the mid-sixties, electoral politics in India showed a rearrangement of the political coalition of dominance, the rich peasants defecting from the Congress and leading a resentful coalition of rural interests under the flag of peasant parties.

Within twenty years after Nehru's death, central conflicts of Indian politics and the discourses expressing them changed unrecognizably. Politics in the Nehru years appeared a tolerable imitation of Western political styles, in which the main disputes occurred between ideological groups of the left, right and centre. In the eighties, it appeared that these were insubstantial differences within a modernist bloc of privilege which was opposed with increasing energy, vehemence, irritation, insolence by a bloc of social groups who were outsiders to the etiquettes of westernized modernity. Politicians of this bloc spoke derisively of the English-speaking modernists in truculent vernacular, wore indigenous costumes, understood, tolerated, at times revelled in premodern rituals of political power,[24] and created politically innovative coalitions which defied description in terms of either modern or traditional alphabets of politics to bring to bear the pressure of numbers on their adversaries and intended victims. Electoral instability played an important part in this change. Politicians like Indira Gandhi, who felt electorally insecure after 1967 defeats of the Congress party, invited these forces onto the political plane; but once they came inside, it was hard to banish them again to the margins of democratic politics.

[23] For a discussion about the ruling coalition, see Pranab Bardhan, *Political Economy of Development in India* (Delhi, Oxford University Press, 1985).

[24] In recent years, successful politicians were honoured by their caste groups or constituencies by being weighed against money. Sometimes they used a symbolism particularly paradoxical in a republican state of presenting successful parliamentarians with crowns.

They came in through a typically opportunistic welcome, which was not meant to be permanent; but once inside they were too powerful numerically to be extruded. On the contrary, they tended to rewrite not merely the agenda, but also the language of democratic politics in India.

Ironically, the logic of democracy has often worked against the stability of the nation-state in recent Indian history; though both nationalism and democracy speak in the name of the people, they invoke it in different ways, with widely different implications. In the period after the emergency, 1975–7, what initially appeared a crisis of government has slowly spread to become a crisis of the Indian nation-state, at least in its current institutional form. A crisis is a kind of persistent difficulty of self-maintenance produced by the operation of the system itself, from which the system cannot come out untransformed. The crisis of the Indian nation-state has several dimensions. Planning, in its early stages simply got remarkable results by rationalizing resource utilization and giving some direction to the economy. But once that plateau was reached, traditional forms of physical planning, based on direct state production, failed to produce growth. On the contrary, entrenchment of vested interests of both public sector managers and a relatively privileged labour force, made these industries indefensibly wasteful. Bureaucratic shielding of their performance and government protection made them immune to criticism, and they gradually became expensive white elephants which undermined not merely the balanced budget, but more significantly, the moral authority of the state sector. The state sector, originally fashioned to counterbalance the mercenariness of the private capitalist, gradually came to represent an economic sphere whose function slipped unnoticed from a predominantly economic to a political one: from distribution of welfare by producing low cost inputs for industries, these became producers of unaccountable funds used by politicians and pliable bureaucrats. Ideologically, this made it appear that it was the welfare function of the state which was bound to produce corruption, and its excesses could be rectified only by the harsh, if purifying, sanctions of an unrestricted market.

A second success of the Nehruvian development design also started turning sour. Industrialization after independence helped strengthen the national economy, but at the cost of intensifying regional inequalities. With the opportunity provided by democratic institutions, resentment against regional unevenness tended to find quick translation into regionalist movements. The response of the central government to these demands fluctuated from uncomprehending repression to attempts at cooptation.[25] Although the central government was occasionally successful in transforming guerrilla leaders into instant chief ministers, such transactions inevitably tried to head off a widespread social resentment by private satisfaction, often leading to a quick isolation of the leaders who defected into a dishonest constitutionalism to the disapproval of their militant followers. Anyway, this pattern did nothing to produce long term political stability. To most cases of threat to political

---

[25] In a large number of cases, one comes across the same sequence of central response: starting with repression, moving to reluctant concessions, finally an attempt to coopt the leadership by offering the allurement of political power. Such 'solutions' usually bring short-term reprieves at the cost of long-term problems. Democratic politics tends sometimes to encourage such shortsightedness, since the incumbent party can enjoy the brief glory of the reprieve, expecting others to come later and count the costs.

stability the standard answer of the nation-state has been a stern centralizing response. Yet political democracy meant that political troubles arising out of regional resentments had to be found a consultative solution. Given India's great regional diversity which is bound to express itself politically in increasing differentiation of interests, only a transformation towards more decentralization can, in principle, produce a political order based on democratic consent.

Unfortunately however the politics of the parties who have controlled the Central regime has inclined in a different direction. Due to India's great size, it is always in principle possible for a party or an interest coalition to gain an absolute majority in the central legislature by winning support of a major part of the country, leaving some enclaves permanently incapable of channeling their grievance into the significance spaces of decision making. Indira Gandhi successfully pursued policies of isolating resentment in Assam and Punjab, outmanoeuvring regional opposition through a formal democratic process. But such operation of formal democracy strengthens the government while weakening the state. Disaffected groups enjoying large regional support become gradually convinced that their interests would remain permanently outplayed and marginalized through the democratic electoral process itself, and they will be reduced to a permanent enclave of helpless resentment. Operation of elective democracy can thus be seen not as a process of representation, but a means by which representation is craftily taken away. It is not impossible to convince people in those regions to turn away from formal processes of electoral democracy, because for them, plausibly, these mean permanent disfranchizement. Consequently, festering of regional sores of this kind in Punjab, Assam, Kashmir have tended to make politics in those states reach a level of volatility which is impossible for democratic norms of restraint and conversation to contain. What is remarkable is the rapidity with which the curve of regional resentment rises from electoral defeats straight to armed militancy, instead of the trend common in the fifties and sixties, of spilling over into large street demonstrations and popular movements. The rise of armed militancy of course does not increase participation; it reduces its scope still further. Punjab offers the best example of a situation where the people of the state were reduced to a state of utter redundancy between the two combatants speaking in the name of contrary nationalisms: Indian armed forces preserving the Indian nation-state and armed militants trying to create a new Punjabi state of Khalistan.

It is possible to combine the two main lines of causality in the trajectory of Indian politics, the silent, insistent movements of political economy, the logic of capitalism working through the state and the market, and the voluble, visible turbulence at the level of cultural expression. The fundamental process at work appears to have been a form of capitalist development which intensified both class and regional inequality and intensified anger against a modernist élite. The loyalty of this élite to its own acclaimed values of democracy, secularism, equity may have been suspect and practically inconsistent, but it is not its disingenuousness that is attacked, but the values themselves. Democratic governance made it possible for the enormous grievance against such cornering of the benefits to express itself. Democracy also encouraged the slow rise of a new idiom of politics which constantly invokes majorities of various kinds to justify a bending of benefits towards some large groups who can hope permanently to outnumber others. Three majority arguments have broken out with great violence in Indian political discourse recently: the majority of Hindus, of backward caste groups and the less evident one of Hindi-speakers: in all of these there is an implied belief that majority can sanction the sacrifice of equity. If a majority legislates rules which are evidently harmful to others, democratic principles of governance legitimize them; and all of these trends wish to turn the level plane of rights of citizens into slopes which favour their own constituent members. Naturally, the response to such threatening language of majoritarianism is an instant reflex to seek spaces where the groups whose seclusion is sought can find a sanctuary in an answering majority. If some linguistic, religious or social groups believe that in a united India the rules of political game and economic distribution would be skewed permanently against them, they will naturally try to create political spaces where they can constitute similar majorities and practise, in retribution, similar iniquity towards others. Under the pressure of these contending majoritarianisms, and the possibility of a convex majority which might combine principles from all these, the original political imagination of independent India is in danger of disruption. But these are not proposals for abandoning the nationalist imagination altogether, but for replacing the Nehruvian imagination of nationalism with other forms.

Thus the central contradiction of the history of the Indian nation-state seems to be, at this point at least, between the logic of economic development and the logic of political identities. Economic change through the centralizing state and the homogenizing market works towards large entities like the commodities and the labour market. Associated institutions of the modern, highly technically sophisticated, armed forces, the large and powerful bureaucracy, a massive managerial and professional middle class the size of the population of big European nations, all understand the advantages of scale; they enjoy the surpluses that only India's scale makes possible. But the processes which produce this coalition of modernist groups and their advantages also produce, in its dark underside, equally constant processes of exclusion, resentment and hostility to its undeserved privilege. Since this élite speaks the language of national integration and unity, the latter speak the negative language of localism, regional autonomy, small-scale nationalism, in dystopias of ethnicity – small, xenophobic, homogeneous political communities. This does violence to the political imagination of the Indian nation-state which emphasized diversity as a great asset and enjoined principles of tolerance and mixture as the special gift of Indian civilization. That narrative of Indian history may have been romantic, but its politics was certainly praiseworthy and it produced the most noteworthy spell of democratic governance for about a fifth of mankind for close to half a century. The present stage marks a crisis in the life of the Indian nation-state in both senses of the term. It is brought on by the unfolding of its own inner tendencies, and therefore, it cannot escape from the crisis by a policy of masterly negligence, precisely because this is not a result of policy failures, but of its limited successes. Secondly, it cannot, it appears, emerge out of it untransformed; simply singleminded pursuit of centralization is apt to make its strains only worse; its apparent suppression at one point would make it erupt elsewhere. The nation-state as it emerged through the Nehruvian design of the fifties can survive only if it allows its dominant imagination to admit amendments, and strive to achieve greater equity between classes and regions, and try to surmount and heal the great cleavage of dispossession by the processes of the cognitively arrogant, socially uncaring, brutal form of modernity. But the crisis of the Indian nation state as it is imagined at present does not of course indicate a depletion of the attraction of the abstract idea of nationalism. The structure of the international system forces all dissatisfaction to seek articulation, however inappropriate, through the obligatory pretence that each minority, each disgruntled group of people, are a nation in waiting, and must break away from one erstwhile nation only to create another. With heroic unreasonableness, they would also believe, in the face of history that their nation would not repeat the tragedies of others. If the present Indian state suffers disintegration, its present space would most likely be occupied by a number of smaller, more homogeneous, less democratic states with their own insecure narratives of being a nation from immemorial antiquity. However threatened the future of the Indian nation-state, the age of the nationalist imagination is far from over. The world of political possibilities in India seems to be simplifying into the frightening choice before most of the modern world's political communities: to try to craft imperfect democratic rules by which increasingly mixed groups of people can carry on together an unheroic everyday existence, or the illusion of a permanent and homogeneous, unmixed, single nation, a single collective self without any trace of a defiling otherness.

The Crises of Southern States

GEOFFREY HAWTHORN

A state, like any agent, is in difficulties if it cannot for a moment do what is expected of it. It is in crisis if it is unlikely into the foreseeable future to be able to do so. Not all Southern states are, in this sense, in crisis. But a large number are finding themselves unable to act as they have in the past hoped to act: in some, customary political practices are under threat, in many, the once common project of 'development' has become more difficult to sustain, and in a few, what has conventionally been taken to be the nature and purpose of modern statehood itself is in jeopardy.

I

The class of Southern states is large. But it is not self-defining. It is no longer a class of states in a third world. Since the second of the three worlds disappeared at the end of the 1980s, leaving only the relics of Cuba and North Korea, there are at most now two. Nor are all Southern states now 'under-developed'. And if they can nevertheless be said still to be 'developing', so also, unless an arbitrary criterion (like membership of the Organization of Economic Cooperation and Development or the World Bank's average *per capita* income) is used to draw the distinction, can those in the North. The class of Southern states, it would seem, is merely residual. There is the 'West' and 'the Rest': those societies and states with the exception now, in this context, of Japan, that do not share what Huntington has recently characterized as the 'civilization' of western Europe and North America.[1]

Huntington's suggestion is that it is the cultural differences between the West and the Rest, not, as in the Cold War years, any difference of economic fortune or political ideology, that will mark the lines of conflict at the end of this century and the beginning of the next. He himself defines the differences in a misleading way. A 'cultural difference' is often marked as much by 'political ideology' and the political history that has shaped that ideology as by language, religion or other less directly political facts. (How else could one distinguish his 'Latin American civilization' from those in Portugal and Spain?) His prediction for the post-Cold War world may nevertheless be correct. The West has unprecedented powers in relation to the Rest, and to preserve these, will take the offensive.

[1] S. P. Huntington, 'The clash of civilisations?', *Foreign Affairs*, 72 (1993), 22–49, at p. 41. Huntington attributes the phrase to K. Mahbubani, 'The west and the Rest', *The National Interest*, Summer (1992), 3–13. In fact it has long been used more or less fondly to describe an introductory history course at Cambridge. J. M. Dunn, 'The identity of the bourgeois liberal republic', in B. Fontana (ed.), *The Invention of the Modern Republic* (Cambridge, Cambridge University Press, 1994), pp. 206–28.

This offensive has already begun. Since 1989, the International Monetary Fund and the World Bank have begun to impose political as well as more purely economic conditions on the financial assistance they extend to Southern governments. An increasing number of governments in the North have followed suit.[2] These conditions are not always precise. The IMF has yet to be explicit about anything beyond expenditure on arms. The World Bank, sensitive still to its formal requirement to stay above politics, talks obliquely of 'the rule of law' and greater 'accountability' and 'transparency' in the administration of economic affairs. It is only Northern governments that have openly asked for a move to 'multi-party democracy' in the South and also made a concerted attempt, under the auspices of the United Nations, to insist on the acknowledgement of a schedule of 'human rights'. (The United States has been the most open of these governments. Members of the Clinton administration now argue that the end of the Cold War makes it possible to try once again to realize Wilson's ambition of spreading the ideals of the liberal Enlightenment, and that part of this project, the extension of democracy, will enhance the economic and political 'security' of the United States.) But even the multilateral institutions' discreet insistence on the rule of law implies the need for a separation of executive and judicial powers, and their demand for greater accountability, a greater readiness of governments to open themselves to popular criticism.

These demands may not in themselves be unreasonable. In the very long run, the bourgeois liberal republic, as Marxists rightly describe it, may have been more effective than any of its competitors in ensuring the security of its citizens and extending and sustaining the conditions for their well-being. There is some reason also to think that states in the South which share the liberal republic's commitment to civil and political rights have more effectively extended similar benefits there.[3] But as some east Asian states suggest, this is not universally true. And even if it were, it is notoriously difficult for Southern states to adopt such rules of rule and sustain them. Nor is it clear, at least in the shorter run, that when they do wish to do so and can, their governments are able adequately to discharge the responsibilities of the modern state.

[2] C. Lancaster, 'Governance and development: the views from Washington', *IDS Bulletin*, 24 (1992), 9–15. World Bank, *Governance and Development* (New York, World Bank, 1992). M. Moore, 'Declining to learn from the East? The World Bank on "governance and development"', *IDS Bulletin*, 24 (1992), 39–50. The European Bank for Reconstruction and Development is the only one of these institutions which stipulates political conditions for assistance in its charter. The insistence on such conditions has so far been distinctively Western. Japan has since 1990 been the largest single bilateral aid donor, and now extends much aid to sub-Saharan Africa, which in 1989 was the first object of the World Bank's attention to 'governance'. Yet although notoriously more severe than Western states in the periodic negotiations it conducts with them about concessions on debt in the meetings of the Paris Club of creditor nations, it has been reluctant to follow their lead on political conditionality. M. Hanabusa, 'A Japanese perspective on aid and development', T. Yanagihara and A. Emig, 'An overview of Japan's foreign aid', in S. Islam (ed.), *Yen for Development: Japanese Foreign Aid and the Politics of Burden-sharing* (New York, Council on Foreign Relations Press, 1991), pp. 37–69, 88–104. G. P. Hawthorn, 'Conditionality: Japan's reservations', unpublished paper, 1993. There will be renewed pressure on the South in the recently concluded extensions and revisions to the General Agreement on Tariffs and Trade which, as one would expect, anyway favours the stronger trading economies over the weak.

[3] Dunn, 'The identity of the bourgeois liberal republic'; P. Dasgupta, *An Inquiry into Well-being and Destitution* (Oxford, Clarendon, 1993).

II

The first difficulty is one simply of the will to democratize. It is a difficulty that arises in the distance between the assumptions that inform the politics of modern liberal republics and those with which states in the South have come to modern statehood, conceptions which the practice of modern statehood itself has done less than might be supposed to extinguish.

In Latin America, these have been the conceptions of ancient liberty.[4] Spanish American republicanism, like its ancient model, was aristocratic, exclusionary, and bellicose. It presupposed a common good, the liberty and honour of the republic itself. Other interests, individual and sectional, were to be resisted. In its early modern European expressions, which passed to those who were angry with colonial rule in the Americas in the eighteenth century, it often insisted that the defence of this liberty against threats of control from without and subversion within was the first political priority. And despite the contempt of some republican theorists for Christian passivity, the republicans' conception of government and its purposes sat easily, in Catholic populations, with the warnings of the Godless and divisive implications of liberalism and socialism that were increasingly pressed in Encyclicals from Rome between 1880 and the late 1930s.

At first, in the movements in the Americas for independence from Spain, the liberty that was at issue was freedom from empire itself. This required perpetual vigilance, which was the responsibility of the military, and since this liberty was the first priority and the greatest good, armies accordingly found it easy, when they wished to, to claim supreme authority. Later, the liberty at issue was a freedom from the pressures being imposed by the once admired post-imperial republic of the United States, which came to seem to many to be assuming imperial powers. This is one reason why the ancient conception of liberty should have persisted in Latin America into the twentieth. This persistence explains why in the conflicts there between the landed classes, the advocates of industrialization, urban workers, and the rural poor, each party should so often have thought its opponents not merely inconvenient but also subversive. It also explains why those who have made demands from outside the political class have either, as with the rural poor, been excluded, or, on the assumption that the good state is the 'organic' state, caressed, coopted, expensively cushioned and then usually subordinated in politics of a 'corporatist' kind.[5]

In the larger countries in the south of Latin America in the 1930s and 1940s, this conception of the state was reinforced in the move away from a dependence on the export of agricultural products and other primary goods towards industry and the development of modern services. In Vargas's *Estado Novo* in Brazil in the late 1930s, for example, in Peronism in Argentina in the 1940s, and elsewhere, the demands of the new industrial and commercial classes were

---

[4] R. Morse, 'The heritage of Latin America', in L. Hartz (ed.), *The Founding of New Societies* (New York, Harcourt Brace, 1954), pp. 123–177. The contrast between 'ancient' and 'modern' liberty is Constant's, 'The liberty of the ancients compared with that of the moderns', in B. Fontana (ed.), *Benjamin Constant: Political Writings* (Cambridge, Cambridge University Press, 1988), pp. 309–28.

[5] A. Stepan, *State and Society: Peru in Comparative Perspective* (Princeton, Princeton University Press, 1978); P. C. Schmitter, 'Still the century of corporatism?', *Review of Politics*, 36 (1974), 85–131.

promoted against those of the landed élites and watched over by the more self-consciously 'progressive' elements in the armed forces. The fact that the armed forces were themselves often divided, and became more so in the arguments that developed in the 1950s and 1960s between economic 'nationalists', insisting on the virtues of protection, and 'internationalists', convinced of the need to attract foreign investment, served to complicate the picture, but it did not radically change it. Only, among the larger states, in Mexico, where after the success of the revolution in 1920 both the army and the Catholic hierarchy were decisively constrained, did this contest subside. There also, however, the ruling Institutional Party of the Revolution has found the attractions of the older republicanism difficult to resist. It has continued to try politically to incorporate all those who have been willing to be incorporated, and exclude those who are not.[6]

The sharpest contrast to the idea of a good for each which is the good for all, the instantiation of the virtue of the *res publica* itself, is with the conception of power as a private prebend. This has been pervasive in sub-Saharan Africa.[7] In conditions there of persistent material scarcity, the object has been to appropriate what surpluses there are and to distribute them to those, one's kin or one's *ethnos* considered more widely, who can be relied upon to sustain one's power in the state. Such economic 'development' as there has been in these countries has done little to reduce the scarcity on which this practice has rested. Where it has occurred, it has been promoted, even into the period of economic 'restructuring' in the 1980s, through powerful executives, executives which, as in the colonial period, have been all but entirely unconstrained by effective separations of power within the state itself or free regular elections. Executive power, and the resources that such power brings, is the prize, and competition for it has been a zero-sum game. This is why armed forces in Africa have so often been tempted to capture it. Their monopoly of force, less incidental to the authority they claim than in Latin America, has often been decisive.

It is nevertheless the case that in both sub-Saharan Africa and Latin America there have been many attempts to institute modern republics. In both continents, indeed, the soldiers have even on occasion transferred their power to such a regime. Over most of the Middle East by contrast, the attempt has been rare. States in this region are all exceptionally artificial. Pakistan, which although it lies beyond the region as that is usually defined has some of the features of a Middle Eastern state, was a hasty invention at the end of British rule after Congress and the Muslim League had failed to agree on the division of powers in an independent India. The countries to its west (apart from Afghanistan and Iran) were divided as they are by the French and the British after the defeat of the Ottoman Empire in 1919. Like many states in sub-Saharan Africa, they include a variety of socially and often economically separate groups. Also like the sub-Saharan states, they have a limited

---

[6] There was a period of internal party democratization in the 1980s, but the party later renewed the PRI's old emphasis on corporate structures: V. Bulmer-Thomas, N. Craske and M. Serrano, 'Who will benefit?', in V. Bulmer-Thomas, N. Craske and M. Serrano (eds), *Mexico and the Nafta: who will benefit?* (London, Macmillan, 1994), pp. 2–31.

[7] J.-F. Bayart, *L'Etat en Afrique: La Politique du Ventre* (Paris, Fayard, 1989, Eng. trans. London, Longman, 1993); G. P. Hawthorn, 'Sub-Saharan Africa', in D. Held (ed.), *Prospects for Democracy: North, South, East, West* (Cambridge, Polity, 1993), pp. 330–53; R. Sandbrook, *The Politics of Africa's Economic Recovery* (Cambridge, Cambridge University Press, 1993).

experience of statehood; the Ottoman administration was distant and loose. And they are states in Islam.[8] In some since the 1920s (Saudi Arabia and what are now the small Gulf states), Islam has been the credal basis of rule. In others (Egypt, Yemen, Syria, Iran, Afghanistan, and Pakistan), the battle for power has been between the clergy and one or another secular party, and each, when successful, has tried to exclude the other. In addition, in almost all (Egypt, Yemen, Saudi Arabia, Syria, Iraq, Iran, the Gulf states, Afghanistan, and Pakistan), the geopolitics of the region since the late 1940s have put large arsenals at the command of whoever does control the state. And even into the 1990s, the incentive in these states to liberalize their politics, and the external pressures to do so, have been slight.

Societies in east and parts of south-east Asia, by contrast, have pre-existing conceptions of politics, and in many cases, a pre-existing experience of actual statehood of a wholly different kind. In some cases, these were well-developed long before the start of the modern state in Europe. In China and Korea, the principles that have informed them are often described as 'Confucian'.[9] In both countries, and in Japan also after the Meiji restoration, this experience took the form of an authoritative and politically exclusive central state. In China, there were considerable differences of emphasis, not least at moments of change and possible reform, between advocates of the Confucian principle of *ren*, of cultivating a personal virtue and harmony and extending it to social relations, and advocates of *li*, of respecting the conventions of social position and the hierarchy of positions. The object, however, in China and elsewhere, was the same. It was to sustain a unitary and exclusionary state dedicated above all to order and stability and to providing as much welfare for its subjects as was consistent with that end.

Such states of course were not always successful. State power was constrained in Korea and Japan before the 1860s by a conservative landed aristocracy that was resistant to directive central rule, and in China by the simple difficulty of maintaining control over vast distances. But even when central power collapsed, as it did in Korea in 1905 and in China in 1911, the ancient aspiration remained. In Japan since the military defeat in 1945, in the two states in Korea since 1948, and in China since the victory of the Communist Party in the civil war in 1949, the resources of the modern state have been used to realize it.

In all the regions of the South, it is only perhaps in Hindu south Asia that pre-existing conceptions of politics sit at all easily with the demands of the modern republic. Many explanations have been offered for India's success in sustaining such a regime. The exceptional size and variety of the country, the legacy from British rule of powers divided between the centre and the states, countering any concentration, and of a relatively highly-trained and cohesive civil service, have all been important. But Hinduism itself may also have played a part. In pre-colonial Indian politics, pre-Mughal as well as pre-British,

---

[8] The enduring experience of many, in a pattern first described by Ibn Khaldun, has been of repeated invasions of the city, the site of what settled political authority there was, by purifying nomads from the desert: E. Gellner, *Muslim Society* (Cambridge, Cambridge University Press, 1981).

[9] G. Rozman (ed.), *The East Asian Region: the Confucian Heritage and its Modern Adaptation* (Princeton, Princeton University Press, 1991).

morality and power were considered to be separate. Morality governed private life, and left the rest to statecraft, which was to be guided by prudence. Priests were responsible for the first, kings for the second. Hinduism, moreover, has no single god, and even in private morality, prescribes no consistent set of precepts. In public life as well as in private, it allows a pragmatic pluralism which readily accommodates itself to the demands of a liberal politics.[10]

III

In most of the states in Latin America and the Middle East, therefore, in many states in sub-Saharan Africa, and until recently in east Asia also, the will to liberal democracy has been weak. In several states, it is absent still. In Latin America, the Middle East and east Asia, this has been because of a reluctance to accept alternative conceptions of the ends of state power and a distaste for the differences and divisions that the promotion of such alternatives produces. In sub-Saharan Africa by contrast, where political arguments of a more principled or 'ideological' kind have been rare, and where expressed, have been more than usually clearly rationalizations of less principled interests, it is because in an all-or-nothing competition, the loss of access to state power could in itself and its material consequences be total.

Even where the will to a liberal republic in the South exists, however, both the transition and success in sustaining it turn on conditions that few political classes have been able easily to meet. This is the second difficulty. The separation of executive, legislative and judicial powers and an agreement to respect the results of competing through regular elections can each only be sustained if politicians who fail at any moment to gain power consider it in their interests to wait to compete again rather than to try to overturn or subvert the system. This, Przeworski suggests, requires institutions that are capable both of accommodating themselves to alternative interests and of proving sufficiently robust to prevent their own subversion. 'Democratic institutions must remain with narrow limits to be successful'.[11] Schumpeter argued that democratic competition could only be sustained if there was widespread agreement on the general shape and direction of the society, if not too many issues were politicized, and if the political class itself and the civil administration were reasonably able and uncorrupt.[12] Dahl and others have insisted on the importance of one or another set of structural pre-conditions. Economic, social and cultural differences, they tend all to agree, should not be too wide.[13]

[10] J. Manor, 'How and why liberal representative politics emerged in India', *Political Studies*, 38 (1990), 20–38.

[11] A. Przeworski, *Democracy and the Market: Political and Economic Reforms in Eastern Europe and Latin America* (Cambridge, Cambridge University Press, 1991), p. 37.

[12] The conditions are Schumpeter's: J. Schumpeter, *Capitalism, Socialism and Democracy* (New York, Harper and Row, 1942).

[13] R. A. Dahl, *Polyarchy: Participation and Opposition* (New Haven, Yale University Press, 1971). There is a number of more elaborate attempts to specify the pre-conditions of 'democracy', variously defined, and their connection with each other. A recent example is A. Hadenius, *Democracy and Development* (Cambridge, Cambridge University Press, 1992), who interestingly finds that the one 'pre-condition' of an economic kind (suggested by others, including Dahl) which seems not to be so in practice is a relative equality of wealth and income.

The example of India tends to favour the strategic explanations over the structural.[14] Structurally, India is as various and unequal as almost any state in the South, and more so than many. It has nevertheless managed to sustain a democratic regime since its independence from Britain in 1947. It is also, of course, a deliberately 'developing' economy. Most observers, however, agree that until 1991 the strategies for development, which favoured the public allocation of resources and a degree of protection for each of the economic interests, were modified in the interests of stability and political continuity. Whatever their other differences, successive governments in Delhi accepted Schumpeter's argument that 'a system – any system, economic or other – that at *every* given point of time fully utilizes its possibilities to the best advantage may yet in the long run be inferior to a system that does so at *no* given point of time, because the latter's failure to do so may be a condition for the level or speed of long-run performance'.[15] One might also argue that this was a decision made easier by the conceptions of political practice with which the country's nominally secular but largely Hindu leadership came to power. Other deliberately 'developing' economies, by contrast, have been led by political classes who were either, as in Latin America, more divided over economic strategy, or, as in parts of Africa and east and south-east Asia, committed to the view that it did make sense to try to 'utilize possibilities to the best advantage' and that to do so precluded compromise. In these cases, the interests tended to dominate the institutions, and not conversely. 'A democracy', their protagonists would have agreed with Tocqueville, 'finds it difficult to coordinate the details of a great undertaking and to fix on some plan and carry it through with determination'.[16]

This second difficulty in moving to a sustainable liberal republic has everywhere except in east and south-east Asia been increased rather than reduced by the nature and speed of the changes that many states in the South have been required to introduce since the early 1980s. This is ironic, since these changes are intended both to utilize their economic resources to the best advantage and to enable governments more easily to effect the transition to a more properly bourgeois liberal republic in which the interests of private commerce in a 'cosmopolitan' or global economy would more readily be met. The argument is that deflation and devaluation, the deregulation of investment and trade, and the denationalization of enterprises will both make economies more efficient and encourage politicians in the societies in which they exist to act more 'democratically'. The evidence for the connection remains uncertain.[17] The experience of the 1980s and early 1990s is that the delay between the introduction of stabilization, liberalization and privatization and the resump-

---

[14] A powerful and persuasive case is made for the superiority of strategic explanations over structural ones for Latin America by A. O. Hirschman, 'Notes on consolidating democracy in Latin America', in *Rival Views of the Market and Other Essays* (New York, Viking, 1986), pp. 176–82.

[15] J. Schumpeter, *Capitalism, Socialism and Democracy*, p. 83 (emphases his). Two acounts of the Congress strategy, from opposite political standpoints, are P. B. Bardhan, *The Political Economy of Development in India* (Oxford, Blackwell, 1984) and F. R. Frankel, *India's Political Economy 1947–1977: the Gradual Revolution* (Princeton, Princeton University Press, 1978).

[16] Quoted by J. Elster, 'Consequences of constitutional choice', in J. Elster and R. Slagstad (eds), *Constitutionalism and Democracy* (Cambridge and Paris, Cambridge University Press and Editions de la Maison des Sciences de l'Homme, 1988), pp. 81–101 at p. 94.

[17] J. Healey and M. Robinson, *Democracy. Governance and Economic Policy* (London, Overseas Development Institute, 1992).

tion of economic growth is usually protracted, that domestic support for these reforms tends to fall unless there are compensating measures for those who are adversely affected, and that the peremptory way in which they have tended to be introduced can threaten the institutions for bargaining and compromise whose consolidation they are expected to support. Thus even though the policies have tended to strengthen the hand of presidents and their ministers of finance, to remove other centres of power that have been dependent on extensive public expenditure, and to create a new political space, those who enter this space have unstable constituencies and little or no procedural security. The economic reforms can thus serve both to deepen the difficulties of a politics of decentralized equilibrium in countries where such a politics has not hitherto been strong and to create difficulties in those in which a degree of democracy had previously been stable and reasonably secure.[18]

IV

The fact remains, however, that for all regimes 'future legitimation', as Przeworski has put it, 'requires present accumulation'.[19] This is the third difficulty faced now by many states in the South. In some, it is not new. Many countries in Latin America, having done well in exporting to the United States between 1939 and 1945, when other supplies of commodities and manufactures were closed, felt themselves to be doing less well once the war had ended, and suffered from often deepening divisions over what could and should be done to redress the problem.[20] In other Southern states, the difficulty has arisen in their more recent political independence. The long economic boom in the North from the outbreak of the Korean War in 1950 to the first oil-price rise in 1973 sustained a demand for the commodities on which the foreign earnings of ex-colonies in Africa and Asia depended. The dramatically increased liquidity of Western banks in the 1970s, which prompted them to extend loans on what seemed at the time to be advantageous (but floating) rates, perpetuated the pervasive sense of optimism and ease. It was the Organization of Petroleum and Exporting Countries' second oil-price increase in 1979, the rise in interest rates, and the by then evident downturn in the Western economies that from the early 1980s together created an increasing number of balance of payments crises and

[18] M. Bruno, *Crisis, Stabilisation and Economic Reform* (Oxford, Clarendon, 1993); A. Prze-worski, 'Economic reform, public opinion, and political institutions: Poland in the East European perspective', in L. C. Pereira Bresser, J. M. Maravall and A. Przeworski, *Economic Reforms in New Democracies* (Cambridge, Cambridge University Press, 1993), pp. 132–220. Examples of the first include some countries in eastern Europe and many in sub-Saharan Africa. Venezuela is an instance of the second. After the imposition of an IMF structural adjustment programme there in 1989, there were urban riots, the president was impeached, the two main political parties collapsed, and sections of the armed forces attempted two coups. In December 1993, Jaime Caldera, one of the architects of the 'democratic pact' which had in 1958 established what proved to be a stable political competition after a period of military rule, stood successfully as an independent candidate for the presidency against what proved against many expectations to be a powerful coalition of the left.

[19] A. Przeworski, *Capitalism and Social Democracy* (Cambridge, Cambridge University Press, 1985), p. 157.

[20] R. Thorp, 'A reappraisal of the origins of import-substituting industrialisation 1930–1950', *Journal of Latin American Studies*, 24 (1992 Supplement), 181–95. J. Sheahan, *Patterns of Development in Latin America: Poverty, Repression and Economic Strategy* (Princeton, Princeton University Press, 1987) is a good general account of the consequences through to the mid 1980s.

budget deficits which in turn prompted the imposition of unprecedentedly severe and far-reaching economic conditions by the IMF and the World Bank.

It is in the 1990s, however, that the full force of the point that the multilateral institutions were already making to Southern states in the 1980s has become clear. No degree of financial stabilization, economic liberalization, and privatization will serve to restore growth if barriers to trade remain between the South and the North, and if direct investment in the South is not forthcoming. In trade, the conclusion of the Uruguay Round of the General Agreement on Tariffs and Trade has done something to redress what by the mid 1970s many feared was becoming a new period of protection. In the agreements on agriculture, which are included for the first time in the General Agreement, domestic farm supports are to be reduced by 20 per cent, subsidized agricultural exports by 36 per cent in value and 26 per cent in volume, and tariffs against tropical products by an average of more than 40 per cent. Those against textile imports will also be dismantled over the next ten years. These will benefit exporters in the South and be to the disadvantage only of those countries (largely in sub-Saharan Africa) which have to continue to import food from the North. Southern countries may nevertheless suffer from new rules to protect intellectual property.

For investment, by contrast, the prospects are much less good. Between 1980 and 1989, the proportion of foreign direct investment in the South by European, American and Japanese companies fell from 25 per cent of the whole to 18 per cent. 75 per cent of the 18 per cent at the end of this period was going to China, Hong Kong, Malaysia, Singapore, and Thailand, all of which were benefiting from the devolution of production from Japan; to Argentina, Brazil, Colombia, and Mexico, to all of which 'flight capital' was beginning to return after the financial panics of the later 1970s and early 1980s; and to Egypt, which was by the end of the decade also the largest recipient of United States aid. The forty or so lowest-income economies, however, which are usually only otherwise able to raise loans for investment from the concessionary International Development Assistance division of the World Bank and one or two favourably disposed bilateral donors, received just 0.7 per cent of the 18 per cent.[21] Even for those governments which are able, as the multilateral donors ask, to extend their tax base and improve their capacity actually to gather more tax, it follows that the likelihood of generating sufficient revenue for the public investment that any modern state has to make to attract investment, to provide the services to maintain the productivity and well-being of its citizens, and to support the quality of administration necessary to implement and sustain these and its other activities, is not high.

V

In so far as those governing (or hoping to govern) Southern states now face a political 'crisis', therefore, this crisis will be most severe where the pre-existing conceptions and practices of politics are most inimical to the kind of liberal democracy now being pressed by the West on what Huntington calls 'the Rest', where the political class is least disposed to take the risk of separating its powers

---

[21] United Nations Centre on Transnational Corporations, *The Triad in Foreign Direct Investment* (New York, UNCTC, 1991).

and opening itself to the possibility of defeat at the polls, and where the prospects of economic growth, necessary to the perceived purposes of the state itself and necessary also (if not always sufficient) for the regime to be accepted by its electors, are poor. Where, by contrast, the pre-existing conceptions of politics, however different they may be from those in the West, are compatible both with the will to some kind and degree of democracy and with the reasonably effective discharge of the functions of the modern state, where members of the political class are secure enough to compete more openly with each other, and where growth is assured, the crisis will usually be short-lived. In these respects, the extremes are the states of sub-Saharan Africa and those of east Asia.

In Africa, the crisis can be total. Some sub-Saharan states, many of them small, and many, including Zaïre, affected by internal war, have reached the point at which the state itself has in most respects ceased effectively to function and the official economy is all but ruined. Others, like Zambia, which had been buffeted by structural adjustment and become increasingly frustrated by non-democratic rule, have returned in relief and desperation to a competitive politics. But there is as yet no evidence that this has improved the quality of government or the performance of those aspects of the economy over which the state retains control. Others again, like Ghana, have concentrated first on economic reform, and in Ghana's own case with what has become a noted success. In 1992, moreover, the Rawlings regime opened itself to elections and received 48 per cent of the vote, largely because the liberalization of agricultural marketing had improved the returns to farmers and those who depended on them in the countryside. It remains to be seen, however, whether once the World Bank has ceased to fund the economy, it will be able to attract the foreign direct investment it needs to sustain itself. Yet others, like Nigeria, which is not economically so disadvantaged as Zambia or Ghana or most of the other states in the continent, have repeatedly failed to establish any enduring, effective and accepted pattern of rule at all. The prospects in sub-Saharan Africa for all but a very small number of privileged states remain bleak.[22]

In east Asia, by contrast, except, for the moment, in China, what might have seemed a decade ago to be an impending political crisis has proved to be no more than a difficulty. All states in the region have been economically strong enough to be able to insulate themselves from the hazards of the international economy. Several do remain dependent on foreign direct investment, but all are receiving it in sufficient quantities. Several have also had to concede in their determination to protect their agriculture and their domestic markets for manufactures and services, but not fatally. Most have large foreign reserves. None, therefore, has been subject to the disciplines of the international financial institutions. All indeed have retained a considerable degree of fiscal latitude, and have been able to commit themselves to comparatively high levels of public expenditure. The main difficulty they have had to face has been political, and has arisen from their economic success.

This success has in most cases been achieved by governments which have taken care to protect themselves from loss of office and retained control over

---

[22] Sandbrook, *The Politics of Africa's Economic Recovery* is a useful recent review.

savings, credit and the direction of investment. These governments were in all cases helped by the Cold War, which allowed them, together (for those in the Western camp) with more direct assistance from Washington, to defend their exceptional powers on grounds of 'national security'. In their economic policies, which came to emphasize the production of manufactured exports for the West, they were helped also until the 1980s by expanding markets. Their success nonetheless threatened the politics which had nurtured it. Economic growth increased the number of skilled and semi-skilled workers and of white-collar employees also, in each case better educated than their parents' generation and over time, irritated by what they took to be the increasing anachronism of absolutist rule, the political distance at which the governments held them, and in many cases, by the overt financial corruption of many politicians. In South Korea in the mid 1980s, and in Taiwan, Singapore and Japan itself later in the decade, established ruling parties were threatened and had in each case to concede. In each of these cases, it is true, except (at the time of writing) Japan, they have successfully re-grouped, and appear to have forestalled an enduring loss of authority. Their price, however, has been reduced authority. For more prosperous states like these, however, this does not now matter. In all four countries, the economies were already becoming too complex to plan, and the larger enterprises, private or public, no longer needed extensive credits; the ministries of finance and industry and although the bureaucracies were able to retain the controls they wished to, the economic planning boards were beginning to relax their direction. The need to retain political authority remains more acute in those other countries, Indonesia for instance, Thailand and (now) Vietnam, in which levels of savings and investment and the growth they can bring are not yet so assured. It is perhaps most acute of all, given the fears of what could happen, economically and politically, if it were to be lost, in China. There is nevertheless no strong reason at present to suppose that there, those who describe themselves as the 'new authoritarians' and argue for a slow transition to a more open and competitive politics along Korean or Taiwanese lines, will not prove to be justified.

Nonetheless, a will to democracy, a disposition in the political class to compete, and some assurance of growth, although together useful to weather the kind of political crisis that can now face a Southern state, may not everywhere be sufficient. These conditions may co-exist with an inability actually to discharge the functions of the modern state. This is perhaps most evident in the southern part of Latin America, where in several countries the battle that began with industrialization in the 1930s and 1940s is still unresolved. A modernizing centre, anxious for financial stabilization to lower inflation and for fiscal reform to reduce the budget deficit; conservatives in the provinces on both left and right, dependent still on patronage and thus fiscal laxity and powerful in the national assembly; and a presidency inclined, to sustain its popularity, to make a more 'popular' appeal across the heads of both, can each refuse to concede and impede the purposes of the others. Brazil is a graphic instance. The constitution of 1988 requires the federal government in Brasilia to disperse three-quarters of its revenue to the states; even so, by 1992 the states owed the centre a total of $49 billion. The budget deficit for 1994 is expected, if there are no reductions in expenditure, to reach $22 billion. An estimated seven million of the 61 million eligible to pay income tax actually do so, causing a shortfall of $35 billion. Meanwhile, inflation was by 1993 running at more than 2,000 per cent. Successive finance ministers have attempted to redress the balance between the centre and the states and to address other aspects of the fiscal crisis. Without the support of Congress, however, and the presidency also, their capacity to do so is restricted.[23]

<h1 style="text-align:center">VI</h1>

It is by no means clear, therefore, that any state in the South, apart from some in east and now also south-east Asia, can reliably expect to be able to do what is expected of it. Even if the pre-existing conception of the purposes of state power and political practice is weaker than it was, and is not inimical to what is expected of a modern bourgeois liberal republic, the practical capacity of a Southern government to deliver what its government and others expect may continue to be weak. If it does, there will only be three options. One is to continue to hope that the weakness will not last. The second is to reduce expectations. The third is to reconsider the sovereignty of the state itself.

The first is at once the least drastic and for most states, the least sensible. All states in the South, except those which are net importers of food, are likely to derive some benefit from the agreement reached at the end of the Uruguay Round of GATT. There is nothing in this agreement, however, beyond a diffuse, unspecific and undated statement of intention at some point to use a new Multilateral Trade Organization to redress the disadvantages that poor exporters suffer, to offset the long-term decline in the terms of trade for primary commodities. If one adds to this the fact that on present indications, the flows of foreign direct investment from North to South will continue disproportionately to concentrate in east and south-east Asia and a few of the larger economies of Latin America (and perhaps also in a new South Africa), it seems clear that whatever degree of economic 'restructuring' the government of a poor country is able to effect, and however much assistance, even on concessionary terms, it is thereby able to extract from the multilateral institutions and bilateral donors, its future as a self-sufficient economy is not promising. Ghana in the 1980s, a model, it is claimed, of economic and now political restructuring, cannot be a recipe for Ghana itself or any other state in a similar predicament in the later 1990s and into the next century. Only those states fortunate enough to have an unusually valuable commodity to export, providing the price of that commodity remains reasonably high, and, if they can stimulate their domestic markets, those with the largest economies, like Brazil, India and China, can hope to sustain themselves by themselves.

It is for this reason that the multilateral institutions and many bilateral donors, informed in this as in other respects by the liberal turn in the North in the later 1970s and 1980s, have told Southern states that they have no choice but to reduce their expectations of what, as modern states, they can do. In one respect, as the IMF now argues, this seems unexceptionable. For many countries in the South, the end of the Cold War might appear to have reduced if not altogether removed the justification for high levels of spending on the armed forces. For others, however, there remains, realistically or not, the

---

[23] A clear general account of this difficulty, drawing on the example of Brazil, is A. Fishlow, 'The Latin American state', *Journal of Economic Perspectives*, 4 (1990), 61–74. One way out of the impasse is the kind of constitutional coup effected by Fujimori in Peru in 1992.

possibility of more local conflicts. And for these, it is by no means yet clear from the examples of the former Yugoslavia, Zaïre and several others, that the West, directly or through the United Nations, will be as willing to intervene as it was in the years between the invasion of South Korea by the North in 1950 and its first and not altogether fortunate forays into 'peace-making' and 'peace-keeping' since 1989. In other respects, however, the request to reduce public expenditure conflicts both with the presumption that has stood since at least the end of the Second World War that the modern state has a responsibility to extend rights of a 'social' as well as a civil and political kind to its citizens and with the more recent presumption, urged by other international institutions, official and non governmental, that it has a responsibility also to extend 'human rights' and the means with which to uphold them. It likewise conflicts with the argument that such expenditures, apart from whatever importance they may have of a moral kind, are an essential investment also in the future productivity of the presently deprived.[24] In response to such concern, and to the apparent increase in the proportions as well as the absolute number of the poor in every country in the South (except India and China) in the 1980s, the World Bank and some bilateral donors have relented and advocated the inclusion in programmes of 'structural adjustment' of compensating provisions for 'social adjustment' also. These, however, can only be temporary alleviations, and it remains the case that even in sub-Saharan Africa, where the Bank and others have remarked on the lack of state capacity, institutional and administrative as well as financial,[25] little effective help is yet being given to improve such capacities.

Even if such help were to be forthcoming, however, the capacities of Southern states would have to be sustained. The question of revenue is crucial. The measures suggested by many to sustain state incomes in the 1970s and even, by the more hopeful, into the 1980s, that Southern states must acquire preferential access to Northern markets, seek to exploit the comparative advantages of labour-intensive industries, try to negotiate more equitable arrangements with multi- and trans-national investors, and pursue what is sometimes described as 'collective self-reliance', co-operation amongst themselves in producer cartels, free trade zones and the sharing of 'appropriate' technologies could never have been sufficient to what was needed. 'Old protectionism' was already being countered in the North by a more sophisticated protectionism of a newer kind, and both have now been pushed back in the conclusion to the latest round of GATT. Southern states, moreover (Zimbabwe is just one recent example), have been moving to make agreements with foreign investors of a less rather than more equitable kind in order to be able to attract investment at all.[26]

It is for these reasons that Southern governments are coming increasingly to think of abandoning the old but never widely-realized intention of increasing

[24] Dasgupta, *An Inquiry into Well-Being and Destitution.*

[25] World Bank, *Sub-Saharan Africa: from Crisis to Sustainable Growth* (New York, Oxford University Press for the World Bank, 1989).

[26] For an intelligent defence of the older view of what the South needs to do, M. Todaro, *Economic Development in the Third World* (London, Longman, 1990); for the contrast between the old protectionism and the new, R. Gilpin, *The Political Economy of International Relations* (Princeton, Princeton University Press, 1987).

economic cooperation with each other and contemplating instead the possibility that has recently, for the first time, been realized in the North American Free Trade Agreement between Canada, the United States and Mexico. The OECD countries' interests in such agreements, at least in Europe and north America, and in the case of the United States, between north America and east Asia in the Asian Pacific Economic Council, are well known. The interests of poorer countries, by contrast, can initially present a puzzle. Mexico's reasons for joining NAFTA, however, are not difficult to see.[27] Against what is commonly expected from such a policy, years of 'old protection' have generated manufacturing and services (including medical care) that are internationally competitive. Mexico's access to other markets to the north will also be easier. There is an effectively unlimited supply of cheap labour from the countryside with which to attract investors. Even more important, at a period where in more and more kinds of manufacturing the comparative advantage of comparatively cheap labour is diminishing in relation to the importance of new technologies and managerial skills, is the fact that it was made clear to the Mexicans by the Japanese that if they did not enter NAFTA, thereby giving Japanese firms an access to the north American market which they might otherwise find difficult, future Japanese investment in Mexico would not be forthcoming. It is not surprising that Chile, excluded from APEC, is keen to join the agreement, and that Colombia and Venezuela have also signalled an interest.[28] Mexico, however, like South Korea before it and China, Thailand, Vietnam and other countries in south-east Asia now, is in the fortunate position of being next to a powerful and complementary economy from which, it believes, it can benefit, and whose government has an unusually strong interest in maintaining good relations with it. Outside the Americas and east and south-east Asia, only the north African countries, which have negotiated some special arrangements with the European Community, and India, in its previous alliance with the Soviet Union, have been in a comparable position. In sub-Saharan Africa, the possibility perhaps only exists for those previously so-called 'front-line' states which are close to South Africa and could stand to benefit (as Malawi and Zimbabwe have been doing for some time) from an association with its more advanced economy; although there, the stronger economy itself has abundant cheap labour.

In all such arrangements, however, and especially for the weaker members, there is a loss of sovereignty: a loss of sovereignty, as analyses of the relations between Mexico and the United States over the three years of negotiations to NAFTA suggest, in both foreign and economic policy. The politics of western Europe in the past few years make it clear that this is no easy matter politically to manage in the more prosperous societies. In these, however, there has usually been more for governments and citizens to lose. There is the memory of a period when domestic control of the economy was much more extensive than

---

[27] V. Bulmer-Thomas, N. Craske and M. Serrano, 'Who will benefit?'. The European Community has of course attempted economic integration; the NAFTA, by contrast, is as yet only a free trade area.

[28] The request of other Latin American countries to join the agreement, however, may be resisted by the United States. The political reasons for consolidating what had become an increasing interdependence between the economies of Mexico and the United States will not necessarily override the objections to extending benefits to others, of less political importance to Washington, from domestic interests in the United States.

it can be now, whether or not one is a member of any kind of economic association, and the memory also of relatively full employment and high rates of public expenditure; the price to be paid for external disciplines, therefore, in employment, for instance, or in prices, or in real or perceived loss of well-being, may politically be higher than in those countries in which expectations have been lower and the facts of dependence more familiar. In many of the latter, in Africa and Asia, there is the memory only of the exhilaration of independence from colonial rule. But this has less and less force for fewer and fewer people over time, and even where there have more recently been strong sentiments of what might be described as a post-colonial kind, as in the arguments against 'dependence' in Latin America in the 1960s and 1970s, these can evaporate in the face of a fiscal impasse and low investment.[29]

VII

A modern nation-state that is not in serious difficulty, let alone in crisis, is one in which the strength of the economy enables it largely to determine its own policy on investment (or to be content with the investment that is uncontrolled), in which there are no insuperable problems of a fiscal kind, in which political competition is sufficient to insure against the excesses of unchallengable rule but not so severe as to raise fundamental questions about the direction of policy and disrupt good government, and in which successive governments can therefore meet what have since the 1940s been taken to be the central responsibilities of the modern state. By this standard, there are few states in the world, in the South or the North, which are not in difficulty. The most striking exceptions are in east Asia. The ones that are in crisis, however, beyond eastern Europe and Russia, are all in the South, even if it is the case that not all states in the South are in crisis. They have inherited the expectations for modern states, and found themselves increasingly unable to meet them. For all but a few in south-east Asia and parts of Latin America, moreover, there is no reasonable likelihood of their being able to do so in any foreseeable future. Economically, they are fated to follow the course indicated in the eighteenth century by Hume rather than Smith (and after Smith, by Marx): that's to say to do what they can by trading in commodities rather than manufactured goods.[30] Where the possibility presents itself, their most rational hope is to enter an alliance with a stronger economy. In this way they can protect themselves against the worst of the increasing international competition for trade and investment, and once they have overcome the more immediate political consequences, in making an economic alliance, of dislocation and adjustment, insure themselves against the turbulence that comes from declining advantage and increasing despair. It may even, as some of those at the head of the PRI in Mexico, for instance, now hope, be possible in time to reach the bourgeois liberal republic.

Yet the political economy of the modern South makes it clear, clearer than

---

[29] Mexico is in this respect in between: there is memory there of greater domestic control and of some greater discretion also over foreign policy, but economic pressures now are strong.

[30] I. Hont, 'The "rich-country poor-country" debate in Scottish classical political economy', in I. Hont and M. Ignatieff (eds), *Wealth and Virtue: the Shaping of Political Economy in the Scottish Enlightenment* (Cambridge, Cambridge University Press, 1983), pp. 271–315.

it yet is in the North, that modern statehood, like 'the Rest' in general in relation to 'the West', is an increasingly residual category: where it is still possible, it may be increasingly less necessary, and where it is necessary, it is so only by default, and increasingly less possible. Where governments can meet the practical responsibilities of the modern state, they will be able to do so in conditions in which governing a separate state will matter less, and conversely. The political economy of the modern South thus raises with some sharpness the question of whether, as the responsibilities of the modern state which turn on governments having some degree of macroeconomic control are increasingly removed from these governments, there remain any more distinctly *political* purposes in statehood beyond the satisfactions of political community (including representation in that community) as ends in themselves, and if there do, how these purposes might be sustained.

A Crisis of Ecological Viability? Global Environmental Change and the Nation State

Andrew Hurrell

The increased seriousness of many environmental problems provides one of the most intuitively plausible reasons for believing that the nation state and the system of states may be either in crisis or heading towards a crisis. Running through much writing on the subject is the sense – sometimes explicit, more often implicit – that the state and the fragmented system of sovereign states are less and less able to guarantee the effective and equitable management of an interdependent world in general, and of the global environment in particular.[1] Environmental issues (and especially second generation 'global' issues) present states and the state system with new challenges of unprecedented complexity. The state is seen to be both too big and too small for dealing with these challenges: too big for the task of devising viable strategies of sustainable development which can only be developed from the bottom up; and too small for the effective management of global problems such as combating global climate change or protecting biodiversity which by their nature demand increasingly wide-ranging forms of international cooperation.

In relation to the environment there are three principal arguments that the nation-state as a political form is either already in crisis, or else heading towards a crisis. The first concerns the state system as a whole. From this perspective, the system of nation-states may be said to be in crisis or to be dysfunctional because it can no longer provide a viable political framework for the collective management of the global environment. Although there is little agreement on alternative paths, there appears to many to be a basic contradiction between a single integrated, enormously complex, and deeply interdependent ecosystem and our still dominant form of global political organization: a fragmented system of sovereign states, normatively built around mutual recognition of sovereignty, and politically forming an anarchical system in which cooperation has been historically limited and in which war and conflict have been a deeply rooted, and for many, an inherent feature. As the Brundtland Report put it: 'Our Earth is one, our world is not'. Or, as Lynton Caldwell has suggested more recently: 'By this time, experience should have taught us that a complex

---

[1] See, for example, Joseph A. Camillieri and Jim Falk who argue that '...First, the principle of sovereignty is an impediment to action designed to ameliorate critical ecological dilemmas. Second, it is itself a major contributing cause of the environmental problems which confront humanity', *The End of Sovereignty? The Politics of a Shrinking and Fragmenting World* (London, Edward Elgar, 1992), p. 179.

planetary biosphere cannot be addressed effectively for protection or for rational management by a fragmented and uncoordinated political order'.[2]

A second argument is that an increasing number of individual nation-states are no longer able to provide localized order and an adequate degree of environmental management within their own borders. The weakness of many states and state structures is all too evident. What is harder to discern is the degree and significance of this weakness. As we shall see, for some the environmental failings of many weak states are merely suggestive of a crisis of particular policies, or, at worst, a crisis of particular political or economic institutions. But for others they suggest something altogether more generalized and far reaching. Ronnie Lipschutz and Ken Conca, for example, believe that we are witnessing 'the emergence of a fundamental new social dynamic, with which governments, their critics, and their observers may be poorly equipped to deal'. Global ecological interdependence is leading both to 'tighter systemic binding among actors in the prevailing international system, and the simultaneous decay and fragmentation of the traditional authority structures of world politics'.[3] Of these authority structures the position of the state is particularly shaky and they speak of 'the fundamental incapacity of governments to control the destructive processes involved'.[4]

The third argument moves beyond the state's practical capacity to deal effectively with new challenges. On this view environmental problems may be contributing towards a crisis of the nation-state by eroding the normative appeal of the state and the idea of the nation state as the primary, if not exclusive, focus for human loyalties. In part this loss of legitimacy derives from the domestic environmental shortcomings of many states. But in part it results from the extent to which increased awareness of global environmental problems and of the deep and unavoidable reality of environmental interdependence have created a new sense of planetary consciousness which is leading to new forms of non-territorially based political identity. Moreover this sense of planetary consciousness is increasingly embodied concretely in the mobilization of new social actors around environmental issues. Undoubtedly tied to other processes of globalization, the consolidation of what is loosely termed the global environmental movement is seen as one of the most significant and substantial pillars of an emerging transnational civil society. On this view we are therefore witnessing the emergence of new forms of non-territorially based political identity and new mechanisms of political organization and action that go beyond the nation state and which challenge the hegemony of statist world politics.

These challenges to the nation-state do not of course stand alone, but are symptomatic of a broader reading of contemporary world politics. First, there is the extent to which the state is caught between two contradictory processes: fusion, globalization, and integration on the one hand; and fragmentation,

[2] Lynton Keith Caldwell, *Between Two Worlds. Science, the Environmental Movement and Policy Choice* (Cambridge, Cambridge University Press, 1992), p. 151.

[3] Ken Conca and Ronnie D. Lipschutz, 'A tale of two forests' in K. Conca and R. D. Lipschutz (eds), *The State and Social Power in Global Environmental Politics* (New York, Columbia University Press, 1993), p. 9.

[4] Lipschutz and Conca, 'The implications of global ecological interdependence', in Lipschutz and Conca, *The State and Social Power*, p. 332.

fission and disintegration on the other. Second, there is the extent to which processes of globalization (economic, technological, environmental, cultural) force us to reopen questions about both the nature and limits of state sovereignty and the solidity of established identities. And third, there is the pervasive sense that the pace and scope of change have undermined the established spatial and temporal categories around which global politics has been traditionally conceived and analysed.

The notion of 'crisis' is particularly problematic when used in relation to the environment. There are, to be sure, many examples of environmental crises that are immediate and very visible, and that have already led to sudden death or widespread catastrophe (for example, the environmental factors centrally implicated in the series of large scale African famines). But many, perhaps most, environmental problems are long-term and their effects and (especially) interactions uncertain. Here 'normality', continuing to adopt the profligate resource use and lifestyles typical of modern industrial societies and continuing to promote traditional notions of economic growth in the developing world, is fundamental to the idea of the environmental crisis. Normality, in the sense of allowing existing trends to continue, is likely to consign the majority of the world's population to a bleak future of grinding poverty and worsening environmental degradation and, in the long run, may well render the planet uninhabitable. Moreover, if humanity waits until forced to change by an acute and immediate crisis, then the available range of options is likely to be drastically reduced. In these senses, then, normality itself comes to form a central element of the 'crisis'. To quote Norman Myers:

> Were environmental problems to strike us like a heart attack, we would rush our ecosystems into intensive-care units and have them restored. Instead they are like a cancer, quietly undercutting our foundations, unseen and unresisted until they eventually burst forth with deep damage all too evident. Or to shift the metaphor, they are like the frog in the experiment. If you drop a frog into a saucepan of boiling water, it will respond to its acutely and suddenly hostile environment by hopping out. If then you put the same frog into a saucepan of cold water and set the pan on the stove, the frog will enjoy its benign environment for a while. It will even think its environment becomes more benign as the water warms up. It will swim around placidly, oblivious to the threat of the rising temperature. As the water gets hot, it will start to feel drowsy. Finally it will succumb to the heat and go into a coma before boiling to death. For us, it is the world outside the window that is steadily heating up.[5]

To what extent do nation states (embodying a set of institutions exercising final authority over a given territory, claiming independence from any external authority, and forming the focus for a territorially defined national identity) and the state system (characterized by interaction between a plurality of sovereign states and by limited forms of institutionalized cooperation) prevent us from understanding what may be happening outside the window and from devising an alternative future to that of the boiled frog? These are large questions that are, at least in part, speculative in nature. This article seeks to

---

[5] Norman Myers, *Ultimate Security. The Environmental Basis of Political Security* (New York, Norton, 1993), pp. 28–9.

specify the three principal arguments of those who believe the nation state to be in crisis and to unravel some of the complexities of the issues involved.

1. The Incapacity of the State System

Although only one aspect of global environmental management, the problem of securing a sufficient degree of inter-state cooperation remains fundamental. Indeed it is clear that the increased seriousness of environmental degradation and the emergence of a new category of global environmental problems demand a qualitatively different kind of inter-state order. Managing global environmental issues involves a dramatic change in the character and goals of international society: away from minimalist goals of coexistence and towards the creation of rules and institutions that embody notions of shared responsibilities, that impinge heavily on the domestic organization of states, that invest individuals and groups within states with rights and duties, and that seek to embody some notion of the planetary good. This switch can be characterized in different ways: in terms of Terry Nardin's distinction between a practical association on the one hand and a purposive association on the other; or Hedley Bull's distinction between pluralist and solidarist conceptions of international society; or the distinction drawn by international lawyers such as Richard Falk or Antonio Cassese between a Westphalian model of international law and a UN Charter model.[6]

Cries of despair should not, however, be taken at face value. Indeed it is perfectly possible to provide an optimistic reading of the evolution of global environmental governance. On this view international society has begun to tackle emerging environmental problems, albeit fitfully and perhaps belatedly, by building on the common interests, common rules and common institutions of international society.[7]

In the first place, optimists can point to the emergence of an increasingly complex structure of global environmental governance and to the increased attention given by policymakers and politicians to international environmental issues. Indeed the UNCED process has helped to crystallize an enormously important change in both popular and political attitudes towards the environment. However varied the level of concern, it is now very difficult to imagine environmental concerns disappearing completely from the agendas of governments. Not only has there been a mushrooming of environmental regimes but the time taken from recognition of a problem to international action has decreased (compare, for example, the Law of Sea negotiations with the emergence of the ozone regime and both with the signature at UNCED of the framework conventions on biodiversity and climate change).

---

[6] Terry Nardin, *Law, Morality and the Relations between States* (Princeton, Princeton University Press, 1983); Hedley Bull, *The Anarchical Society* (London, Macmillan, 1977); and Antonio Cassese, *International Law in a Divided World* (Oxford, Oxford University Press, 1986).

[7] Amongst the large literature on international environmental cooperation see Peter M. Haas, Robert O. Keohane and Mark Levy (eds), *Institutions for the Earth* (Cambridge, Massachussetts Institute of Technology, 1993); Andrew Hurrell and Benedict Kingsbury (eds), *The International Politics of the Environment* (Oxford, Oxford University Press, 1992); Patricia Birnie and Alan Boyle, *International Environmental Law* (Oxford, Oxford University Press, 1993); and Oran Young, *International Regimes for Natural Resources and the Environment* (Ithaca, Cornell University Press, 1989).

Second, we have seen the emergence of a wide variety of new international legal concepts with which to deal with environmental problems. Legal duties to prevent environmental harm, liability for environmental harm, duties to inform and to consult, duty to undertake environmental assessments have all become firmly established. Moreover quite radical principles have appeared on the international scene, albeit usually in a 'softer' form: for example, the precautionary principle, the principle of intergenerational equity; ideas of common heritage, of shared resources, and of common concern; and the recognition by the industrial countries of a duty to help secure sustainability in the developing world through the transfer of funds and technology. Such a normative shift is undoubtedly important and needs to be seen as part of a broader shift in international legal understandings of sovereignty: away from an emphasis on the rights of states and towards a far greater stress on both duties and common interests. Such developments also bring home the extent to which sovereignty needs to be understood not as a single discrete claim based solely on state power, but rather as a historically constituted 'bundle of competences' whose exact definition depends on the changing constitution of the international legal order as a whole.

Third, optimists stress the extent to which environmental regimes need to be understood and evaluated as part of an ongoing process of management and negotiation. For the optimists it is wrong to lay excessive stress on the loopholes of a particular agreement. Rather, the effectiveness of environmental regimes derives from the extent to which states are tied into a continuing and institutionalized process: hence the importance of provisions for regular meetings and for the generation and publication of information; hence the view of regimes as frameworks around which political pressure on states can be mobilized. This sense of an ongoing process of cooperation is central to optimistic assessments of UNCED which highlight the extent to which the framework conventions create institutions for follow-up and further negotiation and which make much of the creation of new institutions such as the Commission for Sustainable Development.[8]

Fourth, optimists can also claim with some plausibility that conflict over sovereignty has eased. Attitudes to sovereignty, particularly in the developing world, have shifted very substantially since the Stockholm Conference in 1972. Developing countries such as India or Brazil have moved away from the rigid dichotomy between environment and development visible at Stockholm. They have come to lay greater weight on the importance of protecting the environment and on moving towards more sustainable patterns of economic development. There is, then, increasing consensus on the ways in which environmental protection can reinforce economic development. There is also increased awareness of the threats posed to the South by unchecked environmental degradation. Indeed the persistent poverty in many parts of the developing world means that the South is less able to afford to put right reversible damage to the environment and also less able to manage the process of adaptation to whatever global environmental changes do occur. In addition, the South has come to accept that environmental degradation within states is a matter of legitimate interest to the outside world, being both a matter of 'international concern' (suggesting that it

---

[8] For details of the agreements reached at Rio see Michael Grubb *et al.*, *The Earth Summit Agreements: a Guide and Assessment* (London, RIIA/Earthscan, 1993).

is legitimate for other states to become involved), and, increasingly, of the 'common concern to humankind'. Recent declarations have also acknowledged the rights of NGOs both to involve themselves within the 'domestic' environmental affairs of developing countries and to participate in global negotiations.

Fifth, a great deal of the optimistic case depends on confidence in scientific knowledge: both to generate solutions to environmental problems, but also to promote and facilitate international cooperation. Indeed one dominant theme of the literature has been the extent to which increasing levels of scientific knowledge can work to redirect state interests, to facilitate international cooperation, and to promote 'environmental learning'. Within this context much attention has been given to the role of transnational 'epistemic communities' of scientists and experts.[9] This is, of course, related to the greatly increased role that non-governmental groups (NGOs) have come to play in global environmental politics: in shifting public and political attitudes towards the environment and placing environmental issues high on the political agendas of an increasing number of states; in publicizing the nature and seriousness of environmental problems; in acting as a conduit for the dissemination of scientific research; in organizing and orchestrating pressure on states, companies, and international organizations; and in providing one of the most important mechanisms for helping to ensure effective implementation of environmental agreements. Impatient as ever with states, liberals are inclined to see the emergence of this transnational civil society as an inherently positive development.

Out of these various arguments a broader case can be made, namely that the environmental challenge is working, not to undermine, but rather to reinforce the centrality of the state. Dominant patterns of managing global environmental change (such as the Brundtland Report) have emphasized the importance of strengthening inter-state cooperation and the institutional capabilities of states. The environment can be viewed as an example of how perceptions of crisis can lead to the reassertion and extension of state authority and how states are increasingly willing to trade a degree of legal freedom of action for a greater degree of practical influence over the policies of other states and over the management of common problems. Moreover, there is a close and important link between inter-state cooperation and domestic political power. Thus, for example, although the Biodiversity Convention recognizes the importance of indigenous peoples for the protection of forest resources, it also gives international blessing to the authority of the state over such peoples.

Thus for modern liberals, the seriousness of environmental problems and the inescapability of ecological interdependence will increasingly force states to cooperate. James Rosenau, for example, talks of environmental issues 'impelling national and sub-national governments towards ever greater transnational cooperation'.[10] The language of environmentalism is full of talk of 'necessities' and 'imperatives' and often rests on the idea that fear of impending catastrophe will inevitably help to bring forth reform.[11] But, whilst it is

[9] See Peter M. Haas (ed.), 'Knowledge, Power and International Policy Coordination', special issue of *International Organization* 28, 2, (1993).

[10] James Rosenau, 'Environmental challenges in a turbulent world', in Lipschutz and Conca, *The State and Social Power*, p. 77.

[11] For an assessment of arguments of 'salvation through necessity' see Ian Clark, *The Hierarchy of States. Reform and Resistance in the International Order* (Cambridge, Cambridge University Press, 1989), pp. 57–66.

impossible to arrive at a definitive judgement on the effectiveness of current structures of global environmental governance, there are unfortunately good grounds for scepticism, for questioning this optimistic picture, and for arguing that traditional patterns of inter-state conflict will be reproduced within the new domain of environmental politics.

In the first place, the weaknesses of many existing legal regimes are too great to be ignored. The numbers of agreements may well be large but sanctions for compliance are weak. There is a marked preference for non-binding targets/ guidelines which states are free to implement at whatever pace they see fit rather than the acceptance of firm and unambiguous obligations. Indeed the agreements negotiated at Rio on Global Climate Change and Biological Diversity are peppered with caveats, qualifications, and escape holes, and lacking in clear measurable commitments. Few existing environmental treaties contain inescapable requirements that states resort to binding third-party procedures for settlement of disputes. States remain extremely keen to maintain firm control over reporting, monitoring and inspection procedures. And although much is made of the increased openness of states to NGO participation, states continue to be extremely resistant to any significant dilution of control.

The negotiations around the Earth Summit therefore illustrate the continued plausibility of realist accounts of the obstacles to effective cooperation: the weakness of most international institutions and the absence of sanctioning power; the unprecedentedly high levels of cooperation and policy coordination required to deal with many of the most pressing environmental issues; the pressures on states and state representatives to place a high priority on their immediate short-term interests and on the protection of political autonomy; the mismatch between the time horizons of politicians and political processes on the one hand and the extended time frames needed to address and deal with many of the most serious environmental problems on the other; the fact that there is no easy link between increased scientific knowledge and the growth of international cooperation; the extent to which the loose rhetoric of 'interdependence' disguises a wide variety of problems whose specific dependence structures may sometimes work to promote cooperation (as in the case of ozone) but may also militate against cooperation (as in the case of global climate change); and finally, the extent to which these difficulties have to be set against the large number of deep-rooted historical conflicts that exist between states and by the cultural, political, and economic heterogeneity of the international system. Moreover it is depressing to note the reappearance in the follow-up negotiations to UNCED of the old clashes over the political control of environmental institutions, over the amount and management of transferred resources, and over the meaning of sustainability.

Second, the concern for sovereignty remains a fundamental factor in global environmental politics in both North and South and the political acceptance of the erosion of sovereignty is less apparent than legal declarations would tend to suggest. This is well illustrated by the impasse at the Earth Summit on those critical issues that threatened to bite deeply into the sovereign prerogatives of governments: the unspoken agreement not to tackle the divisive issue of population growth; the near absolute refusal of the North to accept that sustainability might require a change in its consumption patterns and resource use, especially its use of energy and fossil fuels; or the bitter resistance of developing states to the negotiation of a convention on the protection of forests.

Third, we have to note the inapplicability of traditional techniques (and especially legal techniques) for dealing with most serious environmental issues. These have mostly depended on treating discrete aspects of the environment, often of rather narrow notions of what constitutes environmental problems. International environmental regulation has traditionally relied on separating issues and negotiating particular agreements to deal with particular problems. Yet attempting to give meaning to sustainability at the international level is necessarily about managing the environmental implications of a diverse and highly politicized sets of relationships (for example links between trade and environment, between debt and environment, between military spending and environment). Unsurprisingly international society has found this task to be a daunting one and the most notable step in this direction (the negotiation at Rio of the 400 page Agenda 21) was marked by omissions, by lack of overall coherence, and by a reluctance to prioritize and to specify any too clear link between impressive aspirations and effective action.[12]

This leads to a final problem, which is by far the most serious, namely the capacity of the major states to coordinate the global economy in the interests of ecological rationality. Even those inclined to emphasize markets and market mechanisms as the most effective instruments for environmental policy recognize the importance of continued inter-state cooperation. On a fundamental level global capitalism has long depended on the political structures of the state system (not least for guaranteeing a stable pattern of property rights).[13] Greater economic integration increases both the need for and the complexity of international environmental regulation (for example, in providing stable management of the links between the rules of the trading regime and national environmental policies). Moreover, these challenges will be greatly increased if the dominant reformist liberalism that characterizes so much international thinking on the environment proves to be overoptimistic. On the 'official version' (exemplified by the Brundtland Report or the 1992 World Development Report), a revitalization of global growth (albeit of a more sustainable character) is an essential part of averting future environmental catastrophe and of securing some form of 'global bargain' between the industrialized and developing world. But for those who see a deep contradiction between this continued emphasis on growth and the finite nature of the earth's ecosystem, the distributional conflicts are likely to be far more intense and politically significant than the comforting rhetoric of 'Brundtlandism' and 'sustainable development' would suggest. If the scale of human activity relative to the biosphere is becoming simply too large, then unregulated markets, however efficient they may be in increasing wealth, are unlikely to provide an adequate solution, and the zero-sum character of international politics is likely to be intensified not diminished.

---

[12] The texts of the UNCED agreements and declarations can be found in Stanley P. Johnson (ed.), *The Earth Summit* (Dordrecht, Graham and Trotman/Martinus Nijhoff, 1993).

[13] As Krasner and Thomson note: '. . . the commonplace notion that there is an inherent conflict between sovereignty and economic transactions is fundamentally misplaced. The consolidation of sovereignty – that is, the establishment of a set of institutions exercising final authority over a defined territory – was a necessary condition for more international transactions'. Janice E. Thomson and Stephen B. Krasner, 'Global transactions and the consolidation of sovereignty', in Ernst-Otto Czempiel and James N. Rosenau (eds), *Global Changes and Theoretical Challenges* (Lexington, Lexington Books, 1989), p. 198.

As with domestic policy, the problem is not with what markets and market mechanisms *might* be able to do to secure long-term sustainable development, but rather with the weakness of the political institutions that would enable these prescriptions to be applied in practice. The central difficulty is that states may no longer possess the power to manage the international order because of the extent to which 'power' has been diffused away from states and towards both markets and the players that dominate those markets. Thus, if it is indeed the case that power in the global economy is exercised increasingly by nonstate actors and, in particular, by transnational companies, then the utility of a predominantly state-centred approach to international order is also likely to be limited. Many of the most important environmental policy 'decisions' are not taken by states, but emerge out of the production, technological and trading strategies of a relatively small number of powerful transnational companies. Equally, both the generation of many 'local' environmental problems and the capacity of states to deal with those problems is heavily influenced by the pressures and constraints of an increasingly globalized world economy – for example, linkages between structural adjustment policies and environmental degradation, or more broadly, the transmission via the market of western lifestyles, of a particular vision of modernity and progress, or of particular kinds of environmental knowledge.

If this is in fact the case, what is to be done? Many environmentalists would suggest that the choice is a stark one: either to 'bring the world economy under control' and to move to more centralized political coordination, or to try and reverse the powerful contemporary pressures towards integration and globalization, to decentralize economic and political power, and to build a sustainable future around grassroots democratic participation and locally generated economic transformation. For most environmentalists decentralization is the preferred route and the attenuation of sovereignty as part of a project of radical decentralization forms a common plank of much of the environmentalist agenda.[14] Others, such as Susan Strange, would argue that the world economy is already effectively out of control and that state control cannot be reasserted in the traditional manner.[15] If true, and given the incapacity of the global economy to develop a politically and ecologically sustainable order of its own, then the project of international society is indeed lost and we are faced with a pessimism as profound as that of the gloomiest realist.

2. The Erosion of State Capacity

But even if it were possible to imagine a world in which the process of international environmental regime creation proceeded easily and unproblematically and in which the many barriers to inter-state cooperation had been overcome, dealing with many environmental challenges would still depend on

[14] This case is made at length in Herman E. Daly and John B. Cobb, *For the Common Good* (London, Green Print, 1990). The alternative of global centralism is out of fashion. For an exception see William Ophuls Jr who argues that '[T] the need for a world government with enough coercive powers over fractious nation states to achieve what reasonable people would regard as the planetary common interest has become overwhelming.' In *Ecology and the Politics of Scarcity Revisited* (New York, Freeman, 1992), p. 278.

[15] On the shift of power from states to markets see Susan Strange, *States and Markets* (London, Pinter, 1988).

the effective capabilities of the states that make up that broader order. In an important sense the emergence of transnational environmental issues poses a severe challenge to all states precisely because solutions cannot be found solely within their own jurisdiction. Moreover, for many commentators, the expansion of economic and societal interdependence has served to empower citizens and citizen movements, to promote challenges to existing authority, and to complicate the task of governance in all parts of the world.[16]

Beyond these general trends, it is clear that many of the most serious obstacles to sustainability have to do with the domestic weaknesses of particular states and state structures. In some cases these weaknesses stem from the limits of economic development: the fragility, inefficiency and corruption of government bureaucracies; the absence of appropriate human, financial and technological resources; the prevalence of deep-rooted economic problems; and the increasing susceptibility to international economic forces and the policies of transnational companies. But in many cases the problems are directly political: the opposition of powerful political interests that benefit from unsustainable forms of development and the difficulties of the state in regulating both itself and the many areas of economic life in which it is directly involved.

The old dichotomy between domestic order and international anarchy has therefore been recast in many parts of the world. As international lawyers never tire of pointing out, there is a great deal more 'law and order' internationally than there is on the streets of an increasing number of states, unable to secure even the most minimal conditions of social order. Indeed it is becoming a truism of the post Cold War world that the problem is not the lack of legitimacy between states, but the still greater lack of legitimacy within them.[17] In many parts of the world environmental problems such as extensive urban degradation, deforestation, desertification, water or fuel wood scarcity are helping to undermine the economic base and social fabric of many weak states. Such problems do not stand alone but interact with political instability, economic mismanagement and civil war to produce a deadly downward spiral leading towards disintegration and anarchy. Thus even if few major conflicts can be seen as exclusively 'ecological', environmental factors have come to play an important role in an increasing number of social conflicts.[18]

The net result is to debase further the currency of statehood and to move towards a situation in which the empirical claims to statehood of many

[16] This argument is developed, for example, by James Rosenau who believes that the institutions of world politics are undergoing a profound transformation and sees a general tendency in the international system towards authority crises, 'subgroupism', and the expanded competence of citizens. See his *Turbulence in World Politics: a Theory of Change and Continuity* (Princeton, Princeton University Press, 1990). It is also one of the principal conclusions of Eugene Skolnikoff's recent study of the impact of technological change: 'These technologies tend to support conditions that lead to pluralistic and democratic forms of government, and correspondingly tend to undermine authoritarian political structures.' Eugene B. Skolnikoff, *The Elusive Transformation. Science, Technology and the Evolution of International Politics* (Princeton, Princeton University Press, 1993), p. 226.

[17] Defenders of statist perspectives in International Relations have traditionally noted the weakness of many individual states but took it as a basic assumption that most (or at least a sufficient number of) states were capable of providing the conditions for local order. See, for example, Hedley Bull, 'The state's positive role in world affairs', *Daedalus*, October (1979).

[18] For a recent and wide ranging survey of environmental conflicts see Myers, *Ultimate Security*.

'quasi-states' are being gutted of any real meaning.[19] The problem of states that are states only in name is not of course a new one: it has been central to the analysis of post-colonial politics. But the ecological fragility of many states has added a powerful new twist to an old problem. It is also important to stress that the issue of environmental management and the very complex problems to which it gives rise have forced a reassessment of commonly used distinctions between 'strong' and 'weak' states. Clearly the problem of environmental degradation is acute in many of the weakest states, such as Haiti, El Salvador or many parts of Africa. But the story of the Brazilian Amazon provides a parable of how a quintessentially 'strong' state came to grief: an extensive state-led development programme built around a powerful ideology of national integration and national development; the attempt to achieve direct centralized control, displacing traditional local élites and replacing them with new bureau-cratic structures of control; the gradual erosion of the capacity of the state to control the powerful and contradictory forces that had been unleashed; the present situation in which the writ of the state has ceased to run in many, perhaps most, parts of Amazonia.[20] Moreover the Brazilian case does not stand alone, as shown by the role of environmental degradation and environmental protest in the collapse of communist regimes in the Soviet Union and Eastern Europe. And there are worrying signs that its shaky environmental foundations may yet force a dramatic reassessment of the much vaunted 'Chinese miracle'.

Despite the rhetorical emphasis placed on sustainable development, environ-mental policies in many developing countries suggest little more than the illusion of action and serious attempts to implement the measures discussed at UNCED and formalized in Agenda 21 have been at best patchy. The list of problems facing developing countries is long and depressing. An inadequate summary would include: the weakness of environmentalism and environmental parties domestically; the impact of economic adjustment on public spending and increased poverty; the degree to which incomplete understanding of the long-term costs of environmental damage leads to a reluctance to assume the short-term costs of environmental reforms; the extent to which the pressing nature of existing economic, political and social problems and high levels of institutional instability make any kind of long-term planning extremely difficult to draw up, let alone implement; the impact of the debt crisis and the ascendancy of neo-liberal economics on the capacities of the state and on perceptions of long term planning; the manifold weaknesses of environmental bureaucracies, lacking technical knowledge, political and bureaucratic clout, or financial resources; the critical problems of implementation and enforcement and the fact that the writ of the central government is often confined to limited areas of the country; the extent to which the currently fashionable ideas of democratization and decentralization may not only serve to 'empower' those seeking to improve the environment and the use of natural resources, but by the same token those (often entrenched regional élites) most directly opposed to the implementation of tighter controls over the use of such resources.[21]

---

[19] On this subject see Robert H. Jackson, *Quasi-states: Sovereignty, International Relations and the Third World* (Cambridge, Cambridge University Press, 1990).

[20] For an excellent account of the politics of Amazonian developments see Marianne Schmink and Charles H. Wood, *Contested Frontiers in Amazonia* (New York, Columbia University Press, 1992).

[21] On how to think about state 'strength' and the variability of state presence see Guillermo O'Donnell, 'On the state: democratization and some conceptual problems', *World Development* 21, (1993) 8.

Our Own Agenda, the Latin American follow-up to the Brundtland Report, provided a frank acknowledgement of the scale of the problems involved:

> Any action in the direction of sustainable development will be very difficult whilst any of these conditions prevail: authoritarianism and the incapacity to interpret signals by society; deficient representation; absence of full guarantees on the part of a legally constituted state and the failure to combat corruption; non-professional civil service; lack of formulation and monitoring of medium and long-term policies . . .[22]

Although the seriousness of these problems varies from one country to another, their existence is widely acknowledged. What is contested, however, is what they mean. There are two broad ways of looking at the domestic crisis of ecological viability. The first sees the problem essentially in technocratic terms: the policy levers are assumed to exist and the main difficulty consists of locating the optimum mix of market based and interventionist measures. The dominant orthodoxy leans heavily on the positive role of markets, although it assigns an important role to the state in correcting market failures, ensuring the proper valuation of environmental goods (for example biodiversity or forest resources), guaranteeing the distribution of property rights among individuals and groups, securing the enforcement of environmental legislation, correcting environmentally harmful fiscal policies, and providing macroeconomic stability.[23]

Yet in many technocratic analyses there is a fundamental ambiguity about the role of the state. On the one hand, the extent to which the state has proved to be an environmental villain is widely recognized, as are the political difficulties faced by the state in regulating both itself and the many areas of the economy in which it is involved. Indonesia's transmigration programme, Sri Lanka's Mahaweli scheme and Brazil's Polonoreste programme provide just three examples of large state-led development programmes that caused enormous environmental damage. On the other hand, the technocratic solution clearly depends on reforming the state and turning it into an environmentally more benign actor. This problem is made more acute because demands that the state 'manage' the environment come at a time when the central thrust of international pressure is to restrict the role of the state and to redefine the boundaries between the private and public sectors. How is the circle to be squared? On the technocratic view it is mostly a matter of 'institutional strengthening' and 'capacity building', together with a degree of empowerment/involvement, and a heavy dose of decentralization.

Yet it is precisely the growth of doubts about the viability of this technocratic strategy that has given rise to the alternative 'community approach' favoured by many NGOs. According to this approach, it is grassroots and peoples' organizations that need to play the predominant role in the transition towards a more sustainable society. This view has a strong anti-statist slant, arguing that the state is so implicated in the generation of environmental problems that it is unlikely to serve as the vehicle for their solution. Especially in the developing world, many doubt whether states possess the capacity to control the destructive

---

[22] Development and Economic Commission for Latin America and the Caribbean, *Our Own Agenda* (IDB/UNDP, 1991), pp. 196–7.

[23] See, for example, The World Bank, *World Development Report 1992: Development and the Environment* (Washington, World Bank, 1992).

processes involved or have access to the requisite effective policy levers, especially given the importance of many forms of environmentally destructive development for key state-society alliances.

This view, therefore, emphasizes the political obstacles that block environmental policy reform and points to the social and political conflicts that lie behind many environmental issues – conflicts over access to specific resources but also conflicts over the meaning of 'development', 'environment' and 'sustainability' and the ways in which understandings of these concepts are socially constructed. On more extreme readings, states and the state system are seen as central parts of the 'problem'. As the Indian environmentalist Anupam Mishra has put it: 'It would be folly to think that the Brundtland Commission can find solutions within the "counter-productive framework" of governments, the United Nations, the World Bank and so on. Because the present structures have given us the disease, is it then logical that they should also provide the cure?'[24]

The increased political importance of environmental pressure groups and NGOs has attracted a great deal of attention.[25] The pressure for expanding the role of NGOs has come primarily from the movements themselves, born of protest at the environmental failures of states and international institutions. But they have also come from states anxious to cut their losses, to reduce their role in conformity with the new international orthodoxy, and to divest themselves of difficult problems; and from international institutions anxious to find an alternative channel for aid and a way of deflecting environmentalist criticisms. Not only is an increasing percentage of official aid being channelled through NGOs, but, in several cases governments have wanted the text of international agreements to include the wording favoured by NGOs precisely in order to increase legitimacy.

The empowerment of both individuals and communities, combined with a strong emphasis on decentralized forms of political organization, has become a major theme of environmentalist writing. Decentralization and empowerment facilitate sustainability in various ways: first, by helping to create the political conditions that would make more effective public opposition to existing environmental dangers; second, by strengthening the balance of political forces in favour of greater social equity and justice; and third, because of the extent that local groups and communities possess special knowledge of what forms of development are sustainable and provide the social organizations within which that knowledge can be effectively implemented.[26]

[24] Quoted in Thijs de la Court, *Beyond Brundtland. Green Development in the* 1990s (London, Ned, 1990), p. 118.

[25] For a discussion of the growth of NGO activities in the environmental field see 'Policies and institutions. Non-governmental organizations: a growing force in the developing world', in World Resources Institute, *World Resources* 1992–93 (New York, Oxford University Press, 1992), ch. 14. On environmental movements in the developing world more generally see 'Environmental social movements in Latin America and Europe: challenging development and democracy', special issue of *International Journal of Sociology and Social Policy* 12, 4/5/6/7 (1992); Matthias Finger (ed.), 'The Green Movement Worldwide', *Research in Social Movements, Conflicts and Change*, suppl. 2 (1992); and John McCormick, *Reclaiming Paradise. The Global Environmental Movement* (London, Belhaven, 1989).

[26] For examples of arguments that stress the importance of environmental movements as vehicles for change and emancipation see Camillieri and Falk, *The End of Sovereignty?*, ch. 8; Paul Ekins, *A New World Order. Grassroots Movements for Global Change* (London, Routledge, 1992); John Clark, *Democratizing Development. The Role of Voluntary Organizations* (London, Earthscan, 1991); and Richard Falk, 'The global promise of social movements: explorations at the edge of time', *Alternatives* 12, 2 (1987).

These arguments are important and few would want to dispute the importance of NGOs in developing new forms of political action and social development. But there are also real limits to the role of NGOs. First, there are the difficulties of generalizing and implementing on a larger scale what may be effective and equitable grassroots projects (for example, the concept of extractive reserves in Amazonia). Much of the value of such projects lies in their small size, and they may not easily lend themselves to 'scaling up' to perform larger and more complex roles. Second, as Steve Sanderson has argued, focus on grassroots NGO activity cannot be a substitute for tackling the underlying causes of environmental destruction. 'In Latin America, the development assistance community has been much better at developing small-scale projects than it has been in addressing the more fundamental questions that make their creation necessary.'[27] Third, there is the difficult trade-off between the role of NGOs in articulating criticisms or raising environmental or political awareness on the one hand and the loss of legitimacy that can follow from their becoming too closely associated with the provision of services. As many NGOs are becoming aware, excessive expectations and moves to become the lowest rung on the state bureaucracy are likely to engender a rapid loss of legitimacy.

Finally, and most importantly, despite the rhetoric of new forms of authentic democratic action and political practice, NGOs cannot themselves fulfil the core functions of the state: including the goal of providing minimum public order or protecting property rights. NGOs can usefully supplement but only rarely supplant the state at the local level (still less the national or international), however tempting an alternative this may appear to be. If the state collapses it is all too likely that the warlords and the drug barons will move in instead.

On closer inspection many of the anti-statist arguments of the environmental movement turn out to be calls for reformed and more democratic states. Having denounced 'statism' as a cruel deception and, along with scientism and developmentalism, one of the main sources of our present predicament, Paul Ekins goes on to provide an impressively long list of the functions that states need to be pressed to fulfil:

> State power has a vital role to play in people's self-development. It must provide the basic institutions to encapsulate and frame the market so that the market mechanism may work to general advantage. It must guarantee continuing access for all people to the resources for production and development, both monetary and non-monetary in nature. And it must implement basic norms of social justice which narrow differentials in society by progressively enabling the disadvantaged to provide for their own needs from their own resources and participate fully in its mainstream life.[28]

This is hardly an exit from 'statism': more a call for grassroots pressure to reform and rehabilitate the state.

But does any of this really matter? There are, as there have, always been, many examples of weak states, but this might tell us nothing very interesting

[27] Steven Sanderson, 'Environmental protection in Latin America', in Sheldon Kamiemiecki (ed.), *Environmental Protection in the International Arena* (New York, State University of New York Press, 1993), p. 228.
[28] Elkins, *A New World Order*, p. 208.

about the effectiveness of the state as an organizing principle or about the state system *in toto*. The obvious weakness of many individual states might do nothing to jeopardize the viability of the nation-state as an institutional form.

But there are at least two reasons why the domestic failures of many weak states have far wider ramifications. In the first place, the traditional separation between the domestic and the international overlooks the extent to which domestic weakness is connected to international forces. There is no need to claim here, with crude dependency or world systems theory, that the external is all powerful and that all domestic environmental problems are the result of malign external pressures; only that both the problems themselves and the state's capacity to deal with them are the product of the interaction between domestic and global factors. Examples would include the complex links between structural adjustment and environmental degradation, or between particular sets of agricultural policies and deforestation/desertification.

Second, the capacity of the state system (and of the most powerful states that dominate that system) to deal with the most pressing environmental problems is clearly affected by the fragility of many states. Exactly in what ways, to what extent and with what consequences forms one of the most important issues in global environmental politics. These links are most visible when one considers the impact of domestic weakness on environmental issues that are global in the strong sense that they affect everyone and can only be effectively managed on the basis of cooperation between all, or at least a great majority, of the states of the world: controlling climate change and the emission of greenhouse gases, the protection of the ozone layer, safeguarding biodiversity, protecting special regions such as Antarctica or the Amazon, the management of the sea-bed, and the protection of the high seas. Developing countries are central to many of these problems. With the exception of Australia, for example, the top twelve 'megadiversity' states are all in the developing world: India, China, Indonesia, Malaysia, Brazil, Colombia, Ecuador, Peru, Mexico, Madagascar and Zaire. Equally, global climate change will be critically affected by the future decisions on energy use of major countries such as China, Brazil or India.

But it is not only a matter of these more obviously 'global' problems. The scale of many problems that have often been seen as 'local' has expanded enormously over the past fifty years. According to some estimates, for example, around 10% of the vegetation bearing surface of the earth is suffering from moderate to extreme degradation due to human activity since 1945 (an area larger than India and China combined).[29] Moreover, whilst many environmental issues (particularly questions of resource scarcity) appear manageable when viewed from a global perspective, it is clear that, once disaggregated, 'success' will depend on high levels of cooperation and significant levels of inter-state redistribution. Thus the numbers of individual countries likely to be affected by 'localized' environmental degradation and serious resource scarcity remains alarming. For example, although the 'world' may be able to feed itself, food production lagged behind population growth in 69 out of 102, developing countries between 1978 and 1989. The world's consumption of water more than doubled between 1945 and 1980 and is likely to double again in the next twenty years. Yet already 80 countries with two fifths of the world's population suffer

[29] Crispin Tickell, 'The Earth Summit: a year later', *RSA Journal*, December (1993), p. 41.

from serious water deficits.[30] Such examples underline the extent to which definitions of 'global' are politically constructed and hence politically contested.

It is wrong to believe, with the arch apostles of ecological globalism, that everything matters and matters equally. There are many examples of extreme environmental degradation and human misery that are unlikely to engage the political interests and humanitarian concerns of the core industrialized countries. But too mechanical an understanding of the linkages between North and South, too cynical a definition of interest, and too narrow an understanding of how and why the South 'matters', are equally misleading. For political as much as environmental reasons, it is difficult to believe in a stable international order that condemns a large part of humankind both to material deprivation and to high levels of powerlessness and vulnerability.

The ball is therefore quickly back in the court of international society. Two problems are evident: First, there are the political problems connected with the management of increasing international inequality. Environmental change provides a good example of how globalization works not to erode the power of all states, but rather to create new patterns of inequality and dominance. Environmental degradation works to increase inequality since some states are manifestly more able to adapt, both because of their superior wealth and, especially, technological capabilities, and because of their ability to help frame collective solutions that reflect their own preferences and interests.

Second, increasing pressure is placed on the core capitalist states to intervene and to try and 'do something' about the manifest environmental failings of those developing states which palpably affect their own interests. Part of the difficulty stems from the dubious legitimacy of external intervention. But still more arises from its questionable efficacy. There are by now enough cases of misguided and misdirected external involvement to place in doubt the capacity of the core states to find viable answers to environmental problems. (For example, the repeated environmental catastrophes of World Bank supported projects and the difficulties of securing effective implementation of apparently impressive environmental goals). It is therefore essential to consider just what we mean when we speak of the 'power' of the most powerful industrialized states. For if the 'power' of the core industrialized states is insufficient or irrelevant, then a crisis in the periphery will rapidly become a crisis for the centre.

3. The Erosion of Identity

Increased environmental awareness may have affected the normative appeal of the state in two ways. The first set of challenges undermines the normative appeal of the state from within: by questioning of the ability of large-scale centralized power structures to deal with environmental problems; by arguing for the need to root solutions and identities in local knowledge and local values; by filling the void left by a retreating state wherever the latter is no longer able to perform its traditional functions. There are several powerful and persuasive examples of ecological failures which have been catalysts of a dramatic and widespread loss of legitimacy. Not only was mobilization around environmen-

---

[30] Myers, *Ultimate Security*, p. 18.

tal issues central to political protest in the Soviet Union and Eastern Europe, but the scale of the region's environmental problems helped to expose the hollowness of official claims and formed a major obstacle to bureaucratic reform.[31] In many parts of Latin America environmentalism grew up as part of a broader protest against authoritarian rule and of what O'Donnell has termed 'the resurrection of civil society'.

The second set of challenges derives from the increasingly global character of many environmental issues and from the extent to which this global character has strengthened a cosmopolitan awareness or planetary consciousness. Perhaps the most important shift in the 20 years that separated the Stockholm Conference in 1972 from the Earth Summit in Rio de Janeiro in 1992 was the emergence of the paradigm of *global* environmental crisis. Dominant understandings of the most pressing environmental problems moved from the discussions of the 1970s about the impact of localized pollution and the limits to natural resources (The Club of Rome, 'limits to growth', OPEC etc.) to an increased emphasis on the notion of 'global environmental change' and on the limited capacity of the planet to absorb the wastes produced by economic activity: in shorthand, a shift from 'resource limits' to 'sink limits'. The emergence of global environmental problems and the greatly strengthened awareness of a global common interest amongst all peoples in protecting the environment and safeguarding the future of humanity have provided a powerful stimulus to the growth of a cosmopolitan moral consciousness. The notion of sharing a world, the essential inter-connectedness and interdependence of the global environment, and the scarcity of the resources available to humanity that need to be distributed both within and between generations all create conditions within which it becomes much harder than in the past to accept that community ends at the borders of states. For many people, then, global environmental interdependence has given greater plausibility to visions of a cosmopolitan global community.

The essential claim here is a very important one. The sceptic has traditionally denied the importance of the idea of a global community of humankind by claiming that it is no more than the figment of the imagination, that it has no empirical referent. Attempts (for example by Charles Beitz) to root the existence of such community in the workings of the global economy were never very convincing.[32] They drastically underplayed the difference between the *fact* of being part of a common system on the one hand and the *consciousness* of belonging to a single community on the other. To argue that a global community is coming into being solely as a result of technological change or economic integration is to succumb to technological or economic determinism.

Environmental interdependence, however, is arguably very different. First, because it is 'deeper' in the sense that no state or group of people can cut themselves off from the actions of others, unlike economic interdependence,

---

[31] See Ze'ev Wolfson and Vladimir Butenko, 'The Green Movement in the USSR and Eastern Europe', in Finger, 'The Green Movement Worldwide'; and Philip R. Pryde, *Environmental Management in the Soviet Union* (Cambridge, Cambridge University Press, 1991).

[32] Charles Beitz, *Political Theory and International Relations* (Princeton, Princeton University Press, 1979). For a good discussion of this question see Chris Brown, 'International political theory and the idea of world community' in Steve Smith and Ken Booth (eds), *International Political Theory Today* (Cambridge, Polity, forthcoming 1994).

which is, at least in principle, reversible and where patterns have oscillated over time. Second it is 'deeper' in the sense that interconnections are not simply 'external' relations. Global climate change, for example, is caused by core industrial activities and by the lifestyles of millions of citizens. In the third place, it is different because of the extent to which the global environmental movement now gives concrete political expression to the idea of a global community. Thus we have seen increased attention being given to the import-ance of environmental groups, not just because of their ability to influence state policies but also to create a transnational civil society and to define a new pattern of politics. This attention encompasses both the scientific community and transnational environmental pressure groups concerned with the inter-linked issues of sustainable development, the promotion of grassroots democ-racy, and the protection of indigenous peoples. The strength of such groups rests on their ability to articulate a powerful set of human values, to harness a growing sense of cosmopolitan moral awareness, and to respond to the multiple failures of the state system, both local and globally. The ability to act in this way is clearly assisted by other aspects of globalization in that increased levels of economic globalization provide the 'infrastructure' for increased social communication – the role of communications technologies in facilitating the flow of values, knowledge and ideas and in allowing like-minded groups to organize across national boundaries.

The emerging sense of planetary consciousness is undoubtedly important and adds further complexity to the constant and confusing swirl of contemporary claims to identity. But how far does all this indicate a serious and sustained crisis of legitimacy for the nation state?

How strong are these new loyalties? It is extremely hard to judge how far environmentalism and the global environmental movement are undermining the normative appeal of the idea of the nation state. There is a large body of work on Northern environmentalism, but far less on environmental movements in other parts of the world and less still on the specifically transnational elements of the global environmental movement. What we do know suggests that its impact has increased very significantly but remains uneven, that it varies from one issue to another and can fall as well as rise. Indeed it is interesting to note how many environmental pressure groups believe their influence on outcomes at UNCED to be quite modest.

Second, there is the question of the relative strength of the various 'new' identities that have emerged to challenge the legitimacy of existing states. There are surely powerful reasons to believe that ethnic or nationalist claims exercise far greater sway over the popular and political imagination of many peoples than the arguments of the environmental movement. Such 'disintegrationist' claims may well represent a deep challenge to the stability of the state system – by reopening the criteria for membership and undermining the pragmatic compromise underlying the post-war application of self-determi-nation (colonial self-determination combined with opposition to secession); and by undermining many of the traditional instruments of inter-state order (balance of power, spheres of influence, non-intervention etc.). But they do not challenge the centrality of the nation-state itself as the dominant political form. Indeed nationalist movements continue to be driven by the overriding goal of establishing their own state, however bloody may be the road towards that goal.

Third, much environmental thinking is characterized by an attractive combination of globalism, of solidarity, of 'one-worldism' on the one hand and of diversity, of parochialism, of the importance of small-scale community on the other. Indeed communitarian arguments that stress the importance of particular communities and emphasize pluralism and diversity take on a new dimension in the environmental field: The relationship to nature and the natural world is often a defining feature of a community's sense of itself. Environmentalism may well provide a more promising route towards the reconciliation of these conflicting identities than the ferociously divisive and deeply particularist claims of race, religion or ethnicity. But it will not be easy to achieve this reconciliation. No universal definition of sustainable development can be applied in a mechanistic fashion in all parts of the world. Environmental policies and priorities will inevitably and legitimately vary from one country (and one community) to another. This reflects the immense variation that exists in the physical world, in the nature and scope of environmental challenges, and in the different perspectives on environmental problems that come from different levels of economic development. Equally, sustainability unavoidably requires trade-offs between different priorities: between the maximum preservation of the natural environment and the pursuit of continuously high levels of economic development; between rapid economic growth and the protection of traditional cultures or improvements in equity and social justice; or between the importation of the latest technology and the safeguarding of traditional practices and cultures.

The UNCED process revealed the still very deep divisions (including within the NGO community) over the ways in which these trade-offs are managed. As Tickell notes, in many cases '[T]here is a clash of uncomprehending cultures within and between countries and peoples'.[33] For all the claims to novelty, it may well be, then, that the difference between economic interdependence and ecological interdependence is not so great. It is still very hard to move from participation in a common system, even one in which there are substantial common interests, towards a shared sense of community built around a consensus either on substantive values (what, for example, 'sustainability' might actually mean) or on the procedural mechanisms (whether, for example, greater 'global democracy' would be a help or a hindrance) by which the claims of conflicting sets of environmental values can be adjudicated between different communities, states, and cultures.

Conclusion

The increasing range and seriousness of environmental problems undoubtedly threatens to overwhelm the already frail capabilities of many states and to undermine the extent to which they can form the 'building blocks' of a broader world order. There is a serious tension between seeing the state as both deeply implicated in many forms of environmental degradation and as the vehicle for reform and redemption. Equally the need to reconcile the scope of human activity with the carrying capacity of the biosphere is likely to require historically unprecedented levels of inter-state cooperation. Although the

---

[33] Tickell, 'The Earth Summit', p. 41.

number and scope of international environmental agreements have indeed increased very rapidly, there is no guarantee that such cooperation will be forthcoming. The obstacles to such cooperation remain all too evident and the argument that 'necessity' will 'inevitably' bring forth such cooperation is a shallow one. States and the state system, then, remain indispensable but may well prove inadequate.

Of course global environmental order cannot be usefully understood, still less promoted, solely in terms of the actions and policies of states. On the one hand, there is the central role of the global economy; on the other, the rise of NGOs and of environmentalism. The global environmental movement has certainly become a significant political force. Transnational civil society has also become extremely important both in promoting grassroots community and development and in cultivating and extending a sense of the common world good. It would be absurd to pretend that global environmental politics can be reduced to a narrow statist perspective.

But the image of the Global Forum in Rio as a 'world community in waiting', although a seductive one, is deeply misleading. The state system may well be part of the problem but it is also an essential part of the solution. The lack of global solidarity about resources and environmental issues is not primarily rooted in the state system but in the inability of human beings to agree on the nature and seriousness of the environmental threats, on the meaning of sustainability, and on the principles of global environmental management. Unless the present international system breaks up in some dramatic and unexpected way, these tensions need to be managed on a global basis. Relations within 'a community of communities' (to take Herman Daly's picture of the future) would have to replicate or reinvent many of the institutions of international society. The political and moral tensions that have long been central to international society – above all between the respect for difference and pluralism on the one hand and the cultivation of an overlapping consensus on the nature of a common world good on the other – would not go away, but would merely reappear in a different form. There is no obvious reason for believing that an alternative to the state system would prove a better means of achieving this (already extremely difficult) end.

The Permanent Crisis of a Divided Mankind: 'Contemporary Crisis of the Nation State' in Historical Perspective

It is said that the people are sovereign; but over whom? – over themselves, apparently. The people are thus subject. There is surely something equivocal if not erroneous here, for the people which *command* are not the people which *obey*. It is enough, then, to put the general proposition, 'The people are sovereign', to feel that it needs an exegesis. . . . The people, it will be said, exercise their sovereignty by means of their representatives. This begins to make sense. The people are the sovereign which cannot exercise sovereignty. . . .
(Joseph De Maistre, *Study on Sovereignty*)

Someone was speaking to Sieyès of the scorn that his detractors continually affect for what they call 'grand theories'. 'Theories', he said, 'are the practice of centuries; all their practices are the theory of the passing moment!
(Pierre Louis Roederer)[1]

Is there a 'contemporary crisis of the nation-state'? The answer depends on what one takes a 'nation-state' to be (on how distinctly and clearly one can differentiate it from other forms of community) and on some

* I would like to express my gratitude for the intellectual help and encouragement of all those who in one way or another assisted me in writing this paper. Michael Sonenscher helped me to navigate the hazardous straits of the history of the French Revolution and John Dunn unfailingly encouraged my efforts and aided me in refining my text at every stage. Reinhart Koselleck has kindly discussed with me the first version of this paper in detail, Sylvana Tomaselli, Quentin Skinner, Richard Tuck, Gareth Stedman Jones, Aladár Madarász, Biancamaria Fontana, Hans-Erich Bödeker, Raymond Geuss, Keith Baker, Pasquale Pasquino, Fredric Smoler, David Feldman, Richard Whatmore, Bela Kapossy and Jaikumar Ramaswamy have made a number of very helpful suggestions. Needless to say, none of them are responsible for any errors or misconceptions that may exist in my argument. A first draft of this paper was written in the autumn of 1993, when I was a Fellow of the Collegium Budapest Institute for Advanced Study. I wish to record my gratitude to the Rector and members of the Collegium for their support and hospitality.

[1] Joseph De Maistre, *Study on Sovereignty* Bk. I. Ch. 1 'The sovereignty of the people', in Jack Lively (ed.), *The Works of Joseph de Maistre* (London, Allen and Unwin, 1965) p. 93. The *Study on Sovereignty* was written in Lausanne between 1793 and 98, where De Maistre was in exile after the French had overrun his native Savoy in 1792. Up to 1792 De Maistre was an enthusiastic supporter of the revolution. The text was first published in 1884. Roederer's remark is from 1795, cited in Murray Forsyth (ed.), *The Spirit of the Revolution of 1789 and Other Writings of the Revolutionary Epoch by Pierre Louis Roederer* (London, Scolar, 1989), p. 138.

understanding of what a 'crisis' might be. Given the condition of current academic opinion on the subject even answering the more modest question of 'what *is* the contemporary nation-state?' is quite an ambitious enterprise. Assessing the possibility of a 'crisis' of the 'nation-state' also requires the would-be respondent to pay attention to the temporal dimensions of the identity of the 'nation-state', its *future*. This sets the stakes very high, since in order to say anything about the future of the 'nation-state' one needs not only an analytical understanding of what this entity might be, but also of its past (of what it has actually been). Thus it is crucial to realize right from the outset that assessing the dynamics of the 'nation-state' in terms of a possible *crisis* compounds the difficulty significantly, because it poses the question within the framework of a highly specific model of temporality. This may or may not have been intentional, since it is a characteristic feature of the corruption of modern political language that the notion of 'crisis' is overused, generalized and trivialized. To avoid this trap, a meaningful answer concerning the predicament of the 'nation-state' and its prospective life chances must focus just as sharply on the proper meaning of 'crisis' as on the various theoretical possibilities packed into the conjunction of 'state' and 'nation' to form a single composite term. My attempt to provide a historical perspective for a meaningful discussion of the alleged 'contemporary crisis of the nation-state' thus starts with an outline of such a perspective in terms of the language of 'crisis' itself.

What 'Crisis'?

Crisis implies a moment of crucial decision in the face of acute difficulty or danger. Its meaning is most accessible as a medical metaphor depicting the decisive moment when a patient's fate was sealed. A crisis did not yet signify the 'agonia', or 'being in the throes of death', but the turning point where a road to recovery had to be opened if an irrecoverable descent into oblivion was to be avoided. Miraculous recovery might still remain on the cards and a long course of illness might still lie ahead, but the term carried strong connotations of finality. Although this medical image has a very long provenance, reaching back to Galen, equally stark meanings of crisis preceded it, and then ran parallel to it, in political, juridical and religious discourse. Crisis and judgment (*judicium*) became strongly linked, and the Biblical connection to apocalypse and final judgment endowed 'crisis' with rich eschatological undertones. Early modern usages of the notion of crisis preserved many of these theological and medical associations, but when the phrase came to prominence in the late Enlightenment, and particularly during and after the French revolution, its meaning as Reinhart Koselleck's seminal studies have shown, also underwent a substantial change.[2] From the early 19th century onwards it became a very frequently used category in general political discourse, in historiography and finally, and most conspicuously, in economics. The chief characteristic of 'modern' political language (according to Koselleck) has been a corrupting transformation in

[2] See Reinhart Koselleck, 'Krise', in Otto Brunner, Werner Conze and Reinhart Koselleck, *Geschichtliche Grundbegriffe: Historisches Lexikon zur politisch-sozialen Sprache in Deutschland* 7 vols. (Stuttgart, Klett-Cotta, 1975–93), vol. 3, pp. 617–50.

our 'political' sense of time (unfortunately there is no English equivalent for the more apt German term, *Zeitlichkeit*). Crisis, like so many concepts which previously had a widely accepted and relatively precise theological undergirding, became part of a modern and apparently secular historical eschatology, as the centrepiece of manifold explanations of historical and economic dynamics.[3] Crisis became twinned with the idea of revolution. Each revolution was justified as a solution to a crisis and then seen as the very source of the next crisis. The ultra-radical notion of a permanent revolution only mirrored its much more widely used counterpart: the frenzied (and at the same time melancholy) image of modernity as permanent crisis. Crisis theory has been a fertile ground for successive versions of both modern and anti-modern utopias and very recently has even induced some commentators to announce the 'end of history'.

Any serious investigation of the recurring hysteria over the viability of the 'nation state' should begin by questioning the political language of 'critique and crisis' itself. The problem is not simply in the vast inflation in the range of instances described as 'crises'. The overuse of the term can itself be read as a manifestation of modern (and post-modern) confusion in Western political identity. If the diagnosis of the 'contemporary crisis of the nation-state' stems from the kind of pathological *Krisenbewußtsein* described by Koselleck, then basing the prognosis on this kind of intellectual apparatus simply introduces a vicious circularity into the argument. As a first step, it is necessary to state that many 'crises' which occur in states which are not nation-states and many difficulties in the inner workings of 'nation-states' (the 'crises' of its various social, political or intellectual components) plainly cannot qualify as indicators of *the* crisis of the nation state, at least without very special arguments to support the claim.[4] The real question here is whether the 'nation-state' as a world historical form of political community is undergoing a crisis or not, i.e. whether one can or cannot speak of a *general crisis* of the 'nation-state'. Furthermore, taking one's cue from the underlying medical metaphor of crisis, it is important to focus on the possibility of there being a general crisis

[3] See Koselleck's essays in *Futures Past. On the Semantics of Historical Time*, trans. Keith Tribe (Cambridge, MA, MIT Press, 1985), particularly '*Historia Magistra Vitae*: The dissolution of the topos into the perspective of a modernized historical process', pp. 21–38; ' "*Neuzeit*": Remarks on the semantics of the modern concepts of movement', pp. 231–667; ' "Space of experience" and "horizon of expectation": two historical categories', pp. 267–88.

[4] See the classification of 'crises' occurring in modern governmental efforts of adapting to change in L. Binder, J.S. Coleman, J. Palombara, L.W. Pye, S. Verba and M. Weiner, *Crises and Sequences in Political Development* (Princeton, Princeton University Press, 1971), where the authors find crisis phenomena in virtually all aspects of the political process, and distinguish between 'problems', which are constantly solved by applying the rules of the institutions which deal with it, and 'crisis' as the occurrence of a 'problem' where 'the basic institutional patterns of the political system are challenged and routine response is inadequate'. 'Crisis' is accordingly 'a change that requires some governmental innovation and institutionalization if élites are not seriously to risk a loss of their position or if the society is to survive'. Innovation (renewal), is however, the standard response to crises and the conclusion seems to be that while problems (or problem areas) remain, crises 'may come and go'; see particularly Sidney Verba, 'Sequences and development', pp. 298–303. It is a somewhat similar experience of crisis which David Held points at when he claims that 'We live in a world which is increasingly punctuated by crises which daily affect the welfare and life-chances of countless millions of human beings'. ('A discipline of politics?' in his *Political Theory and the Modern State* (Cambridge, Polity, 1989), p. 244.

in the strictest and most extreme sense. We might consider, that is to say, the danger (or perhaps the glorious prospect) of a transformation in the shape of political communities so radical that 'nation states' become an endangered species. If this is a real prospect, it would be helpful to be told what *crucial therapy* (based on what judgment) should be deployed to avert such a crisis, and if none is likely to be available, how best to prepare for life after death.

It is essential to be able to specify the opposite of crisis: the condition of 'non-crisis', as it were. One might imagine that a crisis is consummated in either a positive or a negative outcome. One idiom of crisis has replaced the religious eschatological end-state of crisis with a secular utopia. According to this scenario the 'nation-state' dies, but something more positive and perfectly healthy takes its place. This healthy post-crisis outcome lay at the very core of the doctrine of socialism (or communism); but it is currently out of favour and it is unlikely ever to return in precisely the form in which it was venerated in its heyday. In another version a genuine crisis of the 'nation-state' may occur in a nuclear holocaust, a descent into a state of international anarchy, or perhaps even in some kind of new barbaric world-wide tyranny. But there is a third, and less stark, possible interpretation: a happy escape from death, which falls short of achieving a utopian return to real health. In such a scenario the patient stumbles from one relapse to the next, the 'crisis' always recurring, yet constantly changing in its precise nature and location. Such an idea, as Koselleck has suggested, has also been widespread in the modern era, serving as the vital source of the modern idea of *critique*, chiefly in the many varieties of the critique of civilization and, at its most pathological, in *Kulturpessimismus*. This is a non-revolutionary model of a permanent *crisis*, without the decisive outcome of genuine crisis theories. If it really is insulated from eschatological or teleological idioms (or indeed from any metaphor of a biological life-cycle), it might perhaps be rescued from the hands of modern 'crisis-mongers'.

It is an index of the *malaise* of modern political language that such a non-pathological interpretation of 'permanent crisis' does not have a commonly agreed name. The only antithesis to crisis which the medical metaphor can suggest is 'health', but this would be entirely misleading and would polarize the field of meaning too much. What is needed is to get away from the medical metaphor as much as possible. For want of a better option one might suggest that a non-teleological process of permanent 'crisis', a sort of process which might lead to survival (or perhaps moderate improvement), but not to full 'health', may best be described as historical normality. 'Normality', if used sceptically and cautiously, would simply re-define most 'crises' as difficulties attendant on 'change', as strategic moves to which political communities might be able to commit themselves in order to adapt to changing circumstances (both internally and externally). If one accepts that 'change', however difficult and 'crisis-like' its actual experience might be, is 'normal', then what is most often called 'crisis' is the normal manifestation of political and economic movement, without ever necessarily reaching a grand 'crisis' with a conclusively positive or irrevocably negative outcome. The use of this term has its own obvious pitfalls. But substituting 'normality' for 'crisis' as an explanatory starting point might be intellectually productive. Even if it does not work, it may help to pinpoint whether we might have good reason to see the current condition of 'nation-states' as 'abnormal'.

If 'normality' or 'change' prove to be descriptively compelling, then portraying each and every difficult step in a process of change as 'crisis' is at best redundant, and at worst a serious intellectual hindrance. Furthermore, if 'normality' itself is seen as a process of change consisting of a sequential occurrence of 'crises', then it must be abundantly clear that the question of whether there is a 'contemporary crisis of the nation-state' cannot be addressed in a short-term intellectual framework. What I shall do in the substantive part of my essay is to consider briefly some aspects of the alleged crisis of the 'nation-state' which seem to require long-term historical scrutiny with particular urgency. My interest here is not in the history of earlier 'crises' of the 'nation-state' *per se*, but rather in how the problems of the 'nation-state' were theorized in the past and in identifying a number of perspectives in the history of political thought dealing with the long term viability of 'nation-states' which seem both to anticipate and run against current opinion.

I wish to inquire whether the language of 'nation-states' is a stable one with a settled historical provenance and to examine how far in Western political theory it might have been used to conceal, rather than reveal, long-standing problems in the history of modern Western European states. In this latter sense, the weaknesses in our theoretical understanding of the salient features of apparently well established 'nation-states' must be recognized not as signs of a distinctive 'contemporary crisis', but merely as practical instances of succes-sive attempts to grapple with the largely unresolved classic questions of modern political theory. Some of the problems facing contemporary 'nation-states' have been recognized as acute difficulties for a very long time; and only by recognizing their longevity can we be in a position to judge whether the various solutions proposed in the past might prove workable.

There are two obvious dangers threatening 'nation-states': either they cannot preserve their territorial integrity, or they cannot provide the people within their territory with adequate welfare and comfort. It is a frequently advanced contention that free international markets, and particularly their recent expansion, necessarily undermine the foundations of the 'nation-state'. But the dangers of free international markets for national states have been recognized as a persistently difficult problem of politics ever since their beginning. In fact, some of the characteristic features of the historical development of 'nation-states' can be more readily understood as answers to problems caused by free trade than to other types of threats. In order to judge the acuteness or otherwise of this problem (sometimes perceived as the most modern and most devastating element of the current 'crisis', but possibly one of the oldest), both theorists and historians have to be able to pass judgment on the merit of the claimed incompatibility between sovereign states and free markets. The powerful notion that in the modern world there are economic limits to politics requires a serious reconsideration of both the political and economic components of the 'nation-state'. The power of any argument which either asserts or denies its 'crisis' must depend on bringing into focus both the long term political and the long term economic argument simul-taneously. In the past I made several attempts to put the political economy side of the problem in a long term historical perspective.[5] In this essay it is the politics of this equation which is in the foreground.[6]

To bring the political-territorial problem of the viability of 'nation-states' into focus, one needs to understand key aspects of the modern notion of popular sovereignty. I take it as given that without a historically informed understanding of the theory of popular sovereignty no clarification of the modern language of 'nation-states' and 'nationalism' is possible.[7] First I ask a very broad question: whether it has ever been possible to justify the existence of 'nation-states' as sovereign occupiers of certain definite tracts of the surface of the globe (whether the territorial security of states could ever be expected to hold in anything but *de facto* terms). If not, then the insecurity of national states and their borders is a generic phenomenon, and cannot be seen as a sign of special and contemporary crisis. Even if the long term crisis of traditional states and empires is not a difficult issue to tackle, the next question I want to consider is whether their crises can be extended to modern West European states as well or whether one is now facing a new kind of 'crisis' situation. In other words, I am interested in asking whether the fact that modern Western European states are democracies of sorts has changed the shape of the long term historical process or not. As an introduction to this argument I wish to discuss how the 'composite' states which emerged in early modern Europe were gradually transformed into unitary states and to what extent Hobbes's theory of sovereignty captured essential features of this process. The central thrust of this article is contained in my attempt to analyse the connection between Hobbesian sovereignty and the notion of national sovereignty which emerged in the French Revolution (generally taken to be the crucial turning point in the development of the modern 'nation-state'). I try to show that the language of

[5] See my 'Free trade and the economic limits to national politics: neo-Machiavellian political economy reconsidered', in John Dunn (ed.), *The Economic Limits to Politics* (Cambridge, Cambridge University Press, 1990), pp. 41–120; 'The "Rich country–poor country" debate in Scottish classical political economy', in I. Hont and M. Ignatieff (eds), *Wealth and Virtue: the Shaping of Political Economy in the Scottish Enlightenment* (Cambridge, Cambridge University Press, 1983), pp. 271–316; 'The language of sociability and commerce: Samuel Pufendorf and the foundations of Smith's "Four Stages" theory', in A. Pagden (ed.), *Languages of Political Theory in Early Modern Europe* (Cambridge, Cambridge University Press, 1986), pp. 253–76; 'The rhapsody of public debt: David Hume and voluntary state bankruptcy', in N. Phillipson and Q. Skinner (eds), *Political Discourse in Early Modern Britain* (Cambridge, Cambridge University Press, 1993), pp. 321–48; (with Michael Ignatieff) 'Needs and justice in the *Wealth of Nations*', in *Wealth and Virtue*, pp. 1–44; 'The political economy of the "unnatural and retrograde" order: Adam Smith and natural liberty', in *Französische Revolution und Politische Ökonomie* (Trier, Karl Marx Haus, 1989), pp. 122–49.

[6] The present essay is an extended version of the first half of the argument which I presented at the 'Crisis of the Nation State?' conference at King's College, Cambridge on the 11th of September, 1993. The second part dealt with two further topics, 'Commerce and the "Nation-State" ' and 'The "Crisis" of Expectations'.

[7] See the oft cited remark of Hugh Seton-Watson in his *Nations and States. An Enquiry into the Origins of Nations and the Politics of Nationalism* (London, Methuen, 1977), that the doctrine of nationalism is simple and quite uninteresting, since 'it is the application to national communities of the Enlightenment doctrine of popular sovereignty' (445) . . . 'with half-digested chunks of socialism added to the broth in the course of time' (p. 3). Seton-Watson nonetheless spent a great deal of his energy distinguishing between various nationalist movements which embraced different doctrines of nationalism; while his view correctly implies that there is no point in investigating doctrines of nationalism without investigating the doctrine of 'popular sovereignty', it suggests that the ability to distinguish between models of 'popular sovereignty' (and their attendant conceptions of political community and political obligation) is a necessary precondition for understanding the predicament of the modern 'nation-state'.

the 'nation' and representation which emerged in the political thought of Emmanuel Sieyès was a continuation of the Hobbesian theory of indirect popular sovereignty. The counterpoint to this is provided by a dissection of the logic of the Jacobin position, in which I try to argue that their notion of the direct sovereignty of the 'people', rather than the 'nation', amounted to an opposition to the idea of modern sovereignty altogether and hence to the idea of the 'nation-state'. A brief survey of the late eighteenth-century notion of 'nationalism' then leads me to consider the implications of the failure of the French Revolution to bring about a terminal crisis of the 'nation-state', and the consequences of the default of Jacobin 'anti-nationalism' into a virulent form of 'ancient' republican patriotism deployed to preserve the territorial integrity of a large unified state like modern France. This implies that some salient aspects of the career of the 'nation-state' and 'nationalism' in the nineteenth and twentieth centuries might be understood better if one compared the period following the collapse of the first French Republic to the aftermath of the demise of late-renaissance Italian republican politics, when central and powerful notions of republican political theory became absorbed into the ideology of the major European states, with both positive and negative effects. Attention will be drawn to the fact that the formation of modern nationalism after the French Revolution cannot be seen as a single process, but as a debate and fight between widely divergent views about connection between nation-hood and state power, which were carried over unresolved from the debates of the French Revolution into the subsequent 'Age of Nationalism'.

The 'Nation State' and the 'National' Origins of Private Property

It is a commonplace of historiography that 'nation-states' replaced territorial states. But all states are by definition claimants of territory and 'nation-states' are no exception.[8] In contrast to the 'territorial state', the idea of the 'nation-state' implies that its territory belongs to the population which actually inhabits it, and to no-one else. The population which lives in a 'nation-state' cannot have a superior power which exercises *dominium* or *imperium* over its territory and hence also over themselves as a collectivity. A state which stands in a relationship of periphery to some other state or power as the core or metropole, is not a 'nation-state', but a province of an empire. The primary sense of the 'nation-state' is that it is the opposite of empire, defined as a kind of territorial state-system within which entire populations or nations (even if they might retain the appearance of being the inhabitants of a distinct and separate territory) are also considered as either superiors or inferiors.[9] In the

---

[8] I use the word 'state' here in its common or 'weak' sense, in which the connection between state and territory is tautological, see Henry Sidgwick: '... it belongs to our ordinary conception of a State that the political society so called could be attached to a particular part of the earth's surface: and should have a generally admitted claim to determine legal rights and obligations of persons inhabiting this portion, whether they are members of the society or not. This is so much the case that we sometimes use the word 'state' to designate the portion of the earth's surface thus claimed'. *The Development of European Polity* (London, Macmillan, 3rd ed., 1920), p. 26.

[9] 'Defining empire', pp. 30–47. 'Empire ... is a relationship, formal or informal, in which one state controls the effective political sovereignty of another political society. It can be achieved by force, by political collaboration, by economic, social, or cultural dependence' in Michael W. Doyle, *Empires* (Ithaca, Cornell University Press, 1986), p. 45. See the entire Ch. 1, section 2 on the issue of whether both formal and informal notions of control should be included in the concept of empire.

old political language of Europe one could say that a 'nation-state' was an empire to itself. Sovereign states exist in the 'state of nature'. Among them are neither superiors nor inferiors: all states are equal with one another.

From this perspective, the rise of the 'nation-state' is the process of sorting out the territorial rights of communities in such a way that ownership of national property in land is ever more legitimate, i.e. distinctly belongs to those who live and work there. It is the devolution of empire, a renunciation of any rights to the territory from the outside or from above. This is obvious in the case of empires of conquest or any other forms of external acquisition, when their legitimacy is questioned. The notion of community underlying the idea of the 'nation-state' is one in which a community is cleansed of empire when its members consider themselves to be members of the same nation. Further devolution into 'nation-states' can also happen to states which are in no sense formalized empires, but whose inhabitants, or some of them, discover that there are, after all, systematic inequalities within their apparent 'nation-state' in which one community is considered or treated as superior to another. This frequently happens in states which themselves gain independence from an empire, and in most cases the tension within the newly 'nationalized' population is itself a residue of the new country's past in that empire. The modern idea of nationalism holds that the bottom line of such devolution is reached when the political community of a state is ethnically homogenized. The ideal typical 'nation-state' is one whose territory belongs to a community whose members share a common origin in the sense of a 'common birth'. Even when populations of different ethnic origin live in an entirely mixed way and without a past of standing in relation of core and province to each other, the territorial logic of statehood means, that once they see themselves as separate and antagonistic groups their conflict can be resolved and their equality re-established only if they are separated as 'nation-states'. Ethnic cleansing is the natural corollary of this line of thought. At the beginning of the 20th century it seemed impossible to observers of the nationality problems of the Austro-Hungarian monarchy that populations which had lived together for a considerable time could ever be unscrambled in a territorial fashion.[10] But to a large degree this is what has actually happened and the current predicament of Bosnia-Hercegovina is a further step in the grisly 20th-century history of the entire region.

Unsettling changes in the boundaries of states around the world might easily be taken as indices of a crisis of the 'nation-state'. They highlight certain weaknesses in territorial legitimation. It is useful to realize how fragile this legitimation really is. Holding territory is a question of property rights, and states, including 'nation-states', are owners of collective property in land. Settling the issue of territorial property would require a clear principle of legitimation capable of specifying precisely who, i.e. which population group, could occupy what territory and for how long. Although the question of private property appears to have been settled for the time being and no longer

[10] See the proposal of the Austro-Marxist Otto Bauer who wished to separate nationality entirely from its territorial basis and make nations within a multi-national state the mere associations of persons, Otto Bauer, *Die Nationalitatenfrage und die österreichische Sozialdemokratie* (Vienna, Wiener Volksbuchhandlung Ignaz Brand, 1907), Ch. 4 'Die Nationale Autonomie', §21 'Das Territorialprinzip', pp. 321–53; §22 'Das Personalitätsprinzip', pp. 353–66.

constitutes the sort of great ideological divide which it was whilst socialism was still powerful as a theory and as a historical movement, it is perhaps useful to remember that this outcome has been due less to a victory of the *theory* of private property over its rival, than to a practical failure of economic regimes based on its alternative. Adam Smith, for example, could not be easily mistaken to have been an opponent of modern economic regimes based on private property. But he nonetheless wisely explained to his students at the University of Glasgow in the 1760s that private property could never be justified to the degree to which one's right to life and personal bodily security could be.[11] But if the legitimation of private property remains contentious, national group property is even more so as we still do not possess a theory that can provide an ultimate justification for it.

This is significant, because most early modern and modern property theorists assumed that the origins of private property must be sought in what they deemed to be the chronologically prior origins of group or communal property. There were very few theorists in the Western tradition who attempted to shortcircuit the legitimation problem of private property by asserting that private property was the naturally (or more precisely divinely) given original condition of man's use of the earth's resources. The dominant and orthodox tradition held that originally there was no such thing as private property, or indeed any kind of property at all: that the territory of the globe was destined for the use of the human species, – that God's gift of the Earth was to mankind in common. The communal origins of mankind's use of the territory of the Earth were supported both by the authority of the Christian tradition and by the most important ancient authorities celebrated by the humanist revival. The difficulty facing those who wished to justify modern regimes of private property was how to explain and then legitimate the world historical change from commonality to firmly private individuation, particularly in land. If our globe 'belonged' to the human species as a whole, then its division between groups of populations, and subsequently between private individuals within such groups, had to be legitimized by some sort of historical explanation. The relationship between the totality of available resources and the whole of mankind was defined as inclusionary, resulting in a notion of general, but indeterminate, entitlement. But the establishment of more durable, or perhaps even permanent, entitlements to definite pieces of land, carved out of a finite pool of resources, was by its nature exclusionary. Its origins, the beginning of exclusion, were theorized as having taken place as 'first occupations'. Although at first sight this had an obvious plausibility as a procedural device for sorting out contending claims to disputed territory, defining its criteria proved to be notoriously elusive. Nor was it easier to explain away the problem that the acquisition of sovereign dominion over territory by virtue of 'first occupation' still represented a leap from 'fact' to 'right'. The weight of legitimation, almost invariably, was shifted over to theoretical histories of mankind, in the effort to show how the ever firmer individuation of basic life resources, under the

---

[11] 'Lectures on Jurisprudence' (Report of 1762–3), in Adam Smith, *Lectures on Jurisprudence*, R.L. Meek, D.D. Raphael and P.G. Stein (eds) (Oxford, Clarendon, 1978), i. 24–5 'The only case where the origin of naturall rights is not altogether plain, is in that of property. It does not at first appear evident that, e.g. any thing which may suit another as well or perhaps better than it does me, should belong to me exclusively of all others barely because I have got it into my power' (p. 13).

relentless pressure of population growth, could be defended by reference to necessity and hence ultimately to the utility of exclusionary property rights.

The ultimate aim of these theories was to explain the necessity of private property within communities, despite its consequence, inequality. The creation of the state was linked to the positive legalization of the development of private property, as the institution which was designed to stop any further contention over the individuation of resources within the community. But the idea of the state as the guardian of private property was a strictly domestic theory. It could not, and did not, explain how the community as a whole came into the possession of its national territory. The early communal aspect of the story, however, did figure prominently in the conjectural histories of property. The image of the ocean, the 'great remaining common of mankind' did not play such a conspicuous role in controversies over the origins and limits of private property simply because it could not be made into *private* property. It was not carved up into *national* or group property either. John Locke, who ended up by constructing one of the strongest defences of private property as the engine of modern civilization, in many ways also regretted the world historical development of private property regimes. He, like many others, argued that the rot had set in with the establishment of tribes or nations carving out communal group property for themselves[12] from the 'negative' community of mankind. Samuel Pufendorf, in his influential discussion of the origins and history of property, also emphasized that property first became prominent as group property of 'positive' (i.e. exclusionary) communities.[13] He added that private property came to be established only when national regimes of communal property broke down under the pressure of population growth and the consequent need to increase productivity.[14]

Legitimating the occupational right of nations was not a peripheral issue for the natural law theorists of the early modern era. Their attempt to develop a system of 'laws of war and peace' took place at precisely the time when rivalry between the first 'nation-states' intensified significantly and they also had a vital interest in justifying a variety of colonial projects which followed the discovery of America. Their explanation of national territorial rights remained that of first occupation theory, as a special case of rights acquired by conquest. The

---

[12] Locke, *Two Treatises of Government*, Second Treatise, §128 '... he and all the rest of Mankind are one Community, make up one Society distinct from all other Creatures. And were it not for the corruption, and vitiousness of degenerate Men, there would be no need of any other; no necessity that Men should separate from this great and natural Community, and by positive agreements combine into smaller and divided associations'. §45 'the several Communities settled the Bounds of their distinct Territories ... and the Leagues that have been made between several States and Kingdoms, either expressly or tacitly disowning all Claim and Right to the Land in the others Possession, have, by common Consent, given up their Pretences to their natural common Right, which originally they had to those countries' (see also §38); §117 'For there are no Examples so frequent in History, both Sacred and Prophane, as those of Men withdrawing themselves, and their Obedience, from the Jurisdiction they were born under, and the Family or Community they were bred up in, and setting up new Governments in other places; from where sprang all that number of petty Common-wealths in the beginning of Ages, and which always multiplied, as long as there was room enough, till the stronger, or more fortunate swallowed the weaker; and those great ones again breaking to pieces, dissolved into lesser Dominions'.

[13] Samuel Pufendorf, *Of the Law of Nature and Nations. Eight Books.* [1688], trans. Basil Kennett (London, Sane, Bonwicke *et al.*, 3rd ed., 1717), 4.4.2., 4.4.13.

[14] Pufendorf, *Law of Nature*, 4.4.6–7.

lack of legitimation for national territorial property was made evident in the commonly held view that national states still inhabited the 'state of nature'. The efforts to develop international law were attempts to regularize the rules of conflict in a world of might, not right. It was for this reason that Kant denounced the early modern classical exponents of natural law and international rights as 'sorry comforters';[15] thinkers who could not finally lift their eyes above accepting the power games of 'nation-states' as an inescapable condition of politics. What Kant showed was that modern international law was ultimately an expression of the principles of 'reason of state'.[16]

What in modern American parlance is known as the 'realist' doctrine of international relations has always been the underlying philosophy of territorial states. In a world ruled by might, not right, 'nation states' have always been compelled to put their own survival first and hence follow their 'national interest'. The lack of territorial security is a real problem for contemporary 'nation-states'; but it is not a problem for them alone. Although states are clearly institutions of territorial property, their entitlement to their own territory could, at best, be legitimized as an acquisition of *res nullius*. In their mythical accounts of their origin some nations referred to such first occupations and tried to use them to justify the acquisition of further (colonial) territory. But it was well understood that all European states were products not of first occupation, but conquest. Their survival had always depended, and would continue to depend, upon their ability to hold on to that territory by defending it in contests of power. This need would only cease, as Kant suggested, when there were no more empires holding other nations in subservience, and none of the 'nation-states' remained in the grip of the 'spirit of conquest'. If the crisis of 'nation-states' is linked to a weakness in the legitimation of their territorial specification, and that is linked to the legitimation of their national property in land, then the idea of the 'nation-state' cannot be *now* in 'crisis', because it has always been in 'crisis'. The only possible world of territorial security is the world of perpetual peace.

If territorial states, including 'nation-states' cannot hope to see a stage at which they can cease to be governed by their 'reason of state', then this narrows the notion of 'crisis' applicable to them to a small range of possibilities. The 'nation-state' would really be in crisis if the current world regime consisting of many independent units of national group property were to be radically undermined. The establishment of very large supra-national states, or ultimately a world state, would be a true end of the 'nation-state'. A full scale attack on 'property' as such would also lead to the end of 'nation-states'. Marx, following Proudhon, denounced earlier communists for presupposing that abolishing private property in favour of national group property (state property) could be the solution to the ills of modern society. In fact, his considered view was that it was more likely to make matters

---

[15] The original phrase is 'Hugo Grotius, Pufendorf, Vattel u.a.m. (*lauter leidige Tröster*)', see Immanuel Kant, 'Perpetual peace. A philosophical sketch' [1795], in Kant, *Political Writings*, trans. H.B. Nisbet, ed. H. Reiss (Cambridge, Cambridge University Press, 2nd ed., 1991), p. 103.

[16] Kant, 'Perpetual peace', pp. 102–5, compare to *The Metaphysics of Morals*, trans. Mary Gregor (Cambridge, Cambridge University Press, 1991), pp. 150–7.

worse. His particular brand of communism required a full return to the 'negative' community of mankind, that is, to a world without either private or communal property. But neither of these two scenarios seems even remotely likely to lie at the bottom of our apparent 'contemporary' crisis. Where there seems more obvious grounds for concern over the territorial integrity of contemporary states is in the devolution of large states into smaller territorial entities. Since the result of such devolutions is invariably new or resuscitated 'nation-states', it is not clear why this should not be seen as a triumph, rather than a crisis of the 'nation-state'. The reason for puzzlement is, however, clear. It seems that the new, and ethnically purer, 'nation-states' have taken the place of states that, at one time or another, claimed to be 'nation-states' themselves. If such a process can be shown to be the decomposition of an empire, rather than previous 'nation-states', then there is much less reason for concern. If the tottering 'nation-state' in question was always in some measure a fraud, then the 'nation-state' is not the source of the crisis, but its most plausible resolution. The escape of the Baltic States from the Soviet Union is simply a reversal of quite recent conquest, and the falling apart of the Soviet Union is the dissolution of a 'nation-state' which was a federal state only on paper and an old style empire in reality. The case of Yugoslavia and Czechoslovakia are also less than pertinent instances of a crisis of the 'nation-state' as such, since both were federal states in the first place, as well as being rather motley results of the very recent decomposition of large empires. In the history of these states there were sustained attempts to turn them into proper 'nation-states' and a study of such failures might be instructive. But they would only become relevant if the events which really have given rise to the suspicion of a 'contemporary crisis of the nation-state' turn out to be as menacing as some fear. The real issue here is the possible devolution into smaller 'nation-states' of states which have hitherto them-selves been classified as the very epitomes of the 'nation-state', and one is invariably thinking of Western Europe in this instance.

If this process of disintegration, which is currently no more than a possibility, began and ended with 'nation-states', different only in size and number, then it too could not be properly called a 'crisis of the nation-state'. There are two other possible scenarios, based on the presumption either that the 'nation-state' which is supposed to be falling apart, or the 'nation-states' which are newly emerging, are not genuine specimens of the species. It may well be that the traditional claimants to the title of 'nation-state', or some of them, will turn out to be concealed empires all along, even if in a far less transparently fraudulent manner than the Soviet Union, or that the new small states will be compelled to end up as *de facto* provinces of a new European super-state (perhaps calling itself the European Union). All three options are theoretically possible, but none of these scenarios can be usefully analysed in relation to a 'contemporary crisis of the nation-state', if the concept of the 'nation-state' itself cannot coherently distinguish between these two varieties of states. Despite the ubiquity of the term in contemporary political science and historiography, it is hard to find a genuinely historical definition of the 'nation-state' which could be consistently applied in conceptual analysis. Most discussions of the 'nation-state', both in its domestic and international aspects, consequently, are riven by contradic-tion and inconsistency.

From the Mixed Constitution to the National Monarchy:
State-Building and 'Absolutism'

One common and influential narrative recounts the rise of the important modern West European states, Spain, Britain and France (perhaps even Russia), as the rise of the 'great powers'. It places the origin of the 'nation-state' in the 16th and 17th centuries and associates it with the birth of the modern doctrine (and practice) of sovereignty. Europe in 1500 included some five hundred more-or-less independent units; the Europe of 1900 approximately twenty five.[17] The rise of nation-states was a grand process of unification. Those national monarchies which became the 'great powers' were the states which managed most successfully to leave behind the weaknesses of the late medieval political systems. They were literally constructed as artifices in a historical manner which can be readily recognized. Everybody knows that the making of modern Italy and Germany involved a deliberate process of creation since this occurred virtually within living memory. But the older national states of Europe, Spain, France, Britain, and so on, were also products of drives for unification. Most people tend to be aware of this fact in the case of their own 'nation'-state, but not necessarily of the others. A German might think of 'England' as a nation state, but the British (and, still more, the Irish) tend to remember that the name of the country is the United Kingdom and to know that its flag, the *Union* Jack, is a simple superimposition of the original flags of England, Scotland and Ireland (thus excluding Wales, which had been first conquered and then annexed by union). Although not even the full modern state titles of Spain and France refer to the historical process of their making, both of them were nonetheless the results of a protracted and elaborate operation of unification out of previously quite separate territorial entities. The historical theory of national states holds that the modern 'nation-states' of Europe are the products of a process of state building, that is the outcome, according to Charles Tilly's tidy summary, of 'territorial consolidation, centralization, differentiation of the instruments of government from other sorts of organization, and monopolization (plus concentration) of the means of coercion'.[18] It is crucial to realize that a possible 'contemporary crisis of the nation-state' might involve the reversal, at least in parts, of this very particular kind of unification process. Such a reversal of four hundred years of history (by no means unprecedented by world historical standards) might meaningfully be seen as the end of those artificially unified or integrated large states which are described by the 'state-building' theorists as the modern state. But if the narrative in question is one of the development of 'supra-national' – and at the point of their birth definitely supra-provincial – entities, then it must be questionable, to say the least, whether it is better to describe some of the states which existed before (and might exist again in the future) as 'nation-states' proper or to reserve that title for those which came after and have lasted until the present.

The theory of 'state-building', as a guide for understanding the 'nation-state', is first and foremost an application of the theory of the state itself. It handles

---

[17] These oft cited figures come from Charles Tilly, 'Reflections on the history of European state-making' in C. Tilly (ed.), *The Formation of National States in Western Europe* (Princeton, Princeton University Press, 1975), p. 15.

[18] Tilly, 'Reflections', p. 27.

the 'nation' prefixed to the dyad 'nation-state', or 'national state', not as a genuinely constitutive agency, but as an important supporting actor playing out a specific role in consummating the teleology of 'state-building'. Modern historical sociology and historiography, following a time-honoured tradition, tends to assume that the history of the nation-state started with the union of crowns of Aragon and Castile. But it is only because of the fixation of 'state-building' theory with that process of unification and territorial consolidation which eventually streamlined the complicated web of nations in Europe so radically that the ascent of the 'nation-state' has come to be seen as beginning with post-medieval supra-national dynastic unions. The history of the 'nation state' is usually seen as the product of three successive stages or waves of state unification and consolidation. The *first* is the creation of early modern composite states under the leadership of a single dynasty, but without administrative and institutional unification. The *second* is the institutionalization of modern sovereignty in its modern monarchical form, known as the rise of 'absolutism' and later of 'enlightened absolutism'. The *third* is the transformation of monarchical absolutism into the popular absolutism of the sovereignty of the 'nation', usually described as the birth of the modern representative republic (which may still have a monarch as the highest public servant of the nation).

According to this sequence the oldest of the European 'nation-states' were composite monarchies, or what used to be called *systems* of states, territorial states made up of distinct 'national' parts that had, for a variety of reasons, a high degree of political and cultural separateness, even if the governments of the parts were controlled on a regular basis by one monarch or legislature, so that the overall political representation of the state became formally unitary.[19]

[19] The term 'system' was used by Hobbes in *Leviathan* (Ch. 22 'Of Systemes Subject, Politicall, and Private') to describe 'any numbers of men joyned in One interest, or one businesse' just like the parts which make up a 'Body naturall' … In a regular system one man or one assembly represented the whole body politic; he called every other system irregular. Pufendorf, using this language, made a distinction between 'system' which are one political body, and 'systems of states', which are made up from several pre-existing states so that they 'seem to compose one body', but they nonetheless retain some degree of their sovereignty (*Of the Law of Nature and Nations in Eight Books*, Bk 7, Ch. 5, §16). As opposed to the policy of some large states which 'vastly increased their dominions by swallowing up their little neighbours, and by reducing to the same body as themselves', which was an exercise in political body building as it were, in a system of states there was the creation of a special kind of 'moral body', which had no natural simile, that is an entity in which several bodies were linked and shared a single head between them. Systems of states were of two kinds, monarchical personal unions (Pufendorf's example being England, Scotland and Ireland) or confederations. The body-builders could retain lower level institutions and customs in their subordinated new 'muscles', but not sovereignty; in the systems of states sovereignty is retained in the several bodies even if a pooling or sharing took place in the head. It was this concept of systems of states which Jean Barbeyrac, in his elegant French translation of Pufendorf restyled as '*Etats composez*' (dropping both the Hobbesian and the Pufendorfian terminology of system); see *Le Droit de Nature et des Gens*, trans. Jean Barbeyrac (Basel, E. and J. R. Thourneisen, 1732), Bk 7, Ch. 5, §16–8, pp. 282–6. The term 'composite state' then became part of 18th and 19th-century historical theories of the state: for the eighteenth century see the article 'Etats composés' by the Chevalier de Jaucourt in d'Alembert and Diderot (eds), *Encyclopédie ou Dictionnaire raisonné des sciences, des arts et des métiers, par une société de gens de lettres*, vol. 6 (Paris, Briasson, David, Le Breton and Durand, 1756), pp. 19b–20a; a particularly clear nineteenth-century definition is in Henry Sidgwick, *Elements of Politics* (London, Macmillan, 2nd ed., 1897), Ch. 26 'Federal and other composite states', §1. The old terminology has been revived in recent controversies by H.G. Koenigsberger, '*Dominium Regale* or *Dominium Politicum et Regale*', in his *Politicians and Virtuosi: Essays in Modern History* (London, Hambledon, 1986), pp. 1–25, and 'Composite states, representative institutions and the American Revolution', *Historical Research* 62 (1989), 135–53,

The process cannot be easily described in the language of voluntarism, although the *modus operandi* has stretched from conquest to dynastic negotiation or coalescence into larger composite state units.[20] The motivation was imperial, but what distinguished the new 'composite' monarchies from pre-modern empires was the effort to avoid the instabilities associated with harsh imperial domination from the centre over the peripheries. Central to this was the endeavour to establish as much equality between the constitutive parts as possible, governing them from the centre as if the monarch were the sovereign of each virtually separate country within the empire. This entailed ensuring the regular presence of the monarch in each of the dependent, but co-equal states, and keeping the governance of each part of the empire under the guidance of its respective customary political culture. There were obvious lessons drawn from this practice, such as to attempt to build composite states from territories as geographically contiguous as possible; and the states which survived into the era of mature 'nation-states' (Spain, Britain, France) were those which were the most successful in this respect. The rise of absolutism, a term invented in German historiography to describe the Stage before the rise of the truly modern civil society of the representative state, can be understood as a further, quite radical step away from traditional empire as a model for organizing and keeping together large territorial states.

The rise of 'absolutism' is often described as the process whereby the modern idea of united and indivisible sovereignty replaced previous notions of divided or fragmented sovereignty, consisting of the mixed constitution internally and the composite multinational kingdom externally.[21] It was driven not simply

Footnote continued
and following him by J.H. Elliott, 'A Europe of composite monarchies', *Past and Present*, no. 137 (1992), 48–71. Conrad Russell uses the term 'multiple kingdoms' to describe the same structure as applied to British history, see his *The Causes of the English Civil War* (Oxford, Oxford University Press, 1990), p. 27. Joseph Strayer occasionally uses the perhaps less fortunate term, the 'mosaic state', see his influential monographs *On the Medieval Origins of the Modern State* (Princeton, Princeton University Press, 1970) and *Medieval Statecraft and the Perspectives of History* (Princeton, Princeton University Press, 1971); a convenient brief summary is in Strayer, 'The historical experience of nation-building in Europe', in Karl W. Deutsch and William J. Foltz (eds), *Nation-Building* (New York, Atherton, 1963), pp. 17–26, the 'mosaic-state' is on pp. 23–5.

[20] See Mark Greengrass, 'Conquest and coalescence' in M. Greengrass (ed.), *Conquest and Coalescence. The Shaping of the State in Early Modern Europe* (London, Edward Arnold, 1991), pp. 1–24.

[21] The term '*Absolutismus*' was first used for the definition of an entire stage of early modern European state formation by Eduard Gans (Hegel's pupil, successor at the University of Berlin and the editor of his *Philosophy of Right*) as an addition to the four stages theory and of the history of monarchy which he developed following Hegel, that is 'oriental despotism', 'Roman despotism', 'feudal monarchy' and 'enlightened or constitutional monarchy'. The new additional type, called 'absolutism', was a transitional type of monarchy inserted between stages three and four, covering two hundred years starting from the end of the sixteenth century. It was the '*ancien régime*' (chiefly exemplified by France) and its historical function was to lay the foundations of the modern constitutional monarchy by unification and freeing Europe from the particularism of the Middle Ages. It could not last, Gans explained, because its spectacular unitariness in form lacked underlying coherence. See Gans, 'Deutsches Staatsrecht' (Vorlesungnachschrift–Sommersemester 1834), in Gans, *Philosophische Schriften* Horst Schröder (ed) (Glashütten, Detlev Auvermann, 1971), pp. 175–9. For the original four stages model of monarchy see Gans' lectures on 'Natturecht' (Vorlesungnachschrift – Sommersemester 1828–9), in *Philosophische Schriften*, pp. 128–9. For an introduction to the formation of the notion of 'absolutism' in German political theory before Gans see Horst Dreitzel, *Monarchiebegriffe in der Fürstengesselschaft. Semantik und Theorie der Einherrschaft in Deutschland von der Reformation bis zum Vormärz* 2 vols, (Cologne, Böhlau, 1991), vol. 2 *Theorie der Monarchie*, Ch. 3, section 2 'Theorien der absoluten Monarchie', particularly

by the need to govern in a more efficient manner, but by the imperative to make the governance of large country-states possible at all under modern conditions of military and economic competition. The composite large states strove to sustain unity of a modern empire from the centre, while still maintaining the diversity of political cultures of its nominally equal (or equally subordinated) component states or provinces. In the composite state the constituent members are equal but different. The 'absolutist' state solved the tension between the centre and the provinces by virtually eliminating the diversity. The response to a number of obvious external and internal challenges converged on the strategy of establishing an ultimate and unchallenged centre of decision-making within any territorially distinct polity, enabling the monarchy to deal with domestic religious and political threats as well as with the centrifugal forces present in all geographically and culturally diversified composite states. Its chief characteristic was a relentless drive for homogenization. Absolutism, in the name of modern sovereignty, implied the build-up of a standardized machinery of government administering the 'fiscal-military state'. It also required that all subjects accept their obligations to the political system and to their united country in the same way, putting loyalty to their state and obedience to its government as paramount among their various duties. This latter point is crucial for understanding the connection between the 'absolutist' and the 'nationalist' stages in the conception of developmental state-building which informs the usual Western understanding of a 'nation-state'.[22]

In the impossibly vague terminology of 'absolutism' two ideas came to be conflated. The first was the process of centralization, homogenization and military-fiscal build-up just described. But in the historical development of most countries in Europe this required the monarchy to crush opposition to these policies, and this second fact is also reflected in the meaning of 'absolutism' as unlimited executive power, exercised without constitutional limits or the consent of representative institutions, in order to achieve monarchical and

---

Footnote continued

pp. 775–7 and Dreitzel, *Absolutismus und ständische Verfassung in Deutschland. Ein Beitrag zu Kontinuität und Diskontinuität der politischen Theorie in der frühen Neuzeit* (Mainz, Philipp von Zabern, 1992), pp. 127–9. The term 'enlightened absolutism' came to prominence not much later, in Wilhelm Roscher's 1847 attempt to rework the ancient classification of state-forms (monarchy, aristocracy, democracy), in which he distinguished three stages in the development of modern 'absolutist' monarchies, 'confessional', 'courtly', and finally, from the middle of the eighteenth century, 'enlightened absolutism', see his 'Umrisse zur Naturlehre der drei Staatsformen', *Allgemeine Zeitschrift für Geschichte* 7 (1847), 79–88, 322–65, 436–73, especially p. 451. A more systematically developed later version can be found in his systematic *Politik: Geschichtliche Naturlehre der Monarchie, Aristokratie und Demokratie* (Stuttgart, Cotta, 1892), Bk. 3 'Absolute Monarchie', and he also presented the idea in his much better known *Geschichte der National-Oekonomik in Deutschland* (Munich, Oldenbourg, 1874), in the chapter on 'Der Nationalökonomik Friedrich's des Großen', pp. 380–1. See V. Sellin 'Friedrich der Große und der aufgeklärte Absolutismus. Ein Beitrag zum Klärung eines umstrittenden Begriffs', in U. Engelhardt, V. Sellin, H. Stuker (eds), *Soziale Bewegung und politische Verfassung* (Stuttgart, Klett, 1976), pp. 83–112, and H.M. Scott, 'Introduction: the problem of enlightened absolutism' in H.M. Scott (ed.), *Enlightened Absolutism. Reform and Reformers in Later Eighteenth-Century Europe* (Basingstoke, Macmillan, 1990), pp. 4–7.

[22] See the distinction between 'state-building' and 'nation-building' in G.A. Almond and G.B. Powell Jr., *Comparative Politics: a Developmental Approach* (Boston, Little Brown, 1966), p. 35, the first refers to 'penetration and integration', the second to 'loyalty and commitment'; also Anthony D. Smith, 'State-making and nation-building' in John A. Hall (ed.), *States in History* (Oxford, Basil Blackwell, 1986), pp. 228–63.

national grandeur. It was long the national myth of Britain that because this country, after 1688, could dispense with 'absolutism' in this second, 'despotic', sense, it also contrived to attain the status of a modern 'nation-state' without the first. Recent British historiography, however, has demonstrated, as generations of German historians and politicians vividly suspected, that Britain had an extremely successful policy of 'state-building', and that she had possessed not only large modern armed forces and a navy, along with a very advanced financial system (these were after all widely known and understood long ago), but also a very effective machinery[23] of a centralized 'state-building' administration. The British limited monarchy, it seems, enjoyed a much higher level of legitimation than its Continental counterparts, while pursuing a course of military and fiscal aggrandizement; and its success in the international arena gave rise to a British patriotism with strong military and imperialist undertones. In terms of the theory at issue the multiple kingdom or composite empire of Britain became a 'nation-state' when the pressures of war manufactured 'Britons' on an ever larger scale.[24] The difference between a modern 'absolutist' state, striving to unite the country and homogenize its institutions, and a 'nation-state' is thus no more than a higher stage of the very same 'state-building' process, a 'nation-state' is merely an 'absolutist' state whose subjects or citizens identify themselves with it, and regard it as a collective expression of themselves as a 'nation'. The pairing of the notions of 'nation' and 'state' makes sense when in people's imagination their nationality and their territorial political unit, which has emerged from a history of 'conquest and coalescence', becomes fused. The belief that a historically forged unitary state with a grisly past of war and coercion has become a true 'nation' (the birth association of *post nati*), could provide it with the greatest political security which any power structure could ever aspire to, the supporting power of public opinion.

The genesis of this popular national legitimation of the state built by the methods of modern absolutism sometimes required a revolutionary domestic political transformation. Thus it is conventional wisdom that the concept of the 'nation' entered the charmed circle of key political concepts in the early phases of the French revolution eventually giving rise to the notion of a 'nation-state'. While it does appear to be true that the term *'nation'* became a cornerstone of the French revolutionary understanding of what their new republican 'state' was it still remains to be shown how, firstly, the notion of the 'state' as a political entity maps on to the spatial definition of the 'state' as constituted by territorial occupation, and secondly, how the concept of the political 'state' relates to what, in the constitutional thought of the French revolution came to be called the 'nation'. The impact of altering the political order and

[23] John Brewer, *The Sinews of Power. War, Money and the English State*, 1688–1783 (London, Unwin Hyman, 1989). For an explanation of the relationship between the thesis of his book and modern theories of the state see Brewer, 'The eighteenth-century British state: contexts and issues', in Lawrence Stone (ed.), *An Imperial State at War. Britain from 1689 to 1815* (London, Routledge, 1994), pp. 52–71.

[24] Linda Colley, *Britons. Forging the Nation 1707–1837* (New Haven, Yale University Press, 1992). Beside warfare itself, it was Britain's aggressively Protestant worldview, Colley insists, the religious identity of a militant and chosen people (a Protestant Israel who were destined to fight Catholic France), which shaped the making of British patriotism. Instead of being a mere expression of anti-governmental politics, British patriotism was a major expression of popular support for the British nation-state (pp. 368–72).

displacing the monarchical system of government by the representative republic as a feasible and indeed the most suitable form of modern popular sovereignty for large territorial country-states (in contrast to city-states) should not be underestimated. But revolution and continuity could and did in many ways go hand in hand. The French revolution was preceded by a failure of the French fiscal-military regime; but the overwhelming majority of the revolutionaries aimed to rescue the integrity of France as a unitary state, rather than dismantle its absolutist territorial heritage. The republic as a territorial state was still constituted by the borders inherited from the *ancien régime*. In the theory of 'state-building' there were already 'national' monarchies. With the revolution a 'national' republic came into being. If one emphasizes the continuity between the two, then it is necessary to explain how the absolutist monarchical state inherited from Louis XIV could be transmuted into what is sometimes believed to be its political opposite, i.e. the modern constitutional republic. To see if the upheavals of the popular revolution have really changed the nature of the entity called '*la France*' in any relevant sense, one needs to deal with the aspects of the 'state' which cannot be captured by a purely spatial definition of it.

Hobbes's 'State' and Popular Sovereignty: the Artificial Moral Person of the People

At the time of its inception the modern idea of the 'state' could not be easily connected to the idea of the 'nation', and despite the universal acceptance of the hyphenated term 'nation-state' today, it would then have been thought of as something of an oxymoron. The nation was mostly understood either as a pre- or non-political category or as a term in Christian political eschatology. It referred to people of common origin, like groups of students from distant countries and regions at universities, or social groups of a certain rank, primarily élites with an influence on the mechanisms of political decision making (in effect the political nation within a territorial state).[25] Sometimes, and with increasing frequency, it was used to describe traditionally accepted and relatively homogeneous parts of composite territorial state formations (such as England or the English nation within the composite British state). The 'state', on the other hand, was introduced as a particular definition of the political community, as an interpretation of the *civitas*, and in the conceptual universe derived from the Roman political and legal heritage *civitas* and *natio* were far from being interchangeable or intimately connected terms (the *civitas* belonged to the *populus*). Originally the term *status* or '[e]state' was not used as a substitute for *civitas* either, and had quite different implications. *Natio* referred

[25] See Moses Hadas, 'From nationalism to cosmopolitanism in the Greco-Roman world', *Journal of the History of Ideas* 4 (1943), 105–11; F.W. Walbank, 'Nationality as a factor in Roman history', *Harvard Studies in Classical Philology*, 76 (1972), 145–68; Guido Zernatto, 'Nation: the history of the word', *Review of Politics* 6 (1944), 351–66; Bendykt Zientara, '*Populus-Gens-Natio*. Einige Probleme aus dem Bereich der ethnischen Terminologie des frühen Mittelalters', in Otto Dann (ed.), *Nationalismus in vorindustrieller Zeit* (Munich, Oldenbourg, 1986), pp. 11–20; Jenő Szűcs, ' "Nationalität" und "Nationalbewußtsein im Mittelalter. Versuch eine einheitlichen Begriffs-sprache', in *Nation und Geschichte. Studien* (Cologne-Vienna, Böhlau, 1981) and a critical review of the latter by J. Ehlers, 'Nation und Geschichte', *Zeitschrift für Historische Forschung* 11 (1984), 205–18. See also chapter 1, 'The nation as novelty' in E. J. Hobsbawn, *Nations and Nationalism since 1780. Programme, Myth, Reality* (Cambridge, Cambridge University Press, 2nd ed., 1990), pp. 14–45.

to a spatially or hierarchically defined group, sharply demarcated from others. *Status* or condition, on the other hand, was a temporally defined aspect of either individuals or communities of any size, capturing their standing in the world at a given time, and serving as a marker by which to evaluate the possible directions of change. It made it possible to assess whether one's position was improving, declining, or remaining the same. But increasingly it came to be associated with the primary aim of avoiding decline, i.e. the deterioration of one's standing, relative to one's previous condition and that of others. The origins of the modern notion of the 'state' can be found in the process whereby the *status* of the *civitas* as a whole, understood as a *respublica* or common-wealth, became privileged over the status of any of its parts (including the *people*). This can be seen as a key move in the formation of the modern doctrine of sovereignty which claimed that ensuring the survival and greatness of a political community required the designation of an ultimate decision making agency within it, whose task was to devise policies which could meet challenges from outside and to stop divisive infighting at home. This idea implied that the various kind of mixed constitutions which prevailed all over Europe had to be remodelled in such a way that the capacity for ultimate decision-making was removed from any of the competing political agencies which might claim primacy over each other (or block each other's power) within the polity. Instead, it suggested that sovereignty must be posited as resting on a shared conception of legitimation, supported by the entirety of the commonwealth, and precluding the privileging of any constituent component (the prince, the aristocracy, the people) of the political regime. The new model thus routed political obligations through a neutralized all-encompassing agency represent-ing the entire political community and made it clear that the task of the sovereign was to preserve the status of the whole political body as a united entity. The working out of this theory started with Bodin in France and reached its classic formulation in the work of Thomas Hobbes. As Quentin Skinner has demonstrated,[26] the deployment of the word '*état*' or '*state*', appearing without a specific attribution to any particular agency within the polity, marks its rise.

The new theory of sovereignty as the theory of the 'state' required two fundamental stages of construction. The first was the re-definition of the political community. The second was the specification of the mechanism whereby the political community became capable of arriving at those crucial decisions which required a unitary will. Making the political community all-encompassing marked the idea off from any strong theory of kingship which conceived the country as the monarch's hereditary estate. The aim, rather, was to highlight the notion that the *civitas* must serve the good of *all* (*salus populi suprema lex esto*), and hence that the people making up the polity individually owed a political obligation ultimately to no-one but themselves in their

---

[26] Quentin Skinner, 'The state' in T. Ball, J. Farr and R.L. Hanson (eds), *Political Innovation and Conceptual Change* (Cambridge, Cambridge University Press, 1989), pp. 90–131. For the complex and protracted pre-history of inventing the 'state' see his *Foundations of Modern Political Thought*, 2 vols (Cambridge, Cambridge University Press, 1978), and for the beginnings of 'state' theory in particular the 'Conclusion', vol. 2, pp. 349–58. For an argument analogous to Skinner's explanation of the emergence of the 'state', see J.H. Burns, 'George Buchanan and the anti-monarchomachs' in Phillipson and Skinner, *Political Discourse in Early Modern Britain*, pp. 3–22.

severalty or their communal capacity.[27] The *civitas*, the *respublica* or *common-wealth* had to be a popular state in the broadest possible sense of the word. This construction, however, undercut traditional notions of popular sovereignty as much as traditional notions of the princely state. As Skinner has pointed out, in the 'pre-state' idioms of popular government it was the actual flesh and blood commonality of the people which was taken to be the depository of rightful ultimate decision making, in just the same way as defenders of princely or monarchical government equated the seat of power with the person of the actual ruler or of the corporate nation of the aristocracy. The 'state' as a refurbished version of the *civitas* or *respublica* destroyed the idea and practice of popular legitimation, as understood previously by the neo-classical republicans of the Renaissance and the monarchomachs. The very purpose of inserting the term *state* as a substitute for, or qualification of, the *respublica* or *commonwealth* was to make this change clear. The notion of a politically organized community having acquired a temporally continuous identity or *status* over and beyond the survival of its current regime form (whether monarchical or republican) is the idea, in the words of Hobbes, of the 'great Leviathan, called a *Common-wealth*, or *State* (in latine *Civitas*)'.[28] It was designed to demonstrate the point that the relationship between the people and sovereignty must be mediated, rather than direct.[29]

This new kind of indirect representation of the entire political community, superior to, and independent of, the form of government, and the sole true source of ultimate authority in any political community, was always easier to understand as a political and intellectual strategy than as a description of actual political reality.[30] How could the people be sovereign indirectly, and how could

---

[27] See a particularly clear statement in *De Cive*, Ch. 13, sections 2–4 (in the contemporary unauthorized English translation *Philosophical Rudiments Concerning Government and Society* Bernard Gert (ed.) (New York, Doubleday, 1972), pp. 258–9: 'Now all the duties of the rulers are contained in this one sentence, the safety of the people is the supreme law ... because dominions were constituted for peace's sake, and peace was sought after for safety's sake; he, who being placed in authority, shall use his power otherwise than to the safety of the people, will act against the reason of peace, that is to say, against the laws of nature'. From this Hobbes develops the whole doctrine of the duties of rulers and the aims of states according to public utility, including the requirements of defence and material flourishing. He also emphasizes that the 'city was not instituted for its own, but for the subjects' sake, and yet a particular care is not required of *this* or *that* man'. Individuals may be sacrificed because of their own fault, or because of unavoidable necessity, and 'it sometimes conduces to the safety of the most part, that wicked men do suffer'.

[28] Hobbes, *Leviathan, or The Matter, Forme, & Power of a Common-Wealth Ecclesiasticall and Civill*, Richard Tuck (ed.) (Cambridge, Cambridge University Press, 1991), p. 9.

[29] 'The *people* is somewhat that is *one*, having *one will*, and to whom *one action* may be attributed; none of these can properly be said of a *multitude*. The people rules in all governments. ... in a *monarchy*, the subjects are the *multitude*, and (however it seems a paradox) the king is the *people*'. *De Cive* Ch. 12, section 8, p. 250. *De Cive*, 'Of the citizen', was a provocative title for a book which aimed at levelling the difference between democracies or republics and other legitimate states, and hence between citizens and subjects, arguing that there was no more liberty in a traditionally understood popular state than in a modern monarchy, see *De Cive*, Ch. 10, section 8, pp. 228–9, *Leviathan*, Ch. 21, pp. 148–50. For a penetrating discussion of Hobbes's theory of liberty and its critical deployment in the debates about the Commonwealth government against those who were 'clamouring for liberty and calling it a birthright' see Quentin Skinner, 'Thomas Hobbes on the proper signification of liberty', *Transactions of the Royal Historical Society*, 5th series, 40 (1990), 121–51.

[30] The connection between the intellectual and the political strategy in Hobbes's construction of sovereignty is brought out clearly and followed through the various versions of Hobbes's political theory, from *The Elements of Law* to *De Cive* and the *Leviathan* by Richard Tuck, *Philosophy and*

the many individuals who make up a community move from being a mere multitude to being a 'people' or '*demos*', unless united by coercion or by fear of a common enemy preying on their territory? The image of the 'state' as a 'Leviathan' – an artificial man, possessing an artificial soul and an artificial will – was an evocative metaphor, but the Leviathan was strictly an imagined community.[31] It had to remain essentially impersonal and disembodied; its intended identity being lost as soon as any attempt was made to equate it with the actual individuals or corporate bodies that composed the *civitas*. This difficulty was not so much solved, as compounded in the theory of how the actual decision-making agency of sovereignty was generated. The sovereign agency as an office-holder appointed or authorized by the entire political community presupposed a community that was sufficiently united to perform this task without tearing itself apart, even though Hobbes himself also insisted that unification of the multitude into a state depended on the successful appointment of a sovereign decision-maker to embody the unity of the 'state'. 'For it is the *Unity* of the Represented, that maketh the Person [i.e. the disembodied artificial person of the state] *One*. And it is the Representer that beareth the Person, and but one Person: And *Unity*, cannot otherwise be understood in Multitude'.[32] He was careful to preclude the possibility of his theory being interpreted as a theory of resistance, disallowing

---

Footnote continued

Government 1572–1651 (Cambridge, Cambridge University Press, 1993), pp. 308–29, see also the 'Conclusion', pp. 346–8. The need for a political 'state' to adjudicate between private judgments and to create a workable moral consensus as a major motivation of Hobbes's theory of sovereignty is also shown, through a different route, in Quentin Skinner, 'Thomas Hobbes: rhetoric and the construction of morality', *Proceedings of the British Academy*, 76 (1991), 1–61.

[31] For a discussion of Hobbes's method of analysis behind his metaphor of the 'state' as an 'automaton or artificiall man' see Noel Malcolm, 'Hobbes's science of politics and his theory of science' in Andrea Napoli and Guido Canziani (eds), *Hobbes Oggi* (Milan, Franco Angeli, 1990), pp. 145–57. Malcolm argues that the emphasis in 'artificiall man' is not on the fact that it resembles a man, but that it is 'an artificial object, an object constituted by the intentions of the people who make it and use it' (p. 151).

[32] *Leviathan*, Ch. 16 'Of *Persons, Authors*, and things Personated', p. 114. For the beginning of the language of 'representation' in Hobbes *De Cive*, and the possible role Sorbière's French translation of *De Cive*'s in 1649 played in this, see Tuck, *Philosophy and Government*, p. 327. Later, in the *Leviathan* the sovereign is consistently called 'the representative'. On the relevance of studying the language use in the Latin and English versions of Hobbes, particularly regarding concepts like the commonwealth, authority, actor, person, etc. see François Tricaud, 'Language and political thought in the XVIIth century: a research on Hobbes as a bilingual philosopher' in Reinhart Koselleck (ed.), *Historische Semantik und Begriffsgeschichte* (Stuttgart, Klett-Cotta, 1978), pp. 303–13. The outlines of the 'personation' or 'representation' theory involved are explained by H. Pitkin, 'Hobbes's concept of representation', *American Political Science Review*, 58 (1964), 328–40, 902–18, and in a more concise version in H.F. Pitkin, *The Concept of Representation* (Berkeley, University of California Press, 1967), Ch. 2. 'The problem of Hobbes', pp. 14–37. See also Lucien Jaume, *Hobbes et l'État representatif moderne* (Paris, Presses Universitaires de France, 1986), pp. 82–117. Some of the conceptual distinctions are also laid out very clearly in David P. Gauthier, *The Logic of Leviathan. The Moral and Political Theory of Thomas Hobbes* (Oxford, Clarendon, 1969), Ch. 4 'Theory of authorization', pp. 120–77, who emphasizes that although Ch. 16 of the *Leviathan* appeared as a somewhat irrelevant appendix to Hobbes's psychology and moral theory to some past interpreters, it contains the cornerstone of his political theory. A reading which aims to correct some of Pitkin's modernist biases is in Deborah Baumgold, *Hobbes's Political Theory* (Cambridge, Cambridge University Press, 1988), pp. 45–55. See also the controversy with Gauthier's interpretation in Jean Hampton, *Hobbes and the Social Contract Tradition* (Cambridge, Cambridge University Press, 1986), Ch. 5 'Authorizing the sovereign', pp. 114–31.

the possibility that the multitude of the people which was shaped into a united entity by the sovereign representative should be able to use this newly founded unitariness for challenging and controlling the decision-making prerogative of the representer.[33] But it was not a necessary corollary of his model that the sovereign agency should be embodied in a single person. Hobbes saw the authorization as coming from the people through choice or election for a special purpose, but he did not insist on any particular principle for determining the precise shape of the sovereign agency so authorized. It could as readily be a committee (of various sizes) as a single man, the final preference for monarchy stemming from considerations of time-honoured arguments about the procedural difficulties and advantages in decision-making associated with various forms of government.[34]

Despite the conceptual elusiveness and abstraction of the disembodied notion of a united people which lay at the heart of this model of representative popular sovereignty, it was designed to serve the very practical political purpose of setting up the sovereign as an agent of legitimate coercion in the name of the imagined unitary popular state. But the new theory of the 'state' rested on the assumption that territories occupied by real people already existed and that it was their survival, individually, which was favoured by seeing them not simply as spatial entities but also as temporally continuous *political* processes of occupation. The new theory said virtually nothing about the legitimacy of the spatial borders themselves. The boundaries were *de facto*; they were functionally connected to the sovereign's ability to perform the task which it was legitimated for, the protection of the population living within its territory. Nor did the theory say anything about the world beyond the sovereign's protection. The state itself was deemed to live in the state of nature, in the realm of might and competing reasons of state.[35] Where the new theory of the state really struck home was by making it abundantly clear that successful states had to homogenize their populations in all those aspects which affected their ability to remain united enough to maintain their citizens' survival. This homogenization required the state's members to accept political obligation in exchange for their own safety. But the size of the state in question was a direct product of

[33] See Noel Malcolm, 'Hobbes and Spinoza' in J.H. Burns and M. Goldie (eds), *The Cambridge History of Political Thought* 1450–1700 (Cambridge, Cambridge University Press, 1991), pp. 541–2, and Richard Tuck, *Hobbes* (Oxford, Oxford University Press, 1989), pp. 66–7.

[34] For Hobbes retaining some features (at the minimum as a procedural assumption) of the principle of an elective creation of sovereignty by majority as the 'institution' of a 'common-wealth' see *Leviathan*, Ch. 18, p. 121. On the comparative merits of monarchy, democracy and aristocracy see Ch. 19 'Of the severall Kinds of Common-Wealth by Institution, and of Succession to the Soveraigne Power', pp. 129–35. The succession issue was important, as Hobbes explained, 'as there was order taken for an Artificiall Man, so there be order also taken, for an Artificiall Eternity of life', pp. 135–8. For a challenge of Hobbes over the comparative merits of monarchical and democratic government and a plan to make the electoral procedures of republican government compatible with a large modern country (in fact making it an explicit precondition of the working of such an electoral democracy that the country should be large enough, around a million voters, to make the corrupting influence of family, kin, local circle of acquaintances irrelevant) see the interesting manuscript by his one time disciple Sir William Petty, in Marquis of Lansdowne (ed.), *The Petty Papers* 2 vols (London, Constable, 1927), vol. 2, pp. 35–9 and in English translation in Frank Amati and Tony Aspromourgos, 'Petty *contra* Hobbes: a previously untranslated manuscript', *Journal of the History of Ideas*, 46 (1985), 127–32.

[35] *Leviathan*, Ch. 13 'Of the Naturall Condition of Mankind, as concerning their Felicity, and Misery', p. 90.

the community's power to hold on to territory. Its boundaries remained indeterminate from all other points of view, including language and ethnic homogeneity. The underdetermined character of these boundaries is particularly relevant if one considers it against the background of state-building. Most of the territorial states of Europe were composite or multiple entities stitched together from different pre-existing territorial units. The 'state', in practice, was invented to underscore the continuous and indivisible identity not of small and self-consciously loyal republican communities (although the theory of internal unification had its point even when applied to them), but of larger units of considerable heterogeneity.

The French constitutional revolutionaries followed the same logic in their search for a means to assert the continuity of France over the enormous divide opened up by political and social revolution. They, or at least some of them, choose the term 'nation' to express an idea that was congruent with Hobbes's state. By and large Hobbes's theory of the state has always been taken as, if not more, seriously in France than in Britain[36] and his ideas were an active presence in the half-century leading up to the Revolution. Central ideas of Hobbes were repeated or critically reviewed, for example, in Diderot's *Encyclopédie*.[37] The Genevan J.-J. Rousseau in particular kept the vital relevance of Hobbes's Leviathan at the centre of debate, repeatedly pointing out that its conception of representation made it a ready vehicle for despotism. Rousseau agreed that the democratic multitude who formed the initial community could be imagined as a unity only if one understood that union as a process generating a single disembodied moral person as their *respublica*. But he refused to accept that this abstract collective singularity of a state-person could be properly animated, endowed with a genuine popular will, through the elective authorization of a representative agency with awesome unifying powers embodied in a chosen number of actual human beings. The essence of creating a state was to give birth to the rule of law, putting all the people of the republic without exception under a set of collectively and individually beneficial disciplines which they themselves agree to create. Rousseau attempted, accordingly, to work out a model of the 'general will' which achieved this effect

[36] For the beginning of this process see Quentin Skinner, 'Thomas Hobbes and his disciples in France and England', *Comparative Studies in Society and History*, 8 (1965), 153–67. Richard Tuck claims that with the *Leviathan* in 1651 'the basic character of Enlightenment politics was already in place ... and the men of the Enlightenment themselves recognized this', see *Philosophy and Government*, p. 348. For a survey of traces of Hobbes' later influence see Yves Glaziou, *Hobbes en France au XVIIIe siècle* (Paris, Presses Universitaires de France, 1993).

[37] See the article *État* written by Jaucourt: 'We can consider the state as a moral person whose head is the sovereign, and whose limbs are the individual citizens: accordingly we can attribute to this person certain specific actions and rights that are distinct from those of each citizen, and that no citizen can arrogate to themselves ... the state is a society animated by a single soul that directs all its movements in a consistent manner, with an orientation towards the common good', *Encyclopédie*, vol. 6, p. 19a–19b. Jaucourt, however, also tried to distance the notion of *état* from the modern notion of *souveraineté* (accusing Pufendorf, and thus *per force* Hobbes with conflating the two) and adopted Cicero's definition of *Société civile* instead: *Multitudo, juris consensu, &. utilitatis communione societa'* (p. 19a). On Diderot's use and critique of Hobbes (in 'Hobbisme', 'Droit naturel', 'Autorité politique', 'Cité', 'Citoyen') via borrowing from Pufendorf and Jacob Brucker's *Historia Critica Philosophiae* and importantly in using it as a vehicle for developing a controversy with Rousseau see Robert Wokler, 'The influence of Diderot on the political theory of Rousseau' in *Studies in Voltaire and the Eighteenth Century*, 132 (1975), 55–111. See also the 'Introduction' and the translation of some of these articles in Diderot, *Political Writings*, John Hope Mason and Robert Wokler (eds) (Cambridge, Cambridge University Press, 1992), pp. ix–xv, 6–21, 27–9.

without involving any special agency within the whole community of the people. This was by no means a simple direct democracy; it was however direct in the sense that it involved all the people or citizens all the time inclusively, without allowing abstention or privileging anybody even temporarily, and it totally proscribed what Rousseau saw as the dangerous and unnecessary representation of popular sovereignty. Rousseau recognized that his ultimate project of positing sovereignty directly in the laws themselves, without any further human actuating agency, amounted to attempting to square the circle, but he believed that he had made the underlying idea far clearer than anyone else and left it as a serviceable tool of patriotic education for his Genevan compatriots. In many ways the ideas of the Physiocrats ran on parallel lines, at least in seeking to generate from their particular and highly idiosyncratic version of natural law theory a very similar conception of placing the laws, and not men, in command of the polity and the economy. But Quesnay, Mirabeau and their disciples, who had France in their mind as a model and not tiny republican Geneva, could see no way of circumventing the appointment of a sovereign despot to enforce the rule of law.[38] When they pressed their theory of *despotisme légale* on Rousseau, the Genevan heaped scorn on their naive failure to recognize that no human individual could safely be placed in this position, since power corrupts and absolute power corrupts absolutely. He was also quite clear about the starkness of available choices. If his own squaring of the circle could not work (and he knew it could not), he preferred a Hobbesian despotism to the illusory and confused attempt either to render it *légale* or to make a large country like France submit to the austere discipline of a direct popular republic.[39] The generation of thinkers responsible for the drafting of the first constitutions of revolutionary France were well aware of

---

[38] The much misunderstood Physiocratic theory of *despotisme légale* was presented in a fully fledged form in Pierre Le Mercier de la Rivière, *L'ordre naturel et essentiel des sociétés politiques* (London, J. Nourse and Paris, Desaint, 1767) and reviewed and defended by the abbé Baudeau in the *Ephemerides du citoyen ou bibliothéque raisonnée des sciences morales et politiques*, vol. 12 (Paris, Delalain and Lacombe, 1767), especially '[Explication des mots: despotisme légale]' pp. 190–209. The essence of the theory soon after became incorporated into the doctrine of the *économistes* in Dupont de Nemours, *Origine et progrès d'une science nouvelle* (London and Paris, Desaint, 1768) and then by Baudeau in his *Première introduction à la philosophie économique ou analyse des états policés. Par une disciple de l'ami des hommes* (Paris, Didot, 1771). The sharpest and most substantial attack on *despotisme légale* came from the abbé Mably, in his *Doutes proposés aux philosophes économistes sur l'ordre naturel et essentiel des sociétés politiques* (The Hague, Nyon and Veuve Durand, 1768). For an outline of the birth of the doctrine and the controversy around it see the classic account of Georges Weulersse, *Le Mouvement Physiocratique en France (de 1756 à 1770)*, 2 vols (Paris, Felix Alcan, 1910), Bk. 3, ch. 2 'Les principes de l'ordre politique' (vol. 2, pp. 36–92) and Bk. 5, ch. 2, §2 'Critique des principes politiques des economistes' (vol. 2, pp. 654–67). For a modern account of the range of 18th-century interpretations of despotism, including *despotisme légale*, see Melvin Richter, 'Despotism in P. P. Wiener (ed.), *Dictionary of the History of Ideas*, (New York, Scribner's Sons, 1973), vol. 2, pp. 1–18.

[39] 'Your system is very good for the people of Utopia; it is worthless for the children of Adam', wrote Rousseau to Mirabeau on 26 July, 1767. 'This is, as I used to see it, the great problem of politics, which I compare to that of squaring the circle in geometry and longitude in astronomy: to find a government that puts laws above man. If such a form can be found – and I confess frankly that I believe that it is not to be found – I believe we must pass to the other extreme, and immediately put man as far as possible above the law; to establish, therefore, arbitrary despotism, and the most arbitrary possible. I wish that the despot might be God. In a word, I do not see any tolerable mean between the most austere democracy and the most perfect Hobbism. For the conflict of men and laws, which puts the state into a continual civil war, is the worst of all political states'. The letter was printed in the 1782 edition of Rousseau's work; for the modern critical edition see

these debates and understood quite accurately both the point of Hobbesian state theory and the nature of the difficulties Rousseau and the *économistes* had encountered in their attempts to modify it.

It has sometimes been claimed that Louis XIV's absolutism corresponded neatly to Hobbesian state theory. The mixed constitution was swept away and the all-powerful monarch stood at the apex of society as the single symbol of a unified sovereignty. This interpretation ignores the fact that French subjects were far from being citizens even in the Hobbesian sense and that Louis in no sense represented that artificial moral person which, according to contractarian theory, had first come into being as a democratic union of individuals. With the failure of Louis' grand project to make France the hegemonic power of Europe, the imperial legacy of aggressive monarchical absolutism went through a protracted crisis of legitimation. In effect, France ran the course described in Hobbes's state-building theory in the reverse. It began with the *de facto* unifying and homogenizing powers of a unitary sovereignty, and then pro-ceeded, under pressure, slowly to reshape the underlying political community into the popular entity which in Hobbes's eyes the unitary sovereign should have represented in the first place. In this retroactive legitimation of the absolutist achievement the starting point was the 'state', understood as the king's *état*, and the substratum which it was increasingly made to correspond to in terms of representation was called the 'nation'. Although the term itself had been in use in a variety of traditional significations for quite a long time, as the Marquis d'Argenson remarked in the 1750s, the prominant deployment of the notions of *état* and *nation* in political discourse would have been inconceivable in Louis XIV's time.[40] In many ways *nation* became the battering ram of the critique[41] of the absolutist monarchy, a word easily associated with rights and the defence of liberties.

Footnote continued

letter 5991 (and 5991bis) in R.A. Leigh (ed.), *Correspondence complète de J.-J. Rousseau*, vol. 31 (Oxford, Voltaire Foundation, 1978), pp. 255–64. pp. 238–46, an English translation of the main passages is in John Hope Mason (ed.), *The Indispensable Rousseau* (London, Quartet, 1979), p. 281; Mirabeau's answer is in letter 5998 (30 July 1767), pp. 255–64.

[40] René-Louis de Voyer de Paulmy, marquis d'Argenson, *Journal et mémoires du Marquis d'Argenson publiés pour la première fois d'après les manuscrits autographes de la Bibliothèque du Louvre*, ed. E. J. B. Rathery, 8 vols. (Paris, Jules Renouard, 1866), vol. 8, p. 315. In English translation see [misdated to 21 June, 1754] the *Journal and Memoirs of the Marquis d'Argenson*, ed. E. J. B. Rathery, trans. K. Prescott Wormeley, 2 vols. (London, Heinemann, 1902), vol. 2, p. 294. D'Argenson claimed that this sort of political language had its source in the parliamentary system of England. For his alternative for the reform of France see his *Consideration sur le gouvernement ancien et présent de la France*, (Amsterdam, Marc-Michel Rey, 1764). The original title of d'Argenson's manuscript book was *Jusques où la démocratie peut être admise dans le gouvernement monarchique*, revealing the author's aim to show that the inclusion of a democratic element into the monarchy would support, rather than subvert, sovereignty. See Nannerl O. Keohane, *Philosophy and the State in France. The Renaissance to the Enlightenment* (Princeton, Princeton University Press, 1980), pp. 376–91, based on her Yale Ph.D. dissertation, 'Democratic monarchy: the political theory of the Marquis d'Argenson' (1967); and Joseph Gallanar, 'Argenson's "Platonic Republics" ', *Studies in Voltaire and the Eighteenth Century* 61 (1967), 557–75.

[41] For eighteenth-century notions of 'critique' see Reinhart Koselleck, *Critique and Crisis. Enlightenment and the Pathogenesis of Modern Society* (Cambridge, MA, MIT Press, 1988), Ch. 8 'The process of criticism', pp. 98–123, Kurt Röttgers, 'Kritik', in *Geschichtliche Grundbegriffe*, vol. 3 (Stuttgart, Klett-Cotta, 1982), pp. 651–75; Martin Fontius, 'Critique', in R. Reichardt, E. Schmidt, G. van den Heuvel and A. Höfer (eds) *Handbuch politisch-sozialer Grundbegriffe in Frankreich 1680–1820*, vol. 5 (Munich, Oldenbourg, 1986), pp. 7–20.

The absolutist legacy of Louis XIV could be attacked from a number of very different political directions. One came from the continuing resistance to hegemonic absolutism and centralism as such, in the name of the mixed constitution which had been overridden in the seventeenth-century, but was still potentially anchored to the functioning corporatist entities of the pre-absolutist regime. The claim to represent the *nation* became a key element of the parlementarian opposition, which believed the *parlements*, particularly in the 1750s and 60s, to be substitutes for the representation of the nation by the Estates General.[42] Another, and in a sense opposite, way of attacking the absolutist regime was to point out that it had failed to modernize itself and to adjust its political institutions to the emergence of the modern economy and modern warfare, and to the new web of social relations to which these gave rise in the eighteenth century. A third type of critique contrasted the absolutist monarchical regime to the politics of free commonwealths and held out the liberty of popular republics as an alternative. It was only the second viewpoint, in effect a theory of the modern civilized monarchy, which could generate a critical concept of the *nation* compatible with the intellectual and political strategy behind the Hobbesian theory of the state. When the abbé Sieyès managed to put the *nation* at the centre of the constitutional invention of a regenerated France in the first revolution, he was not simply attacking the *ancien régime*, but was using his critical powers with intellectually devastating effects against the concepts of the nation embedded both in the pre-modern corporatist tradition of the mixed constitution and in direct popular republicanism. Without understanding the dialectic of this fight it is impossible to understand what the word *nation* in the modern idea of the 'nation-state' might really mean.[43]

---

[42] See Keith Michael Baker; 'Representation redefined', in his *Inventing the French Revolution. Essays on French Political Culture in the Eighteenth Century* (Cambridge, Cambridge University Press, 1990), especially the section on 'Parlementary claims', pp. 228–35.

[43] For histories of the concept of the 'nation' in eighteenth-century France and the revolution see: Pierre Nora, 'Nation', in François Furet and Mona Ozouf (eds), *A Critical Dictionary of the French Revolution*, trans. A. Goldhammer (Cambridge, MA, Harvard, 1989), pp. 742–52, Elisabeth Fehrenbach, 'Nation' in R. Reichardt *et al.* (eds), *Handbuch politisch-sozialer Grundbegriffe in Frankreich 1680–1820*, Vol. 7, pp. 75–107; Bernd Schönemann, 'Exkurs: zur Entwicklung der Begriffe *'peuple'* und *'nation'* in Frankreich (1760–1815)' in the article by Reinhart Koselleck, Fritz Gschnitzer, Karl Ferdinand Weiner and Bernd Schönemann, 'Volk, Nation, Nationalismus, Masse' in *Geschichtliche Grundbegriffe*, vol. 7 (Stuttgart, Klett-Cotta, 1992), pp. 321–25; U. Dierse and H. Rath, 'Nation, Nationalismus, Nationalität' in J. Ritter and K. Gründer (eds), *Historisches Wörterbuch der Philosophie*, vol. 6 (Darmstadt, Wissenschaftliche Buchgesellschaft, 1984), pp. 406–14; P. Sagnac, 'L'idée de la nation en France (1788–1789), *Revue d'histoire politique et constitutionelle* 1 (1937), 158–63; R.R. Palmer, 'The national idea in France before the Revolution', *Journal of the History of Ideas* 1 (1940), 95–111; Eberhard Weis, 'Die Bedeutung von Absolutismus und Revolution für den französischen Nationalstaat und das französische Nationalbewußtsein' in Dann, *Nationalismus in vorindustrieller Zeit*, pp. 101–2; Jacques Godechot, 'Nation, patrie, nationalisme et patriotisme en France au 18e siècle', *Annales historiques de la Révolution française* 43 (1971), 481–501; Jacques Godechot, 'The new concept of the nation' in Otto Dann and John Dinwiddy (eds), *Nationalism in the Age of the French Revolution* (London, Hambledon, 1988), pp. 17–8; C. Buzon and C. Girardin, 'La Constitution du concept de nation', in *Autour de Feraud. La lexicographie en France de 1762 à 1835. Actes du colloque international organisé à l'Ecole normale supérieure de jeunes filles les 7, 8, 9 decembre 1984* (Paris, L'Ecole, 1986), pp. 185–91. Norman Hampson, 'The idea of the nation in revolutionary France', in A. Forrest and P. Jones (eds), *Reshaping France: Town, Country and Region during the French Revolution* (Manchester, 1991), pp. 13–25; Norman Hampson, 'La patrie', in Lucas (ed.), *The Political Culture of the French*

Two Models of French Popular Sovereignty: the 'Nation' of Sieyès and the 'People' of the Jacobins

When the various attempts to rescue the war finance system of the absolutist monarchy from collapse failed, and France was plunged into crisis, the country might have reverted to its pre-absolutist mixed constitution, and directly reconvened its last central institution of representation, dormant since 1614–5, the Estates General. Sieyès' sizzling pamphlet *What is the Third Estate?*, was written with the specific aim of destroying any attempt to revive the mixed constitution as wholly unsuited to the modern conditions of France. Its political rhetoric was designed to mow down the claims of the aristocracy and the Church for separate corporate representation as conclusively as possible (the aristocracy were said to be descendants of conquerors, functionless unproductive labourers or simply a small minority thwarting the will of the vast numerical majority); but the essence of the pamphlet lay in its attempt to recapture the logic underlying the case for undivided sovereignty (i.e. an undivided and all inclusive community as the basis of a single unified decision-making power) as clearly as possible, boldly stating that no Estates General could ever solve serious conflict between the estates without appealing either to a higher agency of representation, in which case that agency would be the real sovereign (as French monarchs had realized when they suspended the Estates general for a century and a half), or going back for a decision to those whom it represented, setting up a vicious circle which could lead to nothing but indecision.[44] A composite representative body such as the Estates General could not really adjudicate between the estates which were its constituent parts. Sieyès explained that the French debate could not be resolved simply by choosing between technical modes of representation, without considering whom or what the contending models of representation were supposed to be representative of. He offered a theoretical history of political communities emerging from a condition solely guided by the laws of nature as the compacted body of free individuals (a union, a society, a people, a nation) to a single body possessing one common will. The sequence led from a mere multitude to a direct

---

Footnote continued

Revolution (Oxford, 1988), pp. 125–38; Maurice Cranston, 'The sovereignty of the nation', in Lucas (ed.), *The Political Culture of the French Revolution*, pp. 97–104; Gary Kates, 'Jews into Frenchmen: nationality and representation in revolutionary France' in Ferenc Fehér (ed.), *The French Revolution and the Birth of Modernity* (Berkeley, University of California Press, 1990), pp. 103–16; Liah Greenfield, 'The three identities of France', in her *Nationalism: Five Roads to Modernity* (Cambridge, MA, Harvard University Press, 1992), pp. 89–188.

[44] Emmanuel Joseph Sieyès, *What is the Third Estate?*, trans. M. Blondel, S.E. Finer (ed.) (London, Pall Mall, 1963), p. 130. Sieyès claimed that even a regularly convened Estates General would be a constitutional *petitio principii*. For commentary on the thought of Sieyès in general see Murray Forsyth, *Reason and Revolution. The Political Thought of the Abbé Sieyès* (Leicester, Leicester University Press, 1987), which is far the best treatment of the political thought of any of the major political thinkers or actors in the French Revolution. Forsyth's book is also the first which used extensively the unpublished writings and the large but unwieldy collection of notes by Sieyès in the National Archives in Paris, some now available in print in various places, mainly in Emmanuel-Joseph Sieyès, *Écrits Politiques* Roberto Zapperi (ed.) (Paris, Editions des Archives Contemporaines, 1985), pp. 45–91. Sieyès' printed works and pamphlets, and some newspaper reports of his speeches are now also available in a three volume collection of photographic reprints, Marcel Dorigny (ed.), *Oeuvres de Sieyès* (Paris, Editions d'Histoire Sociale, 1990).

democracy and then, as the community grew in size, to indirect democracy or a system of representation.[45] For Sieyès the association of free individuals living under the laws of nature, if and when they become united into a single body with one common will, was the 'nation'.[46] To the question where the 'nation' was to be found, Sieyès gave a very simple answer: it was in the '40,000 parishes which embrace the whole territory, all its inhabitants and every element of the commonwealth'.[47] The supporting mechanism of unification in his theory was not Rousseau's patriotic political chemistry of the general will[48] but a theory of the *complete* nation as an embodiment of utilitarian or commercial sociability operating through the reciprocities of the division of labour.[49] A population like this, connected through the unavoidable common effort of economic

[45] *What is the Third Estate?*, pp. 120–3. The third stage was called by Sieyès 'government by proxy' (*gouvernement exercé par procuration*).

[46] *What is the Third Estate?*, pp. 126–8. Sieyès emphasized that the existence of the nation in itself cannot be explained by any theory or myth of creation, including contract theory, since it would involve imagining the nation contracting with itself, which could not be binding. 'Every attribute of the nation', he explained, 'springs from the simple fact that it exists', owing its existence 'to *natural* law alone'.

[47] *What is the Third Estate?*, p. 133.

[48] See a discussion of Rousseau's attempt to express the nature of the *être morale*, or *personne morale* (the institutional entity brought into being by the union of its members) through a chemical metaphor in the Geneva Manuscript of the *Contrat Social* (*On the Social Contract or Essay about the Form of the Republic* [First Version, commonly called the *Geneva Manuscript*], trans. J. R. Masters in Rousseau, *On the Social Contract with Geneva Manuscript and Political Economy*, ed. R. D. Masters (New York, St. Martin's Press, 1978), pp. 159–60) by John Hope Mason, 'Individuals in society: Rousseau's republican vision, *History of Political Thought* 10 (1989), 89–112. For Rousseau's complaint about the 'poverty of the language' to describe adequately the relation between individuals and the political community (the sovereign power) in terms of the *civitas* imagined as a moral person, see Ch. 4 of the *Social Contract*.

[49] For the crucially important theory of the 'complete nation', as the sum total of the private and public activities of a nation capable of material-economic and cultural, as well as military and political, survival see *What is the Third Estate?*, Ch. 1. A more sustained exposition of the connection between commercial sociability and the political constitution of the nation is to be found in Sieyès' introduction of his version of, or more precisely alternative to, the declaration of the rights of man, which he read to the Constitutional Committee on 20 July 1789, and published under the title *Préliminaire de la Constitution. Reconoissance et exposition raisonnée des droits de l'homme et du citoyen. Lu les 20 et 21 Juillet 1789, au Comité de la Constitution*, in *Écrits Politiques*, pp. 192–206; see also the detailed commentary in Forsyth, *Reason and Revolution*, pp. 108–119. In effect this makes Sieyès a 'socialist' in the sense the term was understood in the late 18th century, i.e. as somebody who had accepted Pufendorf's emendation to Hobbes's theory of the state of nature as a state without society and accepted commercial reciprocity as the real foundation of man's ability to form a common social life and provide foundations for politics. A 'socialist' opposed natural sociability and the Christian idea of sociability based on love, and hence accepted that the basis of modern politics was the 'unsocial sociability' described in such critical terms in Rousseau's *Second Discourse*. A 'socialist' was a supporter of the idea that the *état social* was commercial society built on the reciprocal satisfaction of human needs through the division of labour. Among Sieyès' manuscripts there is a note indicating that at some point he planned to write a *Traité du socialisme ou du but que se propose l'homme en société et des moyens qu'il y a d'y parvenir*. (Archives Nationales, 284 AP3 dossier 1[3], undated; I owe this reference to Michael Sonenscher). For an explanation of the idiom see my, 'The language of sociability and commerce: Samuel Pufendorf and the foundations of the "Four-Stages" theory'; for eighteenth-century definitions of the socialist position see Gottlieb Hufeland, *Lehrsätze des Naturrechts und der damit verbundenen Wissenschaften* (Jena, Cuno, 1790), p. 16, and Ernst Ferdinand Klein, *Grundsätze der Natürlichen Rechtswissenschaft nebst eine Geschichte derselben* [1797], p. 356. For commentary on 18th-century usage see See Wolfgang Schieder, 'Sozialismus' in *Geschichtliche Grundbegriffe*, vol. 5 (Königstein, Scriptor, 1979), particularly §2 ' "Socialistae", "socialisti" und "Socialisten" in der rechtsphilosophischen Terminologie der frühen Neuzeit', pp. 924–34; Hans Müller, *Ursprung und*

survival, Sieyès argued, could function as a single body only if its unity as a 'nation' was built on the *political* homogenization of its entire membership. For the French to become a 'nation', the territorial unification of France, inherited from the 'despot' Louis XIV, had to be complemented by civil egalitarianism.

The first step towards this goal was consummated when the Estates General transformed itself not into a House of Commons shaped after the British model, or an Assembly of the Majority, or even an 'Assembly representing the People of France' (as Mirabeau had suggested), but into a united and indivisible *Assemblée Nationale* on 17 June 1789.[50] Defeating the mixed constitution (in effect the second time round in the history of France) was however only the first leg of the argument. The further question was how the homogenized 'nation' could act out its popular sovereignty in a properly functioning unitary political regime. In other words, in the wake of rejecting both absolute monarchical sovereignty and its historical opponent, divided sovereignty, the meaning of 'national' popular sovereignty had itself to be clarified. The clash between the various interpretations came to a head in the drafting of the new constitution and in the debate over allowing a royal veto against the National Assembly. When the first *Declaration of the Rights of Man* was endorsed by the *Assemblée National* at the end of August 1789,[51] its Article III borrowed the

---

Footnote continued

Geschichte des Wortes "Sozialismus" und seiner Verwandten (Hannover, J. H. W. Dietz Nachf., 1967); Franco Venturi, 'Towards a historical dictionary: ['socialist' and] 'socialism' [in 18th-century Italy], in Venturi, *Italy and the Enlightenment: Studies in a Cosmopolitan Century*, ed. S. Woolf, trans. S. Corsi (London, Longman, 1972), pp. 52–62. For the subsequent transformation of this vocabulary into the language of 'individualism' see Arthur E. Bestor, Jr., 'The evolution of the socialist vocabulary', *Journal of the History of Ideas* 9 (1948), 259–302 and Gregory Claeys, ' "Individualism", "socialism", and "social science": further notes on a process of conceptual formation', *Journal of the History of Ideas*, 47 (1986), 81–93.

[50] See Lynn Hunt, 'The "National Assembly" in K.M. Baker (ed.), *The Political Culture of the Old Regime*, vol. 1 *The French Revolution and the Creation of Modern Political Culture* (Oxford, Pergamon, 1987), pp. 403–15; and Eberhard Schmitt, '*Repraesentatio in Toto* und *Raepresentatio Singulariter*. Zur Frage nach dem Zusammenbruch des französischen Ancien régime und der Durchsetzung moderner parlamentarischer Theorie und Praxis im Jahr 1789', *Historische Zeitschrift* 213 (1971), 529–76. The argument against Mirabeau's suggestion turned on the interpretation of the meaning of the French word *peuple*, which for the deputies of the Third meant the *populus*, the entire constituency of the *civitas*, while for the nobility and the clergy it carried the association of the lower orders, the Latin *plebs*. It was deemed that *nation* rather than *peuple* was the correct, that is inclusive modern French equivalent of the *populus*. For the ambivalences of the term see the article 'Peuple' in the *Encyclopedie*, by Jaucourt, which is almost entirely taken from the *Dissertation sur la nature du peuple* in the Abbé Coyer's *Dissertations pour être lues* (The Hague, Pierre Gosse, 1755), for a discussion see the essay of Jean Fabre, 'L'article "Peuple" de l'*Encyclopédie* et le couple Coyer-Jaucourt', in Henri Coulet (ed.), *Images du peuple au dix-huitème siècle: Colloque d'Aix-en-Provence, 25 et 26 octobre 1969* (Paris, Armand Colin, 1973).

[51] The final text of the '*Déclaration des droits de l'homme et du citoyen' décrétés par l'Assemblée nationale dans les séances des* 20, 21, 22, 23, 24, 26 *août et* 1er *octobre*, 1789, *acceptés par le Roi le* 5 *octobre*' and the previous proposals are now conveniently collected in three collections published for the bicentenary celebrations of the revolution, Stéphane Rials (ed.), *La déclaration des droits de l'homme et du citoyen* (Paris, Hachette, 1988), Christine Fauré (ed.), *Les Déclarations des droits de l'homme de 1789* (Paris, Payot, 1988), A. de Baecque, W. Schmale and M. Vovelle (eds), *L'an 1 des droits de l'homme* (Paris, Presses du CNRS, 1988), the most complete selection being that of Rials, whose 473 pages introduction is the best monographic treatment of the genesis of the *Declaration*. From the beginning of the official debate in the Assemblée Nationale there were about thirty projects or comments tabled, Rials publishes another seventeen which were conceived between the declaration of the *parlement* of Paris in May 1788 and the end of June 1789. The most complete list is in Annexe I 'Les Projets de 1789' in Marcel Gauchet, *La Révolution des droits de*

succinct formulation of popular sovereignty first presented to the constitutional committee by General Lafayette: 'The principle of all sovereignty resides essentially in the nation'.[52] Sieyès (who hated the populist American idea of

Footnote continued
l'homme (Paris, Gallimard, 1989), pp. 319–23. The sequence of deliberations, the formation of the three committees entrusted with the editorial work and the final discussion are presented in detail in Ch. 1 of Rials' introduction '*Le travail déclaratoire*', pp. 115–319 and a useful overview is in K. M. Baker, 'The idea of a Declaration of Rights' in Dale Van Kley (ed.), *The French Idea of Freedom: The Old Regime and the Declaration of the Rights of Man* (Stanford, Stanford University Press, 1994), pp. 154–96. See also Georg Jellinek, *Die Erklärung der Menschen- und Bürgerrechte. Ein Beitrag zur modernen Verfassungsgeschichte*, (Leipzig, Duncker und Humblot, 1895), English translation as *The Declaration of the Rights of Man and of the Citizen. A Contribution to Modern Constitutional History*, trans. M. Ferrand (New York, H. Holt, 1901), and Jürgen Sandweg, *Rationales Naturrecht als revolutionäre Praxis. Untersuchungen zur 'Erklärung der Menschen und Bürgerrechte' von 1789* (Berlin, Duncker und Humblot, 1972). For the understanding of the notion of 'right' at the period see Wolfgang Schmale, 'Droit' in Rolf Reichardt and Hans-Jürgen Lüsebrink (eds), *Handbuch politisch-sozialer Grundbegriffe in Frankreich*, vol. 12 (Munich, Oldenbourg, 1992), pp. 78–85.

[52] '*Motion de M. le M^{quis} de La Fayette relativement à la déclaration des droits de l'homme* (11 juillet 89)' see Fauré, p. 87, Rials, pp. 590–1, and with the account of the discussion which followed Lafayette's presentation on the same day in de Baecque *et al.*, pp. 65–8. Lafayette's was the very first draft for the *Declaration* presented to the first special committee in charge of drafting the new constitution and it had a great influence on the decision that the constitution should be prefaced by a declaration of rights after the American model. There are two drafts by Lafayette among the papers of Jefferson, and the final version of the *Declaration* (approved by the Assembly) represents a combination of the wording of the two. In the first (which reached Jefferson as early as January 1789) the word *principe* qualifying *toute souveraineté* is not yet there, in the second it is present, but the word *essentiellement* is replaced by the phrase 'imprescriptibly'. Jefferson, whose comments on the margins on the draft survive, left the future Article III unchanged, nonetheless on the sheet of paper which Lafayette finally submitted for circulation to the Constitutional Committee the word 'imprescriptibly' had been crossed out at the last moment (see the photocopy of Lafayette's original handwritten submission in Fauré, p. 85). Mounier, the monarchist spokesman for the committee, reproduced this second version without change in his own shorter submission for the *Declaration*, and in the longer Article II of the Constitutional Committee's joint draft proposal which he also presented, both of them submitted on the 27th of July (Fauré, p. 109–17; 119–21; Rials, pp. 612–4, 606–8). The final text of the article in question, following the reconstitution of the committee (twice) and the submission of many further proposals, remained virtually the same, except that it again contained the moderating adjective 'essentially' which was there in Lafayette's very first draft. For these drafts, and Lafayette's letter urgently requesting consultation with the author of the American *Declaration of Independence* on the night before presenting his proposal to the constitutional committee see Gilbert Chinard, *The Letters of Lafayette and Jefferson* (Baltimore, Johns Hopkins Press, 1929), pp. 134–42, Julian P. Boyd (ed.) *The Papers of Thomas Jefferson* (Princeton, Princeton University Press, 1958), vol. 14, 438–9, and vol. 15, pp. 230–3, and Rials, pp. 528–9, 567–8. An analysis of the debate is given by Fauré on pp. 313–4 of her edition. For a detailed general analysis of Lafayette's activities in 1789 see L. Gottschalk and M. Maddox, *Lafayette in the French Revolution: Through the October Days* (Chicago, Chicago University Press, 1969), pp. 13–6, 80–99, 220–6. Lafayette's influence on the final draft of the *Declaration* is traced in detail in Chinard, 'Déclaration des droits de l'homme', *Cahiers d'histoire de la Révolution française*, no. 1 (1947), 66–90. Some apparent freemasonic associations are indicated by Serge Hutin; 'Les sources initiatiques de la "Déclaration des droits de l'homme" ', in Jacques Viard (ed.), *L'Esprit républicain*, *colloque d'Orléans*, 4 *et* 5 *Septembre* 1970 (Paris, Klincksieck, 1972), pp. 163–74. The first English translation was perhaps the one attached in the appendix to Richard Price's famous sermon greeting the French Revolution reproducing (inadvertently) Lafayette's shorter first version: 'The nation is essentially the source of all sovereignty', see *A Discourse on the Love of Our Country, delivered on Nov. 4, 1789, at the Meeting-House in the Old Jewry, to the Society for Commemorating the Revolution in Great Britain. With an Appendix, containing the Report of the Committee of the Society; an Account of the Population of France; and the Declaration of Rights by the National Assembly of France* (London, T. Cadell, 1789), 'Appendix', p. 6. This was then repeated soon after in Tom Paine's, *Rights of Man* [1791], ed. G. Claeys (Indianapolis,

drafting a list of basic rights and had to be prevailed upon to draw up one)[53] did not include an item about sovereignty *per se* in his proposal.[54] Although he concurred with the underlying drift of Lafayette's somewhat vague 'national' definition,[55] he preferred to use the language of 'people' and 'power' and

Footnote continued

Hackett, 1992), p. 78. A somewhat different modern English translation of the first sentence of Article III as presented above is by Keith Baker (ed.), in his *The Old Regime and the French Revolution*, University of Chicago Readings in Western Civilization, vol. 7 (Chicago, University of Chicago Press, 1987), p. 238: 'The source of all sovereignty resides essentially in the nation'. For Baker's translation of *principe* as 'source' see his 'Fixing the French Constitution' in *Inventing the French Revolution*, p. 271.

[53] In the 'Délibérations à prendre pour les Assemblées de Bailliages' which Sieyès drafted for the *Instruction donnée par S.A.S. Monseigneur Le Duc d'Orleans, à ses représentans aux baillages* ([Paris], 1789), under the rubric 'Besoins nationaux les plus pressans' he still listed in the first place the need for a 'Déclaration des Droits', pp. 39, 44, because it would give everybody access to the knowledge of the '*grands droits Sociaux*'. An important document of Sieyès' thinking about the nature of rights and the idea of declaring the rights of humanity is in his manuscript draft from 1795 'Sur les Déclaration des droits en général, sur celle de 1789 en particulier, sur leurs bases générales. Écrit en l'an III', printed in Fauré, *Les Déclarations des droits de l'homme de 1789*, pp. 319–24, see particularly Sieyès' critique of the false declarations of the past and his explanation of why he presented his 1789 declaration as a '*reconnaisance*' of the '*fins et des moyens*' of the social state as a 'préliminaire' to the 'Constitution politique', see p. 322. At the end the choice in the National Assembly had to be made between the two genres, one which was sophisticated, coherently developed and satisfying to most 'enlighted minds' (Sieyès'), and the one, descending from Lafayette, which was disjointed and programmatic, but had the merit of simplicity and effectiveness, see Champion de Cicé, archbishop of Bordeaux, National Assembly, 27 July, 1789, *Archives Parlementaires d 1787 a 1800. Recueil complet des débats législatifs et politiques des chambres françaises*, 1ere serie, 1787 à 1799, 127 vols. (Paris, Libraire Administrative, 1875), vol. 8, p. 282. For the debate on the wisdom of following the American model see Gauchet, *La Révolution des droits de l'homme*, Ch. 2 'Surpasser l'Amérique', pp. 36–59.

[54] For the paucity of Sieyès' use of the term sovereignty see Forsyth, *Sieyes*, pp. 181–2. The first time he dealt with the issue of sovereignty *qua* sovereignty publicly was after Thermidor, on 20 July 1795, in his *Opinion de Sieyès sur plusieurs articles des titres IV et V du projet de constitution; pronnocée à la Convention le 2 thermidor de l'an troisime de la République*, reprinted in Paul Bastid, *Sieyès et sa pensée* (Paris, Hachette, 1939), 'Thèse Complementaire', in the section entitled by Bastide as 'Critique de l'idée de souveraineté', pp. 17–8. He announced that sovereignty understood as unlimited powers was a 'monstrosity in politics, and a great error on the part of the French people' (p. 17) and criticized the French idea of the sovereignty of the people modelled on the traditional sovereignty of the king. It is clear that he wished to avoid these associations of the word 'sovereignty' and underlined the idea that his notion of popular sovereignty was not unlimited, but restricted to the final decision-making right of a number of specially elected or constituted authorities with specific functional ends. See also the important manuscript essay of Sieyès, on which the *Opinion* was drawing heavily, 'Bases de l'ordre social ou série raisonée de quelques idées fondamentales de l'état social et politique: an III' (between September 1794 or March 1795), frequently cited by Forsyth, *Sieyes*, for the intellectual position of the manuscripts on sovereignty see p. 181. For an interesting analysis see Bronislaw Baczko, 'Du Contrat social des français: Sieyès et Rousseau' in Baker (ed.), *The Political Culture of the Old Regime*, pp. 493–513, particularly the section on '*Ré-publique*' et *ré-totale*', pp. 507–11.

[55] It is probable that Lafayette's idea of substituting the 'nation' for 'people' as the source of sovereignty was influenced by this parlementarian language. Compare Lafayette's phrasing to American formulations, such as the 'Declaration of the Rights of the Inhabitants of the Commonwealth of Massachusetts' in the Massachusetts Constitution of 1780, Art. V. 'All power residing originally in the people. . . .' in P.B. Kurland and R. Lerner (eds), *The Founders' Constitution*, vol. 1 (Chicago, University of Chicago Press, 1987), p. 12. The Pennsylvania declaration was very similar except using the word 'authority' instead of 'power'. Rials juxtaposes Lafayette's first draft to the '*Déclaration des droits de la nation*' of the *parlement* of Paris from May 1788, which consistently formulates its political agenda in terms of the 'nation', see pp. 522–29. In the last sentence of his proposal Lafayette wrote: 'Since the introduction of abuses, and the rights

emphasized that the nation should be understood as the whole of the people acting as the *pouvoir constituant*. In his discursive explication of the basic principles of society and politics he stated that 'all public powers . . . come from the people, that is to say, the nation', and then added: 'These two terms ought to be synonymous'.[56]

Once it was decided that France had to have a new constitution and that the new regime could not simply modify the monarchy by circumscribing and limiting the monarch's power, it became an uncontested idea that the popular sovereignty of France should be connected to its nationhood. It was nonetheless acutely contentious how strongly and through what mechanism 'nation' and 'sovereignty' could be made to correspond to each other. The debate on the royal veto, following the acceptance of the *Declaration of the Rights of Man and Citizen*, was essentially a clash about the unitariness and indivisibility of national sovereignty and the respective roles of the king and the National Assembly within the new system.[57] The proposal for an absolute royal veto was supported both by proponents of a new ultra-civilized monarchy of the English kind, who thought in terms of separation of powers and checks and balances, and by most of the aristocracy who wished to retain as much of the royal prerogative as possible. A suspensive veto, essentially a moderating and delaying measure like that in the American system, became the cause of those who also disliked, and indeed feared, the idea of unitary representation by the National Assembly, but rejected the idea that the balance should be provided by a strong monarchy possibly thwarting the people's will. The participants of the discussion surveyed repeatedly all the ancient theories of democracy and the more modern examples of resistance and the various institutions which had been invented to limit the use of power and argued at length about the trustworthiness of the people in various situations and the passions which ruled in modern politics. Since the spokesman for the English model, Mounier, incorporated Lafayette's cautious definition of national sovereignty in his own proposals, his opponents on the 'patriot' side tended to express their confidence in the people by rephrasing Article III in a shorter and more radical formulation, stating without any further qualification that sovereignty resided in the nation. The difference, ignoring the word *principe* at the beginning of Lafayette's sentence, lay in the acceptance or denial of the full force of the principle of representation, in the issue of whether the people could ever construe its sovereignty as control over the legislative directly or only through

---

Footnote continued

of succeeding generations necessitate the revision of all human institutions, it should be possible for the nation to call, in certain cases, an extraordinary convocation of the deputies, with the sole object to examine and to modify, if necessary, the vices of the constitution'. In a later published version, entitled *Première déclaration européenne des droits de l'homme et du citoyen*, however, the word '*la nation*' was omitted from this crucial sentence, see Rials, p. 591. For a likely explanation see Lafayette's position concerning the royal veto and the 'appeal to the people' below.

[56] *Préliminaire de la Constitution*, *Écrits politiques*, p. 200.

[57] For a detailed analysis of the debate see Pasquale Pasquino, 'La théorie de la "balance du législatif" du premier Comité de Constitution', in François Furet and Mona Ozouf (eds), *Terminer la Révolution. Mounier et Barnave dans la Révolution Française* (Grenoble, Presses Universitaires de Grenoble, 1990), pp. 67–89; for its apparent connection to the proper location of the sovereignty of the nation see Keith Baker, 'Fixing the French Constitution', in *Inventing the French Revolution*, pp. 252–305. See also W. Näf, 'Die Metamorphose von Königtum und Königin in der französischen Verfassung von 1791', *Historisches Jahrbuch* 74 (1955), 373–82.

various mechanisms of voluntary but binding mediation. The partisans of the suspensive veto accepted that in a large and modern country centralized representative institutions were necessary, but hoped to retain the essence of the idea of the direct popular sovereignty of the nation by allowing the king to appeal to the people against the decisions of the representative body of the National Assembly.

Sieyès saw the danger in reneging on the identification of the 'nation' and 'people' and became the strongest opponent of the idea of the royal veto (in this case along with Robespierre).[58] He saw representation as a fundamental fact of modern society, as something indelibly inscribed in the division of labour and commercial sociability,[59] and political representation as a permanent necessity in any large and populous country in which it was virtually impossible to unite the voice of the people directly. A country based on a single nation had the potential to be united, this was the very essence of his doctrine of the nation, but the actual act of unification for the purpose of decision-making had to be effected through a rigorously unifying representation. To give a single voice to the nation, the constituted body of the representative institution had also be be strictly '*one* and *indivisible*'.[60] To allow an appeal against it directly to the people, in fact to the regional assemblies which were closest to the 'people' in their electoral base, was to introduce a practice which by its very nature was divisive. The representative system was not some second-best option for France, it was the only way for responsible popular rule. A royal veto (whether absolute or suspensive), he claimed, would be an introduction of arbitrariness into the new system, a '*lettre-de-cachet*' directed against the national will, against the whole nation'.

The debate was not simply about the unity of the representative political system. It also had implications for the integrity and unity of France. Lafayette, a supporter of the suspensive veto, feared civil war and saw terrible dangers in the tendency of the reformist *monarchiens* to ally themselves with the aristocratic factions who wished to use their provincial power base to oppose the revolution in case a strong royal centre could not be preserved. He violently opposed the idea of national disintegration and the use of the provinces against centralized reforms, 'I prefer an executive power a little too strong a hundred times more than the plan of federative provinces which will divide France into bits'.[61] Sieyès continued this anti-federalist argument, but he also wished to alert

<hr/>

[58] 'Dire de M. de Robespierre, député de la Province d'Artois à l'Assemblée Nationale, Contre le veto royal, soit absolu, soit suspensif', *Oeuvres de Maximilien Robespierre*, vol. 6, *Discours 1789–1790*, eds. M. Bouloiseau, G. Lefebvre and A. Soboul (Paris, Presses Universitaires de France, 1950), pp. 86–95. According to Robespierre the 'appeal to the people' demanded by the partisans of the suspensive veto was a chimera, which would *de facto* subordinate the judgment of the National Assembly to that of the provincial assemblies (pp. 92–3).

[59] This had been a leading idea of Sieyès since the 1770s when he commenced his intellectual career with a critique of Physiocracy. For a very clear statement see his *Opinion* of 1795 'Everything is representative in the social state. It is to be found everywhere in the private as in the public order; it is the mother of productive and commercial industry as of liberal and political progress. I would go further and say that it is identical with the very essence of social life' (p. 16, see also Forsyth, *Sieyes*, p. 144).

[60] *Dire de l'Abbé Sieyes sur la Question du Veto Royal, & C. A la séance du 7 septembre* 1789, in *Écrits*, p. 242.

[61] Letter to his friend Latour-Maubourg, September 10, 1789, in L. Mortimer-Ternaux, *Histoire de la Terreur 1792–1794*, 8 vols. (Paris, Michel Lévy Frères, 1862–81), vol. 1, p. 43, see also for

the deputies proposing the suspensive veto to the dangerous unintended consequences of their idea of following the example of the United States. If they were allowed to smuggle direct democracy into the new representative constitution by the back-door, they would also have to deal not only with its political, but also its territorial logic. He was as much against the prominence of provincial assemblies as Lafayette. But, equally, allowing an appeal to the people against the National Assembly, he prophesied, would 'cut, chop, and tear France into an infinity of small democracies, which then join together simply by the ties of a general confederation, rather as the thirteen or fourteen United States of America formed a confederation in a general convention'.[62] Any attempt to tamper with the unity of the representative system could put the very survival of the idea of the united nation of France in danger:

> France must not be an assemblage of little nations, governing themselves
> separately as democracies; it is not a collection of states; it is a single whole,
> composed of integral parts; these parts must not enjoy separately a complete
> existence, because they are not merely united wholes, but parts forming but
> one whole. The difference is immense; it is of vital interest to us. All is lost
> if we allow ourselves to consider the municipalities that are being established,
> or the districts, or the provinces, as so many republics united solely by the
> ties of common force or protection. Instead of a general administration
> spreading from a common centre and falling in a uniform manner on the
> furthest reaches of the empire; instead of a legislation formed out of the
> citizens coming together in an ascending scale that reaches up to the National
> Assembly, the sole authorized interpreter of the general will; instead of this
> will that descends once again with all the weight of an irresistible force on
> the very wills that have concurred to form it – instead of all this we will have
> nothing more than a kingdom bristling with every kind of barrier, a chaos
> of local customs, regulations and prohibitions.[63]

Allowing the break-up of France, Sieyès insisted, would undo the work of civilization and enlightenment. Modern nations resembled ancient states very little, European states, he argued, were rather like immense workshops, geared towards the production of wealth and the consumption of goods. Ancient democratic republicanism was not a good guide for understanding the modern condition. When, somewhat later, he was entrusted with the design of the territorial reorganization of French administration, he enlarged on the benefits of keeping France together as a single and indivisible 'nation', instead of allowing it to devolve into a republican federation of small states united solely for the purposes of common defence. His thinking was entirely functional. Large states, he claimed, were in a much better position to provide the nation with the primary goods it needed, i.e. internal peace, external security and common welfare. The disadvantages of small states, and particularly of turbulent little republics, were that they were frequently embroiled in war with

Footnote continued

letters on the same subject in *Mémoires, correspondance et manuscrits de général Lafayette publié par sa famille*, 6 vols. (Paris, H. Fournier Aîné, 1837–8), vol. 2, on the unfolding of the debate on the royal veto, and Lafayette's role in it, see Gottschalk-Maddox, *Lafayette: Through the October Days*, pp. 227–55.

[62] *Question du Veto Royal*, p. 234.

[63] *Question du Veto Royal*, pp. 234–5, the translation by Forsyth, *Sieyes*, p. 137.

each other, a tendency enhanced by their intimate proximity. Thus, for external defence such small states were obliged to enter into treaty systems which were often highly unstable and open to the divisive diplomatic intrigues of other states. Finally they became incapable of carrying out large public projects which could advance their economy and the progress of the sciences.[64]

Sieyès did not believe that stopping the fragmentation of France was simply a matter of political argument. He realized that particularism (whether aristocratic, or democratic) will always rise while the historical territorial formations within which they could operate remained in existence. He urged his opponents in the debate on the royal veto not to decide about the respective merits of the unitary representative system and the 'appeal to the people' until the territorial administration of the entire country had been reshaped in such a way as to become harmonious with the system of representation. In his proposal for the administrative-territorial reform of France Sieyès wished to give support to both the aims which he revealed in that controversy: to make the unitary representative system genuinely possible and to keep France together as a large nation. He advocated a very thorough policy of homogenization, the melting down of the diverse people of France into a single people. The aim was to abolish the ancient territorial divisions of France and to get rid of both the notion and indeed the very word of 'province' altogether.[65] A united nation needed reasonably uniform and internally homogenized primary units, governed by the very same administrative principles. To make the people *one*, a new process of engineering a nation was necessary, and to describe it Sieyès invented the neologism 'political *adunation*'. There could be only one *esprit de corps*, that of France. Sieyès envisaged a system of cantons, communes and departments, built up uniformly and then integrated step by step, so that the civic spirit could be properly exercised and replenished at the lower levels without giving way to a democratic tendency of separatism. Although not all of his ideas were accepted, those which concerned administrative nation-building and electoral reform were on the whole embraced by the National Assembly. But the very success of his unificatory strategy, which proved to be of lasting effect, created paradoxical results. While he was supported in the creation of the departmental system, he lost on the issue of the royal veto. The deputies did not heed Sieyès' message. They wished to keep France together, but in approving the suspensive veto of the king they also voted for a constitutional device which allowed for the possibility of a direct democratic appeal to the people behind the backs of the National Assembly. As Keith Baker has remarked about this complicated and self-destructive deliberative sequence, the National Assembly at this point effectively, if unwittingly, voted for the 'terror'.[66] In 1793 Sieyès warned that if the partisans of republican liberty and direct democracy could discredit the national 'representative system in the name of liberty itself' one might expect the coming of 'a most disastrous

[64] These disadvantages of small states are summarized in Forsyth, *Sieyes*, p. 140, based on Sieyès' manuscript preparatory draft for his *Observations sur le rapport du Comité de Constitution, concernant la nouvelle organisation de la France* (Versailles, Baudoin, 1789).

[65] See Rabaut Saint-Etienne: 'We had no longer any provinces: nay they very word province had disappeared from our vocabulary' in J. P. Rabaut [Saint-Etienne], *The History of the Revolution in France*, trans. J. White (London, J. Debrett, 1793), p. 166.

[66] Baker, 'Fixing the French Constitution', p. 305.

era for the human species'.[67] He had the good fortune to survive the consequent republican holocaust and provided its perfect diagnosis: the experiment of coupling the idea of national sovereignty of France to a regime of direct popular democracy produced not a *ré-publique*, but a *ré-totale*.[68]

For a modern reader Sieyès' attack on the *ré-totale* in the name of the 'nation' sounds remarkably prescient and consequently his accomplishment has enjoyed a powerful renaissance in the revisionist interpretation of the French Revolution and in the history of political thought in general.[69] This is fuelled by the recognition that his type of constitutionalism effectively laid the theoretical foundations of the dominant state form of the second half of the twentieth century: democracy today means a representative republic embedded in commercial society.[70] Thinking about the modern representative republic and Sieyès in a historical perspective, however, implies a reversal of the apparent teleology of this vision. Instead of seeing Sieyès as the precursor of these later developments, one realizes that the essence of much of the later debates on nation-states and nationalism must and can only be seen as the protracted and extremely painful re-play of those fundamental dilemmas which burst into the open in the debates about the *Declaration of the Rights of Man and of the Citizen* and the royal veto. In the short run Sieyès' interpretation of the nation did not prevail. His practical influence was greatest in the wake of the publication of *What is the Third Estate?* His impact on the 1791 Constitution was already much weaker than is sometimes assumed, as many of the new political formulations codified reflected successive compromises between the contending interpretations. Nonetheless, the 1791 Constitution stated his position more clearly than the 1789 *Declaration*, claiming that 'sovereignty ... pertains to the nation' and the 'nation ... may exercise [its] powers only by delegation'. The language of the nation then appeared everywhere and replaced

---

[67] 'Des intérêts de la Liberté dans l'état social et dans le système représentatif', *Journal d'Instruction sociale par les citoyens Condorcet, Sieyès et Duhamel*, no. 2 (8 June 1793), 33.

[68] The innovative term was used in two overlapping texts by Sieyès, in the manuscript 'Bases de l'ordre social' and then publicly in *Opinion* p. 18, see also Forsyth, *Sieyes*, pp. 145–6. The new terms were noticed and popularized by Pierre-Louis Roederer, in a review of the *Opinion* published in his *Journal de Paris* on 12 February 1795 under the title 'Du néologisme de Sieyès', reprinted in *Oeuvres du comte P.-L. Roederer*, (Paris, Firmin Didot Fréres, 1853–9), ed. A.-M. Roederer, 8 vols., vol. 4 pp. 204–7.

[69] See the series of influential articles by Pasquale Pasquino, 'Emmanuel Sieyès, Benjamin Constant et le "gouvernement des modernes". Contribution à l'histoire du concept de représentation politique', *Revue française de science politique* 37 (1987), 214–28; 'Citoyenneté, égalité et liberté chez J.-J. Rousseau et E. Sieyès', *Cahiers Bernard Lazare*, nos. 121–122 (1988–89), 150–60; 'Die Lehre vom "Pouvoir Constituant" bei Emmanuel Sieyès und Carl Schmitt' in Helmut Quaritsch (ed.), *Complexio Oppositorum. Über Carl Schmitt* (Berlin, Duncker und Humblot, 1988), pp. 371–85; 'Le concept de nation et les fondements du droit public de la Révolution: Sieyès' in François Furet (ed.), *L'héritage de la Révolution française* (Paris, Hachette, 1989), pp. 309–33; 'The Constitutional Republicanism of Emmanuel Sieyès' in Biancamaria Fontana (ed.), *The Invention of the Modern Republic* (Cambridge, Cambridge University Press, 1994), pp. 107–17.

[70] Pasquale Pasquino, 'Emmanuel Sieyès, Benjamin Constant et le "gouvernement des modernes", Murray Forsyth, 'Thomas Hobbes and the constituent power of the people', *Political Studies*, 29 (1981), 191–203; John Dunn, 'Liberty as a substantive political value', in his *Interpreting Political Responsibility* (Cambridge, Polity, 1990), pp. 61–84; John Dunn, 'The identity of the bourgeois liberal republic' in Fontana (ed.), *The Invention of the Modern Republic*, pp. 206–25.

the adjective 'royal' in the name of all institutions.[71] But the obscure and difficult characterization of the people as indirectly sovereign through the uniting of wills in an abstract representation of the national 'will' was as difficult to comprehend and sustain in actual political argument as ever. Sieyès was no better understood on this point than Hobbes or Rousseau had been. Neither the Girondins, nor the Jacobins agreed with Sieyès' definition of the political community underlying the 'representative system'. In February 1793 Condorcet gave powerful reinforcement to Sieyès' idea and actually used the formula 'national sovereignty', adding that it was 'essentially residing in the entirety of the people';[72] this latter formulation was accepted in the Girondin *Declaration of the Rights of Man* in May 1793.[73] In his constitutional plan he also repeated the warning about the danger of France breaking up into a multitude of small democratic communities.[74] But the Jacobins, who from the beginning were much more inclined to retain the language of *état* than 'nation', did their utmost to expel the notion of 'nation' from the definition of popular sovereignty. In the debate preceding the 1793 *Declaration* Robespierre suggested that the correct formulation should be that the 'people is the sovereign: the government is its work and its property, the public officials are its agents. The people may change its government and recall its deputies whenever it pleases'.[75] The Constitutional Act of June 1793 then combined Condorcet's and Robespierre's version. It talked about *la souveraineté nationale*, but added that 'sovereignty resides in the people'.[76]

If Hobbes's theory of the 'state' is understood as a defence of absolute monarchy and perhaps even as an advocacy of despotism, then the national

---

[71] See Godechot, 'The new concept of the nation' in Dann and Dinwiddy, *Nationalism in the Age of the French Revolution*, pp. 14–15.

[72] Condorcet, 'On the principles of the constitutional plan presented to the National Convention', in Condorcet, *Selected Writings*, ed. K.M. Baker (Indianapolis, Bobbs-Merrill, 1976), p. 150. The 'Principles', presented to the National Convention on behalf of its Committee on the Constitution on 15–16 February 1793, was never adopted. The '*Projet de déclaration des droits naturels, civils et politiques des hommes*', which was presented together with the 'Principles' (the relevant articles being 26 and 27) is reprinted in Gauchet, *La Révolution des droits de l'homme*, Annexe II, pp. 324–6.

[73] 'Déclaration des droits de l'homme, arrêtée le 22 avril et décrétée le 29 mai 1793', reprinted in Gauchet, *La Révolution des droits de l'homme*, Annexe II, pp. 326–8, the relevant article is no. 26.

[74] Condorcet, 'Principles': 'To divide a single state into a republic of confederated states, or to unite confederated states into a single republic, there ought to be powerful motives of public interest – as, indeed, there ought to be for introducing any change not strictly required for the preservation of freedom and equality. But none of these motives exists among us. We could only want such a change in obedience to systematic views of perfection, to sacrifice the whole in favour of some parts, or to sacrifice the present generation to the uncertain good of generations to come. To effect a new revolution within, to establish a system which would necessarily weaken the means of defense of the nation adopting it, would be to expose the safety of the state to the threats of a league of powerful enemies' (pp. 145–6). See also pp. 170–1 concerning the argument against elected bodies of particularistic representation which would 'transform France into a league of confederated republics'.

[75] *Déclaration des droits de l'homme proposée par Maximilen Robespierre* (24 April 1793) *Archives Parlamentaires*, vol 63 (Paris, Imprimerie et Libraire Administrative, 1903), pp. 197–200, in English translations in J. M. Thompson, *Robespierre* [1935] (Oxford, Blackwell, 1988), pp. 355–6, and in a much less careful version in George Rudé, *Robespierre* (Englewood Cliffs, NJ, Prentice Hall, 1967), p. 55.

[76] *Acte Constitutionel du 24 Juin 1793*, Articles 23 and 25, reprinted in Gauchet, *La Révolution des droits de l'homme*, Annexe II, p. 333. The fullest documentary account of the 1793 debate is in Lucien Jaume, *Les Déclarations des droits de l'homme (Du Débat 1789–1793 au Préambule de 1946)* (Paris, Flammarion, 1989), 'Période de la Convention', pp. 215–309, texts, pp. 240–309.

ré-totale might be understood as a natural successor of his theory of sovereignty. But if one accepts that the thrust of Hobbes's notion of the state was to bring popular sovereignty within the orbit of modern political theory, then his approach should be aligned not with the Jacobin notion of the popular state, but with Sieyès' *ré-publique*.[77] For Hobbes the indirect, that is representative, sovereignty of the people was the 'state', and he introduced the term 'state' to distinguish it from the common understanding of the commonwealth as direct popular sovereignty. Sieyès similarly insisted that the people and the nation were the same, but he specifically redefined the term 'nation' to signify that the people's sovereignty, its 'constituent power' could be exercised only through the unitary representative system of the National Assembly as a constituted agency.[78] This was precisely what Hobbes meant by the 'state'. Twinning these specific versions of the words 'state' and 'nation' in the composite term of 'nation-state' introduces not so much an oxymoron, but a plain tautology. As a political definition of the location of sovereignty, Hobbes's 'state' and Sieyès' 'nation' are identical. Sieyès' 'nation' is Hobbes's 'Leviathan'. Both are powerful interpretations, in a sharply converging manner, of the modern popular *civitas* (*cité* or commonwealth).[79]

---

[77] See the powerful argument presented by Murray Forsyth in his, 'Thomas Hobbes and the constituent power of the people.

[78] One should not be misled here by apparent differences in the theoretical specification of the best representer of the 'nation', the most effective mechanism for ensuring the unity of the constituted sovereign representative. Sieyès (like Kant and Hegel after him) saw the advantage in appointing a single monarchical chairman, president or *chef* for the nation (who could be called a king if that helped): 'What monarchists wish to do by means of individual unity, republicans want to do by a collective body. I do not accuse the latter of being insensitive to the need of unity of action; I do not deny that such unity can be established through a senate or supreme executive council; but I do not think it will be badly constituted in a variety of ways. I think the unity of action requires, if it is not to lose any of the advantages that it provides, to be inseparable from individual unity, etc.', Sieyès' response to Thomas Paine's letter defending republicanism, published in the *Moniteur* on 16 July 1791, together with Paine's letter of 8 July 1791, reprinted in *Oeuvres de Sieyès*, vol. 2, No. 30, cited in translation by Forsyth, p. 178. For Sieyès the essence of republicanism did not lie in the collective as opposed to monarchic institutionalization of the unity of representation.

[79] In the 1799 Constitution, on which Sieyès reputedly had a considerable influence, the general introduction to the description of the republic's institutions bore the title '*De l'Exercise des droits de cité*', see *Constitution de la République Française du 22 Primaire an VIII* in L. Duguit and H. Monnier, *Les Constitutions et les principales lois politiques de la France depuis* 1789 (Paris, Librairie Générale de Droit et de Jurisprudence, 1932), p. 118. The other important thinker who co-operated with Sieyès in constructing this constitution was Pierre-Louis Roederer (see Kenneth Margerison, 'The legacy of social science: Condorcet, Roederer and the Constitution of the Year VIII', in *Condorcet Studies II* ed. D. Williams (Frankfurt, Peter Lang, 1987), pp. 13–30), who during the terror amused himself with preparing a new translation of Hobbes's *De Cive* from Latin (and one of the chief reasons which he gave for undertaking this work was that it was from Hobbes that Rousseau took the idea of popular sovereignty). During the winter and spring of 1793 Roederer gave his famous *Cours d'organisation sociale* at the Lycée de Paris, in which he discussed the general theory of sovereignty in some detail, see the *Oeuvres du comte P.-L. Roederer*, vol. 8, 10th discourse, 'De la souveraineté – De la loi', pp. 241–52, in the form of a direct commentary on the debates concerning the *Declaration of the Rights of Man* in 1793. Before embarking on the Hobbes translation he planned to finish his 12th discourse in which he aimed at dissecting the views of Montesquieu, Rousseau, Hobbes and Sieyès on the difference between monarchical and republican government (including a discussion of the Paine-Sieyès encounter), but as the new constitution was accepted by the National Convention he thought it prudent not to continue with the public exposition of his own ideas. The ideas of this 12th discourse, in the form of an imaginary conversation between Hobbes, Locke, Bayle, Voltaire, Helvétius, Rousseau and Sieyès, entitled

The Jacobin notion of 'national sovereignty' was very different from this. It aimed at reversing the whole development of *modern* popular sovereignty, which gradually emerged from the late 16th century onwards, both in its domestic and its external context. Domestically it not only attacked the restricted franchise underlying the electoral machinery of representative government,[80] it also reversed Sieyès' definition of the popular political community in terms of the indirect and artificial unit of the 'nation', which was incapable of properly acting without representation. Such a notion of popular sovereignty, Robespierre claimed, was the most odious despotism ever invented because it allowed no recourse to the people against their own representative.[81] His definition identified 'national sovereignty' as the people's property, the people's state or, by that point, as the people's republic. Domestic sovereignty was now seen as fully embodied, residing in the real people, acting directly. The people in this vision were not seen as individuals united into an artificial body, the sovereign was the corporation (or community) of people as a living actual body. The nation in this sense could not be paired with a Hobbesian definition of the 'state'. Such a dyad would be not just an oxymoron, an incongruity, but a straightforward contradiction. The Jacobins, using the Rousseauist idiom of popular sovereignty to support their case[82] might have thought that they had squared the circle of the rule of law without representation. In practice they chose the option of a severely austere democratic republic against Rousseau's advocacy of strict Hobbism. What in Sieyès' language was the *ré-totale* was a re-enactment of the republic of the ancients, and therefore inappropriate to large modern countries. Sieyès and Condorcet paid dear for their insistence throughout the relevant debates that France must be kept together as a unitary state, in which the Jacobins were their allies against the so called 'federalists'.

Footnote continued

Entretien de plusieurs philosophes célebrés sur les gouvernements républicain et monarchique, were eventually published in the *Journal d'Économie publique* in 1797 and later reprinted in *Oeuvres*, vol. 7, pp. 61–71.

[80] For Robespierre's indignant attack on Sieyès' separation of the people into active and passive citizens, and for the demand for a full national franchise, see his speech to the Constituent Assembly, '[On the Right to Vote]', March 1791, in *Oeuvres de Maximilien Robespierre*, vol. 7, *Discours Janvier-Septembre 1791*, eds M. Bouloiseau, G. Lefebvre and A. Soboul (Paris, Presses Universitaires de France, 1951), pp. 161–6, English translation in George Rudé, *Robespierre*, pp. 13–22. For commentary see William H. Sewell, '*Le citoyen/la citoyenne*: Activity, passivity, and the revolutionary concept of citizenship' in Lucas (ed.), *The French Revolution and the Creation of Modern Political Culture*, pp. 105–13.

[81] *Lettres de Maximilien Robespierre, membre de la Convention nationale de France, à ses commettants*, 1st series, no. 1, 19 October 1792, article 1 'Exposé des principes et but de cette publication', in *Oeuvres de Maximilien Robespierre*, vol. 5, *Les Journaux: Lettres à son commettants*, ed. Gustave Laurent (Paris, GAP, 1961), p. 19. A useful discussion of the issue, with a list of the occurrences where Robespierre returned to this theme is given in J.L. Talmon, *The Origins of Totalitarian Democracy* (New York, Praeger, 1960), pp. 98–107, 298–99.

[82] See Robespierre's intervention in the debate on 'Sur les principes de la souverainité', discussing article III of the constitution of 1791 in the Assembly National, 10 August 1791, *Oeuvres*, vol. 7, pp. 612–4; 614–7. The subject of the debate was whether the words imprescriptible or inaliénable should be added to characterize sovereignty after the adjectives 'one and indivisible'. Robespierre invoked the authority of Rousseau twice (pp. 612, 615) in support of his claim that the people cannot give all their legislative power over to the delegates unless they wished to create the worst kind of despotism in which the nation would cease to exist. For a detailed analysis of the Jacobin theory of sovereignty see Lucien Jaume, *Le discours jacobin et la démocratie* (Paris, Fayard, 1989), particularly Pt. 3, Ch. 2. 'La localisation de souveraineté, une controverse permanente', pp. 282–323, and the 'Conclusion', pp. 389–403.

Having destroyed the mixed constitution – the traditional framework of earlier arguments for the ultimate sovereignty of the people – the 'people' now had to play out their role in an absolutist political space.[83] Since a large country required a powerful centre to govern it, if it was not to fall apart into its regional parts, the national democracy of the people simply inverted rather than replaced the previous centralization and homogenization of France under united monarchical sovereignty. It did not change the spirit of the latter. As Sieyès complained, the Jacobins replaced this carefully thought out *adunation* with simple old fashioned *integration* and *unification*, and breathed the life of monastic communitarianism into it.[84] Royal despotism gave way to the 'despotism of liberty',[85] and the Jacobins committed themselves to a heavily *moralized* political variant of ethnic cleansing. Conducted in the name of republican virtue, the terror was just an extreme form of the internal homogenization of the republican state.

[83] This is the central argument of Koselleck's interpretation in *Critique and Crisis*. François Furet, *Interpreting the French Revolution*, trans. E. Forster (Cambridge, Cambridge University Press, 1981) particularly Pt. 2, Ch. 3. 'Augustin Cochin: the theory of Jacobinism', pp. 164–204 and 'Révolution française et tradition jacobine' in Lucas (ed.), *The Political Culture of the French Revolution*, pp. 329–38, follows a similar line, ultimately tracing back the argument to Tocqueville. The return to Cochin's work served as the battering ram to break the hold of 'neo-republican' and Marxist historiography on the French revolution and helped Furet to re-introduce an interpretation focusing on the political dynamics dictated by the political (or anti-political) ideas of the main protagonists. The centrepiece of this view is the derivation of Jacobin ideology from the type of sociability which served as the hotbed for the production of pre-revolutionary critiques of politics in the 'philosophical societies' and freemasonic lodges, eventually producing a patriotic model of 'direct democracy' and 'unpolitical natural sociability' with 'pre-programmed' disastrous consequences. See the review essay on this topic by Michael Sonenscher and his analysis of the difficulties inherent in trying to produce a causal explanation of the political dynamics of the revolution mainly out of repeated cycles of historiographical critique, explaining too much and too little at the same time, 'The cheese and the rats: Augustin Cochin and the Bicentenary of the French Revolution', *Economy and Society*, 19 (1990), 266–74. A major difference between Koselleck's line of thought and the Cochin interpretation is the central place Koselleck allocates to Hobbes (rather than Rousseau) as the originator of the political philosophy of the Enlightenment, see *Critique and Crisis*, Pt. I. Ch. 2. 'Hobbesian rationality and the origins of the Enlightenment', pp. 23–40. Lucien Jaume moves in a similar direction, adding Bossuet to Hobbes in the ancestry of the absolutist features of the Jacobin theory and practice of centralist 'representation', see *Le discours jacobin*, pp. 358–85.

[84] 'Why do all makers of plans have an involuntary tendency to monasticize people? It is because they are systematic spirits, and they wish to *unify* and *integrate*, instead of to unite [*aduner*]. It is because they regard the individual as materials for a building, his individual liberty is nothing to them', Sieyès, 'Bases de l'ordre social', cited by Forsyth, p. 127.

[85] Maximilien Robespierre, 'Sur les principes de morale politique qui doivent guider la Convention Nationale dans l'administration intérieure de la République, fait au nom du Comité de Salut Public' (5 February 1794), *Oeuvres de Maximilien Robespierre*, vol. 10, *Discours 27 Juillet 1793–27 Juillet 1794*, eds. M. Bouloiseau and A. Soboul (Paris, Presses Universitaires de France, 1967), p. 357, in English 'On the Principles of Moral Policy that Ought to Guide the National Convention in the Internal Administration of the Republic', speech in the name of the Committee of Public Safety, 5 February 1794, in R.T. Bienvenu (ed.), *The Ninth of Thermidor: The Fall of Robespierre* (Oxford, Oxford University Press, 1968), p. 39. Robespierre made clear that a democratic republican government (he equated the two adjectives) had two faces, or two stages, as it were. In peacetime it was a constitutional regime of justice, order and the protection of individual liberty (see pp. 33–4 for a full description of the republican ideal). 'Here the development of our theory would reach its limit, if you had only to steer the ship of the Republic through calm waters. But the tempest rages, and the state of the revolution in which you find yourselves imposes upon you another task'. Under external challenge and at the time of establishing itself as a regime of liberty the republic had to assume the features of an emergency government and put its interest over the rights of its enemies and detractors. This dualism was characteristic of Robespierre's statement about policy aims throughout the revolution.

Against Nationalism: the Brotherhood of Peoples and the Expected Crisis of the 'Nation-State'

The sharp divergences between the Jacobin republican 'nation-state' and the Hobbes-Sieyès type of 'nation-state' based on indirect popular sovereignty become fully visible only when one also considers Robespierre's general theory of how the people should conduct the external affairs of their nation. Sieyès' position was fairly straightforward on this point. The 'nations of the world', Sieyès explained in *What is the Third Estate?*, were just 'like men living outside society or in a "state of nature", as it is called'. The nation was the constituent power and by definition its will could not be subject to any other decision making agency, including external ones. Although individuals could draw on a certain moral power to form nations, Sieyès explained, the same assumption just could not be made on the level of national groups. A nation of nations was not possible; nations had to remain in the a state of nature forever. Nations cannot escape from living in conditions of acute danger, and under such conditions a nation could 'never have too many possible methods of expressing its will' in relation to the outside world. Consequently, Sieyès pressed home the point, the actions of the nation as a unit had to 'remain independent of any procedures'.[86]

This understanding of what sovereignty meant for the relations between nations was fully in harmony with the tradition descending from Grotius and Hobbes, and it was not in any sense innovatory. All that Sieyès claimed was that replacing the mixed constitution by the indirect popular sovereignty of the nation could not be expected in itself to change the shape of the international arena. But there is a powerful interpretation of the origins of modern nationalism which holds that it was this orthodox retaining of the external and exclusivist meaning of sovereignty which gave the French revolutionary language of the 'nation' its peculiar character. It is an oft repeated complaint by opponents of modern nationalism, perhaps most clearly expressed by Hannah Arendt in her *Origins of Totalitarianism*, that

> the secret conflict between state and nation came to light at the very birth of the modern nation-state, when the French Revolution combined the declaration of the Rights of Man with the demand for national sovereignty. The same essential rights were at once claimed as the inalienable heritage of all human beings and as the specific heritage of specific nations, the same nation was at once declared to be subject to laws, which supposedly would flow from the Rights of Man and sovereign, that is bound by no universal law and acknowledging nothing superior to itself. The practical outcome of this contradiction was that from then on human rights were protected and enforced only as national rights and the very institution of a state, whose supreme task was to protect and guarantee man his rights as man, as citizen and national, lost its legal, rational appearance and could be interpreted by the romantics as the nebulous representative of a

---

[86] *What is the Third Estate?*, p. 128. The same idea is clearly repeated in *Deliberations*, p. 40. For Sieyès' thinking on the question of war see his *Rapport du Comitée Défense générale pour organiser le Minstère de la Guerre* (Paris, Imprimerie nationale, 1793), where he clearly states the common view that the powers given to the military are ultimately indefinite in their nature, because the supreme law is the '*salut de la République & de l'armée*' (p. 4). He clearly acknowledged that the defence of the country has to be democratic in its character, but he was concerned that the normal operations of the army should be conducted not democratically, but in the spirit, and under the guidance, of representative government, so that the temptation of dictatorship could be avoided.

'national soul' which through the very fact of its existence was supposed to be beyond or above the law. National sovereignty, accordingly, lost its original connotation of freedom of the people and was being surrounded by a pseudo-mystical aura of lawless arbitrariness.[87]

It is crucial to realise the historical provenance of this judgment. In historical terms Arendt's interpretation of the French revolutionary 'nation-state' is paradoxically identical to the radical Jacobin denunciation of the 1789 and 1793 *Declarations of the Rights of Man*. On 24 April 1793, Robespierre, in a critical speech on the Girondin version of the *Declaration*, first targeted their absolute notion of private property, but at the end went out of his way to note that the most glaring discrepancy between the stated intentions of the *Declaration*, as a document putatively addressed to man in general, and its actual social and political content was in the adoption of the notion of national sovereignty. They had completely neglected 'to record the obligation of brotherhood that bind together the men of all nations, and their right to mutual assistance'. 'It would seem that your declaration has been drafted for a human herd planted in an isolated corner of the globe', he continued, 'and not for the vast family of nations to which nature has given the earth for its use and dwelling'. Accordingly he proposed adding four articles to the *Declaration* to remedy this state of affairs. The enemies of any one local national section of the 'people', he claimed, had to be seen as the enemies of the people of all nations. If sovereignty meant anything, then it had to be all inclusive, uniting, rather than dividing peoples. The 'sovereign of earth', he claimed, was the 'human race' and the 'legislator of the universe' was 'nature'. The expression 'nation' still played a significant role in Robespierre's text, but only denoting the local branches of the human species understood as the 'people'. The source of conflict between nations was in those human agents who set themselves apart from the people of their nation in order to dominate them locally (and in due time other countries as well). These were the kings, aristocrats, tyrants and other enemies of virtue and popular rights – criminals against mankind. Against them Robespierre posited the notion that 'the men of all countries are brothers, and the different peoples must help one another, according to their power, as citizens of the same State'.[88] What the doctrine required was political homogenization on a world scale and moral cleansing of a totally universal character.[89]

When after Robespierre Saint-Just was called to speak to present his constitutional draft to which Robespierre's version of the *Declaration of the*

[87] Hannah Arendt, *The Origins of Totalitarianism*, (New York, Harcourt Brace, Jovanovich, 2nd ed., 1968), pp. 230–1.

[88] *Déclaration des droits de l'homme proposée par Maximilien Robespierre*, *Archives Parlementaires*, vol. 63, pp. 197–200. Robespierre also printed the text (with minor revisions) in the last number of his *Lettres à ses comettants*, 2nd. ser., no. 10 (23 April, 1793) in *Oeuvres*, vol. 5, pp. 360–3. The draft *Déclaration* was reprinted several times in the nineteenth century, most prominently in Ernest Hamel, *Histoire de Robespierre*, 3 vols. (Paris, Librairie Internationale and the author, 1865–7) vol. 2, pp. 685–8. In English (with commentary) see Thompson, *Robespierre*, Ch. 12, sections 3–7, pp. 349–66. The four clauses, articles 34–7 of the *Déclaration*, are on p. 353, the whole *Déclaration* on pp. 354–7. Another translation, under the title 'On Property' (April 24, 1793) is in Rudé, *Robespierre*, pp. 51–7.

[89] See Hans Kohn, *Prelude to Nation-States. The French and German Experience, 1789–1815* (Princeton, van Nostrand, 1967), pp. 53–4. The meaning of Robespierre's clauses was the subject of considerable controversy in early twentieth-century French revolutionary historiography, Thompson cites Alphonse Aulard's view that the four clauses were 'violent,

Rights of Man was the introduction, as it were, he revealed the full extent of the Jacobin attack on sovereignty.[90] He produced a theoretical introduction to the constitution, just like Sieyès in 1789, which was based on an earlier preparatory essay of his, entitled *'De la nature, de l'état civil, de la cité ou les règles de l'indépendance du gouvernement'*.[91] The draft constitution itself injected the maximum of radicalism into all the issues concerning sovereignty. It made it clear that the people's sovereignty could not be represented, that it belonged directly to the body of the people as organized into local communes, that sovereignty was emphatically not an expression of territoriality[92] but a property of peoples, and that the French territory had to remain united and indivisible precisely because it was under the protection of the indivisible sovereignty of the people's general will. In terms of external relations the draft constitution declared the French to be the friend of all other peoples, providing extensive asylum rights (except for murderers and tyrants) and forbade the use of the army to oppress others or the signing of treaties whose aim was anything but the peace and happiness of nations. Its last sentence was: *'Le peuple français vote la liberté du monde'*.[93]

Saint-Just provided an extensive theoretical back-up to his notion that the French *patrie* had to be kept open for all the people of the earth, and identified the division of the globe between separate nations as the ultimate source of the ills of mankind. His text was not so much Rousseau's *Social Contract*, but the *Second Discourse* and his aim was to engineer the return of mankind not to a state of nature, but to that happy early stage of society which Rousseau claimed

Footnote continued
intolerant and intolerable propaganda' (p. 366), but the judgment of Albert Mathiez was to the contrary, claiming that it was 'an outline of a Society of Nations' which could be used for setting the limits of policy-making: see his discussion of Robespierre's four clauses in 'La Constitution de 1793' in his *Girondins et Montagnards* (Paris, Firmin Didot Fréres, 1930), pp. 101–2.

[90] For this sequence of events in the Constitutional Assembly see *Archives Parlamentaires*, vol. 63, p. 200. Saint-Just spoke immediately after Robespierre.

[91] Louis-Léon Saint-Just, 'De la nature, de l'état civil, de la cité ou les règles de l'indépendance du gouvernement' in *Ouvres Complètes*, ed. Michèle Duval (Paris, Editions Gérard Lebovici, 1984). The dating of the manuscript is somewhat controversial and the most likely is the one suggested by Miguel Abensour which places it between September 1791 and September 1972, see his 'Saint-Just and the problem of heroism in the French Revolution', in Fehér, *The French Revolution and the Birth of Modernity*, pp. 133–4. The significant borrowing of the *Discours sur la Constitution de la France* (24 April 1793) from *De la nature* is accepted generally and, as Abensour warns, we would be 'inevitably dumbfounded' in our attempts to interpret Jacobin thought if we did not take the interaction between the essentially anti-political theories expressed in Saint-Just's text and his subsequent political practice seriously (p. 134).

[92] He repeated this important argument in his 'Discours sur la division constitutionelle du territoire, prononcé a la Convention Nationale dans la séance du 15 Mai 1793', emphasizing that the territorial principle of division was a monarchical principle aimed at making the people divided and charged that the United States therefore was not an embodiment of the true republican principle of the people's unity, see *Oeuvres Complètes*, pp. 443–6. On this issue he, like Robespierre, was very close to Sieyès.

[93] 'Essai du constitution', *Oeuvres Complètes*, pp. 425–42. For the possible origins of Robespierre's critique of the *Declaration* as 'drafted for a human herd planted in an isolated corner of the globe' see Saint-Just's attack on the state of the world as depicted by the social contract tradition: 'By the contract everyone lives armed against everyone else like a herd of animals from different species, each unknown to the others, each ready to devour the others. The security of each person lies in the possible annihilation of everyone else, instead of simply in their independence' ('De la nature', *Oeuvres Complètes*, p. 924).

existed until right replaced violence and nature was subjected to law.[94] Like Rousseau, Saint-Just saw the modern world as thoroughly Hobbesian and taking a leaf from the Christian critique of modernity opposed it in the name of the pure natural sociability of universal love.[95] The social state was a relationship between man and man, while the modern Hobbesian system, the political state, was a relationship between peoples. The political state emerged under the pressure of population growth and became the new system when princes usurped the people's sovereignty and instituted the politics of reason of state expressing the spirit of conquest. He was against reciprocal dependence of people and social contracts, these were instruments of the political, not the social state. Saint-Just's 'anarchism' was thoroughgoing. He literally wanted to rescue the social from the political, to create a world without power altogether, where the lack of coercion did not imply anarchy, since 'laws merely repel evil; innocence and virtue walk in independence in the world'. For Saint-Just the task of republican institutions was to re-establish the nexus of benevolence and the patriotic love of mankind.[96] The only concession he made to the political world was allowing the government to exercise the function of external preservation, but even for this he wished only to institute a sort of temporary military dictatorship. For this recklessly ambitious system of the anti-politics of love and independence the relevant category was not the nation, but the entire human species.

Arendt's striking argument suggests a general awareness that Sieyès' 'nation' could indeed be paired with Hobbes's notion of the 'state', but her claim is precisely that such a pairing must entail a sinister tension at the very foundations of the modern 'nation-state'. As with Robespierre and Saint-Just, her objection to *national* sovereignty is really a complaint about the notion of modern sovereignty *tout court*. What confuses the reader at first is the strange inversion of the categories. In this idiom it is not the case that the doctrine of state sovereignty corrupts the 'nation', but the other way round, it is the 'nation' which corrupts the 'state'. Her consequent definition, that 'nationalism is essentially the expression of this perversion of the state into an instrument of the nation and the identification of the citizen with the member of the nation' is an expression of this polemical idea. Lafayette's Article III of the first *Declaration of the Rights of Man*

---

[94] See Ch. 6 of 'De la nature', entitled 'Du principe de la legislation': 'I am confident that one can distinguish between a democracy where the people are subjected to themselves, from the social state where it should be said that there is no prince rather than that the people are prince. I do not see any difference between the different forms of legislation; in the one the people are subjected to a single person, in another to several persons, and in this one to themselves' (*Oeuvres Complètes*, p. 929) Saint-Just's rejection of the *Contrat Social* was quite violent. In his search for the means against slavery Rousseau forged the weapons of tyranny, he claimed, and ended up with the most vigorous imaginable model of a state (*Oeuvres complètes*, p. 929). For a commentary see B.C.J. Singer, *Society, Theory and the French Revolution. Studies in Revolutionary Imaginary* (Basingstoke, Macmillan, 1986), Ch. 9 'Saint-Just against the social contract: society without a polity', pp. 109–23.

[95] See Ch. 3 of 'De la nature', entitled 'De homme social, ou des premiers hommes' (*Oeuvres complètes*, pp. 926–7), where Saint-Just engages with Hobbes via Montesquieu's critique of Hobbes in Pt. 1, Ch. 3 'On the laws of nature' of *The Spirit of the Laws* [see the translation of A.M. Cohler, B.C. Miller and H.S. Stone (Cambridge, Cambridge University Press, 1989), p. 6], and then criticizing Montesquieu's critique as well. Saint-Just's deep debt to Montesquieu is obvious in his *Esprit de la Révolution et de la constitution de France*, in *Oeuvres complètes*, pp. 276–348.

[96] 'Fragments d'institutions républicaines', *Oeuvres complètes*, pp. 966–1009.

grew out of a debate on the correct location of sovereignty within a state.[97] It did not question the fact that there were such entities as separate and sovereign countries. What it stated was that in each and every state sovereignty had to be deposited not in the hands of kings, but in those of the 'nation'. Similarly, in Sieyès' theory of the nation it was not the ordinary sense of the word 'nation' which was in dispute. As we have seen Sieyès had apparently no difficulty in describing those entities into which France might devolve as 'small nations' or 'small states' and in the same vein it is not clear why the term 'nation-state', anachronistic as it is, could not be equally applied either to what he called his *ré-publique* or the Jacobin *ré-totale* (both of which referred to the same spatial entity, France). This confusing lumping together of national entities, which existed then as now, is best avoided. Sieyès' entire intellectual and political effort went into distinguishing his 'nation' as the embodiment of indirect popular sovereignty from its democratic alternatives. *Both* the alternatives he rejected were democratic options, although the damage they could inflict differed greatly. If democracy was to lead to 'small-nationism', then it would roll back not only the negative, but also all the positive effects of the previous two hundred years of state-building, destabilizing the international order and reversing the growth of commercial society and material civilization. On the other hand, if the large state of the French empire was retained, but made democratic, a new era of despotism would come into being, exacerbating rather than ameliorating the ills and vicious tendencies of the monarchical absolutism which preceded it. In contrast, it is quite clear that 'nationalism' in Arendt's definition does not refer to these constitutional debates seeking to define sovereignty within a state, but rather to the ordinary signification of the word 'nation', to describe the fact that the world consists of 'nations' in the sense of distinct political communities independent of each other. This kind of use of the notions of 'nation' and even 'nationalism', however, is not at odds with the Jacobin critique of the sovereignty of the nation, it is rather an authentic borrowing from the political imagery of Jacobin direct democratic political thought.

The curiously worded formulation *'nationalisme'* was a borrowing from German sources. Its only relevant occurrence in French in the late 18th-century can be found in the Jesuit counter-revolutionary Augustin Barruel's investigations into the origin and nature of Jacobinism. *'Nationalisme'* was a translation from an initiation manual to the Bavarian secret society of *Illuminati*, written by its founder Adam Weishaupt,[98] which Barruel aimed to connect to the Jacobins as part of his explanation of the revolution as a giant intellectual conspiracy. The *Illuminati* had indeed produced an argument which was very close to the tenor of Robespierre's four clauses in his *Declaration of the Rights of Man* and even more

---

[97] See this clearly in Richard Price's sermon on 'The Love of Our Country', where he praised Article III of the *Declaration of the Rights of Man* as clearly stating that 'civil laws are regulations agreed by the community', after discussing at length the problems created by external sovereignty, obviously failing to see that the sovereignty of the nation might vitiate the *Declaration*'s cosmopolitan credentials; see *A Discourse on the Love of Our Country*, pp. 20–2.

[98] Weishaupt's text was entitled '*Discourse of the Hierophant for the Degree of Priest or Epopt of the Illuminées*', which surfaced in a tranche of secret documents captured, and subsequently published, by the Bavarian government. For a general background of this event and the Bavarian *Illuminati* see Ch. 10 'The conspiracy theory of the Revolution' in Klaus Epstein, *The Genesis of German Conservatism* (Princeton, Princeton University Press, 1966), especially pp. 504–5.

to Saint-Just's ideas. When in his version of the history of mankind, shadowing Rousseau's *Second Discourse*, Weishaupt reached the period when the dispersed individuals of the species reunited and formed nations, he claimed that as a consequence

> they ceased to acknowledge a common name – Nationalism (*nationalisme*), or love for a particular nation (*amour national*), took the place of general love (*amour général*). With the division of the globe and of its states, benevolence was restrained within certain limits, beyond which it could no longer trespass. Then it became a merit to extend the bounds of states at the expense of the neighbouring ones. Then it became lawful to abuse, offend, and despise foreigners, to attack that end – and this virtue was styled patriotism; and he was styled a patriot who, just toward his countrymen, and unjust to others, was blind to the merits of strangers, and believed the very vices of his own country to be perfections. In such a case, why not restrain that love within a narrower compass, to citizens living in the same town, or to the members of one family; or why even should not each person have concentrated his affections in himself? We really beheld Patriotism generating localism, the confined spirit of families, and at length Egoism. Hence the origin of states and governments, and of civil society, has really proved to be the seeds of discord, and Patriotism has found its punishment in itself.[99]

[99] Abbé Barruel, *Mémoires pour servir à l'histoire du jacobinisme*, 4 vols (London, l'Imprimerie Française, 1797–8), English translation as *Memoirs Illustrating the History of Jacobinism*, 4 vols (London, printed for the author 1797–8), vol. 3, Pt. III 'The anti-social conspiracy', Ch. 9, p. 181. Compare this to the article 'Cosmopolitain, ou cosmopolite' in the *Encyclopédie*, which cites the views of an 'ancient philosopher': 'I am a Cosmopolite, that is a citizen of the universe. I prefer ... my family to myself, my fatherland to my family, and the human species to my fatherland' [vol. 11 (Neuchâtel, Samuel Faulche, 1765), p. 279b]. Views very similar to Weishaupt's on the international state-system were already cited in Ernst August Anton von Göchhausen's attack on the cosmopolitanism of the *Illuminati*, entitled *Enthüllung des Systems der Weltbürger-Republik. In Briefen aus der Verlassenschaft eines Freymaurers. Wahrscheinlich manchem Leser zwanzig Jahre zu spät publiziert* (Rome [Leipzig], 1786), pp. 235–6, where the Master of the Lodge defines as a chief aim of the masons the abolition of political slavery: 'When nations are no longer separated from one another; when citizens are no longer influenced by the exclusive interest of any state or the parochial system of patriotism, which binds them to a particular plot of earth and thereby makes them useless for the great concerns of mankind; when we have finally ceased to be slaves in any sense of the word; when the whole world has become one band of brothers – will not all despots with their special interests disappear? together with the numerous evil conditions which have been created for the sole purpose of serving the interests of despots?' (cited by Epstein, p. 98). For an interpretation of Weishaupt's theories and Göchhausen's report of the ideas of the *Illuminati* see Koselleck, *Critique and Crisis*, pp. 131–7. For a French example see the Grand Master's announcement in 1740: 'The entire world is only one great republic, of which each nation is a family and each individual an infant. It is in order to revive and spread these essential maxims found in the nature of man that our society was first established', cited by Gaston Martin, *La franc-maçonnerie française e la preparation de la Révolution* (Paris, Presses Universitaires de France, 1926), p. 47. Similar instances are cited by Margaret C. Jacob, *Living the Enlightenment. Freemasonry and Politics in Eighteenth-Century Europe* (Oxford, Oxford University Press, 1991), pp. 147–50. There is a rather futile debate about the status of Barruel's book as admissible evidence for serious historical study, which mixes up the use of his text as a source of contemporary ideas with acceptance of his conspiracy theory. The latter was effectively dispatched as early as 1801 by J.-J. Mounier (of 'Declaration of the Rights of Men and Citizen' fame) in his *On the Influence Attributed to Philosophes, Free-Masons, and the Illuminati on the Revolution of France*, trans. J. Walker (London, J. Wallis, 1801), see also the famous review of Mounier's book by Francis Jeffrey in the very first number of the Edinburgh Review No. 1 (October 1802), 1–18. Barruel himself was quite

Barruel, naturally, opposed this kind of exaltation of cosmopolitanism and pointed at the genuine diversity of the globe and its population, which made the notion of separate nations both necessary and useful. For him the anti-nationalism of the freemasons, illuminati and the French revolutionaries represented the highest and most vicious level of plotting against the existing order and religion of Europe, and characterized their 'Anti-Social Conspiracy' as an anarchist movement 'against every government, without even excepting the republican, against all civil society and all property whatsoever'.[100] People who held such views, he charged, notwithstanding what they claimed publicly, were false patriots.

It was indeed the case that beside standing for virtue and fraternity, the Jacobins saw patriotism as the crucial supporting passion of the people's republic. Virtue, Robespierre exclaimed echoing Montesquieu's definition of republican manners, was nothing else than the love of one's country. However, in the discourse within which Robespierre and Saint-Just were operating the brotherhood of nations and patriotism were quite compatible notions. It was a significant feature of late eighteenth-century critiques of the European state system dominated by 'reason of state' to dismiss ordinary patriotism as a dangerous and divisive sentiment, the 'last refuge of a scoundrel' and the source of crass xenophobia. Voltaire, in his *Philosophical Dictionary* was quite clear in his regret 'that men often become the enemies of the rest of mankind in order to be good patriots'. 'To be a good patriot', he continued his argument, 'is to want one's city to enrich itself by commerce and to be powerful in war.... This, then, is the human condition: to wish for the greatness of one's country is to wish evil to one's neighbours. The man who would wish his country never to be either larger or smaller, richer or poorer than it is, would be a citizen of the world'.[101] It was clearly claimed by many, and the article '*Paix*' in the *Encyclopédie* was a good example, that reason of state was fuelled by the passion of kings,[102] and patriotism was an easily exploitable sentiment to foster their aims. It was also well understood that there was a kind of republicanism, enamoured of the examples of Sparta and Rome, which turned republicanism into a patriotism suffused by a spirit of conquest and military virtue. To be a citizen of the world, as well as one's own country was an oft repeated statement in opposition to narrowminded patriotism and the competitive ambitions of governments. A *cosmopolite* was someone who wished for the good of all nations and ultimately the good of mankind.[103] The radical republican version

---

Footnote continued

a sophisticated political theorist; for an analysis of his *Question nationale sur l'autorité et sur les droits du people* [1791] see Marc A. Goldstein, *The People in French Counter-Revolutionary Thought* (New York, Peter Lang, 1988), pp. 21–37.

[100] Barruel, *Memoirs*, vol. 1, p. iv.

[101] Voltaire, *Philosophical Dictionary*, trans Peter Gay, 2 vols (New York, Basic, 1962), vol. 2, 'Patrie', p. 413.

[102] 'Paix', *Encyclopédie*, vol. 11, pp. 768b–9a.

[103] From the vast literature see Gerd van den Heuvel, 'Cosmopolite, Cosmopoli(ti)sme' in *Handbuch politisch-sozialer Grundbegriffe in Frankreich*, vol. 6. pp. 41–55; Max H. Boehm, 'Cosmopolitanism' in E.R.A. Seligman and A. Johnston (eds), *Encyclopaedia of the Social Sciences* (New York, Macmillan, 1931), vol. 4, pp. 457–61; Thomas J. Schlereth, *The Cosmopolitan Ideal in the Enlightenment. Its Form and Function in the Ideas of Franklin, Hume, and Voltaire, 1694–1790* (Notre Dame, Indiana, University of Notre Dame Press, 1977), Virginie Guiraudon, 'Cosmopolitism and national priority', *History of European Ideas* 13 (1991), 591–604. See also Hans Kohn, *The Idea of Nationalism: A Study in Its Origins and Background* (New York, Macmillan-Collier, 1967), ch. 7.

of this idea embraced this transcendence of narrowminded patriotism and war-mongering as an essential element of proper modern republican patriotism. Richard Price, for example, in his famous *Discourse on the Love of our Country* decried 'that spirit of rivalship and ambition which has been common among nations', but asserted that true patriotism implied the best care of one's own country as much as considering oneself as a citizen of the world, caring 'to maintain a just regard for the rights of other countries'.[104]

It is a common belief that the other widely known occurrence of the term 'nationalism' in the late eighteenth-century, in a text by Johann Gottfried Herder in Germany in the 1770s, came from a completely different intellectual world in which, as Arendt remarked, the sovereignty of the nation was turned into mystical and nebulous nationalism. This, however, is not quite the case. Herder, in his brilliant attack and satire on Enlightenment conjectural histories of mankind (entitled *Yet Another Philosophy of History for the Education* [Bildung] *of Mankind*) did indeed defend the sort of narrow-minded xenophobic patriotism which his enlighted contemporaries thought was the shame of modern civilization. When nations come into contact with one another, Herder pointed out ironically, one is indeed bound to find the sort of 'prejudice! popular agitation! [*Pöbelei*], narrow-minded *nationalism!*'[105] which spokesmen of Enlighted cosmopolitanism complain about. This was natural; it was there among ancient Egyptians when they came into contact with pastoral nomads and the Greeks; and Herder maintained that at the proper historical place and time such prejudices played an essential role in the formation of national communities. This was the way for the people to acquire a cultural identity, a bounded universe within which it could attain a modicum of happiness with its own lot. He

---

[104] Price, *Discourse on the Love of Our Country*, pp. 4–5; 10. Price's critical view of the standard designation of patriotism corresponds to what the *Illuminati* meant by *nationalism*: 'What has the love of the country hitherto been among mankind? What has it been but a love of domination; a desire of conquest, and a thirst for grandeur and glory, by extending territory, and enslaving surrounding countries? What has it been but a blind and narrow principle, producing in every country a contempt of other countries, and forming men into combinations and factions against their common rights and liberties? This is the principle that has been too often cried up as a virtue of the first rank: a principle of the same kind with that which governs clans of Indians or tribes of Arabs, and leads them to plunder and massacre. As most of the evils which have taken place in private life, and among individuals, have been occasioned by the desire of private interest overcoming the public affections; so most of the evils which have taken place among bodies of men have been occasioned by the desire of their own interest overcoming the principle of universal benevolence: and leading them to attack one another's territories, to encroach on one another's rights, and to endeavour to build their own advancement on the degradation of all within the reach of their power. ... What was the love of their country among the old *Romans*? We have heard much of it; but I cannot hesitate in saying that, however great it appeared in some of its exertions, it was in general no better than a principle holding together a band of robbers in their attempts to crush all liberty but their own' (pp. 5–6). On Richard Price's attack on sovereignty and empire see Peter N. Miller, *Defining the Common Good. Empire, Religion and Philosophy in Eighteenth-Century Britain* (Cambridge, Cambridge University Press, 1994), pp. 373–91.

[105] J.G. Herder, *Auch eine Philosophie der Geschichte zur Bildung der Menscheit* [1774], with an afterword by Hans-Georg Gadamer (Frankfurt, Suhrkamp, 1967), p. 46. In Riga, where he got his first job after his studies in Königsberg, Herder became the secretary of the local lodge of freemasons, the North Star, and he was familiar with the freemasonic critique of egotistic patriotism. He became a republican patriot in the Baltic city, which he compared to Geneva. The *Auch eine Philosophie der Geschichte* is from his Bückeburg period, written after his eye-opening travels in France in the late 60s, and after abandoning his earlier theological libertinism in favour of Christian moral theology. The best biography of Herder is still Rudolf Haym, *Herder nach seinem Leben und seinen Werken*, 2 vols (Berlin, Rudolph Gaertner, 1885–87).

condemned the empty phrase of the brotherhood of men as mere individuals and refused to support the general society of mankind.[106] For Herder the proper seat of cultural development was always the locality and the nation where one was born and destined to live. But despite this his politics had a great deal in common with the kind of patriotism that contemporaries counterposed to reason of state and in some respects his theoretical inspiration was quite close to Saint-Just's desire to return from the *état politique* to the *état social*.

Underlying Herder's notion of the nation was a Christian notion of natural sociability which was pitted against the artificial sociability of the political state. He was an implacable enemy of the Hobbesian kind of central authority and attacked his teacher Kant for apparently accepting the false causation that because man was an animal living in the perpetual antagonism of 'unsocial sociability', he was in need of disciplined political rule. For Herder human beings needed no master, ideally everyone must govern themselves, and the state should become dispensable.[107] The modern world, he claimed, 'finds its most sublime political expression in the new-fangled concept of *sovereignty*. If you want to know what this so-called political sovereignty rests on, you only have to look at our coins with their famous sun-eagle, their crowns and royal insignia, their drums, standards, bullets and the caps of servile soldiery'.[108] Herder was an enemy of the homogenization of populations attendant on the building of large modern states and criticized the leading lights of the metropolitan Enlightenment for fanning the flames of a new enthusiasm by becoming the party of the worldwide propagation of the metropolitan intellectual and social milieu of civilized monarchies. He despaired at the prospect of the aggressively sceptical culture of the Enlightenment provoking a backlash of superstition in the nineteenth century and his idea of the nation was part of an effort to find a way to prevent this 'wretched vicious circle' of action and reaction.[109] His understand-

---

[106] It is revealing of the intellectual background of the subsequent famous slogan of the Jacobins in the French Revolution, that Herder used the word 'sociability' interchangeably with 'brotherhood' or 'fraternity': 'Liberty, sociability and equality, as they are sprouting everywhere at present, have caused, and will cause, a thousand evils to be committed in their name.' (In English translation as *Yet Another Philosophy of History for the Enlightenment of Mankind* (selections), in F. M. Barnard (ed.), *J. G. Herder on Social and Political Culture* (Cambridge, Cambridge University Press, 1969), p. 219.) The deterioration of 'sociability' into universal 'brotherhood' Herder specifically associates with the worst kind of reason of state: 'The garment of generalities which characterizes our philosophy and philanthropy can conceal oppression, infringements on the true personal freedom of men and of countries, of citizens and peoples, in a manner which would have appealed to Ceasar Borgia' (p. 220).

[107] See his *Ideen zur Philosophie der Geschichte der Menschheit* [1784–9], in *Sämmtliche Werke*, ed. Bernard Suphan, 33 vols. (Berlin, Weidmannsche Buchhandlung, 1877–1913), vol. 13, pp. 338–9; 383–4. The *Ideen* was first translated into English by T. Churchill as *Outlines of a Philosophy of the History of Man* (London, J. Johnson, 1800), the passages cited here are available in a new translation in *Ideas for a Philosophy of the History of Mankind* (excerpts), in *J. G. Herder on Social and Political Culture*, ed. F. M. Barnard, pp. 309–10, 322–3. Herder was attacking Kant's 'Idea of a Universal History from a Cosmopolitan Point of View' [1784] 'Sixth Proposition', in *Political Writings*, pp. 46–7. Kant answered Herder in his review essay of Part Two of the *Ideen*, see *Political Writings*, pp. 213–20, especially p. 219. For an analysis of this debate see H. D. Irmscher, 'Die geschicht-sphilosophische Kontroverse zwischen Kant und 'Herder', in Bernhard Gajek (ed.), *Hamann-Kant-Herder: Acta des Vierten Internationalen Hamann-Kolloquiums* (Frankfurt am Main, Peter Lang, 1987), pp. 111–92. It is clear that without a clear grasp of theories of 'sociability' the debates in political theory in the second half of the eighteenth-century (and in the French revolution) cannot be properly understood.

[108] *Yet Another Philosophy of History*, p. 197.

[109] *Yet Another Philosophy of History*, p. 221.

ing of the causal origins of the modern European order was very clear, including the political role of the towns, the crucial impact of commerce and both the positive and the dangerous consequences of inter-state rivalry.[110] Under competitive pressure despotic regimes transmuted themselves into constitutional monarchies, but at the same time they entered into the spiralling logic of colonization, increasingly brutal warfare and a heavily camouflaged and vulgarized monarchical Machiavellianism.[111] Herder's sympathies were republican and anti-aristocratic, he welcomed the French revolution and whether he was disappointed by the terror or not, he continued to think in terms of the fate of the whole of humanity even more explicitly than before.[112] As he put it eloquently in an essay on ancient and modern patriotism published with his *Letters on the Advancement of Mankind*: 'Cabinets may deceive each other; political machines may exert pressure on each other until one is shattered. *Fatherlands* do not march against each other this way; they lie quietly side by side and help each other like families. ... The idea of fatherland against fatherland in blood feud is the most horrible barbarity that can be expressed in human language'.[113]

[110] See his *Ideen zur Philosophie der Geschichte der Menscheit* [1784–91], Bk. 20 'The Origins of modern Europe', available in the abbreviated version of Churchill's old translation edited by Frank E. Manuel under the title, *Reflections on the Philosophy of the History of Mankind* (Chicago, University of Chicago Press, 1968), pp. 357–98. For a very clear statement on the political relevance of the division of Europe into modern nations see Herder's assessment of the unitariness of Christendom in the Middle Ages and its apparently chaotic aftermath, in the conclusion of the book: 'Had Europe been rich as India, unintersected as Tatary, hot as Africa, isolated as America, what has appeared in it would never have been produced. ... The pressure of the Romish hierarchy was perhaps a necessary yoke, an indispensable bridle for the rude nations of the middle Ages. Without it Europe had probably been the prey of despots, a theatre of eternal discord, or even a Mungal wilderness. Thus as a counterpoise it merits praise: but as the first and permanent spring it would have converted Europe into a Tibetan ecclesiastic state. Action and reaction produced an effect, which neither party had intended: want, necessity, and danger, brought forward between the two a third state, which must be the life-blood of this great active body, or it will run into corruption. This is the *state of science, of useful activity, of emulative industry in the arts*; which necessarily, yet gradually, puts an end to the periods of chivalry and monasticism' (pp. 397–8). Instead of seeing Herder as a hero of the counter-Enlightenment, or some similar imaginary entity, it is more productive to investigate his links to Montesquieu, whose *Spirit of the Laws* he intended to revise and reorganize in a new form, and to the two *Discourses* of Rousseau, whose impact on the later eighteenth-century (including the French Revolution) was far greater than that of the *Contrat Social*, generating one of the most important new philosophical genres of the period, the various 'histories of mankind'.

[111] Herder despised the *Anti-Machiavel* of Frederic the Great and Voltaire's praise for it, see the scathing irony: 'Doubtless Machiavelli would not have written in our century as he wrote in his own, and Caesar in other circumstances would not have been able to act as he did; nevertheless, basically, there has only been a change of clothing. But even such a change is gratifying. For if in our century anyone wrote what Machiavel wrote, he would be stoned'. (*Yet Another Philosophy of History*, p. 221.) For the background of Frederick's 'refutation' of Machiavelli and the connections with Voltaire see the 'Introduction' by Paul Sonnino in Frederick of Prussia, *The Refutation of Machiavelli's Prince or Anti-Machiavel*, trans. Paul Sonnino (Athens, Ohio, Ohio University Press, 1981).

[112] See Frederick C. Beiser, *Enlightenment, Evolution and Romanticism. The Genesis of Modern German Political Thought 1790–1800* (Cambridge, MA, Harvard, 1992), Ch. 8.7 'Herder and the French Revolution' pp. 215–21. In the early part of the revolution Herder supported a patriotic defensive war in defence of the constitution as a just war. After the execution of the king and the queen he talked about mob rule and mob government, and he criticized the Jacobins for resurrecting despotism, but even after that he criticized foreign interference in French affairs, and later put his hope in Napoleon.

[113] *Briefe zur Beförderung Humanität*, in *Sämmtliche Werke*, vol. 17, 5th Series [1795], Pt. II of the Supplement to letter no. 57, on the peace plans of Comenius and the Abbé St. Pierre, '*Haben wir noch*

It has been necessary to discuss these debates about sovereignty and 'nationalism' in the French Revolution in some detail in order to clarify how the notion of the 'nation' and 'nationalism' entered European political language with such lasting effect at that time. It helps to arrive at a more satisfactory way of formulating Arendt's point, that modern nationalism is the perversion of the state into the instrument of the nation. We have already seen that in her cosmopolitan opposition to nationalism she effectively sides with the Jacobins and the logic of her argument leads her to put the responsibility for the rise of nationalism on the proponents of *national* sovereignty. It has always been somewhat surprising that such an argument could find its place in a book on *The Origins of Totalitarianism*, so that the blame seemed to have been pinned not on the authors of the *ré-totale*, but the *ré-publique* in the French Revolution.[114] Arendt's wish – in fact one with that of the Jacobins and in a way also with Herder – was to see the world as a brotherhood or family of republics. What revolted her was the actual realization in the 'Age of Nationalism' (and eventually by the National Socialists of Germany) of what Herder had seen as the nightmare of the future, the bloodfeud of *patrie* against *patrie*, fatherland against fatherland, one popular state fighting a patriotic war against another. In this context she saw properly constructed sovereign states as more stable and reliable entities than 'nations', the 'people' or the *Volk*. Alienation from the state could be handled more easily than alienation from the 'people'.[115] Arranged around this axis the valorization of the opposition between national sovereignty

Footnote continued

das Vaterland der Alten?', p. 319. Meinecke cites this particular sentence in support of his view that Herder did not genuinely belong to the 'pre-history' of modern nationalism, because of his staunch opposition to the state and most forms of power, see *Cosmopolitanism and the National State* [1907], trans. R.B. Kimber (Princeton, Princeton University Press, 1970), p. 29. Although the 1795 publication date is significant, the essay annexed to the letter on the famous peace-plans was the resurrection of an old piece, first written as a voluntary offering to the Czarina Catherine II, on the occasion of her visit to Riga in October 1765, virtually as Herder's first serious writing on politics, see 'Haben wir noch jetzt das Publikum und Vaterland der Alten? Eine Abhandlung zur Feier der Deziehung des neuen Gerichthauses' in *Werke*, vol. 1, pp. 13–28 and included a call for the reprint with commentary of Gabriel Naudé's famous reason of state tract, the *Considérations politiques sur les coups d'etat* (p. 324). In the fifth series of the *Letters* Herder was running a serialized commentary on important contemporary political writings on politics and culture in order to facilitate a rethinking of the political theory of the last two hundred years. Letter 58, which followed the reprinted essay questioning the possibility of having ancient patriotism in modern times was a commentary on Machiavelli. The early and the later versions, however, are quite different and the horror of inter-patriotic warfare in a modern world of semi-resurrected ancient politics appears in the 1795 version only. The subject of Letter 59 was Grotius, whom Herder considered, in contradistinction to Frederick the Great, the author of the true *Anti-Machiavell*. For a background and analysis of Herder's concept of humanity see Hans Erich Bödeker, 'Menschheit, Humanität, Humanismus' in *Geschichtliche Grundbegriffe*, vol. 3 (Stuttgart, Klett-Cotta, 1982), pp. 1063–128; and F.M. Barnard, *Herder's Social and Political Thought. From Enlightenment to Nationalism* (Oxford, Clarendon, 1965), Ch. 5 'From nationalism to internationalism: Humanität', pp. 109–27.

[114] In her later book, *On Revolution*, Arendt condemned the Jacobins as the precursors of the one-party state of the Russian Bolsheviks and painted them as relentless centralizers in the name of the fallacious principle of popular sovereignty 'one and indivisible'. Her sympathies were with American republican federalism and the ideas of Jefferson. In the French context she saw the *sociétés populaires* as the only institutions which could have served as the basis of a true revolutionary spirit. She acknowledges that the Jacobins, and particularly Saint-Just supported them until they came into power, but she regarded their activities afterwards as the establishment of a tyranny against popular societies; *On Revolution* (Harmondsworth, Penguin, 1973), pp. 239–48; 254–5; 266.

[115] Arendt, *Totalitarianism*, p. 231. She refers here to the viciousness of the Pan-German distinction between '*Staatsfremde*' and '*Volksfremde*', aliens of the state and aliens to the people or the nation. On

and the people's democracy changes places. Sieyès' nation appears as a bulwark against the worst kind of nationalism, while the Jacobins emerge as contributors to its rise. It is one of the most well known facts of modern history that the Jacobin experiment of radical republicanism has gone disastrously wrong and the two faces of the Jacobin contribution to the development of 'nationalism' and the shaping of the modern 'nation-state' reflect the dynamics of their failure. What concerns us here is the conceptual mapping of this dynamics with reference to a possible crisis of the 'nation-state'.

Ancient Republican Patriotism and the 'Age of Nationalism'

Contrary to the drift of Arendt's interpretation, the Jacobins understood 'nationalism' not as the contamination of the state by the nation, but the other way round, as the *état politique* corrupting the *état social*. The historiographical common-place, that the French Revolution is the origin of nationalism does not tally with the evidence concerning the use of the word 'nationalism', rare as it was, in this period. The two relevant and oft quoted occurrences of the word *nationalism* in the late eighteenth century (even Herder did not use the more heavy-handed term *Nationalismus*, which is of later coinage), clearly referred to phenomena which characterized the period before the French Revolution. What they point to is the entire history of the existence of separate territorial entities of peoples and in particular to the rise of modern states in Europe in the post-medieval period. Even more specifically, they express a critique of that phase of modern state-building (or nation-building) whose hallmarks are the notion of modern sovereignty and reason of state. The meaning of 'nationalism' thus understood signifies the entire system of inter-state power-relations in the modern era. There are two kinds of histories, or interpretations, of nationalism in modern scholarship. One variety, perhaps the majority view, is that nationalism is a post-French Revolution development. There is another variety, however, for which the process starts with the formation of the new post-Renaissance composite states of Europe and which virtually equates the rise of nationalism with the rise of absolutism in its various 'national' manifestations. In this view Henry VIII of England, Louis XIV of France, Gustavus Adolphus of Sweden or Frederick the Great of Prussia are seen as makers of modern 'nation-states' and hence the makers of modern 'nationalism'.[116] This is precisely the understanding which informs the cosmopolitan critique of nationalism as much as the criticism of republican patriots, including the Jacobins. This use of the word 'nationalism' expressed a total opposition to monarchical politics which borrowed the politics

---

Footnote continued

Arendt's complicated views on nation, state and the 'decline of the nation-state', particularly within the context of her work on totalitarianism, see Margaret Canovan, *Hannah Arendt. A Reinterpretation of Her Political Thought* (Cambridge, Cambridge University Press, 1992), especially pp. 28–36, 243–9.

[116] Medievalists extend this backwards to the thirteenth-century, see Ernst H. Kantorowicz, *The King's Two Bodies. A Study in Medieval Political Theology* (Princeton, Princeton University Press, 1957), Ch. 5, Pt. 1. '*Pro Patria Mori*', pp. 232–72; Gaines Post, 'Two Notes on Nationalism: I. *Pugna Pro Patria*, II. *Rex Imperator*', *Traditio*, 10 (1953), 269–300, '*Ratio Publicae Utilitatis, Ratio Status*, and 'Reason of State', 1100–1300' in Post, *Studies in Medieval Legal Thought: Public Law and the State*, 1100–1322 (Princeton, Princeton University Press, 1964), and Strayer, 'Historical Experience', p. 23, 'where a whole *regnum* became a state, nationalism developed early and naturally', in his view England was a nation-state by the fifteenth century (p. 24), on the latter issue see G.R. Elton, 'English national selfconsciousness and the Parliament in the sixteenth century', in Dann, *Nationalismus in vorindustriellen Zeit*, pp. 73–82.

of the late-Renaissance Italian city-states as captured by Machiavelli's *Prince*. Quentin Skinner, when explaining the rise of Bodin's and Hobbes's notion of indirect popular sovereignty as the 'state' called this movement a 'counter-revolution' against popular republican politics and theories of resistance. In the second half of the eighteenth-century there was a rising opposition to the modern international regime and the republicanism of the French Revolution aimed at reversing this Hobbesian 'counter-revolution'.

The rise of the large 'national' monarchies in the wake of the military revolution and their policies of internal homogenization and external military and economic competition drew a great deal of criticism throughout the seventeenth and eighteenth centuries. In France such thinking was perhaps more prevalent and continuous in the eighteenth century than anywhere else in Europe, precisely because it was France, under Louis XIV, which developed the new kind of 'nationalist' statecraft to its highest level. The failure of Louis' bid for making France the leading military and economic power in Europe, his experiment in establishing a universal European monarchy under French leadership, required a long process of rebuilding of the French fiscal-military regime and it also generated a sustained theoretical effort through three generations of French political thinkers to develop the foundations for a possible radical reform of the absolutist state system and its political economy. The immediate cause of the monarchy's collapse, the failure of the public debt system sustaining French power and quest for grandeur, was intimately connected with the nature not only of the domestic institutions of the French state, but also with the structure of the international world, or more precisely to the interaction between the two. The Revolution, from the beginning, was also a revolution against the prevailing 'nationalist' system of international relations. It was absolutely clear to virtually all participants of this revolutionary period that France's relationship to the international power system would have to change and it was well understood that if a major power like France changed its position on international relations, this must have repercussions on the operation of the entire system. It was a widely held opinion that the modern system of international relations, particularly the policy of the balance of powers, needed reform. Those radical revolutionaries, however, who opposed the modern concept of sovereignty also hoped that the Revolution signalled not only a modification of inter-state politics, but the crisis of the 'nation-state' altogether. They would have thought it absurd to see the Revolution as a beginning of the career of the 'nation-state'. What they fervently hoped for was that it was the beginning of its end. They genuinely desired that it would enter its *crisis*.

For the Jacobins this was an absolutely crucial issue. It was not simply the question of survival in a hostile world. Building a new republic, even more a democracy, in one country was an obviously difficult enterprise and crucially depended on a favourable external political environment. But the issue of patriotism went to the heart of their political system. Nationalism, as the ruling political passion of the subjects or citizens of the 'nation-state' is often understood as the opposite to patriotism, and even when the two are seen as connected, it is assumed that nationalism is the pathology of patriotism which develops under specifically modern conditions and chiefly after the French Revolution. Patriotism in the republican vocabulary is the key political virtue which determines the citizens' devotion to the republic as self-government according to the rules of reason and justice. The critical notion of 'nationalism' as developed in the second half of the eighteenth-century specifically stated that patriotism became vitiated when it was conceived within the constraints of single nations or states, in isolation from others.[117] Accordingly, in a world divided among peoples patriotism could be regarded as ultimately a species of egoism, as collective *amour propre*, xenophobic, competitive, and militaristic. The love of the country always reflected what the country was at any given moment, and the popular patriotism of the modern monarchies expressed faithfully their new power politics guided by reason of state. For the Jacobins it was an essential constitutional requirement that their democratic republican system was not built on a patriotism of this kind, but on a love of the country which was neither exclusive, nor competitive. This was not simply a policy issue, it had to be embodied in the *Declaration of the Rights of Man* and in the Constitution. Opting out from the international system of competing and aggressive nationalist monarchies was a necessary precondition of the success of their revolution. But if opting out turned out to be impossible, then the survival of the new republic of virtue increasingly came to depend on forcing a change in the international environment.[118]

The Jacobins, however, were not the party of war. France was in the aftermath of the colossal debt crisis of the monarchy and the new paper money system could best operate in a *geschlossene Handelsstaat*.[119] Robespierre not

---

[117] Mary Dietz argues that the 'blurring of patriotism into nationalism, or even the acknowledgement of nationalism as a "species" of patriotism, reveals that we have literally lost touch with history, with a very real past in which real patriots held to a particular set of political principles and their associated practices – to a conception of citizenship that bears scant resemblance to modern nationalism' ('Patriotism', p. 191). Compare this vision to the attempt to reconstruct the very same British commonwealthmen tradition which Dietz now echoes by the veritable commonwealthman Andrew Fletcher of Saltoun, who was forced to see quite clearly in 1703 that fixing the problem of 'nationalist' patriotism within republicanism is practically identical to the reconstruction of the entirety of the modern political theory tradition: 'Not only those who have ever actually formed governments, but even those who have written on that subject, and contrived schemes of constitution have, as I think, always framed them with respect only to particular nations, for whom they were designed, and without any regard to the rest of mankind. Since, as they could not but know that every society, as well as every private man, has a natural inclination to exceed in everything, and draw the advantages to itself, they might also have seen the necessity of curbing that exorbitant inclination, and obliging them to consider the general good and interest of mankind, on which that of every distinct society does in a great measure depend. And one would think that politicians, who ought to be the best of all moral philosophers, should have considered what a citizen of the world is', *An Account of a Conversation concerning the Right Regulation of Governments for the Common Good of Mankind. In a Letter to the Marquiss of Montrose, the Earls of Rothes, Roxburg and Haddington, from London the first of December, 1703* [1704], in Fletcher of Saltoun, *Selected Writings*, ed. D. Daiches (Edinburgh, Scottish Academic Press, 1979), pp. 105–37. For a background to Fletcher's republicanism and the *Conversation* see John Robertson, 'Andrew Fletcher's vision of union', in R.A. Mason (ed.), *Scotland and England 1286–1815* (Edinburgh, John Donald, 1987), pp. 203–25, and my 'Free trade and the economic limits to national politics: neo-Machiavellian political economy reconsidered', pp. 113–9; on his civic humanist credentials J.G.A. Pocock, *The Machiavellian Moment. Florentine Republican Thought and the Atlantic Republican Tradition* (Princeton, Princeton University Press, 1975), pp. 426–47.

[118] See T.C.W. Blanning, *The Origins of the French Revolutionary Wars* (London, Longman, 1986), particularly Ch. 3 'The origins of the war of 1792', pp. 69–130; Gunther E. Rothenberg, 'The origins, causes, and extension of the wars of the French Revolution and Napoleon', in R.I. Rotberg and T.K. Rabb (eds), *The Origin and Prevention of Major Wars* (Cambridge, Cambridge University Press, 1989), pp. 199–221.

[119] J. G. Fichte, *Der geschlossne Handelsstaat* Ein philosophischer Entwurf als Anhang zur Rechtslehre, und Probe einer Künftig zu liefernden Politik (Tübingen, Cotta, 1800) was an intellectually authentic extrapolation of the Jacobin idea. See particularly his introduction: 'Vom

only feared for the finances of France, but saw war as a weapon for increasing the power of the executive, and he also pointed towards the great danger of the people being seduced into traditional patriotism. The only proper way war could energize the people into virtuous patriotism was through defending their country. Defending the revolution by carrying it abroad through a war of liberation, or the idea of establishing a universal republic (with Paris as the centre, as preached by Anacharsis Cloots[120]), was not what the Jacobins envisaged as their model of political prudence. Robespierre did not believe in the magic liberating force of flying the tricolor 'on the palaces of emperors, sultans, popes and kings' and opposed the war plans of the government and the Girondins.[121] The Jacobins were against the accelerating adventure of liberating

Footnote continued

Verhältnisse des Vernunftstaates zu dem wirklichen, und das reinen Staatsrechts zur Politik'. In English see 'The relationship of the rational state to the actual state, and of pure constitutional law to politics' in H.S. Reiss (ed.) *The Political Thought of the German Romantics 1793–1815* (Oxford, Basil Blackwell, 1955), pp. 86–7.

[120] For the ideas of Anacharsis Cloots [Jean-Baptiste, Baron de Cloots du Val-de-Grâce] see his *Oeuvres*, ed. Albert Soboul, 3 vols (Munich, Kraus Reprint, 1980), vol. 3, *Écrits et discours de la période révolutionnaire*. The two most ambitious and important pamphlets are *La République universelle ou adresse aux tyrannicides par Anacharsis Cloots, orateur de genre humain* (1793), pp. 331–89, and the *Bases constitutionnelles de la republique du genre humain* (1793), pp. 605–52. In the latter book Cloots claimed that he took his inspiration from Sallust: '*Studium reipublicae omnia superat*' (p. 629); he wanted 'perpetual liberty' under '*une nation, une assemblée, un prince* (the latter, he emphasized, to be understood strictly in the philosophical sense, p. 346), with the universal republic replacing the catholic church as the unifying institution, and the national assembly the ecumenical council, forming a truly free version of the Roman empire (which was an empire of servitude) with a billion co-citizen brothers, instead of the 25 million of France alone.

[121] Maximilien Robespierre, 'Sur le parti que l'assemblée Nationale doit prendre relativement à la proposition de guerre, annoncée par le pouvoir exécutif, prononce à la Société le 18 Decembre 1791', in *Oeuvres de Maximilien Robespierre*, vol. 8 *Discours Octobre 1791–Septembre 1792*, eds M. Bouloiseau, G. Lefebvre and A. Soboul, (Paris, Presses Universitaires de France, 1953), pp. 47–52; 58–64. English translation 'On war and peace' (18 December 1791) in Rudé, pp. 32–9. The speech, in which Robespierre turned against the majority opinion in the Jacobin Club for war, was a reply to Jacques Pierre Brissot de Warville's speeches on 9 and 16 December. Brissot spoke again on 29 and 30 December and Robespierre answered on 2 and 11 January 1792. On 20 January, after Brissot's last great speech for the war, Robespierre and Brissot apparently made peace with each other, but from then on the gulf between them became more and more unbridgeable. Brissot's judgment of the international situation and the likely domestic effects of the patriotic war was much more optimistic than Robespierre's, but in any case his support for a 'crusade for universal liberty' fundamentally rested on two assumptions. First, he relied on the republican idea of the superiority of a patriotic national militia: '. . . every advantage is on our side – for now every French citizen is a soldier, and a willing soldier at that! And where is the power on earth, where is the Genghis Khan, is the Tamerlaine, even with clouds of slaves in his train, who could hope to master six million free soldiers?' (29 December, 1791, *Archives Parlementaires*, vol. 36, p. 607.) Second, he counted on the expected positive response of the ordinary foreign soldier to revolutionary liberation: 'Each soldier will say to his enemy: Brother, I am not going to cut your throat. I am going to free you from the yoke you labour under; I am going to show you the road to happiness. Like you, I was once a slave; I took up arms, and the tyrant vanished, look at me now that I am free; you can also be so too; here is my arm in support' [cited by Alphonse Aulard. 'La diplomatie du premier comité de salut public', *Etudes et leçons sur la Révolution française* 3rd ser. vol. 3 (Paris, Félix Alcon 3rd ed., 1914), p. 53]. Brissot's ally, Isnard made the same point: 'Let us tell them that conflicts begun between peoples on the orders of despots resemble blows exchanged in the dark by two friends against each other by some evil intriguer; once day has dawned, they throw away their weapons, embrace and then take revenge on him who deceived them (noise and applause). In the same way, at the moment that the enemy armies begin to fight with ours, the daylight of philosophy will open their eyes and the peoples will embrace each other in the face of their dethroned tyrants and an approving heaven and earth (spirited applause)' (29 November 1791, *Archives Parlementaires*, vol. 35, p. 442). For the shape of the debate see Blanning,

annexations by conquest, and Lazare Carnot, later the 'organizer of victory' under the Jacobin regime, in February 1793 made it clear that the kind of sovereignty of the 'universality of mankind' would also imply that France was 'no more than a portion of the sovereign' either and 'consequently she has no right to establish at home the laws that suit her best'. The guiding principle was the preservation of France's new system of liberty and any dilution of France's new system with the inclusion of neighbouring states with their unreformed populations in it was to be avoided. Under the prevailing conditions of the world the best defence was to 'adhere to the principle that every people, however small the country it inhabits, has an absolute right to be its own master'.[122] The Jacobins saw that the principle of state sovereignty was a protective device which they would better uphold in order to gain time for their domestic revolution. Echoing the spirit of Saint-Just's assertion that independence from the system of *état politique* was the key to the new world, Carnot actually stated that as a first step what was needed was not a *Declaration of the Rights of Man* but a *Declaration of the Rights of the Citizen*, and Article II of his draft announced 'every people has the right to isolate themselves'.[123] Even when

Footnote continued

'The Brissotin campaign for war' and the 'Conversion of the Deputies', in *Origins of the French Revolutionary Wars*, pp. 99–113; François Furet, 'Les Girondins et la guerre: les débuts de l'Assemblée législative', in François Furet and Mona Ozouf, *La Gironde et les Girondins* (Paris, Payot, 1991), pp. 189–206; and in *Interpreting the French Revolution* pp. 64–9; Lucien Jaume, 'Le duel Robespierre-Brissot sur la guerre', in his *Le discours jacobin*, pp. 71–5; Michael L. Kennedy, *The Jacobin Clubs in the French Revolution: The Middle Years* (Princeton, Princeton University Press, 1988), Ch. 9 'Peace or war', Ch. 12 'England: friend or foe?', pp. 123–32, 150–6; Thompson, *Robespierre*, Ch. 7 'The opponent of war (November 1791–April 1792), pp. 195–226. On Brissot and his brand of republicanism see two articles by Patrice Gueniffey, 'Brissot', in Furet and Ozouf, *La Gironde et les Girondins*, pp. 437–64, 'Cordeliers and Girondins: the prehistory of the Republic?', in Fontana (ed.), *The Invention of the Modern Republic*, pp. 86–106; and the chapters on Brissot by Norman Hampson in *Will and Circumstance. Montesquieiu, Rousseau and the French Revolution* (London, Duckworth, 1983), pp. 84–106, 171–92.

[122] See Lazare Carnot's report in the name of the diplomatic committee concerning the annexation of the Principality of Monaco etc., 14 February 1793, *Archives Parlementaires*, vol. 58 (Paris, Imprimerie et Libraire Administratives, 1900), p. 547. Florence Gauthier, in her 'Universal rights and national interest in the French Revolution'(in Dann and Dinwiddy, *Nationalism in the Age of the French Revolution*, pp. 34–5) and repeated in her *Triomphe et mort du droit naturel en Révolution 1789–1795–1802* (Paris, Presses Universitaires de France, 1992), pp. 128–45 claims that Carnot was refuting in advance, as it were, not only Cloots, but also Robespierre and Saint-Just's ideas as presented in their draft *Declaration of Rights* and the project for the new Constitution in April, and announced a 'new political theory, that of national interest and untrammelled sovereignty' (p. 35). In fact Carnot was rehearsing time honoured arguments about the primacy of the right of self-preservation of both individuals and nations (which were just like individuals in the state of nature), claiming that the law of nature did not oblige individuals to sacrifice themselves for their fellows and that the first law for nations was the '*salut de l'État*', which also allowed encroaching on the interest of others if '*necessité pour soi-même*' required it. The interest of the republic, he argued, 'may consist in the increase in strength or national prosperity; in greater security on the frontiers or a simplification of the means of defence; or indeed the glory which a powerful nation may derive from attaching to itself a people which is weak but worthy of the benefit of liberty'. (p. 547). For some of the issues involved in the annexation debates, particularly the annexation of Belgium, see Sophie Wahnick, 'Les Républiques-soeurs, débat théorique et réalité, historique, conquêtes et reconquêtes d'identité républicaine', *Annales historiques de la Révolution Française*, no. 296 (1994), 165–77.

[123] '*Projet de déclaration des droits du citoyen*' (19 February 1793), in Lazare Carnot, *Révolution et mathématique*, ed. Jean-Paul Charnay (Paris, L'Herne, 1984), p. 230. In the preamble Carnot stated that since in the state of nature the primitive rights of man were indefinite, the notion of rights as defined for such conditions was necessarily illusory, it was only a discussion of the rights (and even more the duties) of citizens which could make any sense, in the context of a tacit social pact which has

the continuation of war had become an inescapable reality and the Jacobins took charge of the republic, their rhetoric of war remained resolutely defensive, and although patriotic, it was also anti-nationalist and anti-imperialist. If France was dismembered or destroyed, Robespierre claimed, the whole world would be defeated, and the whole of Europe would be in chains. If she was victorious, the whole world would benefit. The Republic and her citizen army was acting only on behalf of the peoples of the world; revolutionary France was not only the defender of her own liberty, but of true humanity and civilization. However, as the terror started, nothing was more striking than the turning of Jacobin republicanism into the most dramatic form of national patriotism, quickly establishing the systematic persecution of foreigners and 'cosmopolitans' within France. Robespierre specifically complained about the malign influence of international finance, which made the public order of the republic 'dependent on the whim of foreigners'. Facing civil war and foreign war, the two classic problems for whose solution the idea of modern sovereignty was invented, the Jacobins displayed the most spectacular application of reason of state. Those who ran the *Comité de Salut Public* could hardly fail to understand that *salus populi* was the supreme law, and ruling directly in the name of the *populus* it was their duty to put their safety before any other consideration. The revolutionary government had the right to act with less constraint and more energy, than normal government, Robespierre

---

Footnote continued

been established for mutual protection. From these quasi-Hobbesian origins Carnot went on to discuss Rousseau's principles in the *Second Discourse*, reiterating that the *amour de soi-même* was the final motivation of all individuals, and *l'utilité commune* of the state (pp. 227–29). Cloots, like Florence Gauthier today, saw a contradiction here between this idea and the *Declaration of the Rights of Man*, and in his swan song *Appel au Genre Humain, par Anacharsis Cloots* [en réponse à Robespierre et à son exclusion de la Société des Jacobins, le 12 decembre 1793], *Oeuvres*, pp. 689–708, denounced Robespierre as a hypocrite, referring to the latter's agreement with him on the 'sovereignty of the world' in his April 1793 draft for the *Declaration of Rights*, and referring to Robespierre's complaint then that the *'droits de l'homme'* should not be simply *'les droits du français'*, leading to Robespierre's adoption in the draft *Declaration of 'la souveraineté du genre humain'* (p. 695). See Cloots' long visionary speech and proposal for a decree of human rights in the National Convention on 26 April 1793 (*Archives Parlementaires*, vol. 63, pp. 389–403), just two days after Robespierre's, suggesting that the only kind of sovereignty which was acceptable was the 'sovereignty of the human race' (p. 402) and announcing that otherwise those who 'say sovereign, say despot' (p. 391) On that particular day the 'nationalist' patriotic line against the idea of declaring the rights of man and the sovereignty of mankind was voiced not by Robespierre, but the more clearly 'republican' François Robert who spoke just before Cloots. Robert announced that: 'Let us leave to them the problem of examining humanity in all its relationships: we are not the representatives of the human race. I wish therefore that the legislator of France would forget the universe for a moment to concern himself with his country alone. I desire that kind of national egoism without which we shall be false to our duties, without which we shall legislate here for those who have not mandated us, and not in favour of those for whose profit we can legislate on all matters' (*Archives Parlementaires*, vol. 63, p. 385). The short term policy of the Jacobins, and particularly Robespierre, had always been based on prudential considerations anchored in the interest of revolutionary France, eventually the complaint against the 'cosmopolitan' line was in essence against the dangers of imprudential and naive adventurism precipitating a possible failure of French self-preservation. See Robespierre's final critique of Cloots (shortly before the latter's execution): 'Such a man, who was calling France to the conquest of the world, had no other goal than to call the tyrants to the conquest of France. The foreign hypocrite, who for five years has been proclaiming Paris the capital of the globe only expresses, in another jargon, the anathemas of the vile federalists who dedicated Paris to destruction', in 'Sur les principes de morale politique' (February), *Oeuvres*, vol. 10, p. 361, English translation in Bienvenu, *The Ninth of Thermidor*, p. 43.

claimed, because it was authorized by the most indisputable of entitlements, *'la necessité'*.[124]

Those histories of the nation-state and nationalism which stress modernity as their most essential characteristics usually start their history from the impact of the undoubted successes of the Jacobin republican army and the subsequent history of the revolutionary wars of the *'grande nation'* and the 'world war' of Napoleon's conquests. The usual sequence runs from the establishment of the principle of national sovereignty in the first *French Declaration of the Rights of Man and the Citizen* and Sieyès' concept of the 'nation' in the *What is the Third Estate?* to the successes of the French *national* army and then to the reaction, both positive and negative, to these developments in the rest of Europe. Such a picture not only ignores the crucial distinction between the concepts of the nation and sovereignty involved in the various steps of this sequence, it also obliterates the specifically Jacobin contribution to this process. From the point of view of *their* expectations, the European impact of the revolution as the creation of the 'Age of Nationalism' was an unmitigated disaster. The *crisis* for which they hoped failed to materialize. It is important to realize that, as we have seen earlier, the French Revolution, or more precisely its aftermath, is the historical period when the modern language of crisis was firmly established. The notion of crisis became inflated by the hope (or fear) that the original demand for the disappearance of national state boundaries and narrow-minded nationalism might finally be realized. The anti-political and internationalist vision of the Jacobins passed straightforwardly into the modern socialist tradition and became a hallmark of Marxism.[125] What needs to be appreciated is the degree to which the failure of Jacobinism itself contributed to the frustration of the anti-nationalist dream. When the Jacobins insisted that France should be kept together as a united and indivisible republic largely within its inherited monarchical boundaries they laid the foundations to the success of the French armies. France as a large, populous and wealthy state could wage war with far better chances of success than any of the smaller units could have, had the country fallen apart to smaller state entities. When their army marched they hoped that it would be motivated by friendship towards other peoples and hatred towards tyrants and the aristocracy. Their worry, however, that the war would prove to be a vehicle of unifying patriotism of the nationalist kind was well founded. Rather than selflessly internationalist, the symbolic and sentimental motivation of the French army was all too passionately republican.

As the internationalist army defaulted into an army of republican patriotism, the brotherhood of nations gave way to a re-enactment of the imperial conquests of the ancient Roman Republic. Critics of the Jacobins understood this corruption quite clearly. Since the French Revolution every modern revolution is analysed, and in many cases had analysed itself, in terms of its model of political dynamics. Something quite similar, however, was true in late eighteenth-century

[124] Robespierre, 'Rapport sur les principes du gouvernement révolutionnaire, fait au nom du Comité de Salut Public' (25 December, 1793), *Oeuvres*, vol. 10, p. 275; English translation in Rudé, *Robespierre*, p. 60.

[125] See Gregory Claeys, 'Reciprocal dependence, virtue and progress: some sources of early socialist cosmopolitanism and internationalism in Britain, 1750–1850', in F. van Holthoon and M. van der Linden (eds), *Internationalism in the Labour Movement* 1830–1940 (Leiden, Brill, 1988), pp. 235–58; Théodore Ruyssen, *Les Sources doctrinales de l'internationalisme*, (Paris, Presses universitaires de France, 1961), vol. 3, *De la Révolution Française au milieu du XIX siècle*, pp. 462–529.

France too: the fate of republican revolutions was understood to have been prefigured all too precisely in the fate of the ancient Roman Republic. As the Jacobins achieved success in war, the future of their policy of reason of state needed to be explained more thoroughly. Robespierre was compelled to dispel the idea that 'the plan of the French revolution was written out in full in the books of Tacitus and Machiavelli' and that the prudence of 'the people's representatives' could be sought 'in the histories of Augustus, Tiberius, or Vespasian, or even that of certain French legislators; because, except for a few nuances of perfidy or cruelty, all tyrants are alike'.[126] He was answering, almost point by point, Camille Desmoulins' critique of the terror which revived the well-rehearsed republican critique of the final phase of the Roman republic, drawn from classical sources, chiefly from Tacitus (through the mediation of the British commonwealthmen tradition, particularly the commentaries on Tacitus by Thomas Gordon). Publishing the first three numbers of the six numbers of the *Le Vieux Cordelier* with an epigraph from '*notre grand professeur Machiavel*'[127] Desmoulins accused the initiators of the terror of placing so thick a veil over the statue of liberty that it had become a funeral shroud, and suggested that their indiscriminate use of the 'jurisprudence of despots' was bound to destroy virtuous republican spirit to such a degree that a corrupt decline into a traditional tyranny might easily follow. In the last number of his flysheet drafted after his expulsion from the Jacobin Club (and not much before his arrest and execution) Desmoulins recorded faithfully how quickly his initial diagnosis of the republic turning into a warlike empire materialized in Robespierre's policies. Referring to Robespierre's frenzied attack in the Jacobin Club on both the despotism of the English government and the slavish patriotism of the English people, he denounced him as a total hypocrite. Robespierre denounced Brissot, because he wanted to 'nationalize the war' and Cloots because he wanted to 'municipalize Europe', but now he himself became, claimed Desmoulins, the tyrannic apostle of a 'democratizing' war to liberate the English people by force.[128] Was this the same

---

[126] 'Sur les principes de morale politique' *Oeuvres*, vol. 10, p. 351, English translation in Bienvenu, *The Ninth of Thermidor*, p. 32.

[127] Camille Desmoulins, *Le Vieux Cordelier*, ed. Pierre Pachet (Paris, Belin, 1987), no. 4, p. 67. See particularly, nos. 3, 4 and 6, as well as the proofs of no. 7 (with handwritten emendations) which have survived, although their publication in the spring of 1794 was impossible. For the chronology of the *Le Vieux Cordelier* from no. 1 (December 1793) to no. 6 (effectively 25 January, 1794) see Pachet's 'La restitution du texte de Camille Desmoulins: une exigence politique', pp. 13–31. *Gordon sur Tacite* is mentioned in no. 3, p. 60 and no. 6, p. 100, and the epigraph might have been derived from Machiavelli through Gordon as well. The French translation of Gordon's *Discours historiques, critiques et politiques sur Tacite* appeared in 1742, printed in Amsterdam, the English original was *The Works of Tacitus in Four Volumes, to which are prefixed Political Discourses upon that Author* 4 vols. (London, T. Woodward and J. Peele, 2nd ed., 1737). For some of the republican background see Michael Sonenscher, *Work and Wages. Natural Law, Politics and the Eighteenth-Century French Trades* (Cambridge, Cambridge University Press, 1989), Ch. 10 'Artisans, "sans-culottes" and the politics of republicanism', pp. 333–61; for a general overview of Tacitus in eighteenth-century French culture see Catherine Volpilhac-Auger, *Tacite en France de Montesquieu à Chateaubriand* (Oxford, Voltaire Foundation, 1993). Herder in Letter 52 of the 4th series of his *Briefe zur Beförderung Humanität*, published in 1794, also discussed 'Thomas Gordon über dem Tacitus' at length, claiming that the book was one of Diderot's favourites and citing it from the German translation of 1764, interestingly entitled *Die Ehre der Freiheit der Römer und Britten nach Gordons Staatskluge Betrachtungen über dem Tacitus*, see *Sämtliche Werke*, vol. 17, pp. 252–6.

[128] Desmoulins was referring to the debate which followed Robespierre's request on 7 January 1794 that the Jacobin Club discusses the crimes of the English government and the vices of the British Constitution. On 28 January Robespierre interrupted the debate by announcing that the participants

Robespierre, he asked, who in December 1791 declared his fundamental opposition to war and saw war as the 'resource of despots' and who declared that people cannot be given their liberty by the sword?[129]

The success of military republicanism was not unexpected. The superiority of citizen armies over the professional armies of monarchical 'nation-states' in terms of defence had been one of the central beliefs of republicans ever since Machiavelli affirmed it so eloquently in *The Prince*. It was also understood that military success in the modern age of large national states depended on the degree to which monarchical armies could utilize the sentiment of 'nationalist' patriotism for motivating their soldiers. James Harrington, writing in the middle of the seventeenth-century, saw the essence of post-modern politics (modern for him meant the Gothic era after the ancients) as a return to the politics of the ancients and casting a cool eye over the accelerating competition

---

Footnote continued

had missed his point entirely and that their trust in the patriotic brotherhood of the English people was in vain. No appeal to the English people could succeed, he argued, because it was corrupted by a divisive sort of patriotism: The members of the Club only deceived themselves if they thought that the English people are as 'moral and enlighted' as themselves. 'No, they are two hundred years behind you. And they hate you, because . . . for centuries the policy of their government has been to arm the English against the French and to use war as a means of defeating the opposition party. It does not follow that the English will never have a revolution. They will, because they have been opressed and ruined. The revolution will be the work of French navy [he referred to a possible French naval blockade ruining English trade] and it will come about because the British Ministry is corrupt. Pitt will be overthrown, because despite his vastly inflated reputation, he is an imbecile'. (See Société des Amis de la Liberté et de l'Égalité, Séance du 9 Pluviose en II (28 Janvier 1794), 2e intervention, 'Sur les moyens de dénoncer les crimes du gouvernement anglais', *Oeuvres*, vol. 10, p. 345). At the next session, on 30 January, Robespierre objected to the naive Anglophile view that the reputation of the English people should not be tarnished because of the crimes of their government. The question was not the character of individuals, but of an entire nation and emphasized that there could be neither peace nor truce with corrupt or jealous peoples. His *profession de foi* was to detest the English people for their servile support of their despot. 'As a Frenchman, as a representative of the people, I declare that I hate the English people (applause). I will increase the hatred of my compatriots against it as much as I can. What do I care what they think! My only hope is in our soldiers and in the deep hatred which the French have for the English'. ('Séance du 30 January 1794, 2e intervention, 'Sur la difficulté de séparer le peuple anglais de son gouvernement', *Oeuvres*, vol. 10, pp. 348–9.)

[129] *Le Vieux Cordelier*, no. 7 [February–March 1794, with handwritten additions to the proofs], pp. 116–7. In a last section (which is also handwritten), entitled '*Suite de mon credo politique*' Desmoulins also makes the point that Montesquieu was in palpable error claiming that virtue was the foundation of the republic, for who would have needed a republic if the citizens were already virtuous? In developing his conclusion he depicted a sequence of politicization, nationalization and then militarization, showing how the corrupting effects of the governmental enforcement of virtue and patriotism would lead to the ruining of the republic and eventually to the use of the '*l'énergie nationale et l'impetuosité française, doublée par le révolution*' for imperialistic military exploits by a new model mass citizen army under the command of vainglorious generals imprudently following the worst kind of ancient examples (pp. 142–4). Robespierre in his speech at the Jacobin Club in January 1792 said that 'No one likes an armed missionary, and no more extravagant idea ever sprang from the head of a politician than to suppose that one people has only to enter another's territory with arms in its hands to make the latter adopt its laws and Constitution'. In 1794 he was still essentially repeating the same argument, and emphasized the need for armed 'nationalist' patriotism in conscious opposition to the old Brissotin republican 'internationalist' doctrine. While Brissot supposed a patriotic French army, but a soft monarchical enemy whose army could be turned into an anti-despotic revolutionary force, Robespierre now had to prepare the French patriotic citizen army to fight similarly patriotic armies, however misguided their patriotism was. The motivating force was now not 'internationalist' patriotism, but its ordinary 'nationalist', albeit revolutionary, version.

between modern monarchical states for European domination declared that the winner would be that modern state which best succeeded in adopting for its purposes the principles of ancient Roman patriotic politics. The military power of such a patriotic modern state would prove invincible. He feared that it would be the French monarchy which would first accomplish this feat.[130] Those observers of the French Revolution who were schooled in neo-Harringtonian politics understood the sequence all too well. As they saw it, the revolutionary armies and Napoleon had succeeded where Louis XIV failed, because they followed the patriotic example of the ancients much more faithfully.[131] The impact of this discovery explains a great deal of the paradoxical origins of *modern* nationalism. For the failure of the crisis of nationalism did not mean that Europe simply returned to the *status quo ante* of the seventeenth and eighteenth-century state system with its traditional nationalist patriotism, denounced by the Jacobins, raised to a new height by the necessities of protracted warfare. This would have been merely to continue a process which began in earnest with the experience of the Seven Years War. The new element was the revival of the spirit of *ancient* patriotism under modern conditions, and it was this spectacular neo-classicist reintroduction of the passions and the politics of the ancients which provided nineteenth-century nationalism with its energy and to some degree also with its deadliness.

The infusion of this 'ancient' element into the making of post-revolutionary nationalism is reflected in a way in the kind of modern historiography which sees not the absolutist and enlightened absolutist monarchs like Louis XIV or Frederick the Great as its most notable predecessors but the republican patriotism of Machiavelli, Rousseau and the Jacobins.[132] This is garbled

---

[130] 'Though the people of the world, in the dregs of the Gothic empire, be yet tumbling and tossing the bed of sickness, they cannot die, nor is there any means of recovery for them but by ancient prudence, whence of necessity it must come to pass that this drug be better known. If France, Italy and Spain were not all sick, all corrupted together, there would be none of them so, for the sick would not be able to withstand the sound to preserve her health without curing the sick. The first of these nations (which, if you stay her leisure, will in my mind be France) that recovers health of ancient prudence shall assuredly govern the world, for what did Italy when she had it?', James Harrington, *The Commonwealth of Oceana* [1656], in *The Political Works of James Harrington*, ed. J.G.A. Pocock (Cambridge, Cambridge University Press, 1977), p. 332.

[131] For an exemplary analysis in this idiom see the Scottish Adam Ferguson's manuscript essay on the options open for Britain in dealing with Napoleon, entitled 'Of the French Revolution with Its Actual and Still Impending Consequences in Europe', in 'Collection of MSS Essays in the Possession of Sir John Macpherson, Bt', Edinburgh University Library, Dc.1.42[14]. For a discussion of the various connotations of empire at the time of Napoleon's assuming the title 'emperor' and the transformation in its republican meaning see Richard Koebner, *Empire* (Cambridge, Cambridge University Press, 1961), pp. 276–85. The classic analysis of the Napoleonic experience of militaristic post-revolutionary empire and its connection to the political ideologies of the age is Benjamin Constant's *The Spirit of Conquest and Usurpation and Their Relation to European Civilization* [1814] in Constant, *Political Writings*, ed. B. Fontana (Cambridge, Cambridge University Press, 1988), pp. 45–173. Constant did not have a developed theory of the 'nation'; for an attempt at piecemeal reconstruction see Maria Zenner, 'Der Begriff der Nation in den politischen Theorien Benjamin Constants', *Historische Zeitschrift*, 213 (1972), 38–68.

[132] Rousseau is a favourite nominee for being the chief eighteenth-century forerunner of nationalism, the rather regrettable examples are many, see for example the otherwise 'realist' E.H. Carr: 'The founder of modern nationalism as it began to take shape in the 19th century was Rousseau, who, rejecting the embodiment of the nation in the personal sovereign or the ruling class, boldly identified "nation" and "people"; and this identification became the fundamental principle both of the French and American revolution', *Nationalism and After* [1945] (London, Macmillan, 1968), p. 7; this view was anticipated in the famous *Nationalism. A Report by a Study Group of Members of the Royal*

history, but it is not difficult to understand how the failed Jacobin experiment generated these images. The Jacobins' contribution to the revival of neo-classical patriotism became associated with the essential features of their revolutionary *ré-totale*, with the emphasis on reason of state as the uncompromising defence of the people's and the republic's interest, and also with the direct democratic opposition to the system of representation.[133] Many nationalist movements of the subsequent period fought for their cause under the banner of renewed Jacobin democratic republicanism and their political thought suffered the same deformation as that of their French revolutionary predecessors when they substituted the direct sovereignty of the people for the system of indirect popular representation. But it would be a mistake to narrow the impact of the revival of neo-classical republican patriotism to the republican nationalist movements of the later period. Its impact was far wider and reached all the different segments of the modern state-system. In many ways the impact of the French Revolution and the revolutionary wars of the republic and Napoleon resembled that of late-Renaissance neo-classical republicanism on the political thought of Europe after the decline of the Italian city-republics.[134] Revolutionary politics became transplanted into a post-revolutionary world and its principles became absorbed into the politics of the large 'nation-states'

Footnote continued

Institute of International Affairs (London, Oxford University Press, 1939) which was supervised by Carr, see Rousseau's ideas looming large in the Chapter on 'The Growth of the idea of nationalism', pp. 23–34; probably providing Seton Watson with his belief that the connection between the doctrine of nationalism and eighteenth-century ideas of popular sovereignty had been clarified adequately. See also popular accounts such as Anthony H. Birch, *Nationalism and National Integration* (London, Unwin Hyman, 1989), pp. 14–6, or Roman Szporluk, *Communism and Nationalism. Karl Marx versus Friedrich List* (Oxford, Oxford University Press, 1988), pp. 82–3. A somewhat more balanced, but nonetheless misguided, account is in Anne Cohler, *Rousseau and Nationalism* (New York, Basic, 1970).

[133] All these themes appeared together in a manuscript work of Mme de Staël written in 1798 (and revised with the help of Benjamin Constant in 1799), entitled *Des circonstances actuelles qui peuvent terminer la révolution et des principes qui doivent fonder la république*, ed. Lucia Omacini (Geneva, Droz, 1979). For an analysis see Biancamaria Fontana, 'The Thermidorian republic and its principles' in Fontana, *Invention of the Modern Republic*, pp. 118–38. 'The first basis of the republic is national patriotism', wrote Staël, 'Now, as long as the French government makes appeal to circumstances to resort to revolutionary means, the spirit of a free people will never be formed. In France, while the continuation of the war will force six hundred thousand men to remain in arms, the government will never need public opinion, and public opinion will never regain strength. France will be governed in a hundred years' time as it is now and the nation will never become republican' (*Des circonstances actuelles qui peuvent terminer la révolution*, p. 321, cited by Fontana, p. 134). For an analysis of the inability of the Thermidorians to stop the combined patriotic war legacy of the Girondins and the Jacobins see Furet, *Interpreting the French Revolution*, pp. 71–2.

[134] Tuck, *Philosophy and Government 1572–1651* charts this change very clearly, continuing the account of the foundations of modern political thought from the 'Conclusion' of Skinner, *Foundations of Modern Political Thought*, vol. 2. See also Maurizio Viroli, 'The revolution in the concept of politics', *Political Theory* 20 (1992), 473–95, and at greater length *From Politics to Reason of State. The Acquisition and Transformation of the Language of Politics 1250–1600* (Cambridge, Cambridge University Press, 1992). Viroli's 'revolution' is an aspect of what Skinner called a 'counter-revolution' in politics and his account provides a useful background for the understanding of Robespierre's definition of the two faces of republicanism, in peace and in war (or revolution) in his speech 'On the Principles of Moral Policy that Ought to Guide the National Convention in the Internal Administration of the Republic', 5 February 1794. For the origins of the image of the supremely peaceful constitutional republic see also Viroli's, 'Machiavelli and the republican idea of politics' in G. Bock, Q. Skinner and M. Viroli (eds), *Machiavelli and Republicanism* (Cambridge, Cambridge University Press, 1990), pp. 143–73.

of Europe which stood against the revolution. Herder, and many others, complained about the enormous damage inflicted by the misunderstanding and misconstruction of Machiavelli's politics by applying reason of state to the politics of large modern monarchies.[135] What the opponents and victims of the neo-classical republican imperialism of the French learnt was how effective the innovations of the Revolution could be as tools of power politics. The success of the French patriotic army was seen as a combination of patriotism and the thoroughly homogenized unity of the French state behind it. The way forward was to persevere in the quest for national power with the policy of unification and homogenization which had begun with the 'absolutist' monarchies and been preserved and reasserted by the French revolutionaries.[136]

The language of the 'national-state' or 'nation-state' came into prominence in the nineteenth-century to describe the consequences of learning this lesson.[137]

[135] See Herder, 'Letter 58', 'Von den Meinungen des Völker in der verschiedenen Zeiträume ihrer Geschichte. Von Machiavells Fürsten' in the 5th series of *Briefe zur Beförderung der Humanität, Sämmtliche Werke*, vol. 17, pp. 319–24. Herder complains of two hundred years of misunderstanding Machiavelli (compare this to Gans' two hundred years of 'Absolutismus'). Herder clearly understood that Machiavelli's *Discorsi* was republican, and that *The Prince* was a source for 'Staatsraison (*la ragione del stato*)' (p. 322). Cicero and Machiavelli were taken up in Germany in the 1790s and the beginning of the 19th century, see particularly Fichte's essay on Machiavelli and his publication of a selection from his writings in his periodical, the *Vesta*, in 1807 ('Über Machiavell, als Schriftsteller, und Stellen aus seinen Schriften' in J. G. Fichte, *Machiavell. Nebst einem Briefe Carls von Clausewitz an Fichte*, ed. Hans Schulz, 2nd ed. (Leipzig, Felix Meiner, 2nd ed., 1918, 11 vols.). For the background of 'Über Machiavell' and the international reference to continuing Herder's Interpretation of Machiavelli see D. Moggach, 'Fichte's engagement with Machiavelli', *History of Political Thought* 14 (1993), 573–89. Shortly before publishing his *Machiavell* Fichte wrote in his dialogue *Die Patrioten*: 'Cosmopolitanism is the will that the purpose of humanity be really achieved. Patriotism is the will that this purpose be fulfilled in that nation to which we ourselves belong and that the results spread from it to entire humanity. ... Cosmopolitanism must necessarily become patriotism' [in *Nachgelassene Werke*, ed. I. H. Fichte 3 vols. (Bonn, Adolph Marcus, 1834–5), vol. 3, pp. 228–9].

[136] The shape of this policy and its disastrous dynamics were laid very clearly in the famous 1862 essay of Lord Acton on 'Nationality', in John Emerich Edward Dalberg-Acton, *The History of Freedom and Other Essays*, ed. J.N. Figgis and R.V. Laurence (London, Macmillan, 1907), pp. 270–300. For a very clear modern statement about the military-ideological consequences of the French revolution see Theda Skocpol and Meyer Kestenbaum, 'Mars unshackled: the French Revolution in Word-Historical Perspective', in Fehér, *The French Revolution and the Birth of Modernity*, pp. 13–29.

[137] English readers of Hegel can read in his *Philosophy of Right* that the 'nation state is mind in its substantive rationality and immediate actuality and is therefore the absolute power on earth'. This is an expression, and indeed a celebration, of the importance of the modern doctrine of absolute 'popular' sovereignty (it can be found in Hegel's chapter on external sovereignty), and accordingly Hegel's expression was '*das Volk als Staat*', the 'people *qua* state', and not 'nation-state' (§331, see the translation by T.M. Knox [1942], *Hegel's Philosophy of Right* (Oxford, Oxford University Press, 1952), p. 212. H.B. Nisbet in his new translation defers to Knox's distorting but time-honoured translation and registers the possible conceptual discrepancy by simply giving the German original in brackets, see A.W. Wood (ed.) *Elements of the Philosophy of Right* (Cambridge, Cambridge University Press, 1991), p. 366, see also §344, 347, etc., but quite inconsistently not in §347 where '*welthistorischen Volk*' is given as 'world-historical nation', etc. Although the word *nation* was available for and used by Hegel in some contexts (such as 'civilized' and barbarian nations), see §351, 355 etc., it is the case in general that German usage deployed *Volk*, the people, where the French and the English, at least from the 18th century onwards, would use the term nation: see Wilhelm Traugott Krug's *Allgemeines Handwörterbuch der philosophischen Wissenschaften nebst ihrer Literatur und Geschichte, nach dem heutigen Standpunkt der Wissenschaft* (Leipzig, Brockhaus, 2nd ed, 1833), vol. 3, p. 13–14, who lists eleven combinations of 'national' with various nouns and names of institutions, but not the *Nationalstaat* (compare this with his article '*Staat*', where the concept of 'nation' also fails to appear, vol. 4, pp. 1–8). Heinrich von Treitschke, at the end of the century still informed his students that *Nationalität* was a French

The term itself was almost certainly devised to foster the unification of Germany and Italy and then to celebrate the outcome. It signified the formation of large states with an ambition of national homogenization from the residual web of old state particularism which survived the first, pre-French Revolution, phase of absolutist state consolidation.[138] First and foremost the use of the terms 'national state', and in an Anglicized form 'nation-state', became associated with the rise of the unified German state as a world power under Bismarck, who assumed the mantle in the iconography of state-building theory of such great former 'nationalists' as Louis XIV or Frederick the Great.[139] The

Footnote continued
word which the Germans only borrowed, although he took pride in the robustness of the German language in assimilating French concepts so accommodatingly, see his lectures on *Politics* [1897–8], Hans Kohn (ed.), B. Dugdale and T. de Bille (trans) (New York, Harcourt, Brace and World, 1963), ch. 8 'Races, tribes and nations, p. 122. The Swiss-German Johann Caspar Bluntschli, in his famous *Staatswörterbuch Deutsches* 11 vols. (Stuttgart and Leipzig) had a separate article about '*Nation und Volk, Nationalitätprinzip Expedition des Staatswörterbuchs, 1857–70*' (in vol. 7 (1871), pp. 152–60) repeating that the term 'nation' in French and English usage is equivalent to the German '*Volk*', while '*Nation*' in German means a cultural or an ethnically defined community, '*Volk*' refers to a political community (*populus*) living in a state (although, due to foreign influences on the German language, '*Nationalsouveranität*' corresponded to the '*Volk*' and '*Volksouveranität*' to the politically unorganized '*Nation*'). For Bluntschli the proper theory of popular sovereignty of the *Volk* was the Bodin-Hobbes theory of state sovereignty, emphasizing that the nation was the unorganized multitude of individuals, while the state was the *Volk* represented as a single state-person (a *Volksstaat* standing for the most free version of it, as the republic or free state; see the article 'Staat', vol. 9, pp. 612–28). The '*national Staat*' was a mere, and quite unfortunate, modern sub-category of the State as popular sovereignty, expressing the application of the 'principle of nationality' to the state: 'Every People has a call at a right to form a State. As mankind is divided into a number of Peoples, the world must be divided into the same number of States', See the first volume of Bluntschli's *Allgemeines Staatsrecht* which under the title *The Theory of the State*, D. G. Ritchie, P. E. Mathieson and R. Lodge (trans.) (Oxford, Clarendon, 1885) served as the Oxford textbook for political theory, particular ch. 4 'Nationality as a principle in the formation of states', p. 125. In this text Bluntschli noted that the 'principle of nationality' had little to do with the French Revolution, where both '*nation*' and '*peuple*' were interpretations of the collective body of the citizens, the *demos*, and not of ethnic nationhood. See also his pamphlet *Die nationale Staatenbildung und der moderne deutsche Staat* (Berlin, Lüderiss'sche, 1870), which freely acknowledges his debt to the German-American moral and political philosopher, whose text, written in English, now reads more modern than that of his German contemporaries, see Francis Lieber, 'Nationalism and internationalism', in vol. 2 of his *Miscellaneous Writings*, entitled *Contributions to Political Science, including Lectures on the Constitution of the United States and Other Papers* (Philadelphia, J.B. Lippincott, 1881), pp. 225–43.

[138] For a long-term political geography of European state consolidation and for a revival of the genre of eighteenth-century conjectural history for explaining the relative lateness of the unification of Germany and Italy in terms of their unusually dense network of surviving Roman cities see Stein Rokkan, 'Cities, states, and nations: a dimensional model for the study of contrasts in development', in S.N. Eisenstadt and S. Rokkan, *Building States and Nations. Models and Data Resources* (Beverly Hills, Sage, 1973), pp. 78–87.

[139] The first selfconscious and self-descriptive use of 'nationalism', according to the *Dictionnaire alphabetique et analogique de la langue française* par Paul Robert, comes from the period of the Boulanger and Dreyfus affairs, in the work of Maurice Barrès, collected in his *Scènes et doctrines du nationalisme* in Philippe Barrès (ed.), *Oeuvres*, 2 vols (Paris, Plon, 1925). See particularly 'Que le nationalisme est l'acceptation d'un déterminisme, vol. 1, pp. 3–21. Barrès' right-wing '*national-isme*' expressed a disappointment with the republican ideology of the 'nation' to deliver France's greatness, and grew out of a fear of decadence, social decomposition, loss of international status and the (German inspired) internationalism of the working-class movement. On Barrès and the development of the vocabulary of 'nationalism' see Ernst Robert Curtius, *Maurice Barrès und die geistige Grundlagen der französischen Nationalismus* [1921] (Hildesheim, Olms, 2nd ed., 1962) and Zeev Sternhell, *Maurice Barrès et le nationalisme français* (Paris, Armand Colin, 1972); for an

Oxford English Dictionary gives the use of the term by the Oxford historian J.A.R. Marriott as its first relevant example in the English language. Although these citations for first use are somewhat unreliable, it is worth noting that in the book in question, entitled *The European Commonwealth*, Marriott was grappling with the effects of the first World War: the role of German 'nation-state' looms large on his pages. His aim was to denounce the English admirers of the 'unification of great States on the basis of nationality', the adherents of the Teutonic school of history like Stubbs in Oxford and Seeley in Cambridge, who helped to fan the flames of 'the cult of the great Nation-State' and predisposed the minds of their students to become the admirers of Bismarck.[140] As a historian of diplomacy and state formation in modern Europe, he had no difficulty in seeing that the Germans were attempting to achieve just what their predecessors had failed to secure, establishing a universal empire which would secure peace in Europe under the domination of a single state. He quoted the most extravagant German rhetoric of imperial nationalism, which claimed that the German sword would give peace to Europe of a kind which 'it has never known since the dissolution of the Empire of the Caesars' and would 'realize the ideal at once of Dante and Machiavelli'; but he also warned that it would be folly to ignore the passion and idealism behind this bombastic rhetoric.[141] Even the most sober and thoughtful thinkers of Germany at the time realized the dilemmas of the 'nation-state' and saw, as Max Weber had sharply proclaimed in his inaugural address at the University of Freiburg, that the policies of the German national state must be guided by its national interest in power and consequently that the standard by which it must formulate its policies had to be 'reason of

---

Footnote continued

overview of the new French nationalism of the *fin-de-siècle* see Raoul Girardet, *Le nationalisme française* 1871–1914 (Paris, Armand Colin, 1966), Eugene Weber, *The Nationalist Revival in France 1905–1914* (Berkeley, University of California Press, 1968) and Caroline C. Ford, 'Which nation? Language, identity and republican politics in post-revolutionary France', *History of European Ideas*, 17 (1993), 31–46. For the development of the German usage see Reinhart Koselleck, 'Nationalismus', Section XIV, article 3, in 'Volk, Nation, Nationalismus, Masse' in *Geschichtliche Grundbegriffe*, vol. 7, pp. 398–402. In Germany the self-consciously positive usage appears after 1918, unlike in France where the turning point is 1871, and it is associated with the 'constructive hatred' of the *Pöbel*, the crowd or the rabble, and it also has an open militaristic and imperialist connotation. As Ernst Jünger, one of the first self-confessed German nationalists put it: 'The father of this nationalism is war' (p. 400).

[140] J.A.R. Marriott, *The European Commonwealth. Problems Historical and Diplomatic* (Oxford, Clarendon, 1918). Ch. 7, 'The problem of small nations and big states' [originally published in 1915], p. 143. He quotes Seeley's *Life and Times of Stein*, where the latter claimed that the German wars of 1813, 1866 and 1870 'in a manner, reconciled the world to war, for they have exhibited it as a civilising agent and a kind of teacher of morals'. Marriott repeated this attack in a more extended form during the Second World War, in his *Federalism and the Problem of the Small State* (London, Allen and Unwin, 1943).

[141] Marriott, *European Commonwealth*, Ch. 1 'Nationalism, internationalism, and super-nationalism', p. 6–7. Marriott's view was that the Germans were following the footsteps of the wars of the French Revolution and fighting a war of 'an armed doctrine' in Burke's sense (p. 113). For a reaction of the German left to these developments see the formulations of Karl Liebknecht, who argued that '"Militarism", together with the Catholic Church, is the most highly developed Machiavellianism in the history of the world, and the most Machiavellian of all the Machiavellianisms of capitalism', cited in Nicholas Stargardt, *The German Idea of Militarism. Radical and Socialist Critics 1866–1914* (Cambridge, Cambridge University Press, 1994), p. 101.

state'.[142] After completing his history of German nationalism under the title *Weltbürgertum und Nationalstaat* before the first World War, Meinecke wrote its intellectual sequel in the aftermath of the war on *The Idea of Reason of State in Modern History*, which begun the story not with the cosmopolitan and humanitarian tendencies of the French Revolution, which in his eyes prompted the rise of German conservative nationalism in reaction, but with Machiavelli and *The Prince*.[143]

It would be an intellectual fallacy to construct a history of the modern world and modern nationalism out of the impact of the revival of neo-classical republicanism in the French revolution or to blame the resuscitation of popular reason of state in modern history on the Jacobins. But any history of the 'nation-state' and nationalism which ignores the peculiar internal dynamics of the revolution itself and its Janus-faced impact – and either sees them as a straightforward continuity in state-building since the early modern period or presumes a rupture at the time of the French revolution, with their history commencing with its aftermath – will fail to explain the modern conundrum of popular sovereignty. Whether the large 'nation-states' of Europe can preserve their territorial integrity against internal pressure; whether they break-up or not, depends on whether their populations accept them as their own 'state' or whether they see it as in their interest to secure a 'state' more authentically of their own. In other words, it depends on the intersection between democracy and reason of state at the very core of the state in question. A historical perspective on the debates in the French revolution on democracy and reason of state, and a simple comparison between the perspectives of Sieyès and the Jacobins, can still direct our attention to the most fundamental of issues facing the contemporary 'nation-state'.

---

[142] Max Weber, 'The nation state and economic policy [1895] in Weber, *Political Writings*, eds P. Lassman and R. Speirs (Cambridge, Cambridge University Press, 1994), pp. 1–28. See Nicholas Xenos, 'Nation, state and economy: Max Weber's Freibing Inaugural Lecture', in M. Ringrose and A.J. Lerner (eds), *Reimagining the Nation* (Buckingham, Open University Press, 1993), pp. 125–38; and Harry Liebersohn, 'Weber's historical concept of national identity', in H. Lehmann and G. Roth (eds), *Weber's Protestant Ethic: Origins, Evidence, Contexts* (Cambridge, Cambridge University Press, 1993), pp. 123–31, which reports Weber's exasperation with the way sociologists and race theorists attempted to deal with the concept of nationhood in the 1910 and 1912 Annual Meetings of the German Sociological Association (pp. 129–30). See also his elucidation in §5 'The Nation' in his chapter on 'Political Communications' of Part 2 of his *Economy and Society. An Outline of Interpretive Sociology*, eds. Guenther Roth and Claus Wittich, 2 vols. (Berkeley, University of California Press, 1978), vol. 2, pp. 921–6. Following through the implications of his argument concerning the *Nationalstaat* as an embodiment of reason of state Weber remained a consistent 'political nationalist', seeing the 'nation-state' as a political concept reflecting the meeting point, as it were, of 'political events and the state'. Correspondingly he defined 'politics' as the proclivity of 'striving for a share of power or for influence on the distribution of power, whether it be between states or between the groups of people contained within a single state' ('The [Profession and] Vocation of Politics' in *Political Writings*, p. 311).

[143] Friedrich Meinecke, *Machiavellism: The Doctrine of Raison d'Etat and Its Place in Modern History* [1924], trans. D. Scott, ed. W. Stark (London, Routledge, 1957). 'Machiavellism' was added to the title by the editor of the English translation only, in order to 'help' the English reader to position the strange and foreign concept of 'reason of state'.

Index